Peter Behrens
and a
New Architecture
for the
Twentieth Century

Peter Behrens. Berlin, AEG Turbine Factory (1908–1909).
Exterior from the southeast.

Peter Behrens
and a
New Architecture
for the
Twentieth Century

Stanford Anderson

The MIT Press
Cambridge, Massachusetts
London, England

This book was set in Adobe Garamond by The MIT Press and was printed and bound in the United States of America.

Library of Congress Cataloging-in-Publication Data

Anderson, Stanford.
    Peter Behrens and a new architecture for the twentieth century / Stanford Anderson.
        p. cm.
    Includes bibliographical references and index.
    ISBN 0-262-01176-X (alk. paper)
    1. Behrens, Peter, 1868–1940—Criticism and interpretation. 2. Architecture, Modern—20th century—Germany. I. Title.
    NA1088.B4 A827 2000
    720'.92—dc21   99-049154

Endpapers: Peter Behrens. "Behrens Kattune": printed cottons from Gebr. Elbers, Hagen (used in a room by Behrens at the St. Louis world's fair, 1904).

Contents

Acknowledgments

Professors Edward Kaufmann, George Collins, Henry-Russell Hitchcock, and Robert Rosenblum gathered for my dissertation defense at the apartment of George Collins, an unusual location necessitated by the closure of the Columbia University campus due to the student unrest of May 1968. Following the usual custom of dismissing the candidate while the vote was taken, I awaited the decision with Christiane Collins, seated on the marital bed. After a notably brief time, the referees kindly voted my dissertation a "distinction" and then advised that I leave it for a time and do something else. I owe much to these gentlemen, especially Professors Kaufmann and Collins of Columbia, but, at this distance in time, they might join in some regret about that advice.

With the unduly long preparation of this work I incurred debts to more persons and institutions than I can recognize in the short compass of an acknowledgment page. I must then beg the indulgence of many, asking that they know of my grateful recollections and recognize themselves in my collective thanks as I explicitly recognize the few who have been important in the full duration of the project or in its culmination.

My study of Behrens began with a Fulbright Fellowship to Germany in 1961–1962. Of institutions that supported me throughout, I must recognize the AEG-Archiv (which I had occasion to use in Berlin, Braunschweig, and Frankfurt) and the Rotch Library and Rotch Visual Collections of the Massachusetts Institute of Technology, noting especially the long-time Rotch Librarian, Margaret DiPopolo. The MIT Department of Architecture was the constant setting of my work. I recall with gratitude and pleasure a long series of devoted assistants, for the last eight years the excellent, indefatigable, and much beloved Anne Simunovic. John Cook was ever ready with photographic services. Resourceful, indispensable research assistants of recent years include Sandy Isenstadt, Brian McLaren, and Tom Beischer. Ann Vollmann Bible compiled the index. My colleague Julie O'Brien Dorsey generously prepared the digital simulation of the Behrens wall-covering design used as the endpapers.

Henry Millon, colleague throughout these years even as he serves as Dean of the Center for Advanced Study of the Visual Arts at the National Gallery of Art in Washington, still gives constant support to me and my efforts. When I allowed this work to languish, Kenneth Frampton revived it first with partial publication in *Oppositions* and later in unsolicited advocacy with the MIT Press. Having agreed to publication in 1968, the Press, especially in the person of Roger Conover, showed remarkable tenacity and generosity in renewing the publication program. In the realization of the book I received the excellent editorial work of Matthew Abbate and design services of Yasuyo Iguchi.

I owe most to the families who patiently bore with the long, cumbersome realization of this work. I dedicate the book to the memory of my mother and father.

Stanford Anderson
Deer Isle, Maine
1 July 1999

Introduction

This book is still markedly close to the dissertation I completed thirty years ago. I owe the reader an account, beyond personal anecdote, of why the book appears now, and how it has changed from its original form.

The work that I undertook in 1961 was the beginning of the historical study of Behrens (as distinct from the notable monographs of Behrens's active years). More years have passed since that beginning, in the year of the Berlin Wall and a time when the war was still palpable in the cities and life of Germany, than had passed between the death of Peter Behrens in 1940 and the initiation of my study. To established German historians, I was attempting a study that was not yet historical; but I was young and foreign and my distance from Behrens seemed ample. The ensuing years brought additional perspective, but also a change in the attitude of German scholars. The historical study of the twentieth century is no longer questioned, and with that have come three decades of extensive study of Peter Behrens.

I happily acknowledge our debt to this recent scholarship, but there are reasons why my earlier study may survive. That it has an underground existence within Behrens scholarship can be recognized—is sometimes acknowledged—in the later works. Publication thus brings an underground source to light; but there are more fundamental reasons to attend to my original study. A condition for its survival is that, despite the emergence of lost records and much detailed information on Behrens, no new resource has appeared to invalidate or marginalize my work. Its strongest claim for survival is, however, a sustained critical attitude. Recent scholarship ranges from the descriptive, through the reflective glory of Behrens within local histories, to global recuperative studies. A global critical study of Behrens remains a different enterprise.

Before describing how this book is altered from the dissertation, one may also reflect on how the original study may appear different due to the changed context of its reading.

While I had the privilege of personally meeting Walter Gropius and Ludwig Mies van der Rohe and of listening to Frank Lloyd Wright and Le Corbusier, my initiation into architecture was at the hands of the following generation. That is to say, I am of the generation that witnessed, with some alienation, the fading enthusiasms of modern architecture in the decade following the Second World War. Something had gone wrong, and that was both the impetus and the condition for critical historical studies rather than propagandistic stories and criticism. What I sought then and now is both an understanding of architecture in and for itself—what I like to call the discipline of architecture—and of the reciprocities of that discipline with society. I turned to Behrens as a notable figure at the roots of architectural modernism and found him to be interestingly problematic both for the discipline and for its social condition. I sought an understanding that might be helpful in sorting out those continuities that we could value. Writing critical history was worth the trouble precisely because one was not practicing a wholesale rejection of a modernist past. But it is also my generation, working over the last thirty-five years, that opened just that spectrum from critical history through naive rejection—with a reflected spectrum of advocacy and practice. Consequently, the ways of looking at the past, and thus of looking at Behrens or a study of Behrens, multiplied. I recall Philip Johnson, with Robert Stern at his elbow, standing before a group of photographs of works of Peter Behrens at a conference at Columbia University in the late sixties. Johnson rejected Behrens's AEG Turbine Factory (frontispiece), the building that was the universal icon of Behrens's early mastery in modernism. On the contrary, Johnson provocatively endorsed the AEG Small Motors Factory (figure 7.27) and even the German Embassy in St. Petersburg (figure 8.46). No argument from the discipline of architecture was offered, still less a consideration of architecture in its relation to culture and society. It was an instance of projective taste-making, which Johnson himself was notably successful in implementing. Thus the work of Behrens can be seen from new, if empty, perspectives. But if we look more deeply, even where Behrens appears problematic, where, for example, he transforms architecture in complicity with selfishly motivated political and economic power, there are continuing reasons to consider his achievements. In our own period of intensifying international capitalism, for example, the Deutscher Werkbund (and Behrens's signal role within that organization) bears renewed attention—and not only as a cautionary tale. Within the Deutscher Werkbund, and in contemporary criticism such as that of Adolf Loos, unusual intelligence was brought to bear on modern production. The shift from complicity to contribution may be subtle. A refusal to learn from such endeavors is more likely to lead to abject complicity than is a renewal of that past intelligence.

Finally, descriptively, the book is this. Chapters 1–8 are the original dissertation, supplemented in two identifiable ways: detailed and magisterial studies such as that by Tilmann Buddensieg and his colleagues on Behrens's AEG work or Gisela Moeller on Behrens's Düsseldorf years cannot be subsumed, but are acknowledged in "Postscripts" to the most closely related chapters. Studies on more specific topics are incorporated by references in new or expanded notes. Chapter 9, on Behrens's work between the wars, is new except as it incorporates a small part of what had been the "Conclusion." The new conclusion elaborates the original one.

Chapters 1, 4, and 8 of the original were never published. The publication record of the other chapters will be found in the last section of the bibliography. All chapters have been edited. Chapter 3 is cut significantly in its coverage of the theater in Behrens's career; it is now better balanced for a role in a book, but some specialist readers may wish to consult its publication in *Perspecta*.

Peter Behrens
and a
New Architecture
for the
Twentieth Century

1

A Context for the Early Work of Behrens: The Emergence of a New Architecture in Germany and Austria around 1900

Comprehension of the development of the architect Peter Behrens requires a general understanding of the progressive movements in European art and architecture between 1890 and 1910. To evoke such a context with economy, I will emphasize only two representative issues: the almost universal concern, around 1900, with line as a formal element; and the frequently cited importance of Vienna for the origins of the new architecture which culminated in the so-called International Style of the 1920s.

The early stages of a new architecture in Germany and Austria around the year 1900 may be recognized in Vienna, Dresden, and Munich, on through south and west Germany to Darmstadt and Düsseldorf, and even as far as Oldenburg in the lowland area of northwest Germany. Only in Vienna did this revolution center on a trained architect, Otto Wagner (1841–1918), and on his students, especially Joseph Olbrich (1867–1908) and Josef Hoffmann (1870–1956). In 1899, Olbrich, who had designed the Secession Building in Vienna (figure 1.1), became the architect of the important new German experiment in environmental arts, the Darmstadt Artists' Colony. According to many critics, the major public manifestation of the colony, the Darmstadt exhibition of 1901 (see chapter 3), initiated the so-called modern movement in architecture.[1]

The standard works on the history of modern architecture indicate that Vienna had an important influence on the new architecture of Germany. The most obvious agent of this influence would be Olbrich; the most obvious recipient would be his artist-colleague at Darmstadt, Peter Behrens, who was shortly to be considered Germany's leading architect. On consideration, however, one may question whether the influence of Vienna upon Germany was either as early as is claimed or of the wholly beneficial character that is implied. The Viennese Secession (1897) was, after all, the last of the major national manifestations of that international renewal termed Art Nouveau.[2] Movements in England, Belgium, and France preceded it. In Germany, the elegant, avant-garde journal *Pan* had been founded in 1894, the popular *Jugend* in 1895. Munich had its Secession in 1892;

1.1 Joseph Maria Olbrich. Vienna, Secession Building (1899). Perspective by Olbrich.

1.2 Franz Schwechten. Berlin, Kaiser Wilhelm-Gedächtniskirche (1891–1895).

Germany then distinctly celebrated the new manner with several exhibitions and new periodicals in 1897. Furthermore, at the Darmstadt colony, Peter Behrens became an antagonist, not a disciple, of Olbrich. Behrens transformed himself into an architect, built his own house at the colony (figure 3.7), and won critical acclaim while Olbrich was commonly dismissed by the critics for his Viennese frivolity.[3]

To understand Behrens's development, or, for that matter, what influence Vienna did have upon the new architecture of Germany in the early twentieth century, it is necessary to offer a more general characterization of both the new endeavors in art and the conservative state of architecture in Germany around 1900.

In the late nineteenth century, German architects engaged in a search for an architectural style appropriate to the new German Empire. This search resulted in an eclectic, retrospective manner—the adoption and manipulation of any historical prototype thought to manifest northern, as opposed to Mediterranean, spirit. The movement encouraged *Alt-Deutsch,* that is, "Old German," motifs and assembled these elements in chiaroscuro compositions, consciously opposed to the well-drawn forms of the Mediterranean tradition.[4] Franz Schwechten's Kaiser Wilhelm Memorial Church of 1891–1895 in Berlin (figure 1.2) typifies such *Alt-Deutsch* design.

The prevalence of an *Alt-Deutsch* sensibility among German architects of the 1890s is dramatically clear in two examples. The only architectural designs published in the first volume (1897–1898) of the important nationalist, avant-garde periodical *Deutsche Kunst und Dekoration* (published by Alexander Koch and intimately involved in all the subsequent endeavors at Darmstadt, including the Artists' Colony of 1899 and its later exhibitions) were *Alt-Deutsch* designs. Again, at Berlin in 1898, the young Hans Poelzig (1869–1936), who was properly trained in architecture at Berlin's Technische Hochschule and who was later to be one of Germany's most inventive architects, succeeded in winning the coveted prize that bore the name of Germany's greatest classicist architect, Karl Friedrich Schinkel, with an *Alt-Deutsch* design (figure 1.3). With his prize money, Poelzig traveled through Germany and Austria; his biographer, Theodor Heuss, reports that "Poelzig also went to Vienna and came into the circle of the students of Otto Wagner. Poelzig, in a lecture sometime later, recounted that he had been disillusioned by this early encounter with the Vienna circle and had not taken part in the enthusiasm for the 'new line.' He remained cool, skeptically interested; what he saw appeared to him to be too much a graphic formalism."[5] Thus even one of the daring young architects of Germany could continue an exploration of medieval and German Renaissance forms, remaining skeptical about the Wagner circle.[6]

To consider the people who were in those years distinctly open to new ideas, one must turn to those Art Nouveau artists who were working their way through graphics and crafts to become self-taught architects. An almost obsessive concern with line has long

1.3 Hans Poelzig. Project for a *Stadthaus,* Schinkel Prize, 1898. Section and partial elevation.

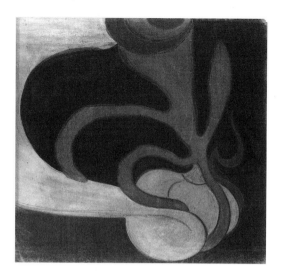

1.4 Henry van de Velde. Abstract plant composition (1892–1893). Pastel.

1.5 Otto Eckmann. *Five Swans* (1897). Tapestry.

been noted as a characterizing feature of Art Nouveau artists. Within the period itself, and recurrently in later discussions of Art Nouveau, the particular character of an artist's line served as a key to a theoretical position. Schmutzler preserves an old theoretical polarity that can be labeled in many ways.[7] Hermann Muthesius had suggested, derisively, that the poles were dominated by the "geschwungene Linie" and the "Blümchenornament," or as we might say, "the whiplash curve" and "nice little floral ornaments."[8] Henry van de Velde (1863–1957), the Belgian artist who worked in Germany after 1899 and who is generally considered the epitome of the school of the so-called "Belgian line," made the same distinction more earnestly.[9] He opposed his own "abstract" or "linear" approach (figure 1.4; these artists were also called *Konstruktionisten*) to the Germanic "floral" direction (figure 1.5; these artists were also called *Naturalisten*) epitomized by Otto Eckmann (1865–1902), a Munich artist.[10]

The stimuli for these polar distinctions are clear enough if we concentrate on particular works of van de Velde and Eckmann. Even for these artists, however, the division of "linear" versus "floral" confuses the situation. Both artists were overtly concerned with line, though in different ways; to insist that Eckmann and the German Jugendstil were "floral" is to mistake a mere motif for their more general concern. On the other hand, the simple characterization of van de Velde's work as "abstract," or as "functionalist," has tended to confuse his work with later works of regular geometrical form that are more closely connected with the so-called "floral" school. Finally, if we try to understand other artists of the time in terms of this linear-floral division, the situation becomes hopelessly muddled. To articulate more adequately the artistic attitudes that were operative around 1900, it is possible to structure four (admittedly still schematic) positions, as presented in table 1.

Table 1. Recognizable Artistic Attitudes in German Art Nouveau (Jugendstil)

	Patheticists		Idealists (intellectualists)	
	Nonobjective	Abstract	Lyric "Dionysian"	Hieratic "Apollonian"
General Concept of Form in Art	Form as a tangible given of experience that solicits a response from the observer through a physiological mechanism	Form as a tangible given of experience that the observer "feels with" through the involvement of all levels of the psyche	Form as an a priori, ideal conception of the artist, used to give order to raw experience; conventionalism	Form as an a priori, ideal power of the creator through which sprit is given to inert matter
Typical Attitude toward Formal Elements	Straight lines, planes, and colors as basic, constructive formal elements	Forms (especially line) and color as affective forces	The "line" of dance, music, and poetry as a formal model	"Unnaturalness" of geometry and architecture as formal model
Response of Subject to Art	Empathy as an original and synthetic phenomenon without reliance on association Empathy as subjective response to external stimuli	Empathy as a process in which the subject contributes to the form—but not as mere association Empathy as a give-and-take process	May involve empathy in the original sense of "feeling in" (psychological projection of one's self); reliance on association and sentiment	Mystic projection of spirit
Subject-Object Relationship	Object as a given for the subject	Subject-object indivisibly fused	Subject as the organizer of the object	Subject as creator of the object
Artist Active within Such Attitude	Endell (fig. 1.13)	van de Velde (fig. 1.4)	Eckmann, early Behrens (fig. 1.5)	Beuron school (fig. 1.6)

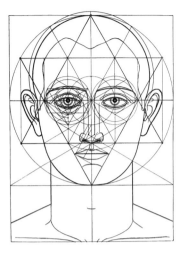

1.6 Father Desiderius Lenz (1832–1928). Canonic head (ca. 1870–1871). Drawing.

One can begin with a somewhat arcane but brief presentation of the artist monks of Kloster Beuron on the upper Danube. These monks, especially their artistic leader, Father Desiderius Lenz, absolutely opposed any naturalistic theory of art. They sought rather to overcome the world and to reveal the ideal beauty of original creation; this could only be achieved through an art of unapproachable loftiness, whose mysterious symbolism would reveal the essence of life rather than its details. Models for this "hieratic art," as they called it, were the arts of Egypt, of "Apollonian Greece," of the Roman catacombs, and of Byzantium. The "unnaturalness" of architecture and of geometry led the monks to a mystic geometry, the occult meanings of which served to breathe spirit into the lifeless matter of man and of building—as in Lenz's canonic head (figure 1.6) and the St. Maurus Chapel built by the monks in 1870 (figure 2.14).[11] Form, in the hieratic art of Beuron, was thus an a priori ideal, an intellectual power manifested in geometry, through which the artist participated in a mystic spiritualization of nature. This spiritualization, they claimed, is what we call "style."[12]

Among the groups that were active in Munich of the 1890s, one recognizes positions that, like the monks of Beuron, opposed naturalistic theories of art, shared an interest in line as a formal element, and yet were to be distinguished one from another. These groups may be termed the idealists (or intellectualists) and the patheticists.[13] Each of them may in turn be subdivided.

In table 1, "idealist" is used to designate the conviction that form is an ideal conception of the creator, an organizing and controlling pattern that is brought to and imposed upon experience. Among idealists, the monks of Beuron represented a preference for an absolute, mystic, and hieratic conception of form. If the mystic sense of preordained order is abandoned, an idealist may still conceive of ideal forms and patterns as the conventions by which one does, in fact, comprehend experience. The restructuring and manipulation of these patterns is a mental process and is not complicated by solicitations from, or contributions to, a world of forms external to the subject. Obviously this is not a new theory; it underlies the classical conception of art.[14] The contribution of an artist such as Otto Eckmann to this old tradition was the establishment of an ideal pattern or form that had not been so fully exploited before—the curved line, as in his famous *Swans* wall hanging (figure 1.5). The ideal line was a graphic means; when it appeared alone it was often drawn with a pen that maintained a constant line width in order to minimize the natural ebb and flow of the ink supply and the pressure and movement of the hand. There was a tendency to use the line as a contour; in this way the line became an outline and thus more ideational, since the eye now gave substance to the enclosed surface rather than to the line itself. The ideal line became the mental and artistic control of the world; the outline could enclose representations of nature. Among the things that were represented were flowers, the blossoms of which could also be rendered with an orderly and repetitive geometry. As in Peter Behrens's *Blaue Blume* (an overt homage to early nineteenth-century romanticism; figure 1.7), the idealistic school of Jugendstil tried to hold numerous factors in a self-conscious, stylized tension: a representation of nature controlled by an as yet

1.7 Peter Behrens. *Blaue Blume* (Fall 1897). Color woodcut (endpapers for Otto Julius Bierbaum's *Die vernarrte Prinzessin*).

incompletely explored artistic form, the wavy line, which in turn was often controlled by a regular geometry. The model for this type of form was to be found in those arts that are extended in time and possessed of strong conventions, especially dance and lyric poetry. In the case of Behrens, this program developed in close collaboration with the lyric poets Otto Julius Bierbaum and Richard Dehmel.

Henry van de Velde was the central figure of the patheticists, and especially of those—noted in table 1 as "abstract"—who accepted the idea of a complex interaction of form and observer. Since van de Velde felt no need to prove that our aesthetic responses stem from nonobjective forms, it was acceptable that a form be merely abstracted from nature and that it partly rely upon our experience (figure 1.4). In van de Velde's works it is usually impossible to specify that a given motif relies upon wind-blown sand or a specific muscle connection, and yet his works are abstracts of natural experience which are affective partially through *our* response as organisms. Van de Velde went beyond such innate or universally learned responses to a conception of line as an entity. Something of the quality of his search emerges from his description of his wonderment when introduced to Seurat's *Grande Jatte* in 1887. Van de Velde understood the conscientious use of line as well as the theoretical significance of the change from chemical to optical mixing of color. His commentary reveals even more about himself: "The impressionist technique is better suited than any other for the expression of vital abundance and radiant fullness. It was at one with my vibrant and spontaneously reactive nature." Van de Velde experimented with neoimpressionist painting and studied the quality of line as he experienced it in his garden or on the beach. When he gave up painting, he remarked, "The daemon of the line did not leave me, and as I created my first ornaments [figure 1.8], they arose out of the dynamic play of the elemental power of line."[15]

Whereas the graphic, ideal line assumed various appearances, none of which insisted upon its own reality, van de Velde's line asserted its reality by existing as abstract form and by pulsing with immanent energy. His position is epitomized in his famous statement,

1.8 Henry van de Velde. Title ornament, *Van nu en straks* (1893).

1.9 Victor Horta. Brussels, Tassel house (1893–1895). Stair landing.

1.10 Henry van de Velde. Uccle, near Brussels, architect's own house Bloemenwerf (1895).

1.11 Henry van de Velde. Dining room furniture (1895).

"The line is a force."[16] In architecture, a similar attitude to line was first evidenced by Victor Horta (1861–1947) in his famous Tassel house of 1893–1895 in Brussels (figure 1.9). By the spring of 1896, van de Velde had moved into his house "Bloemenwerf" in Uccle (figure 1.10), which marked his entry into both architectural and furniture design. Van de Velde termed his furniture (figure 1.11) "a lively image" of the method that he always followed. Through what he liked to call *vernunftgemässe Gestaltung* (rational form-ing), he sought to find "the satisfactory constructions and forms that would please the eye with their elementary and primitive independence." Prior to this statement, van de Velde had claimed that his furniture shared its *vernunftgemässe Gestaltung* with ship design, and

1.12 Hermann Obrist.
Column (1898; destroyed).

that it was the unconscious recognition of this that led Edmond de Goncourt to characterize the work of van de Velde, negatively, as a "yachting style."[17]

Van de Velde's words and works reveal a vitalistic and dynamistic attitude and a sense for the primacy of the life force. His primitive forms and constructions were possessed of that dynamic, elemental power of line by which the viewer is in turn possessed. The "vibrant and spontaneously reactive personality" of both artist and viewer play back and forth upon the form until subject and object are indivisibly fused. This is not the rather sentimental "feeling in" of earlier empathic theory, but rather a complex "feeling with" that involves the psyche at all levels. One cannot say whether viewer or object controls the encounter. Between the artist and the world of form—especially the line—there is approximately the relationship that exists between an inventive person and electrical energy.

Van de Velde quickly succeeded in establishing a theoretical and practical position. He won international renown through both his own efforts and those of S. Bing and Julius Meier-Graefe in Paris. Through the interest of these men, van de Velde's work was shown at Dresden in 1897. From that time, his renown was especially high in Germany, where he worked from 1899 until the First World War. The important interiors of the Folkwang Museum in Hagen of 1902 (figure 1.21) show the consistent development of his abstract, *pathetisch* architecture. It was architecture such as this that was called "functional" at the time, in reference to its vitalistic sense of organic function rather than to any insistence on pragmatic efficiency, for which the word "functional" was later used in architectural discourse.

Although its effect was delayed, a *pathetisch* theory still more abstract than that of van de Velde can be recognized in Munich prior to van de Velde's prominence in Germany. This position is indicated under the heading "nonobjective" in table 1 and was stated most clearly—as it concerns architecture at least—by August Endell (1871–1925) beginning in November 1897.[18] Endell was a philosophy student who also studied the psychophysiologists of the late nineteenth century,[19] and who subsequently learned both artistic theory and practice from Hermann Obrist (1863–1927).[20] Obrist, himself a student of the natural sciences turned artist, had founded a shop in Florence in 1892 producing embroideries with motifs abstracted from nature. There he must have known of the artistically prominent German (Munich) circle of Konrad Fiedler (1841–1895) and Adolf Hildebrand (1847–1921). Fiedler had already emphasized the concept of pure form in painting; in 1893 Hildebrand extended these ideas to sculpture and also evidenced a reliance on contemporary theories of empathy.[21] In 1894 Obrist moved his shop to Munich and turned to Hildebrand's activity, sculpture. Obrist executed an almost nonobjective sculpture in 1898, a column emerging from live rock (figure 1.12). This work evidences a response to contemporary vitalistic concerns with becoming, but the highly abstract capital is also an illustration of Endell's theory of nonobjective artistic form:

> Formal structures [*formale Gebilde*] are the goal of the whole of decorative art—not stylized plants and animals. These formal structures are developed freely, setting line on line, plane on plane, in accordance with the character which is sought. . . . A feeling for form is the basic requirement of the person who appreciates as well as of the one who creates. For any particular purpose, the creator must have a fantasy so full with forms that they flow effortlessly to him in great numbers, out of which he chooses and constructs his formal structure.[22]

Endell also set out a psychology of perception that hypothesized neural stimulation by physiological reactions to the viewing of lines. Straight lines would arouse the feeling of quickness—the longer and thinner the line, the quicker. A vertical line is light and carefree; the horizontal has quiet strength. These psychic feelings, Endell suggested, are stimulated by actual physical movement of the eyes and are in accordance with the comparative strains they induce. All feelings are said to be composed of tempo and tension, all nuances of which can be stimulated by visual forms; it can be shown that all forms are finally only modifications and combinations of straight lines. Endell noted that complexes of lines are necessary to arouse and sustain effects; consequently he did not offer any table of correspondences between particular lines and feelings. But he did go on to a demonstration of his straight-line structures in comparative house facades, where he recognized such qualities as expansiveness and tension (figure 1.13).[23]

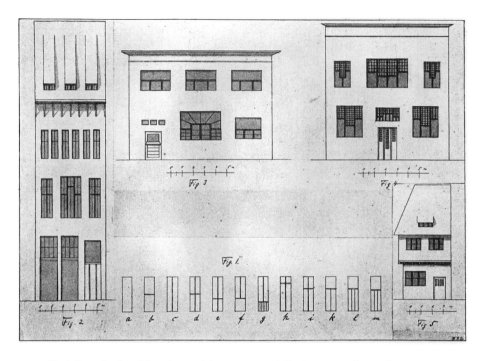

Endell made the claim that architecture especially is an art of pure form:

The naturalists and the stylizers [a slap at Eckmann] may make very pretty things in the crafts; but they totally collapse on an architectural problem. . . . A capital, or a door surround—with these one demonstrates whether one is really a *Formkünstler* [form-artist] or whether one is only capable of reducing the forms of nature to simpler lines. . . . The architect must be a *Formkünstler;* the way to a new architecture must be achieved through the art of pure form [*reine Formkunst*]. We have, of course, very few works of pure *Formkunst*, that is, very few formal structures, which, like the tones of music, *are* nothing, and *mean* nothing, and which affect us directly without any intellectual mediation.[24]

In describing a method of architectural design, Endell began by directing his fantasy upon the interiors until every space fulfilled its purpose, had a formal character attuned to its purpose, and was in proper relation to the other spaces. He then turned to the exterior of the building: "Avoiding all painterly arrangements and without any poverty of effect, it is possible to achieve an aesthetically valuable effect solely through the lines of what is absolutely necessary—very simple walls, naked windows with their divisions, and the lines of the roof and chimneys." Aside from such fundamental forming, "ornament does give to the architect the opportunity to enliven the basic character of the building through a series of nuances."[25]

1.14 August Endell. Munich, Atelier Elvira (1896–1897). Facade.

1.15 Joseph Maria Olbrich. Darmstadt, Artists' Colony, architect's own house (1900–1901). View from street.

The extraordinary ornament on the front of the Atelier Elvira (figure 1.14), which may be contrasted with the ornament of one of Olbrich's houses (figure 1.15), is rendered more comprehensible by the following principles of ornament which were advanced by Endell: To divide a plane in small units and then to fill these with single ornaments is to destroy the original surface. Decoration must be at a scale to work with the plane in which it is to be seen. Ornament based on the human figure is limited because of the strict proportions involved. Free forms are needed, and when at all possible, on every place a new form—especially in the vertical where one expects an event (*ein Geschehen*), a crescendo or a decrescendo. Ornament should not be used just for tonal effect, that is, for the mere desire to enliven a plane without emphasizing any point. Endell finally sums up: "All our endeavors seek: free reign for the fantasy, to indicate the goal and at the same time to set aside all dogmas. We seek free forms without any tradition, forms that ascend from the soul of the individual and therefore are his forms, his creations."[26]

The Elvira ornament, and Endell's acknowledgment that the free creative endeavor of the true *Formkünstler* might result in plantlike or animal-like forms, indicate how the distinction between van de Velde's and Endell's approaches could be blurred. Many variations were explored by the rapidly expanding number of patheticists in Munich, including

1.16 Richard Riemerschmid. Chair (1898–1899).

such men as Richard Riemerschmid (1868–1957; figure 1.16), Bernhard Pankok (1872–1943), and Bruno Paul (1874–1954) as well as Endell and Obrist. Soon formal parallels with rococo, and then with late Gothic and with Celtic art, were recognized by the critics or even overtly exploited by the artists. These events also blurred the historical attitude of both van de Velde and Endell. Their formal endeavors, conceived independent of historical time both theoretically and practically, were captured by men like Karl Scheffler under whose hand even the inappropriate label of the "Belgian line" (referring to work by, or related to, van de Velde) could be transformed into the modern expression of "northern spirit." Scheffler felt this non-Mediterranean spirit to be demanded by historical destiny and by the imperatives of the historical moment.[27] Thus even the concept of pure form was taken out of its timeless state and inserted in a historicist framework where it has been held captive ever since.[28]

The division of artistic attitudes in the Jugendstil period presented in table 1 is neither exhaustive nor absolutely categorical; nevertheless, this division does appear to correspond more closely with the historical evidence than the old "abstract" and "floral" poles. A further advantage of the division here proposed is that it is especially helpful in understanding the collapse of Art Nouveau and the ensuing period of reconstruction.

As early as 1901, distinctly in 1902, a crisis arose in the new art and architecture. This crisis involved strife within the artistic world, but was worsened and partially provoked by an event external to the artists: the vulgarization of their distinctive formal element, the freely curved line. When exploitative manufacturers and craftsmen took the new art as a model, they produced objects of more questionable value than when they borrowed from styles that offered more secure conventions. These derivative new works often incorporated motifs from other styles and indiscriminately used linear elements from both the patheticist and idealist schools. The creative artists within the new art thus suffered a double blow: their program to supplant derivative and eclectic production with creative, original manufacture had collapsed; their own formal contribution had been debased.

Significantly, this vulgarization of the freely moving line, and of the new art generally, reinforced the claims of those who favored *Sachlichkeit,* the meaning of which will emerge in the context of this paragraph. As early as the late 1890s in Munich, the main center of German Secessionist activities, an attitude toward architecture appeared that was radically different from the Art Nouveau involvement with form. The pages of the international, avant-garde publication *Dekorative Kunst* incorporated reports from Hermann Muthesius (1861–1927), a cultural attaché of the German embassy in London from 1896 to 1903. From its founding in 1897 on through the entire period of Art Nouveau, *Dekorative Kunst* published thoughtful essays and information on English arts and crafts, on the necessity of modern industry and related social concerns, on Port Sunlight (figure 1.17), and on such architects as Voysey, Ashbee, and Baillie Scott.[29] Essayists and critics including Alfred Lichtwark, Julius Meier-Graefe, and Karl Scheffler contributed articles on the importance of machine art and on the acceptance of needs and functions as generators of any work in the applied arts. Nevertheless, these *sachlich*—that is, matter-of-fact, pragmatically conditioned, or objective—concerns remained only an undercurrent in the

1.17 Port Sunlight, England, the Lever company town (founded 1887). Street view.

1.18 Rudolph Alexander
Schröder. Munich, A. W.
Heymel apartment (1899–
1901). Entrance hall.

1.19 Schröder. Heymel
apartment. Bedroom.

German-language magazines; these concerns stimulated reports and informed analyses
rather than an active program. However, coincident with the crisis of Art Nouveau in
1901–1902 when it appeared that the wrath of God had been visited upon those who had
slighted the honorable simplicities of life, the directives which need, purpose, material,
structure, economy, and straightforwardness can give to architecture were programmatically restated. Muthesius's teachings, based on what he had learned in England, seemed
increasingly persuasive. Still more impressive, both Muthesius and Meier-Graefe could
publish eulogies for a German work that contributed to the cause of *Sachlichkeit.* Early in
1901, Meier-Graefe published in *Dekorative Kunst* the elegant but simple interior that the
poet Rudolf Alexander Schroeder designed for his fellow editor of *Die Insel,* A. W. Heymel
(figures 1.18–19).[30] The critics saw in these interiors a frank, earnest use of materials
intensified to a stylistic elegance by the use of a controlling geometry. Meier-Graefe
acknowledged the related significance of Adolf Loos (1870–1933), the important and
vociferous Viennese enemy of the superfluous.[31] Loos drew upon both the geometric rigor
of Viennese Secessionist idealism and the *Sachlichkeit* of several domestic styles he had
experienced: especially those of America, England, and the Germanic "Empire Style"
which is called Biedermeier. By 1904, the old campaigners of the Viennese Secession had
founded a new journal, *Hohe Warte.* Its format was simple, and the subject matter concentrated upon the homely rightness of English endeavors, garden cities, the love for
Biedermeier, restoration of monuments, city-building, and other such obvious virtues.

It is notable that the crisis of Art Nouveau was not equally critical for all those concerned. The freely curved line was now anathema. For the idealist school, the loss of the
wavy line was merely the loss of one possible formal device, a device they had, in any case,
usually employed under other formal controls (figure 1.7). For these artists, alternative formal devices were at hand; they quickly turned to regular geometries as a familiar tool (figure 1.20). Such geometries were, after all, better attuned to their attitude than was the
moving line. Under the impact of this situation, the intellectualist, formal line became at
once both more ideal and more compelling. As in the case of Peter Behrens, it was not even

1.20 Josef Hoffmann. Vienna, Beer-Hofmann house (1905–1906). Upper hall.

necessary for the idealist to attempt an accommodation with *Sachlichkeit.* After Behrens's few early experiments in the mode of van de Velde, the crisis of the curved line settled him, for a time, as the most severe of all idealists. His Oldenburg pavilions (figure 2.6) concede nothing to physical reality; they are an absolutely ideal, geometrical conception, a conception with significance beyond mere exhibition pavilions. It was at this time that the monks of Beuron found considerable satisfaction in noting that Behrens's close friend Otto Julius Bierbaum, whom the monks termed "lascivious" and "of the innermost camp of the sexualists," had nevertheless been astonished and edified when he stood before the hieratic works of the school of Beuron at Monte Cassino in 1903.[32] On that same Italian trip, Bierbaum wrote to Behrens of his recognition that the rituals and festivals, the conventionalized forms of the Catholic Church, succeeded in uniting Italian art and life. He also wrote of his enthusiasm for the exalted effect of the church of San Miniato (figures 2.13, 2.16) on the edge of Florence.[33] A few years later Behrens completed a hieratic crematorium in Hagen (figure 2.12), which is simultaneously controlled by regular geometries and derivative from both Beuron's St. Maurus Chapel (figure 2.14) and San Miniato (figure 2.13).

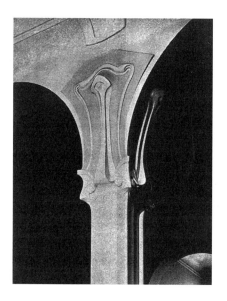 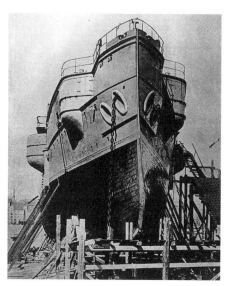

1.21 Henry van de Velde. Hagen, Folkwang Museum (1900–1901). Capital.

1.22 German warship. This image and that of the capital from his Folkwang Museum (figure 1.21) were the only catalog illustrations to van de Velde's programmatic exhibition "Linie und Form," Krefeld (1904).

For van de Velde and the patheticists generally, there was no easy solution to the crisis of Art Nouveau. A commitment to the idea that "line is a force" demands the full exploitation of the free line. The degradation of the energetic line delivered a blow to the patheticist school from which it never fully recovered. Its hope for recovery was in the restoration of respect for that energetic line, a restoration attempted in an exhibition called "Line and Form" held at the Kaiser Wilhelm Museum in Krefeld in 1904. Van de Velde and the director of the museum, Friedrich Deneken, exerted all effort to reinstate the validity of the curved line. The frontispiece of the catalog illustrated a capital from van de Velde's Folkwang Museum in Hagen (figure 1.21).[34] Deneken's essay in the catalog discussed color and line as the most important expressive means of the plastic arts, insisting on the power and beauty of line. The exhibition attempted to document the verity of these claims in works of art ranging from Greek vases to the early nineteenth-century paintings of Philipp Otto Runge as well as in forms from nature and from the marvels of modern industry. The tailpiece was a German Imperial Navy photograph of a warship (figure 1.22). It is at this point that the old term "yachting style" becomes a program; van de Velde's architecture, along with nature's forms and the engineers' bridges, all become works of *vernunftgemässe Gestaltung*. As before, the programmatic base was the rational organization of forces, now reinforced by more hardheaded examples.

The artists of the Vienna Secession were more constant in their embodiment of the idealist position than Eckmann or Behrens, both of whom sometimes experimented with the patheticist line.[35] Furthermore, the Secession, centering as it did on three architects (Wagner, Hoffmann, and Olbrich), illuminates the significance of this idealist position for architecture.

The early architectural projects of the Secession architects revealed the same graphic line as is found in Eckmann and Behrens. Architectural rendering was not treated simply as a literal depiction of the proposed building; rather, it was treated as an art with the same demand for integrity as any other graphic art. The style of the rendering had to be the appropriate counterpart to contemporary painting, sculpture, and architecture—not merely a descriptive device for the architect. Since design and rendering precede execution, this attitude to architectural graphics tended to influence the form of buildings and landscapes. To preserve the sense of line in three dimensions, both silhouette and surface ornament were emphasized. Small trees were trimmed into spheres which maintained a constant outline, and the naturalistic filigree of the dome of the Secession Building was also spherical (figure 1.1). Wagner insisted that architecture was distinct from the other arts in not taking nature as its model; but it could discipline nature, as in the Secession Building or in Wagner's city railway station on Karlsplatz (figure 1.23). Similarly, the new line often controlled traditional architectural elements rather than controlling nature. The massing of many Secession buildings was either severely geometrical or candidly reminiscent of neoclassical composition (figure 1.24); what was new could be in the ornament alone. Even one of Wagner's students and admirers wrote of the "frequent eruptions of a joyous, genuinely Viennese instinct for play, with a spontaneous pleasure in exaggerated flourishes."[36]

1.23 Otto Wagner. Vienna, City Railway Station, Karlsplatz (1898–1899).

1.24 Otto Wagner. Vienna, City Railway Station, Hietzing (1897–1898).

1.25 Beuron, Germany, Beuron Monastery, chapel. Interior (plan by Father Mauritius Gissler, 1898–1899; paintings by Father Paul Krebs).

1.26 Otto Wagner. Vienna, Steinhof Asylum, church (1905–1907). Interior.

At Vienna, sensuous form had been only a counterpoint to a governing geometry. After the crisis of the freely curving line and the ascendance of things *sachlich,* geometry distinctly dominated; however, the situation encouraged the search for possible justifications, such as claiming that things which are clearly geometric are also *sachlich.* A spiritual justification was offered in an exhibition of the hieratic art of the monks of Beuron (figure 1.25) at the Secession Building in Vienna in 1905.[37] The monks offered an occult understanding of geometry and prototypes of an art and architecture that combined austere principle with a lush surface. This tension between a regulated form and an extravagant surface was very much to the taste of early twentieth-century Vienna. A rather close reflection of Beuron's form and content may be seen in Wagner's church for the insane asylum at Steinhof (figure 1.26). The figures atop Josef Hoffmann's Palais Stoclet in Brussels (figure 1.27) crown a work otherwise reduced to simple Secessionist geometry. Gustav Klimt's wall encrustations for the dining room of the Palais Stoclet (figure 1.28) are also consistent with this predilection for a simultaneity of symbolism, geometry, and a rich ornamental surface. Even Wagner's Postal Savings Bank of 1904–1906 (figure 1.29), famous for its simplicity, culminated in winged victories and wreaths. These would be rather literal lessons from the idealist tradition as exemplified at Beuron. But if one turns to the famous main hall of the Savings Bank (figure 1.30), a more sophisticated application of idealistic, or even hieratic, principle is evident. The material of this world—the

1.27 Josef Hoffmann. Brussels, Palais Stoclet
(1905–1911). Exterior.

1.28 Hoffmann. Palais Stoclet. Dining room.

1.29 Otto Wagner. Vienna, Postal Savings
Bank (1904–1906). Detail of exterior.

1.30 Wagner. Postal Savings Bank. Main hall.

metal and glass of the modern world—is bared to us; yet material and technique have been overcome. The details of an engineered building are not placed before us in the *sachlich* manner of nineteenth-century exhibition halls or railway sheds; the concept of an engineered building is revealed instead through the building's own modernist symbols of exposed industrial materials, structure, and equipment. The "reading" of this immediately sensible but rather mystically rationalized hall parallels Father Ansgar Pöllmann's observation that, like the Latin of the Roman liturgy, the symbolism of hieratic art can only be fully appreciated by the initiate, by the adept. Pöllmann went on to say that every art must be sensuous—or better, sensible. *Hieratik,* however, is only sensuous in the most elevated manner; it is more possessed of intellectual sense than of sensuousness.[38]

Considering the idealist, classical preference that even Secessionist decoration did not obscure in the essentially academic work and teaching of Wagner, it is not surprising that the Viennese, Olbrich, and Behrens increasingly relied on an overt classicism (see frontispiece). Behrens came to think of himself as the Schinkel of the twentieth century. As Schinkel was the artistic fulfillment of Winckelmann's understanding of antiquity, so Behrens was the fulfillment of the modern understanding of antiquity as formulated by such men as Schliemann, Nietzsche, and Riegl.[39] Through Behrens's classicizing factories, this modern understanding could encompass an idea such as Loos's statement that the "engineers are our Hellenes."

When Julius Meier-Graefe wrote his developmental history of modern art in 1904, this former advocate of van de Velde had become a mild critic.[40] The entire multivolume text ends with a projection of Behrens (then in his most idealizing, geometric period) and the Viennese as the hope of the future. Thus, even the inner circle now dismissed the patheticist program in favor of the more conservative idealist program. Although not alone, the academically trained Viennese had constantly offered a strong idealist example in both theory and practice. They never wavered from a belief in the primacy of artistic form—an attitude that was both justified and strengthened by the collapse of Art Nouveau.

Concerning the *sachlich* program, up to this time the architects of Germany and Austria offered little in the way of practical or technological innovation; only a few architects such as Muthesius and Loos avidly admired what more pragmatic (especially American and English) architects had achieved. In Germany, the interest in nonobjective form was not reinterpreted within the new preference for *Sachlichkeit;* even the potential contribution of van de Velde's thought to the organization of operative systems of forces was temporarily submerged. Germans and Austrians alike contributed to the new attitude of restraint through a predilection for the simple architecture and furnishings of the Biedermeier times and through an interest in the new idea of the garden city. In addition, Vienna offered the sensitive, traditional city-building concepts of Camillo Sitte (1843–1903)[41] and the antidecorative program of Adolf Loos.[42] However, in the main Germany and Austria received the strict *sachlich* program from England and America, primarily through such intermediaries as Muthesius and Loos. Under the influence of Muthesius's book *Stilarchitektur und Baukunst* (an invidious contrast of the classically derived word *Stilarchitektur* and the "arty" architecture of styles with the Germanic word *Baukunst* and its suggestion of a wholesome art of building), Otto Wagner changed the name of his famous book from *Moderne Architektur* to *Die Baukunst unserer Zeit.*[43] Without changing the content of his book, Wagner was accepting a change of attitude— from a rebellion concerned with the freedom of the artist toward a practical, *sachlich* program that would fulfill and represent the historical moment, "The Art of Building of Our Time." Wagner's book under its new title and his famous main hall in the Postal Savings Bank (figure 1.30) sum up what the Viennese and, more generally, the idealist school gave to modern architecture. (1) They gave a concerted idealist conception of art that manifested itself in the strict rule of geometry, often incorporating such academic conventions as symmetry and axial composition. (2) They gave a concerted historicist conception infused not only in the new title of Wagner's book but in the whole of his teaching; to cite just one instance: "One may indeed take it as proved that art and artists always represent their own epoch."[44] (3) The idealist and historicist conceptions were united, made plausible, and developed into a forceful program by the exercise of idealist geometrical control over the modern materials and simple surfaces advocated in the name of *Sachlichkeit.* This program did not advocate a mere pragmatic approach to current problems through current possibilities. The Viennese sought to give ordered and consistent artistic form to materials and functions that would be taken as typical of our time; they wished to create symbols of our era just as they understood the Parthenon to symbolize its era. Our time was interpreted as chiefly concerned with the efficient fulfillment of need; consequently, the image of this fulfillment was also thought to be the best symbol of our age. In practice, the theory and the symbols dictated to the need.

Both in theory and practice, Wagner appears to have been the first to offer idealist and historicist control of symbolically modern technology, materials, and functions. Behrens reasserted this attitude in the Turbine Factory of 1909—his most prominent building in the period when Gropius, Mies van der Rohe, and Le Corbusier (then Jeanneret) came into his office. Most of what came to be known as modern architecture subscribed, even if unconsciously, to this theory and practice, which can be summarized in Wagner's own words:

> As always, art will have the power to hold before the eyes of mankind its own ideal mirror image. . . .
>
> This new style, the modern, in order to represent us and our time, will have to bring to clear expression in all our works a distinct change from traditional feeling—the nearly complete decline of romanticism and the advance of the fulfillment of function to the point of usurping almost everything.[45]

Wagner was the first to present a fusion (one might say a confusion) of an intellec-tualist, geometrizing form with a use of materials that could be accepted as typical of, and therefore symbolic of, modern times. This attempt to express something about modernity through formal control of a symbolically modern material, technique, or function was bequeathed by Wagner, and then by Behrens, both to the later so-called functionalists and to an entire wing of expressionism.

This characterization of the emergence of a new architecture in Germany and Austria around 1900 may well seem rather implausible to those who have been taught to think of modern architecture as basically concerned with the simple fulfillment of physi-cal needs. A careful look at some of the endeavors that typify the career of Peter Behrens may serve to make the situation clearer and more plausible. There are, of course, nuances not yet mentioned; there is also the apparent difficulty of accounting for Behrens's rather diverse oeuvre. The following chapter is a brief résumé of the first decades of Behrens's career which may facilitate the detailed examination of his work.

Postscript

The exhibition "Art Nouveau" at the Museum of Modern Art in New York in 1960 marked the resurrection of an art movement to acceptance after decades of neglect under the disrespect of mainstream modernism.[46] Numerous exhibitions ensued in Europe and America, both general and specialized by country or medium. In the course of writing this essay, I came to feel, however, that the term "Art Nouveau," or even the distinctly German names of "Secession" or "Jugendstil," masked fundamental differences behind various for-malisms that were not subject to generalization. Much of the revival of interest served only to make collectible what had been too readily denigrated as merely decorative.

If one looks more deeply at the best of the artists and architects working in the period designated as "Art Nouveau," one finds both distinct differences among them and major achievements by them. It was they who made the definitive break with overt reliance on academicism and historical precedent, and in doing so had perforce to invent concepts of abstraction and nonobjectivity that were not exhausted within the few years of Art Nouveau. It was in these circles that appreciation of Ruskin and Morris also led to new attempts at reconciling the dilemmas posed to cultural production by industrialization. This first chapter of my essay was motivated by these concerns. While directed to opening the discussion of a new architecture in Germany, it offers a more general argument about the interpretation and significance of continental Art Nouveau. Still, it is focused on northern Europe and oriented toward architecture. Here I want to acknowledge some later studies of greater generality.

Jan Romein's chapter "Art Nouveau" continues to see such artistic work as defined by the wavy line, but it is only a part of a monumental, interdisciplinary study of Europe at the turn of the century.[47] Hans-Ulrich Simon's *Sezessionismus* is a penetrating study that takes a broader view of both the literary and visual arts of the period in the German-speaking realm.[48] Jost Hermand provided both a critical assessment of research on Jugendstil and a collection of such writings.[49] Gert Selle puts both the Jugendstil period and its new appreciation after midcentury in an economic and political focus.[50]

A cross-disciplinary study that gives due attention to the visual arts in a major center of the period is Carl Schorske's *Fin-de-siècle Vienna*.[51] In this chapter I gave some attention to the affinities of Behrens with the noted Viennese architect Josef Hoffmann, but only the slightest mention of Adolf Loos. This neglect is owing to my perception that Loos represents a fundamentally different position in architecture from that of Peter Behrens; my appreciation of Loos and the contrast with Behrens appears elsewhere.[52]

Munich around 1900, the locus of Behrens's activities of that time, was studied by Maria Makela but with slight attention to him.[53]

2
Behrens's Changing Concept of Life as Art:
A Review of the Early Work

Historical convention has made Behrens's name almost synonymous with the Turbine Factory of 1909, designed for the Allgemeine Elektricitäts-Gesellschaft (AEG) in Berlin. Interpretations of this building differ, but almost all claim that it was a fine building which stood apart from others of its time and came to be influential on later developments. It is usually noted that three great masters of the next generation, Walter Gropius, Ludwig Mies van der Rohe, and Le Corbusier, were in Behrens's atelier at the time when the AEG factories were in process.

That Behrens's work as exemplified in the Turbine Factory is paradigmatic is thus established opinion, and the line of descent from the paradigm is stated. But the question "Paradigm of what?" does not have such an established answer. Nikolaus Pevsner refers to the Turbine Factory as the most beautiful industrial building erected up to that time, stressing Behrens's imagination and visualization. "The result," he says, "is a pure work of architecture, so finely balanced that the huge dimensions are scarcely realized."[1] In contrast to this praise of inventive "pure architecture," Henry-Russell Hitchcock finds the Turbine Factory so influential because it is "a masterpiece of frank industrial architecture."[2] Similarly, J. M. Richards refers to this factory as the first piece of modern architecture, for "it provides a rational solution to a typically modern industrial problem; it makes logical use of modern materials."[3] Sigfried Giedion follows Pevsner rather than the wholly pragmatic apologetics of the American and English authors, and goes on to claim also a social role for the Turbine Factory: "Behrens consciously transformed the factory into a dignified place of work."[4] Finally, Pevsner joins the formal and the pragmatic claims for Behrens's factories in a forthright historicist statement: "The style and the spiritual attitude of the twentieth century had indeed been achieved (functional directness)."[5]

Some European critics and art historians have found it difficult to discuss the same material without noting other possible formulations and interpretations. To cite just one example, in 1940 Peter Meyer, the editor of the Swiss journal *Werk,* wrote, "In its time,

2.1 Grand Duke Ernst
Ludwig of Hesse and his
wife Viktoria Melita (1899).
(Court photographer C.
Ruf, Darmstadt; decorative
frame by M. v. Brauchitsch.)

the Turbine Factory of the AEG was felt to be epoch-making; one saw in it the epitome of a modern functional architecture of the Machine Age. Today, with our fingers burned, we have sharper ears for slogans; we feel the false pathos of the ponderous Egyptian-like stylization even in the apparent 'simplicity' of this machine shop. Or, more specifically: it is genuine pathos in the wrong place, sacred glorification of the machine; that is, idolatry."[6]

Leaving aside for the moment the question of whether Behrens's pathos was misplaced, it does appear that he was much more concerned with "glorification of the machine" than with "frank industrial architecture." In accepting the challenge of designing factories, Behrens's concern was not with recasting all of architecture in terms of a modern industrialized approach to building. His concern was rather with elevating so dominant a societal force as the factory to the level of established cultural standards. What makes his work interesting and important, independent of the quality of the actual achievement, is that he understood that the established cultural standards must be transformed in the process of assimilating modern industry. Behrens was committed to a lofty art, but also to the demand that this high art participate directly in life. It is the changing attempts at a marriage of art and life that relate the apparently disparate periods of his career.

In July 1899, Behrens's friend and advocate, the acute art critic and Parisian editor for Munich's *Dekorative Kunst,* Julius Meier-Graefe, published the following assessment of the international situation in the decorative arts. The England of William Morris was dead. The new movement in France had come to naught. Even the great promise of

Belgium had been reduced to van de Velde, who was then making his foothold in Germany rather than Belgium. Meier-Graefe concluded, "Germany is in the happy situation that it has not yet shown its strength. . . . Here it is indeed the early morning that we experience. Perhaps the midday can bestow beautiful things upon us."[7]

In thus paraphrasing the closing lines of Nietzsche's *Also sprach Zarathustra,* Meier-Graefe was proclaiming the impending triumph of the German artistic movement of the 1890s. One of the sources of Meier-Graefe's immediate enthusiasm was the announcement of established support for this new artistic movement in Germany. A prince, the grand duke of Hesse, Ernst Ludwig, had determined to make his Residenz the center from which would radiate a new life formed in the image of the revitalized visual arts (figure 2.1). Peter Behrens was one of the seven artists called to Darmstadt to realize the prince's dream.[8]

The Darmstadt Artists' Colony was simultaneously the artists' residence, their place of work, and an exhibition of the ideal life completely formed by art; its opening ceremony (15 May 1901) was held in the main mall of the colony, which had been designed by the young Viennese Secessionist Joseph Olbrich. The ceremony was written by Georg Fuchs and directed by Peter Behrens. It was called *Das Zeichen* (The Sign).[9] Figure 3.5 shows the moment at which the formerly unknown prophet has descended from the golden portal above and is about to reveal the shrouded sign—a great crystal. The symbolism of the crystal relies on a metaphorical relationship between transformations that take place at the micro- and macrocosmic levels; for example, just as mere carbon under intense conditions assumes a particular crystal structure and becomes the prized diamond,[10] so the power of art may transform everyday life into a resplendent life filled with meaning.[11]

The theme of the ceremony and the specific symbol were chosen by Behrens, who used precious stones as the leitmotif of his work at the colony.[12] A meticulously drafted diamond forms the frontispiece of the *Festschrift* (figure 2.2) that Behrens wrote and designed for the exhibition.[13] A priestess of the new cult of life-as-art holds aloft a gem on Behrens's poster for the exhibition (figure 2.3). Elsewhere in his work she reappears as a lamp (figure 2.4).[14] Ritual figures with crystals appear again as more abstract decorative devices in the music room (figure 3.9) of Behrens's own house at the colony. This room was the grandest space and the symbolic focal point of Behrens's earnest and hieratic household.

Just as the house had to find its culmination in a sober ceremonial room, so the colony—and implicitly, any community—should have as its climactic experience solemn festival celebrations of noble, rhythmic total-art works performed in austere, symbolic temple-theaters on dominant sites. Behrens explicitly proposed all this, drew a plan for the festival cult house (figure 3.13), described it in enthusiastic terms, and choreographed Richard Dehmel's poem "Eine Lebensmesse" as the first work to be offered. The stage was seen as a sanctuary, not a mere place of entertainment. None of this came to be realized at Darmstadt. The opening ceremony of the colony (figure 3.5) gives us the clearest idea of the rites that were to have been celebrated, and Behrens's second architectural work strongly suggests what the physical character of the festival house might have been.

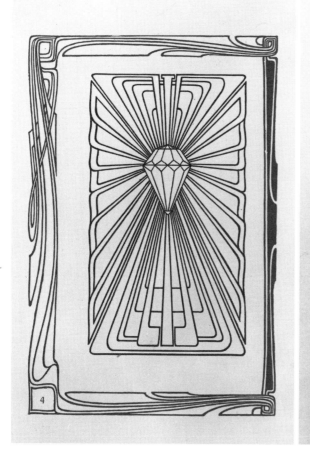

ERNST LUDWIG
DEM GROSSHERZOG VON
HESSEN UND BEI RHEIN

ꞮHM sei Ehre IHM der Dank, denn
Dank gebühret dem, der großen
Willen hat und die Macht, daß dieser
Wille sich in That und schöner Größe
erhebt. Ein hoher Geist erkannte
das, daß über allen Künsten eine
Kunst steht, die Kunst verstehen und
genießen heißt. Das Meisterlichste,
das es geben kann: Kunst genießen
in dem Sinn, daß alles Leben
Schönheit wird, und Schönheit
jedes Leben giebt. Die meisterlichste
und im Großen schöpferische Kunst.
Ein hoher Fürst ist heute Meister
dieser königlichen Kunst.
Es ist in jedem künstlerischen Werke,
das entsteht, so klein es sei, ein gött=
licher Gedanke, und nur die innige
Tiefe des Gedankens giebt die Größe
eines Werkes kund, doch trotz der
Größe seines Werthes kann es

2.2 Peter Behrens. *Ein
Dokument deutscher Kunst*
(1901), pages 4–5. Text, typeface, and design by Behrens.

2.3 Peter Behrens. Poster for the Darmstadt Artists' Colony (1901).

2.4 Peter Behrens. Lamp (1901–1902).

This second work by Behrens was the vestibule to the German section of the Exposition of Decorative Arts at Turin in 1902 (figure 2.5). Here the theme was still more overtly Nietzschean. A copy of *Also sprach Zarathustra* was on exhibit, bound in a massive cover designed by Behrens and employing as its decorative motif *das Zeichen*—the crystal. Figure 2.5 corroborates the comments of viewers that this vestibule was cavelike—dark, cool, damp, its stucco walls and ceiling molded into continuous yet hard, stalactitic forms. This ponderous, scenographic mood-making was then given contrast in the stained glass sunburst of the central vault. It is perhaps not too much to see in all this an illustration of the conclusion of the last section of *Zarathustra*—a section titled "Das Zeichen."

> 'This is *my* morning, *my* day begins:
> *rise up now, rise up, great noontide!*'
> Thus spoke Zarathustra and left his cave, glowing and strong, like a morning sun emerging behind dark mountains.[15]

It is said that the *Hamburger Vorhalle* (Behrens's vestibule at Turin) was known as the "grave of the unknown Superman."[16] Irony aside, Georg Fuchs, one of the propagandists of the Darmstadt colony, eulogized Behrens's *Vorhalle* as the Ideal Palace of Power and Beauty—an architectural symbol that suggested for him neither more nor less than the contemporary German Empire.[17] Thus, as early as his first works in the Darmstadt period, Behrens was involved not only with art in some limited or abstract sense but also with the form of life of the citizens, the representational needs of the state, and the whole expression of a culture.

Behrens's intention to uplift and intensify life through his work may be illuminated by Stendhal's theory of crystallization.[18] Stendhal had visited a salt mine near Salzburg, where he saw a very ordinary twig that had come to be covered with salt crystals and thus had been transformed into a ravishing diamond-studded wand. Personal circumstances of the time led him to formulate a parallel theory of love: that the all too natural woman underwent a process of "crystallizations" in the eyes of the lover, and that only in this way could woman be transformed into the idealized image that would provoke the passion of the lover. As we have seen, Behrens chose the crystal—a substantial object that nevertheless seems to transcend natural experience—as his symbol of *life as art*. Both his program and the formal aspect of his work at Darmstadt and Turin can plausibly be seen as a process of "crystallization." Behrens felt that life was mundane and nasty, yet he was anxious to be a willing partner in the beneficial deception that art could perform—adorning life and the environment with a crystalline veneer that would enable a certain élite to indulge in a passion for life.[19]

In 1903, at a time when the Art Nouveau, including the German Jugendstil, had been declared a mere fashion, Behrens left Darmstadt to become the director of the School of Applied Art (Kunstgewerbeschule) at Düsseldorf.[20] He brought to Düsseldorf the architect J. L. M. Lauweriks, a member of the Dutch geometric school centering on H. P. Berlage. Figure 4.14 shows the section of a church designed by Christian Bayer under Lauweriks influence.[21] The same geometrical pattern, at various "powers" or scales, served for the floor plan, elevations, site plan, and even the details of the church. Berlage himself considered that Lauweriks went further than anyone else in controlling design with geometry—due, perhaps, to Lauweriks's more intense mystical justification for his geometrical schemes.[22] Behrens, being involved in the reaction against the Art Nouveau line and being also an autodidact in architecture, was able to learn from the example of his Dutch colleague. Following the move to Düsseldorf, Behrens devoted himself wholly to a crystalline stereometry intended to capture the eternal verities of geometry and geometrically defined space. His masterpiece of this time was the complex of pavilions and gardens for the 1905 Northwest German Art Exhibition at Oldenburg (figures 2.6–8). In this work, Behrens arrived at a totally abstract conception of architecture. The boxes suited any purpose equally and could be made in any material. There were no walls; what one sees are the conceptual planes that bound a conceptual geometrical solid. Here, as in the 1906 Dresden tempietto

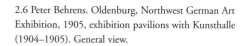

2.6 Peter Behrens. Oldenburg, Northwest German Art Exhibition, 1905, exhibition pavilions with Kunsthalle (1904–1905). General view.

2.7 Behrens. Oldenburg, Kunsthalle. Entrance.

2.8 Behrens. Oldenburg, Kunsthalle. Interior.

2.9 Peter Behrens. Prospectus for Delmenhorst Linoleum Pavilion, Third German Arts and Crafts Exhibition, Dresden (1906). The tempietto-like pavilion was built on the exhibition grounds.

for the display of linoleum (figure 2.9), Behrens celebrated the victory of his personal artistic will over the exigencies of material and purpose.[23]

Having achieved this complete ideality, Behrens was then able to honor both this ideal *and* the exigencies of building by turning to an emulation of extant buildings that were highly abstract. This process can be observed in his design for a crematorium in Hagen (figures 2.10–12), where he took for his model San Miniato in Florence (figure 2.13) and, perhaps more covertly, the St. Maurus Chapel at Beuron (figure 2.14). The Florentine church and the crematorium preside over cemeteries on similar sloping sites. The silhouettes of the buildings are similar; the chimney of the crematorium imitates the position of the campanile. The crematorium was originally clad in dark and light marble set in simple geometric patterns, as in San Miniato. This encrustation, or its simulation, also characterizes the interior wall surfaces (figures 2.15–16). Ornate floors and wooden roofs are common to both. The crematorium even imitates the alabaster windows of San Miniato. The axial termination of each basilica is an apse with a symbolic mosaic. The principal feature of the crematorium, the catafalque, imitates the lines of its counterpart, the early Renaissance tabernacle of San Miniato. As late as the 1920s, Müller-Wulckow could see in this, the first crematorium in Prussia, "the seed of a future common faith in life and in the immortality of the spirit."[24] It is no doubt true that Behrens sought such a faith. On the other hand, he was here more deeply involved in his own artistic problem of

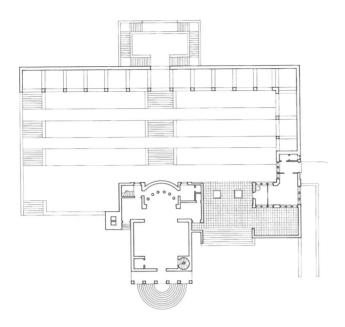

2.10 Peter Behrens. Hagen, Crematorium (1905–1908). Plan of the main level, with projected subsidiary building and columbarium.

2.11 Behrens. Hagen, Crematorium. Perspective with unbuilt subsidiary structures.

2.12 Behrens. Hagen,
Crematorium. Facade viewed
from cemetery below.

2.13 Florence, San Miniato al
Monte. Exterior.

2.14 Father Desiderius Lenz. Beuron Monastery, St. Maurus Chapel, architecture and paintings (1868–1870). Exterior.

working out an accommodation of his crystallizing stereometry (as exemplified at Oldenburg) with the exigencies of building construction. San Miniato had suggested the possibility of a building that articulated material considerations and was also governed by an idealizing aesthetic. In emulation of San Miniato, Behrens accepted the compound geometry of the basilica as well as the material expression of substantial, earthy, rock-face masonry in the rear portion of the crematorium.

In 1907, Behrens was called to be the artistic consultant to the Allgemeine Elektricitäts-Gesellschaft, the large Berlin corporation with a name and role similar to that of the General Electric Company.[25] His first building for the AEG was a special pavilion for the German Shipbuilding Exhibition of 1908 in Berlin (figure 5.4). Continuing his search for plasticity within his geometric system, Behrens again chose highly idealized and symbolic prototypes, the Palatine Chapel at Aachen (figure 5.5) and the baptistery of Florence. The electrical machine industry—science, engineering, electricity, industry, the machine—was so awe-inspiring that it seemed completely appropriate to emulate these noble centralized buildings of octagonal plan. Just as Charlemagne would once have celebrated his own power at the octagonal chapel of Aachen, so Kaiser Wilhelm II himself opened the new AEG pavilion (figure 5.6).

Basic to these buildings by Behrens are two ideas that are also discernible in the Turbine Factory. First, he had accepted the idea that architecture, as a phenomenon that brings together art and life, is the clearest index of the spirit of a time (*Zeitgeist*). This being so, the architect should then fathom his own zeitgeist in order to create buildings that would eventually be appropriate archaeological monuments. The desire to formulate the zeitgeist had led Behrens to Nietzsche and crystal-gazing around 1900, and to a mystic geometry in the Düsseldorf period.[26] Second, specifically following the Viennese art historian Alois Riegl, Behrens accepted the primacy of the "artistic will" (*Kunstwollen*).[27]

Restating Behrens's development in terms of "crystallization," at Darmstadt his artistic control had been a mere crystalline veneer. At Oldenburg, the buildings were crystalline to the point of being astral and superior to the tangible world. Finally, by emulating the most idealizing historical precedents, Behrens made formal accommodations—that is, achieved buildings that were at once ideal, traditional, and physical.

The belief that architecture is a manifestation of something called the zeitgeist, and the belief in the primacy of artistic will over material conditions, are finally only plausible if the zeitgeist manifests itself to the *artist*. The artist can then impress what he takes to be the corresponding artistic form upon the world. Thus far the world had resisted the spirits and the forms that Behrens had prepared for it at Darmstadt and Düsseldorf. Then, at a time when his buildings were becoming increasingly traditional and material, and therefore acceptable, Behrens received the AEG position that also provided him with the stimulus for a compelling zeitgeist. The modernity of the machine, of industry, and of electricity was apparent. The power that was shaping modern politics and modern civilization was manifest in these great technological developments. Through his charter membership in the Deutscher Werkbund, Behrens was linked to the political thought of the leader of the National Social Union, Friedrich Naumann, who had provided the intellectual impetus for the founding of the Werkbund in 1907. Naumann's political position has been characterized as follows:

> The role of the Emperor is the unification and coronation of the national will to power and will to life—but how can this transpire when hostility and misunderstanding reign between the upper classes and the benighted masses? Devotion to the Nation can no longer involve only the external visage of the State . . . it must also possess an internal visage. The role of social politics is not to be understood as a responsibility for social welfare, but rather as the realization by the State of an important new power through the development in the unpropertied classes of a freely held sentiment for the Fatherland. Democracy could be used to help these classes to learn to love the State as *their* State, to want to see the State great, strong and just.[28]

Just as Naumann was seeking to integrate the too earthly masses into a grand hierarchical system which was crowned in the emperor and all of which existed for the sake of a strong national state, so Behrens and the AEG were seeking to incorporate the whole of the worldly realm of industry and engineering into the same great hierarchy.

2.15 Behrens. Hagen,
Crematorium. Interior with
casket platform open.

2.16 Florence, San Miniato
al Monte. Interior.

It is in the Turbine Factory that we can see the brilliant resolution of the numerous problems Behrens had set for himself. A modern national state, if it is to be of importance, will of necessity be shot through with the physical realities of modern science and engineering. Nevertheless, perfection of technique alone, impressive as it may be, is to be termed culture no more than is raw nature. Art must elevate technique into culture.[29]

Thus, it was Behrens's problem to discover the plasticity and flexibility that would not violate his abstract aesthetics, but would allow him to use modern industrial materials and techniques in a synthesis that would proclaim architecture as the immanent order of the great forces of state, capitalism, industry, and technology. Otto Wagner had provided an impressive example in the main hall of his Postal Savings Bank (figure 1.30); but Behrens also turned for inspiration to the inventive, strong, plastic, and abstract neoclassical forms of Friedrich Gilly (figure 7.16). The comparatively simple but carefully confined main body of the Turbine Factory culminates in a grand facade of high pathos (frontispiece). The industrial iron and glass wall of the side elevation (figure 7.11) abuts one of the massive, battered pylons of concrete, which is evocatively confined with iron bands suggesting rustication. The crystalline plane of the central window is held outside the plane of the wall, supported like a solitary gem. The vertical ascent of the pylons, as in the design by Gilly, is abruptly stopped; in the Turbine Factory the entire composition is definitively enclosed by the large gable, which is shaped like a multifaceted bezel.

With a zeitgeist eulogizing power as manifested in the cooperation of technology, industry, and the state, and a concept of artistic will imposing abstract geometrical form on the merely physical, Behrens succeeded in creating a magnificent temple of power—the modern industrial situation cast in a faceted, crystalline form. As in Naumann's politics, one seeks to order the givens of the modern world into a hierarchy that will appear to have been immanent.

Robert Breuer may serve as a contemporary witness of this interpretation. In 1908 he analyzed Behrens's new problem of giving aesthetic form to industrial products:

> Technical form [e.g., a factory] is not so objective that it is independent of the personality of the man who discovers that latent form. Consequently, it is not insignificant whether it should be Behrens or someone else who speaks the magic word that delivers this form. The character and the intensity of this formal revelation is doubtless determined by the power of the utterance and the grandeur of the gesture with which the prophet allows the rhythm which is concealed within necessities to comprehend and materialize itself. On the other hand, . . . the form that finally crystallizes is only one predestined variation of the single possible theme; it is a clearly cut facet through which one receives an insight into the aesthetic heart of the condition of tension of the powers that have been bound in material but have been brought to form. . . . It may be that Behrens and van de Velde are the only ones who could win a classic formal expression for electrical current. Behrens must be named a forerunner of that future religion of form, a man who knows how to grasp the sacred desire of our day in the pathos of his lines and in the radiant tension of his spaces; he appears to be called to build an optical shrine, a temple. As Behrens sets out to achieve compelling symbols for electricity, he feels more strongly than ever that sacred will that would erect a festival house on the high mountain of which Behrens himself, as a world-priest of beauty, said: "Here above we are filled with the impression of a higher purpose that can only be translated into what is sensible; it is our spiritual need, the gratification of our metaphysical sense."[30]

Thus, if by "frank industrial architecture" one means that engineering principles, material conditions, and functional purpose have played the determining role in the shaping of the building, then the Turbine Factory does not fall into so limited a category.

If by "dignified place of work" one implies that immediate social welfare played a distinctive role in the conception of building, then again the Turbine Factory must be excluded.

Similarly, the fairly frequent insistence on Behrens's originality in the use of concrete, iron, and glass can only be accepted under a rarefied aesthetic interpretation. That is, if, when one says that the Turbine Factory was the first modern building, one means that it was the first building to attempt to "crystallize" peculiarly modern materials, techniques, and needs into aesthetically willed strict, idealized forms in the symbolic service of what was taken to be the will-to-power of industry, State, and the era, then the Turbine Factory may indeed fulfill the role that is claimed for it.

3

Behrens's Highest *Kultursymbol,* the Theater: Darmstadt, 1900–1903

Friedrich Nietzsche's writings mounted a brilliant attack on the positivistic science and history that he saw increasingly dominating the entire fabric of nineteenth-century Germany. When Nietzsche envisioned a better German society, he reckoned the first generation of this new society had to be brought up in the "mighty truth" that Germany could not build a culture based on its positivistic education. In contrast to mere knowledge about culture (the German's desire "for the flower without the root or the stalk"), art and a genuine culture must spring from a natural ground. "Life itself," Nietzsche wrote, "is a kind of handicraft that must be learned thoroughly and industriously, and diligently practised. . . . 'Give me life, and I will soon make you a culture out of it'—will be the cry of every man in this new generation, and they will know each other by this cry. But who will give them this life? No god and no man will give it—only their youth."[1]

At the end of the nineteenth century, many young artists read Nietzsche; his influence and the search he encouraged were not restricted to Germany,[2] but interest in his writings was especially strong there. The young enthusiasts of the new artistic movement appropriated Nietzsche's critique of what they felt was a fragmented, incoherent, and artless civilization.[3] These negative characteristics were revealed in a divorce of the artist from society and in the dominance of easel painting and independent sculpture, which isolated contemplation in the laboratory atmosphere of museums and salons, thus making the role of art in Western civilization submissive. The work of art, it was felt, must be removed from its aesthetic, physical, and psychological isolation, even if this endangered the independence of the artist. Supplying the decoration that would create a pervasive and significant environment was considered a higher calling than producing individual works that had no social role. The artist might now become an architect in order to control the environment, or at least painting and sculpture should play a part in such a larger program. The effort to realize this end brought an emphasis on decorative modes of working; the very words "decorative" and "ornamental" took on exalted meaning. Even as individuals, these artists turned from the culturally divisive fine arts and took up the decorative arts, which were then acclaimed for contributing to the construction of a superior culture.

Aside from the grand murals and decorative painting of Puvis de Chavannes, even the most inventive artists of the latter nineteenth century offered no models for the new culture.[4] The impressionists, essentially naturalistic, skimmed over the surface of life; post-impressionists, symbolists, and others appeared to retreat into private worlds of invented images and symbols. Anecdotal and realist artists accepted the world uncritically. Conservatively traditional artists, attempting to operate within conventions that stood above the realities of life, made no attempt at a communication between art and modern life. For the artists of the new society, every grand historical paradigm (e.g., the Greek temple) was understood to have been unified with the life of its time. To emulate the great paradigms was considered a matter of cultural integration rather than mere formal imitation. The motto above the entrance of the Secession Building in Vienna (1899; figure 1.1) was:

For each time, its art;
For art, its freedom.

The new culture, conceived as the natural efflorescence of contemporary life, and as exerting a reciprocal, uplifting effect on that life, placed art in a new position. Art had once again to attain a universal cultural role. At the turn of the century, Behrens (figure 3.1), a young artist just then embracing architecture, was exploring the theater—as architecture and as cultural institution—as the apogee of that earnestly sought new culture.

The houses by Victor Horta in Brussels (figure 1.9) and the house and furniture of Henry van de Velde in Uccle (figure 1.10) were early, unusual, and impressive contributions to the realization of the new cultural program. Nonetheless, artists of the time often had to be content with more modest works that might be considered as steps toward an environmental art: the design of interiors, wallpaper, fabrics, linoleum, furniture, glassware, ceramics, silver, and stained glass. Other forms of acceptable artistic production were decorative carvings, murals, and even smaller paintings if they made, through their decorative frames and insistence on surface, the greatest possible concessions to the walls upon which they were placed.

Even the late nineteenth-century prints by Peter Behrens, referred to as "decorative woodcuts," were acknowledged to have environmental intent. Through generous size (*Victory* is 86 by 61.5 cm.) and flat color areas, Behrens sought to insure these prints a place on a wall, not in a portfolio. Their multiple production and still more the conscious exploitation of surface design distinguished these works from traditional easel painting. The art historian and critic Julius Meier-Graefe described the power of their easily recognized images as resulting from the *Reflexerscheinungen* (empathic phenomena) caused by the strong lines that control their surfaces: what is conveyed, he noted, is a bold expression

of movement despite its having no true visual counterpart.[5] Beyond this portrayal of cosmic movement, there is a related iconography. The woodcut titled *Victory* (figure 3.2)
obviously portrays Prometheus—he "who foresees," the creator of man, he who stole for
man the holy fire from the forge of Hephaestus on the island of Lemnos, and who gave
man the arts and sciences. Prometheus had appeared on the title page of the first edition
of Nietzsche's *The Birth of Tragedy*.[6] Behrens represented this great figure of the "unseasonable" Greek mythology, so appropriately related to the birth of a new culture unifying
life and art, with a nonnaturalistic line intended to express the cosmic energy of the story
and yet achieve a flat, decorative quality uniting the image with its immediate architectural
surroundings.[7] His technique, printing from broad surfaces of wood blocks, enhanced the
desired play of line on a flat surface.

Another woodcut, variously called *Storm* or *Eagle* (figure 3.3), fulfilled Meier-
Graefe's idea of Behrens's formal intent even more completely. With suggestive imagery,

Zarathustra, the spokesman for Nietzsche's theory, had exhorted the higher men to be like the storm-wind under which the seas tremble and leap.[8] Behrens, a founding member of the Munich Secession, may well have been inspired by Zarathustra's words:

> Watch and listen you solitaries! From the future come winds with a stealthy flapping of wings; and good tidings go out to delicate ears.
>
> You solitaries of today, you who have seceded from society, you shall one day be a people: from you, who have chosen out yourselves, shall a chosen people spring—and from this chosen people, the Superman.[9]

The influential cultural entrepreneur Karl Scheffler, in discussing not this woodcut but Behrens's first architectural work, his own house at Darmstadt (1900–1901; figure 3.7), wrote that Behrens's "grandest wish is to create a uniform, high standard, a *Kulturmilieu* in which he could move naturally like a bird in the air."[10] It was this concerted, "unseasonable" desire not just to grasp life but through this to create a new *Kultur*—a totally integrated culture as one imagined it to have been exemplified in ancient Greece—that set the *Secessionsstil* and what I would term the "idealist faction" of Jugendstil apart from contemporary developments elsewhere. The *culture* of Greece was to serve as a model, not the particular Greek forms. Nevertheless, it was tempting to use certain classi-

3.2 Peter Behrens. *Victory,* color woodcut (1897).

3.3 Peter Behrens. *Storm, color woodcut* (1897).

cal motifs or concepts as crutches. Such a programmatic work as the exhibition building for the Secession in Vienna, for instance, was organized along a strict axis; its individual volumes are clear geometric forms. Greek vase painting found a recurrent echo in Secessionist painting. The very insistence on *line* was a classicizing program. Later, when the formal ingenuity of Jugendstil was vulgarized and suspect, the ground was prepared for a retreat to a safer and more conventional neoclassicism.

That the visual arts should be the key to a creative new life suddenly came to public prominence in Germany in 1897. The established magazine of crafts, *Kunstgewerbeblatt,* showed a complete change of content with the 1897–1898 volume. The annual exhibition at Munich's Glaspalast contained for the first time a section devoted to crafts, and Dresden's great exhibition introduced the work of van de Velde to Germany. Several new journals devoted to the decorative arts were founded: Bruckmann's *Dekorative Kunst* in Munich and Alexander Koch's *Deutsche Kunst und Dekoration* in Darmstadt. Nevertheless, it was rare for an artist to realize more than isolated, overstudied interiors, and the entire movement stood in danger of falling into a shallow formalism without having the chance to attempt to reach its goals. The searchers for a new *Kultur* needed either a god or a man to give them life. In the Artists' Colony (*Künstler-Kolonie*) at Darmstadt, the life-giver they found may at first appear an unlikely sort: the grand duke of Hesse, Ernst Ludwig.

Born in the 1860s (like most of the characters in this story), Ernst Ludwig had commissioned two residential interiors by the noted English architect M. H. Baillie Scott.[11] Recognizing the contemporary awakening of the applied arts in Germany, the grand duke took an increasing interest in their potential. With the advice and encouragement of the publisher Alexander Koch and the writer Georg Fuchs, the grand duke sought to preempt the greater established "art cities" by making his seat, Darmstadt, the prominent center of the new movement. As Fuchs wrote in the pretentious volume memorializing the colony, it is a matter of consequence that it should have been a prince of an ancient ducal house who was the first to devote his power and his person to the realization of "the great thought of our time . . . the complete union of life and art."[12] That Ernst Ludwig became the patron and apologist for a new cultural program Fuchs claimed to be a logical parallel to what Kaiser Wilhelm was achieving in the realm of national material productivity and well-being. He also claimed that a creative group gathered at the Residenz would be the stimulus for a revitalization of handicraft industries throughout Hesse. Actually the principals had greater cultural ambitions than either of these arguments would indicate.

The grand duke called seven painters, sculptors, and architects to Darmstadt during the latter half of 1899. The two best-known artists were Joseph Olbrich, the designer of the Secession Building in Vienna and a former student of Otto Wagner, and Peter Behrens, who had already received favorable attention, especially in the pages of *Dekorative Kunst.* The first concerted task of the colony was a bold, inventive project, conceived to explore the desired union of art and life. The artists were to design, build, and furnish their own permanent quarters in a fine, hilly park, the Mathildenhöhe, on the edge of Darmstadt. These quarters, a common studio building and a number of private dwellings, were to form the first exhibition of the work of the colony. Thus an entire small community, formed according to artistic principles—from the site plan to the silverware—would be exhibited programmatically to the nation in the spring of 1901 under the imposing title "A Document of German Art."

Olbrich, the only member of the colony who had trained and worked as an architect, assumed almost complete control of the planning and architectural form of the colony. He designed all the buildings except Behrens's house. The permanent buildings were principally grouped about a main axis that ran up the slope of the Mathildenhöhe (figure 3.4). Individual dwellings of Olbrich's design flanked the axis, the lower end of which terminated in a dramatically formed but shallow temporary exhibition building. The other members of the colony joined in the design and execution of the interiors of the permanent buildings. This complex formed the largest part of the colony and was to exemplify for the public the benefits of a milieu in which art and life were one.

A ceremony by Behrens and Fuchs opened the Artists' Colony on 15 May 1901—*Das Zeichen,* with its emphasis on the symbolism of the crystal and the diamond—as described in the preceding chapter (figure 3.5). More revealing for his future career, Behrens designed and furnished his own house at the colony (figures 3.6–12).[13] The first

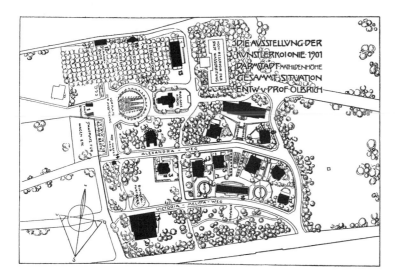

3.4 Joseph Maria Olbrich. Darmstadt, Artists'
Colony (1900–1901). Site plan. The main axis
runs from the Ernst-Ludwig-Haus (artists' studios, 7) down to the exhibition building (10),
flanked by houses by Olbrich. Behrens's house
is to the west (3).

3.5 Peter Behrens. Darmstadt, Artists' Colony,
Behrens's production of Georg Fuchs's *Das
Zeichen* before the Ernst-Ludwig-Haus as the
opening of the 1901 exhibition "Ein Dokument
deutscher Kunst."

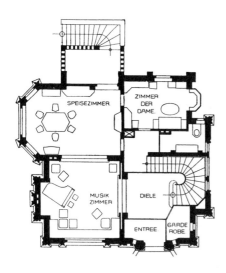

GRUNDRISS VOM ERDGESCHOSS

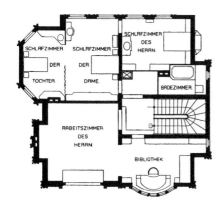

GRUNDRISS V. 1. OBERGESCHOSS

3.6 Behrens. Darmstadt, Artists' Colony, Behrens house (1900–1901). Plans.

3.7 Behrens house with banners hung (1901).

work of a man not professionally trained in architecture, Behrens's house is, not surprisingly, eclectic. Nonetheless he showed an inventiveness both in the sources of his eclecticism and in the formal control he brought to the apparently disparate parts (figure 3.7). Behrens's faith in the formal power of line, manifest in his graphics, is here revealed in three dimensions. The profiles of the bricks that "draw" the lines of the house indicate the source of this architectural use of line: the brick Gothic of northern and central Europe.[14] Such precedents and Behrens's own use of profiled bricks emphasize ribs that provide the linear formal structure of the building; the white stucco walls are treated as an infill. This is, of course, not an exposition of the actual physical structure, which is simply a masonry box, but rather a stylization, an uplifting, of that simple material structure and of anonymous building types (figure 3.8).[15]

3.8 Taufers, Tyrol. Monastic building.

In the main front of the house, and in the ogive gables, the lines are certainly more than boundaries; they have a force of their own, as in van de Velde's work. Behrens's dining room (figure 3.11), too, indicates that he was then not closed to the ideas of the Belgian, but neither the interiors nor the exterior are consistent in this patheticist inclination. For example, at the rear of the house are brick piers that are simply the basic structure and free of the vitalizing Gothic moldings. Again, the underlying prismatic form of the house, an occasional exterior molding, and some of the interiors (e.g., the *Zimmer der Dame*, figure 3.12) are experiments in what was earlier referred to as the idealist wing of Art Nouveau. In this stage of Behrens's development, with its simultaneous and competing explorations, the clearest manifestation of his own thought is the music room (figure 3.9), which occupied the most prominent position in the moderately open plan of his house (figure 3.6). Behrens's symbolism reappears in the concept of the room itself and in

3.9 Behrens house. Music room.

3.10 Behrens house. Music room, draperies.

3.11 Behrens house. Dining room.

3.12 Behrens house. *Damenzimmer*
(lady's parlor).

its details. Ritual figures with diamonds become abstract decorative devices; throughout the music room, notably in the drapes pierced to admit rays of light (figure 3.10), the diamond is the basis of the ornament. This room, with its red and gray marble walls, its blue mirrors, parquet flooring of seven different woods, gilded ceiling, and doors of aluminum-bronze, was indeed the great space and the symbolic culmination for a hieratic conception of domestic life.[16]

What the music room was to his house, Behrens felt, the theater should be to the community—or better, vice versa. Even before his house was known, Behrens sent forth from Darmstadt a program combining his awakening interest in architecture with a concept of theater. Theater became the subject of his three earliest publications. Before attempting to indicate how Behrens's sense of the theater culminated, and thereby dramatized, the program of life as art, we may briefly consider the contemporary state of the theater.[17]

Indictments against the perspectival and pictorial stage—the illusionistic, "peep-show theater" composed of a deep perspective stage viewed by spectators, often from disadvantageous positions, through a kind of picture frame—were so common that we need not dwell on its perceived faults. Advocates of the naturalistic theater had been harsh critics; their ideal was a stage like a room with one wall missing, a simple box set behind the proscenium opening. By limiting the conditions to be simulated, the illusion was more successful; but the naturalistic stage, too, remained essentially a picture of the real world. Besides the uncomfortable disparity between the reality of the canvas sets and the desired illusion, there remained unresolved an even more serious objection. Compared with the architectural, unchanging stages of antiquity and of Shakespeare, the pictorial scene within the frame of the proscenium arch represented a complete divorce of viewer from actor. This lack of contact minimized communication by the actor and sympathetic participation by the viewer. It denied the union of art and life that the artists of the new romantic movement sought.[18]

How, then, did Behrens plan to realize theater as the highest *Kultursymbol*? What were his motives? Who were his influences? As a painter and graphic artist during the 1890s, he had evolved from luminist-impressionist oil paintings to ever more linear, abstract designs, accomplished in the flat media of woodcut or tempera paint, though still representing persons, landscapes, birds, and butterflies. Increasingly, however, he considered nature unworthy of imitation. In his program, nature was to provide strong emotional stimuli; the role of the artist, rather than to ape nature, was to raise experience to a new, higher, abstracted, harmonious, and rhythmic expression. Behrens's artistic battle was not so much against any remaining overreliance on historical precedent as it was against naturalism—a progressive attitude in European figurative and dramatic arts since the 1870s.

In May 1900, Behrens challenged naturalism in his earliest publication, "Die Dekoration der Bühne" (The Decoration of the Stage), a preliminary formulation emphasizing the use of ornamental rather than illusionistic paintings for stage sets.[19] His theater ideas were more fully and systematically presented in a booklet he wrote in June of 1900,

Feste des Lebens und der Kunst: Eine Betrachtung des Theaters als höchsten Kultursymbols (Festivals of Life and Art: A Consideration of the Theater as the Highest Cultural Symbol). Two men, the Darmstadt author and critic Georg Fuchs and the noted lyric poet Richard Dehmel, were important influences on this work; like their friends of the *Neuromantik,*[20] both were strongly opposed to late nineteenth-century naturalism in the theater and the arts. Dehmel, in theory and in poetic works, provided a virile quasi-philosophical basis for the exploitation of life as art. Fuchs's aristocratic ideals, and the implications of those ideals for the social role and physical form of the theater, directly shaped Behrens's proposal. In an article published in 1899,[21] Fuchs already insists on the ceremony of the theater, the importance of stylized, contemporary works, the site of the building, amphitheatrical seating, and an expression of "heimatlichen Geist": "You see before you an edifice which already in its external forms reveals that it is the temple of a Mystery, of the ceremonial revelation of the *Good Life,* of its *Meaning,* and of its *Beauty.* We must erect the edifice itself as a witness of the vital, creative power of the German spirit."[22]

In the summer of 1900, Dehmel, returning from a Mediterranean trip, chose Heidelberg as a temporary residence. With Darmstadt nearby, the opportunity was at hand for Behrens and Dehmel to renew and deepen their acquaintance.[23] Soon two works on the theater appeared under Behrens's name: the book *Feste des Lebens und der Kunst,* and a magazine article containing a proposal for a theater and the staging of Dehmel's poem "Lebensmesse."[24] Behrens treasured the idea that the entire forming of life must be the highest measure of value for the art of a people and a time. Like Dehmel, the members of the Künstler-Kolonie strove to manifest the beauty and the power of the whole of life— and none of them with more fury and determination than Behrens. Consequently, when Behrens expressed these attitudes and proclaimed his belief that a ceremonial theater is the apex and union of life and art, he elevated and stylized his publication itself to a total work of art. Behrens's grandiose proclamation, his *Feste des Lebens und der Kunst,* appeared on fine paper, in an elegant format with typeface, multicolor ornamentation, and binding all designed by Behrens.[25]

Behrens's theater, this place holy to the "gesamten Kunst," "symbol of our surfeit of vigor," dedicated to the "celebration of our culture," was not built, and we have only a published plan (figure 3.13). Yet with this plan and the descriptions in *Feste des Lebens und der Kunst* and his article on staging the "Lebensmesse," we can fully picture Behrens's ceremonial theater for the "cult of the beautiful life."[26] The theater would be situated on a commanding site overlooking a valley, its walls brilliant with color, its columns ringed with garlands, and from seven masts were to flutter long, white banners. The centralized plan of the circular building symbolized the oneness of actors and viewers, easily perceived from within and without. The great main entrance, the "Portal of the Sun," faced south; its decoration, although mysterious, divulged the arts of an abundant land. Though smaller, the east and west entrances—portals of the morning and evening stars—similarly served to welcome the partakers who would both offer and receive at the *Fest.* Through the north

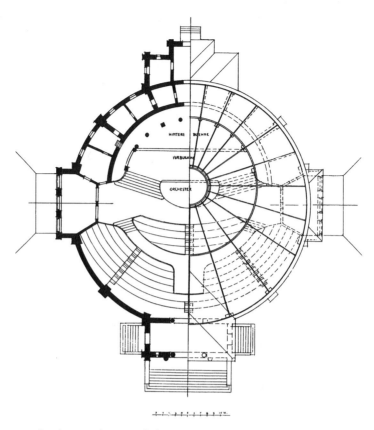

portal, whose architectural decoration designated it as the Portal of the Moon, the personnel of the theater gained access to the backstage rooms. The cupola over the great circular chamber was pierced with windows. High above, trumpeters would stand in glowing raiment sounding their call far over the land and forests below.

The theater was entered by a ramp under the highest of the seats, coming into the high space of the theater where the color range was deeper. The seating approximated that of an antique theater. Each participant had clear, easy, and direct contact with the simple, broad, and shallow stage. A small orchestra was centered in front of the stage and between the two broad ranks of low marble steps that allowed passage between the stage and a processional area on the cross axis. This processional area served both the movements of the actors and the arrival and departure of the congregation. Symbolically it merged the two parts of the theater. The forestage, for Behrens the most important part of the stage, was architecturally united with the auditorium. "We do not want to separate ourselves from our art."[27] The breadth of the stage served the relief-like ordering and movements of the figures and processions. Relief was for Behrens the most striking, the most concentrated expression of line and movement, "which in drama is everything."[28]

Chamber and stage were one space—emphasized by the harmonious architectural and decorative handling of the whole. The marble floor of the stage echoed the pattern of the ceiling vault. By day the stage was naturally lit by the cupola windows and balanced by artificial lighting. At night an even, diffuse illumination revealed the overall cooperation of the arts while being itself consistent with that ideal. There were neither coulisses nor soffits to provide naturalistic illusion or slur the sound. Beyond the slightly elevated rear stage, the vista was closed first with a colonnade and then by a wall—semicircular in plan and permanent. The locale and time lay in the poetry and were to be evoked in the viewer's imagination, not represented in naturalistic sets.

Yet the mood of the piece should be emphasized through manipulation of the background. Great tapestries, which might bear symbolic motifs, could be hung between the columns. If one tapestry were omitted, a portal would open onto the wall beyond, which would then form a second, undifferentiated background. The curving space between the colonnade and the wall would be either darker or brighter than the stage, and though its color could be changed with wall hangings, Behrens preferred in most cases a pure gold ground. For figural relief, the brighter foreground would be used. To emphasize the moving line, a dark silhouette would be used on a bright ground, in which case all tapestries would be omitted and a brilliant golden ground would ascend to the vaulting without interruption. This space must also serve the entrances and exits of the performers, "the priests of the word, of the beautiful gesture, and of the dance; for this, in one person, is what the actor would be."[29]

Behrens claimed that mime and dance were the origin of the theater and must again become its basis. The pure form of the figure and the movement of the dance would be enhanced if only white, or at most a single color, were used for the costumes. Music should be held equal in this collaboration of the arts, even though there are emotions that only music can express. Through these self-imposed limitations, each art would come to full expression and together the arts would attain a harmonious total effect. Faithfulness to real or historical conditions and the unlimited juxtaposition of colors and light, "so artful as this may be, is in principle naturalism; that is, non-art."[30] Naturalism had displaced decadent styles yet was not able to renew art. In theater, for example, the actor's purpose is greater than merely presenting observations of nature. Every word, every movement should be stylized and beautiful; the actor compresses and poetizes his role until all is "Pathos und Pose," until all conforms to the actor's own strong form, his ideal of beauty, his style. "The artistry begins at the point where a phenomenon simplifies itself to the sovereign form that can be the inclusive symbol for all related phenomena."[31]

Behrens called for free and beautiful spaces for communion among the participants during intermissions. These, however, were not accommodated in his project. Perhaps the plan was so idealized that a subsidiary function could not be allowed to disturb the absolute centralization.[32] To imagine most clearly what the physical appearance of Behrens's theater edifice might have been, we can refer to his only public work of this time, the vestibule for the German section at the first International Exposition of Decorative Arts at Turin in 1902 (figure 2.5).

In addition to describing his reconstitution of the theater, Behrens also set out his ideas on the role of theater in society.[33] High on the hill, in the festival hall, everything was to be organized to satisfy the spiritual needs of the participants. The bold forms, the organ, the victorious trumpets would cause one to put aside all secondary matters and prepare for the great art of the *Weltanschauung*. There would be a play of life in which all participants would play. Behrens claimed that poetic and spiritually uplifting dramatic pieces were at hand for his theater; he had in mind Dehmel's "ethical cantata," "Eine Lebensmesse—Dichtung für Musik" (A Mass of Life—Poem for Music).[34] The cantata was to be staged in an extraordinarily ceremonial fashion. The "priests" of the poetic word, universalizations of human types, revealed the Mass of Life in noble processions and earnest declamation. Symmetry reigned in both the visual and the temporal ordering of the performance; Behrens's stage diagram (figure 3.14) hinted at the aura of solemn and pathetic celebration. This solemnity was more clearly expressed, however, in the opening ceremony of the colony (figure 3.5).[35] The appreciation of symbolic ceremony appears again in Behrens's summation of his plan for staging the "Lebensmesse":

> Dehmel's "Lebensmesse," through its liturgical quality, is a work peculiarly predestined for presentation in such a new theatrical style. Since the poet wrote with this intuition, the work actually inaugurates the new style. If drama has derived from religious cults, then I see a great sign for the evolving theater style in the fact that again poets live who can give us and our times the forms for a Cult of Life. We will build the house from its foundation. Dehmel's "Lebensmesse" is a cornerstone, most solemnly formed.[36]

Certainly much of the Fuchs-Behrens-Dehmel theater, its antinaturalism and antidemocracy, its idea of an elite, poetic stylization, the elementary expressiveness of the dance, and above all the reckless grasp of life as its own creator of philosophical and moral criteria, echoes Nietzsche, despite the fact that one can hardly imagine Nietzsche caught up in the naïveté of parts of the Cult of the Beautiful Life.[37] He would nevertheless have understood the endeavors of the Cult:

> And Zarathustra began to speak once more. "O my friends," he said, "you strange men, you Higher Men, how well you please me now,
>
> "since you have become joyful again! Truly, you have all blossomed forth: for such flowers as you, I think *new festivals* are needed.
>
> "A little brave nonsense, some divine service and ass festival, some joyful old Zarathustra-fool, a blustering wind to blow your souls bright.
>
> "Do not forget this night and this ass festival, you Higher Men! You devised

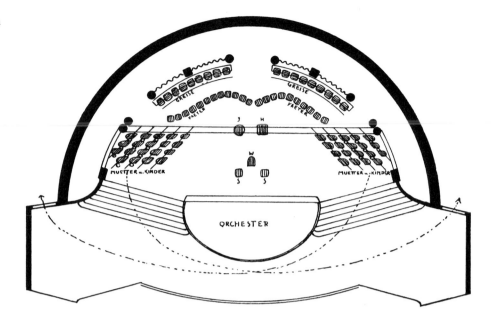

3.14 Peter Behrens. Diagram for staging of Richard Dehmel's "Lebensmesse" (Mass of Life) (1900).

that at my home, I take that as a good omen—only convalescents devise such things!

"And if you celebrate it again, this ass festival, do it for love of yourselves, do it also for love of me! And in remembrance of me!"

Thus spoke Zarathustra.[38]

In 1900, when Behrens wrote his *Feste des Lebens und der Kunst,* Adolphe Appia's proposals within the Wagnerian tradition were the revolutionary but unrealized new theories of stagecraft which, though they urged a freedom of scenic creation, bent toward an intensification of the dramatic line and an absorption of the actors and viewers into an illusion—into an emotional, nonrational total experience.[39] Behrens, too, claimed that his theater was to give an illusion—"Kultur heisst diese Illusion!" But viewed theatrically, not theorized metaphysically, Behrens's proposals, rather than illusionistic, were intended for a sensate immediacy between the actor and viewer. The shallow stage with the consequent emphasis on forestage acting, the proximity of seating and acting areas, the lack of definition between these areas and their inclusion in one architectonic space, the simplicity and architectural permanence of the stage background, the emphasis on dance and movement, and the simple illumination all serve to establish that theatrical contact which became the prime interest of revolutionary twentieth-century stage and theater designers.

The telling difference is that with Behrens, although the "offering and receiving partaker" is presumed to dress and comport himself, offer, and receive as a true "Mitkünstler" in the Cult of the Beautiful Life, he nevertheless participates without an emotional submission to the enacted work. In Behrens's theater the increased contact serves to eliminate illusion and to provide clear presentation of the individual arts; Appia (and later Gordon Craig and most succeeding designers) availed himself of the various techniques for increasing contact with the audience, but to a different end. Appia sought, especially through elaborately controlled evocative lighting, to create a space for the actor and to *immerse* both the actor and the viewer in an ambiance and a mood. For Appia it is desirable that the viewer be a participant, but a participant in the presented work. There is a temporary submission of one's self to the emotional force of the piece. With Behrens, one freely and exaltedly participates in the high mass of the cult to which one is perpetually submitted.[40]

Appia sought to adapt all visual means for the underscoring of the dramatic line. The visual realization exists for the sake of the poetry; the word stands preeminent above the other arts. In contrast to this, one of the characteristics of the Jugendstil's attempts to bring art to the whole of life was the disappearance of hierarchy in the arts. The most worthless of texts could receive painstaking typographical and decorative treatment. The picture frame participated in the expression of the work that it enclosed, and often the whole was intended to be subservient to the decor of the room in which it was placed. Architecture could become a mere scaffolding for decoration. Behrens's theater proposal contained the germ of this same unordered total beautifying. The "Lebensmesse" was clearly of great importance to Behrens. Nevertheless, his insistence on the independent beauty of each part of his total art form—of the space, the materials, the decor, the stage furniture, the costumes, the dance, the gestures, the declamation—could only imply a relative decrease in the importance of the word.[41]

In 1909, through the support of the banker and avid patron of the arts Karl Ernst Osthaus, Behrens received the opportunity to produce a theater work according to his principles. The production was to be part of a festival celebrating the opening of the Stadtgartenhalle in Hagen. Behrens chose to stage *Diogenes,* an uncompleted verse comedy by his late friend Otto Erich Hartleben.[42] The play had not been staged previously, and it was an apt work for the Behrens program—at least in its thematic implications, if not in its dramatic possibilities. Diogenes, "the dog," grasps life at its most elementary and sensual level and shocks the citizens of Athens with his rejection of all conventions and his shameless acts. The beautiful Aspasia, beloved by the nobles of Athens, is won from both her suitors and her superficial love of riches by the words and example of Diogenes. But Diogenes is not unaffected by Aspasia. While the resolution of the attraction of Diogenes and Aspasia for one another is not given in Hartleben's fragment, the direction it would have taken is clear. One need not choose between the acceptance of life and the love of beauty—forward to the Cult of the Beautiful Life!

3.15 Peter Behrens.
Production of Otto Erich
Hartleben's *Diogenes,* scene I,
the banquet (1909).

The *Diogenes* production reflects the tone of Behrens's 1907 statement rather than that of the *Feste des Lebens und der Kunst:* the emphasis is specifically on the stage problems; the social implications are less present here than they were with Fuchs at the same time. Formally, Behrens pushes his "relief stage" to the limit. The photographs of the production show the tiny shelf on which the actors performed in a highly stylized manner. Here at last all is *Pathos und Pose* (figure 3.15). Yet this apparently unpromising production merits consideration.[43]

Theodor Lessing's critique in *Die Schaubühne* minimizes the artistic value of Hartleben's comedy and suggests that Behrens chose a work of insufficient gravity and quality for a trial of his theater reform. It may be that Lessing's personal commitment to the symbolist theater (and the inadequacies of the Hagen experiment) blinded him to some potentially excellent qualities of Behrens's program, but his criticism still appears quite sound. He makes light of Behrens's exaggerated stylization and of the insistence on genuine objects and materials for props. He also criticizes the idea that the auditorium and stage are one space. He accuses Behrens, as a man from the visual arts, of considering staging merely as an end in itself. This visually oriented staging results in a stage space that is not, according to Lessing, the space in which drama takes place. While we don't want a naive illusion of nature in the theater, we must still differentiate between understanding the symbol as real and symbolically understanding reality. Whereas Behrens properly avoids the former, he fails to achieve the latter. The result is an overemphasis on visual factors at the expense of the drama.

Nonetheless, the severity of Behrens's relief-stage production of *Diogenes* may reflect his consideration of the problem of the theatrical depreciation of the word. He wished to retain the beautiful word, yet he did not want to subject the other arts to a subservient theatricalism. Behrens's resolution was to exercise his original program within the most rigid limits. In this way his beautiful production contracted until the whole performance became virtually a recitation in fine but simple surroundings, with rhythmic, expressive movements and gestures by the actors. For the audience and the performers there was a spatial immediacy; the physical impediments and the sensations of theatricalism were largely avoided; with adequate actors the dramatic and imaginative creation of the poet could be recreated in the auditor. This would be at least the potential of Behrens's endeavor. An austere production, however, at once stylized and yet simple enough to give the proper, unified emphasis to the poetry, relies on great literature for its effect. In 1907, Behrens had suggested that the classics be used for the initial trials of his program. Whether *Diogenes* was sufficiently monumental to succeed in fulfilling this program is doubtful; the Hagen experiment had no direct successors.[44]

Behrens's goal of cultural integration was not his alone. The closest thing to a manifesto, to my knowledge, was the *Programm* issued in 1900 by the Eugen Diederichs publishing house, which had also accepted Behrens's *Feste des Lebens und der Kunst* for publication:

As the leading publisher of the *Neuromantik,* I would like to emphasize that this movement is not to be confused with that of the decadents in literature. The new cultural direction does not favor primitivism, nor unrealistic dreams; rather, succeeding the age of specialization and one-sided intellectualization, it wills to observe and enjoy the world as something whole. By once again conceiving the world intuitively, it overcomes the materialism and naturalism that have been the fruit of intellectualism. The romantics of the early nineteenth century opposed the cold smoothness of antiquity and believed that they would find a more natural Man in the Middle Ages, to which they returned in song and legend. We moderns, however, seek our ideals in the time when the energy of the people expressed itself in the unfragmented personalities of the humanistic age. My monographs on the history of German culture are intended to be a landmark on this course, and in a few years the era of the fifteenth and sixteenth centuries will have its place not only in the minds of scholars, but also in those of the people. The old romantics strove for much knowledge, for the universality of man; and inasmuch as they sought not only to think their ideals but also to live them, they gave life to their knowledge. The *Neuromantik* will follow the same course if it goes back to and continues the naturalness, the originality, the art, and the joy of existence common to the men of the age of Paracelsus and Dürer. The cultural philistine who merely decorated himself with patches of culture, and whom Nietzsche has rightly criticized, will be overcome, and the new movement will instruct him in the artistic culture of the twentieth century. The desire of the soul for something that will give meaning and content to life leads directly to the deepening of the individual. From this profundity man develops, as shown by Goethe, to harmony with his environment; the apperceptive life leads to the fulfillment of the latent energies and talents, to the healthy and joyous man whose life is an unconscious work of art. No longer dead knowledge, but art shall transform the soul and the feeling of man and lead him to practical activity. Only in this way did Ruskin lead English culture to its present influential position.[45]

The times of Dürer and of Goethe, recalled by Diederichs, are the two *Blütezeiten,* the two "springs," of German civilization, nourishing the flowering of culture in which the integration of life and art will find its origin in art. The course of the Jugendstil was to envision an artful life without need to check artfulness against existence. The Darmstadt Artists' Colony was the most productive center for this endeavor, Behrens's theater proposal the most ambitious application of its principles. It makes overt what otherwise might have been only implicit.

Primitive acceptance of the symbol or image as reality itself, however important a role in life this might give to the arts, seemed an obvious anachronism in the late nineteenth century. An alternative, the symbolic understanding of reality, placed too much emphasis on a reality that was judged not to deserve this primacy. Furthermore, symbolic understanding was thought too private in the case of the artist, too abstract in the case of the scientist. A remaining alternative was to make reality symbolic. The invention, energy, power, and self-consciousness of modern man could reunite reality and symbolism by transforming life into art.

The endeavor to dramatize the world, to make the whole of life artistic, to make every act symbolic, was a high goal. But it was an endeavor in constant danger of destroying what it most highly valued. All hierarchy threatened to disappear; the frame became as important as the picture. What was meant to be artful risked being only artificial. The step from everything achieving symbolic meaning to being "merely symbolic" was discovered to be dangerously short. Heralded as the model of a new cultural era, the Darmstadt colony turned out to be a huge stage set. Houses were mere coulisses; monumental buildings and even people formed a backdrop before which danced the most artful creation of all, a neoromantic modern zeitgeist. Almost immediately the *sachlich* ("objective," "matter-of-fact," "down to earth") reaction set in. Still another solution to the problem of cultural integration, the endeavor to find the seeds of a new art within the situation of twentieth-century life, now took the lead. So *Zarathustra,* the book that had been for everyone, became a book for no one.

Nietzsche foresaw this condition:

The unhistorical [the power to forget] and the super-historical [art and religion] are the natural antidotes against the overpowering of life by history; they are the cures for the historical disease. We who are sick of the disease may suffer a little from the antidote. But this is no proof that the treatment we have chosen is wrong.

And here I see the mission of the youth that forms the first generation of fighters and dragon-slayers; it will bring a more beautiful and blessed humanity and culture, but will have itself no more than a glimpse of the promised land of happiness and wondrous beauty. This youth will suffer both from the malady and its antidotes; and yet it believes in strength and health and boasts a nature closer to the great Nature than its forebears, the cultured men and graybeards of the present. But its mission is to shake to their foundations the present conceptions of "health" and "culture," and erect hatred and scorn in the place of this rococo mass of ideas. And the clearest sign of its own strength and health is just the fact that it can use no idea, no party-cry from the present-day mint of words and ideas to symbolize its own existence; but only claims conviction from the power in it that acts and fights, breaks up and destroys; and from an ever heightened feeling of life when the hour strikes. You may deny this youth any culture—but how would youth count that a reproach.[46]

Was Darmstadt, then, just the suffering of the first stage of convalescence? Could Nietzsche's treatment, with continued application, indeed be the cure? Perhaps; but I think it is worth indicating that the Nietzschean problem also suggests a quite different treatment. Nietzsche, and most of the men mentioned here, were aware of the limitations of nineteenth-century science (*Wissenschaft*), which they saw as inductive and positivist. With Ranke had come also an inductive, positivist history (*Geschichtswissenschaft*). Now there was also such art history and theory (*Kunstwissenschaft*). These sciences have their material triumphs, it was acknowledged; but against this positivistic intellectual world one must assert the "unhistorical" and the "superhistorical." History and art, and with them, life, must be pulled away from the materialist grasp of positivism. New triumphs, it was hoped, would be achieved through this freedom from *Wissenschaft*. The hubris of the positivist was matched by that of the poet. The other treatment might have been a nonpositivistic reinterpretation of *Wissenschaft*.

Failing any such reinterpretation of science, the *Neuromantik*-Jugendstil movement was no more able to come to terms with the increasingly important intellectual and social role of science than was the society against which these artists had rebelled. Consequently, the movement was never as far removed from its nineteenth-century predecessors as it had sought to be.

Postscript

Readers particularly interested in theater are referred to an earlier publication of this essay with more extensive notes.[47] The principal studies of Behrens and theater subsequent to the initial version of this essay are by Jutta Boehe and Elisabeth Motz.[48]

There is still no study on Behrens's early career as a painter. His color woodcuts immediately won better critical reception and have been more accessible;[49] one, *The Kiss* with its two androgynous figures framed in their own entwining hair, is frequently employed to represent Jugendstil graphics. Nonetheless, there is no concerted study of these works either.[50]

Behrens's transition from painting to crafts in many forms was welcomed and seen as foreshadowed in his woodcuts. The extensive literature of the period is now joined by many entries in exhibition and museum collection catalogs. The most extensive single presentation is in the excellent catalog for the 1980 Behrens exhibition in Nürnberg.[51]

The peak of Behrens's activity in the crafts and the demonstration of its intended focus comes in the design of his own house in Darmstadt. In this chapter, I discuss the house principally in its role as a domestic microcosm of Behrens's vision of the relation of festival to city and collective life. This program yielded both the hierarchy of rooms and the demand for the thoroughness of design invention throughout the house. The earnestness of this effort gave every detail significance beyond that of an element of decor and caused virtually all critics, from 1901 to the present, to see Behrens's house as radically different from the houses of Olbrich, in both intention and result. In retrospect, the house can be seen as a telling first step in Behrens's self-definition as an architect; however, I find no significant contribution in terms of planning, spatial organization, tectonics, light, or other fundamental architectural concerns. There are, however, more appreciative and detailed assessments, including that of Tilmann Buddensieg.[52] A quite different interpretive position leads Ellen Spickernagel to a discussion of Nietzsche's gender differentiation and its representation in Behrens's design of bedrooms for himself and his wife (and in the *Damenzimmer* versus study/library in the Darmstadt house).[53]

4

Theory and Teaching of Architecture: Düsseldorf, 1903–1907

Assessing the late nineteenth century as intellectually and historically overripe, Art Nouveau and Jugendstil artists had turned away from the too naturalistic, derivative, and overladen work of the *Gründerzeit*. The new artists looked for new beginnings and consequently looked to other great beginnings—especially the archaic period of ancient Greece, the Quattrocento, and the art of China and Japan. These precedents shared an expressive use of line that seemed instinct with vitality. This youthful spring of the artistic forms complemented the assignment of archaic Greece and the Quattrocento to the stage of youth in a cyclical yet evolutionary scheme of the history of art.

The fact that the artists' new spring was then nipped in the bud was especially distressing. The Zarathustrian enthusiasm and hubris could not be sustained as a broad artistic movement in the face of a modern cultural and economic organization that thrives on the development, not to say exploitation, of new ideas. The success of the new illustrated magazines with which the artists worked so closely may itself have been prejudicial to the maturation of their proposals. Although not yet prepared to face this organizational problem squarely, those artists who had been the driving force in the movement were the first to acknowledge that the bloom was gone—and not as a natural evolution into a mature period. A classic or baroque phase in continuation of the Jugendstil cycle was not the plausible extension of their movement; furthermore, such an endeavor would confuse their work with that against which they had just rebelled.

The artists could note that the Jugendstil movement had been overly ambitious. For all the youthful verve of the works of the Greek archaic period or of the early Renaissance, these were, after all, evolved art forms—immediately preclassic. It had been wrong to attempt to begin life at puberty rather than in infancy.

The fall of Jugendstil was followed by a still more concerted endeavor to begin at the beginning. Everything that was judged to be archetypal, primitive or elemental, and charged with simple but fundamental distinctions came to be of prime interest. These interests do not begin abruptly in 1902, but they do take on new urgency then. Historic periods of intensified interest included prehistory, the ancient Near East, Egypt, the Geometric Period of ancient Greece, early Christianity including early Byzantium, and selected early medieval periods such as the Carolingian, Ottonian, and Tuscan Romanesque.[1] "Primitive art" was of concern: the *Völkerwanderung,* art of contemporary aboriginal peoples, the art of the child and of the naïve adult. The architectural parallel was anonymous architecture and everything that was *sachlich.*[2] There was also the primitivity of new materials and a new technology, engineering construction of all sorts, machine building, the American skyscraper, and everything that was functional; for example, the sailboat and the bicycle.[3] Specifically in architecture there was the elemental and prismatic late medieval, north European brickwork.[4] In psychology, Freud lent new significance to primitivity, and in psychophysiology there was the continuing interest in the elemental experience of pure form, pure color, and abstract space.[5] The studies of Riegl were of special interest because they were simultaneously concerned with establishing a teleological understanding of the artist's volition, interpreting early medieval art as a new beginning, and understanding the origin of such an art in the confluence of the forms of a full-blown ancient culture with the forms of culturally less developed peoples.[6] This constellation of problems seemed indeed to be the model for the modern situation. Consequently, any modern event that seemed to participate in the convergence of thought and feeling, developed culture and primitive instincts, was also of interest. The period to have accomplished this with the greatest degree of success was the romantic period, with Goethe and Schinkel as the heroes. Biedermeier was the heir to this development and exemplified the possibility that such a desired union of cultural sophistication and anonymous sensibility could thrive as a bourgeois generalization.[7] The preservation of a noble but simple domestic life in England and that country's new domestic architecture were interpreted similarly.[8] Yet another twist of the theme, the new American domestic architecture, was seen as the evolution of a healthy domestic culture in a new and primitive land.[9] Finally, it was as easy to read such writers as Nietzsche, Langbehn, and Steiner in connection with a still more primitive beginning, as it had been earlier in connection with Jugendstil.

In the search for the elemental in experience and in art, anything that was overtly geometric was studied. Things that were not overtly geometric, whether organic life, a complex art form, or the abstract conception of space, were studied in order to discover their underlying geometry. Fundamental geometric forms represented the elemental union of primitive instinct and developed reason.[10] Supposedly at the age of eight, Rudolf Steiner "knew happiness for the first time" when he learned through the study of geometry to "lay hold upon something in the spirit alone." At the same time, through analytical discovery and artistic projection, this became the connection between inner and outer experience.[11] One easily recognizes this same connection in student projects done under the direction of Behrens (figures 4.1–2).[12]

4.1 B. Albers. Student
project at Behrens's
Kunstgewerbeschule,
Düsseldorf (1903–1904).

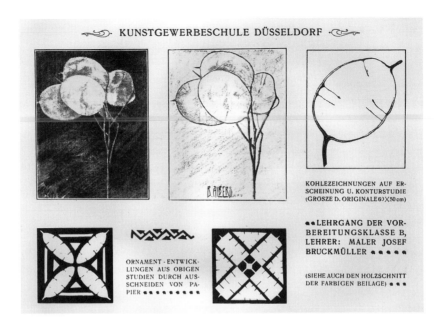

4.2 W. Kürten. Student
project under Behrens,
design for a reception room,
at the Kunstgewerbeschule,
Düsseldorf (1903–1904).

Before examining this student work, it will be well to consider the conditions under which Behrens entered into teaching. His position at Darmstadt had not required any teaching, but Behrens led two master's courses in Nürnberg in 1901 and 1902.[13] There the program called for directing mature, technically experienced craftsmen into creative production according to the best principles of the new art. There was in this a conscious intention to honor technique and to circumvent the artificiality of handicraft draftsmanship as taught in the schools. Wilhelm Schaefer forcefully expressed the disenchantment with the schools of arts and crafts in reviewing the Düsseldorf exhibition of 1902.[14] A quick glance—a sensitive eye can bear no more—at the works exhibited by the *Kunstgewerbeschulen,* Schaefer wrote, convinces one that the state instructs its youth in such a way that nothing good can come of these crafts. It is not that the schools are particularly *retarditaire,* he continued; they are simply the expression of what has been dominant in Germany for a few decades: science in art. This is a very questionable science at that, one that cannot treasure the vital powers involved in art. Germany will not progress in this matter until the scholars are turned out of the crafts, until artistic education is again practiced by means of artistic stimuli rather than through pedagogy.[15]

By January 1903, the reform program for the Kunstgewerbeschule in Düsseldorf was sufficiently advanced that the replacement of Director Hermann Stiller by Peter Behrens could be announced.[16] Behrens had the summer session of 1903 free for preparations. With school about to open in the fall, Schaefer already anticipated radical change for the better.[17] Rather than the old school's inappropriate imitation of "unserer Väter Werke" or "unseres Jugendstils Werke," one could now look forward to Behrens's new school participating in the dynamics of machine construction, iron bridges, and railroad cars—objects that had enjoyed a healthy development because they lacked models in "unserer Väter Werke." Now the school would produce modest but capable servants of life. Schaefer saw this as especially important in the Ruhr district, where the masterful works of the engineers and machine builders made all this style rubbish laughable. The steam engine, the iron girder, the arch of a bridge, and the railway station all develop from their inner necessities, from their construction. From these the students should learn the necessity of working rather than drawing. They would learn that rules are neither arbitrary nor in one's head but are in the things themselves.

Among those on the faculty, Schaefer especially admired the architect Karl Geyer. Behrens was also able to appoint a number of new teachers. From the Darmstadt colony he brought the sculptor Rudolf Bosselt. From Berlin he won Fritz Hellmuth Ehmcke, one of the founders of the Steglitzer Werkstatt (1901), an artist with a broad range of activities but especially renowned for his book and typeface design. There was a distinct geometrical preference in Ehmcke's work, a preference one could also expect in the two young men fresh from the Kunstgewerbeschule in Vienna: the interior and furnishings designer Max Benirschke, a pupil of Josef Hoffmann, and the painter Josef Bruckmüller, a pupil of Alfred Roller.[18]

The contrast between a teacher such as the sculptor Bosselt and the Viennese designers can also be seen in Behrens's work of this time. In cooperation with the City Library of Düsseldorf, Behrens designed a reading room which, before permanent installation in Düsseldorf, was exhibited at the world's fair in St. Louis in 1904 (figure 4.3).[19] The figures of *Day* and *Night* in dark red marble, flanking the clock, and the wooden grotesques at each table are by Bosselt. Together with the heavy consoles and dentils, these are reminiscences of Behrens's Zarathustra style. In sharp contrast, the strict orthogonality, planar surfaces, and subdued ornamentation of the chairs, tables, and lamps indicates his new direction. Obvious as these differences are, they did not result in a mere compromise but rather in one of Behrens's finest interiors.

In retrospect, we can see that the complex structure of Behrens's faculty and work in 1903–1904 mark a transitional phase in his development. The reading room, like the

4.3 Peter Behrens. Düsseldorf, City Library, reading room (1903–1904); exhibited at world's fair, St. Louis, 1904.

earlier hall in Turin, employed a plastic delimitation of space; yet it was occupied by light, abstract, almost dematerialized objects. By the end of his tenure in Düsseldorf, Behrens completely inverted this relationship (figure 4.15). Despite the irresolution in questions of form, he and his faculty initiated a program aimed at solving two criticisms frequently made of this type of school. One was that students usually came into the advanced, essentially professional, courses without either adequate background to make the choice of specialization or enough sensibility and skill to perform at a high standard. Consequently, the school was sending forth unfinished students. On the other hand, Behrens had no doubt found that his mature Nürnberg craftsman could easily produce a technically creditable work that, however, too often accepted Behrens's motifs without challenging the fundamental formal questions.

In the new Düsseldorf program, advanced classes increased the emphasis on "doing," and students were to arrive better equipped. To accomplish the latter, the preliminary schooling was greatly elaborated. There was still an introductory class in drawing, including perspective, light and shadow, and other such matters. However, the emphasis was now on the *Vorbereitungsklasse,* the preparatory class. *Vorbereitungsklasse B,* taught by Bruckmüller, owed much to Alfred Roller of the Kunstgewerbeschule in Vienna. Here the student learned to see, to master the basic artistic techniques, and to glimpse the many aspects of artistic activity. The student made a basic series of studies on ever-changing subjects. Figure 4.1 shows part of one such series. The series always began with studies in *Erscheinungszeichnen* (representational drawing). This group began with a charcoal sketch to convey the *Gesamteindruck,* the painterly total impression of the subject (figure 4.1, upper left). An oil painting followed the charcoal sketch, still intentionally painterly and enforcing the differentiation of color. The next studies, though still considered representational drawings, were increasingly simple. Various techniques were used—painting with a palette of two or three colors, or black-and-white studies with brush and ink or paper and shears. Next the subject was modeled plastically, with rather full naturalistic detail. Only after several such essays in representational drawing and modeling could one attempt the hardest problem: seeking out the contour and fixing it by means of line (*Konturzeichnen*). One could now proceed to the study of parts of the subject, even very small details. A butterfly's wing might be drawn at ten times its actual size to enforce observation of minute detail. Such studies were usually done in pen and ink. At various stages, but especially at the end of such a series, the student made practical use of the studies. All that had been seen and learned in both nature and detail studies was now employed in *compositional studies* in such various materials as wood, plaster, embroidery, or, as in our illustration, simply on paper as an ornamental unit that might be used in many ways. Finally, having learned to see the essential, and having developed technique, the students also undertook studies of movement. Some of the steps mentioned are better illustrated by other student work,[20] but our example does show how, "through analytical discovery and artistic projection, the sense for geometry becomes the connection between inner and outer experience."

It comes as no surprise that one of the student lettering exercises read: "Alle Schönheit beruht auf den Gesetzen natürlicher Formen" (All beauty is founded in the laws of natural forms).

Vorbereitungsklasse A, under Benirschke, was similar to Bruckmüller's class, except that here were grouped those students who evidenced a particularly marked talent for tectonics. Consequently, Benirschke especially emphasized experience of materials and techniques, and the constructive and systematic aspects of the studies.

The advanced classes emphasized still more the theme of art in crafts. Theory and practice, studio and workshop always complemented one another. As often as possible, Behrens wanted to see student projects carried to fruition; e.g., marble benches executed in Bosselt's sculpture class were used in Behrens's exhibition garden at the Düsseldorf exhibition of 1904.

Architectural drawings done under Benirschke, and occasionally those under Behrens, evidence a knowledge of Josef Hoffmann, Charles Rennie Mackintosh, and even of Japan. However, the projects under Behrens more often have a formal independence which is, I believe, explained by the following description of a problem in his class. The student is to structure a given surface (perhaps a square or a rectangle) harmonically, by dividing it into smaller surfaces. This is to be done in such a way that the individual small planes retain their distinct forms and that an ornamental effect is achieved solely through the proportions that are established and the interrelation of the parts to one another and to the whole. This systematic approach commended itself as being, it was said, equally applicable to plans, sections, and elevations, and virtually assured a unity of form. A few, quite papery designs from the first year of Behrens's directorship were published (figure 4.2).[21]

The emphasis that Behrens's school placed on *Vorbereitungsklassen*—courses that simultaneously taught the elements of form and introduced students to several media— was recognized as an innovation in education in the applied arts. With still greater sophistication in the elements of form, such a program was the cornerstone of the curriculum of the Bauhaus and remains a common feature in schools of applied art and architecture.

Behrens's own interest turned increasingly to architecture and the geometrical ordering of form. It did not escape his attention that the nearby Netherlands possessed a tradition of these combined interests. Dutch artists of the turn of the century never quite fitted the Art Nouveau image. In fact, the Dutch had nurtured concerns that were only now coming to the fore in Germany. The Dutch colonies fed an interest in Oriental art of a type that appealed through its exotic formal conventions (for example, batik). Furthermore the Dutch had a master builder who gave new vigor to their tradition of fine brickwork, Hendrik Petrus Berlage. Berlage himself designed within rigid geometric guidelines and elaborated his buildings with a discerning use of studiously elemental and primitive incised ornament, sans serif block letters, exposed iron, and stout craftsman furnishings.[22]

Already in 1904, Behrens, failing to enlist Berlage, brought the Dutch architect J. L. M. Lauweriks (1864–1932) to the faculty at Düsseldorf. Lauweriks, appreciative of

Berlage's work and theory, had worked eight years in the office of the other great Dutch master of the Berlage generation, P. J. H. Cuypers, before joining in partnership (1895–1900) with K. P. C. de Bazel. From January 1898, Lauweriks edited with de Bazel *Bouw- en Sierkunst,* a "bi-monthly journal of ancient and modern art." Published in both Dutch and French, *Bouw- en Sierkunst* was a source for exotic inspiration. Its fine plates illustrated Assyrian, Egyptian, and oriental art, Persian and medieval miniatures, buildings like those of Torcello, and modern work of the editors and their Dutch contemporaries. After four years of teaching in Haarlem, Lauweriks accepted the position under Behrens, bringing with him the theories of geometry and art he had learned, further developed, and practiced in Holland.

The significance given to geometric systems of design is attested in Berlage's book *Grundlagen und Entwicklung der Architektur,* four lectures held in relation to a course at the Kunstgewerbemuseum in Zurich in 1907.[23] Berlage explained his own use of geometric grids; in the case of his renowned Exchange in Amsterdam the grid was based on the "Egyptian triangle," an isosceles triangle with an altitude-to-base ratio of 5:8. The use of this triangle in locating the principal points in the elevations of the Exchange can be seen in figure 4.4. Berlage assured his audience that many of the modern architects of Holland used such systems. "For example," he said, "at the Kunstgewerbeschule in Düsseldorf, under the direction of the Dutch teacher Lauweriks, all designs are executed according to a similar, but very special method [with emphasis on the square with inscribed and circumscribed circles]. In this Lauweriks, goes further than anyone." Berlage set aside an evaluation of the method employed by Lauweriks, saying he had not had sufficient opportunity to study the system. However, he did show his Zurich audience both furniture and architectural design by the Düsseldorf students. The published lectures illustrate an elevation of a great domed central-plan building by an unidentified student and a plan for a house on a repetitive grid of squares with inscribed circles and smaller squares (figure 4.5) by Adolf Meyer, who was later the enigmatic partner of Walter Gropius in all his important early works.[24] Berlage continues: "In the disposition of a ground plan, it will always be found practicable to divide the plan into squares. 'Will that always work?' you will ask. Of course not . . . but it is indeed remarkable how often such a division is successful when one attempts it. It all depends on choosing the correct unit, the basic square, which can, of course, be subdivided if necessary." Berlage then suggests that for the elevations a more complex system is required, usually some form of triangulation as he had used on the Exchange.[25]

That Behrens sought out Lauweriks and gave him the principal teaching position in architecture at Düsseldorf is strong evidence for Behrens's interest in idealist theories of the relationship of geometry to nature and art. Among others, Behrens's close friend Julius Meier-Graefe was a contemporary witness to the fact that Behrens concerned himself with both the theory and practice of Lauweriks.[26] A fine work by Behrens at this time reflecting these ideas is the corner oriel sitting room he designed for Haus Schede at Wetter an

4.4 H. P. Berlage. Amsterdam, Stock Exchange (1896–1903). Elevation.

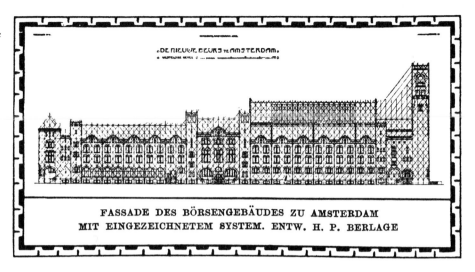

4.5 Adolf Meyer. Student project under Lauweriks, plan for a house, Kunstgewerbeschule, Düsseldorf (latest 1907).

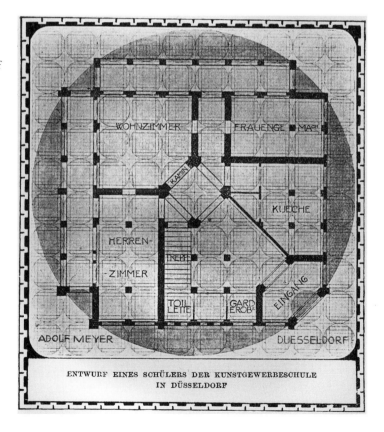

der Ruhr (figure 4.6). The favored mystic geometric relationship of a square with inscribed and circumscribed circles[27] is played out in the following series: circular oriel in square building block; line of building reestablished in ceiling recess and square rug by Behrens; circular table resting on the rug which continues other permutations of squares and circles. With all this, it is still a charming room, filled with light, possessed of a fine view, and almost totally free of the stolid *Zarathustrastil* earnestness.[28] An institutional square-and-circle theme is the Lecture Room designed by Behrens for Osthaus's Folkwang Museum in Hagen (figure 4.7).[29]

Both Gropius and Mies van der Rohe, in conversations about Behrens, volunteered comments on his use of geometry. Both referred to the crematorium in Hagen (figure 2.12) and allowed that perhaps geometry had played too determinative a role. But Gropius immediately said that such endeavors were beneficial—that he himself had profited from similar studies as a young man.[30]

While in Düsseldorf, Lauweriks explored a means of translating his abstract mathematical systems into material construction as directly as possible. This he attempted with sticks one unit square in cross section and multiples of that unit in length. Prior to 1909, in a little collection of simple proportional rules and diagrams illustrating combinations of unit sticks (figure 4.8), Lauweriks designed pieces of furniture that appear prophetic to later eyes (figure 4.9; and the more classicizing version of Behrens, figure 4.10).[31] The desire to hold to a basic element with standard-unit cross section is suggestive of de Stijl furniture; for example, Gerrit Rietveld's dining room chair of 1919 (figure 4.11).[32] However, the assembly of the elements is different. In Rietveld's work, the members pass one another, thereby preserving their identity as elements. The members of Lauweriks's furniture intersect and thus are closer to the de Stijl-influenced furniture of the Bauhaus.[33]

Considering the Düsseldorf *Vorbereitungsklassen* again, the series of student exercises, moving from a natural plant arrangement to a strict geometrical design, precedes by a decade and more similar series in the work of Piet Mondrian and Theo van Doesburg (figure 4.12). The action and the language of the Düsseldorf school and of the de Stijl group indicate that they both sought, through analysis, to discover what is elemental in form and then to reconstruct these elements according to universal harmony.[34] It is important to acknowledge that de Stijl achieved a stricter set of elements, reassembled these elements in an inventive asymmetrical balance, and simultaneously avoided all mere decorative effects. In terms of a formal structure, that is, de Stijl was more emphatic and more resourceful; still the searches were of the same kind. Van Doesburg and the architects of de Stijl sought diligently, and with considerable success, to extend their formal vision to the physical world of furniture (figure 4.11) and buildings.[35] In terms of formal structures, Behrens is less compelling but not totally naïve in matters related to de Stijl's later awareness. Consider the composition of the restaurant Jungbrunnen at the Gartenbau- und Kunstausstellung in Düsseldorf (1904),[36] and especially the excellent Obenauer house in Saarbrücken of 1905–1906 (figures 8.13–20).[37] The fundamental symmetry of these

---

4.6 Peter Behrens. Wetter an der Ruhr, Schede house, sitting room (1904–1905).

4.7 Peter Behrens. Hagen, Folkwang Museum, lecture hall (1904–1905).

4.8 J. L. M. Lauweriks.
Schematic drawing of furniture built with modular units
(before 1909).

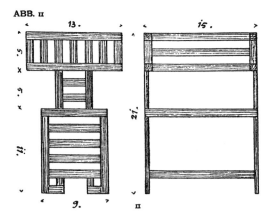

4.9 Lauweriks. Bookshelf and
chair (before 1909).

4.10 Peter Behrens. Garden
table and arm chair; by
Beissbarth & Hoffmann
A.G., Mannheim-Rheinau
(1907).

4.11 Gerrit Rietveld. Dining room chair (1919).

4.12 Theo van Doesburg. "Aesthetic Transfiguration of an Object"; typography by László Moholy-Nagy (1925).

ÄSTHETISCHE TRANSFIGURATION EINES GEGENSTANDES
Abb. 5: Photographische Darstellung. Abb. 6: Formgebundene Akzentuierung von Verhältnissen.
Abb. 7: Aufhebung der Form. Abb. 8: Bild

4.13 Peter Behrens.
Mannheim, International Art
and Garden Exhibition,
1907. Garden (1906–1907).

designs makes the occult asymmetries of their forms all the more provoking. Behrens and the Düsseldorf school, like de Stijl, were concerned with formal structures that related not only to visual criteria, but also to intellectual and mystic criteria which should control all of experience.[38]

Behrens ardently pursued the assembly of unit sticks into larger constructs in garden furniture and pergolas.[39] In this pursuit, his ultimate essay in pure form defining abstract space was the group of pavilions for the Northwest German Art Exhibition at Oldenburg in 1905 (figure 2.6)[40] and the gardens for the same exposition and that of Mannheim in 1907 (figure 4.13). The Oldenburg pavilions are the embodiment of what Meier-Graefe was just then publishing about Behrens:

> Wouldn't it be possible to build in such a way that nothing of the form but only the esteemed, cool spirit of the Greeks would once again arise? Indeed, there is no form that one could borrow. The true Hellenism exists more clearly as an ideal than in the reality of the ruins.
>
> . . . The way to the antique lies within our sphere, it cannot end in Greece but rather must bring Hellenic clarity, Hellenic rationality—or let us simply say beauty—into our forms.
>
> That Behrens attempts.
>
> . . . Culture, which bases itself on lawfulness, opposes itself to the arbitrariness of personality. It is no longer a matter of the enrichment of the fantasy, but the enrichment of geometry. . . .
>
> If they succeed, these endeavors go well beyond the interest of art. The union of the arts can only be achieved through a community of principle. This inevitably rests in geometry. . . . If architecture can demonstrate this healthy sense, then one may expect that the other arts will recognize their infirmity.[41]

Meier-Graefe makes rather extravagant claims for architecture, closely reflecting the ideas of his friend Behrens; even more difficult to credit is the claim that geometry would serve as a simple panacea for all the gravest problems of life and art. And yet we should not fail to see that Lauweriks and Behrens were leaders in the endeavor to change the revolutionary architectural debates, and artistic education, away from a concern with "ornament" and "decoration."[42] About 1903, notably in the development of the teaching program at Düsseldorf, *Gestaltung* was becoming a popular word. This term, with its elevated sense of the act of forming and structuring, and with a more general connotation than van de Velde's *vernunftgemässe Gestaltung,* pointed to new concerns and new activities. Rather than emphasizing the origin and elaboration of ornament, such artists now sought an abstract structuring of experience, of space, and of the material forms that define the space. The geometric structures chosen were so rigid that they seem to inhibit any sense of rewarding experience or the necessities of material and function. However, principal attention had

been shifted to a distinctly architectural scale, to an abstract conception of the structuring of experience through architectural form, to *Gestaltung;* and this conception called out for imaginative elaboration. In this sense, it is not surprising that we can suggest the connections of the ideal geometry of Lauweriks and Behrens to such important contributors to twentieth-century architecture as Gropius and Meyer, Le Corbusier, and the de Stijl group, the latter of which would also have had Dutch sources in common with Lauweriks.

At the time of the Oldenburg exhibition, Meier-Graefe, who had then known Behrens for ten years, wrote that no matter how assertively Behrens might hold a particular position, he did not promise to hold it the next time you met; he would only promise to be better.[43] Whether or not his changes were always for the better, it is true that the whole of Behrens's career is marked by distinct changes of principle. A relatively modest but important change—the endorsement of corporeality—followed shortly upon the words of Meier-Graefe.

The teaching program at Düsseldorf claimed to emphasize the workshop, technique, material, and function as well as theory. Yet the student designs and even the Behrens-executed pavilions at Oldenburg seem to sacrifice all sense of materiality to the rigidly abstract *Gestaltung.* A Christian Bayer–J. L. M. Lauweriks project of 1909 (figure 4.14) is *still* obsessively tied to a single, systematic geometric grid that shapes the site, the plans, the sections, and the elevations of the church.[44] About 1905–1906, Peter Behrens began to search for a means to integrate the act of building and the fact of materiality into his idealistic formal structure. Earlier I suggested how he partially achieved this by a closer emulation of historical buildings which themselves hold the real and the ideal in uneasy tension—for example in his crematorium at Hagen (1907), emulating S. Miniato in Florence (figures 2.12–13). Documents exist that interestingly recreate Behrens's development of an appreciation of corporeality. Admittedly, his work at Turin and his continuing association with Rudolf Bosselt evidence an acceptance of weightiness in his aesthetic of earlier years. Indeed, he was, around the turn of the century, an avid admirer of Egyptian sculpture.[45] But in all these cases, it was their plastic stylization that made them acceptable within his contemporary aesthetic position. Now he desired a corporeality that would stand as the antipode to his newly mastered abstract space.

This interest emerges in his preparation for the exhibition room he was to provide at the Mannheim International Art Exhibition of 1907. On 17 December 1906, Behrens wrote to his friend and patron, the great art collector and founder of the Folkwang Museum, Karl Ernst Osthaus of Hagen. Explaining that he had undertaken the design and execution of a festival hall, a temporary exhibition space, in the new Mannheim Kunsthalle, Behrens wrote that the monumental forming of the hall would provide an excellent opportunity to use sculpture to especially beautiful effect. "I would like to structure this space in such a way that my artistic convictions come to expression, and would consequently also like to seek a complete harmony between that expression and the exhibited works of art. . . . For this purpose the most suitable sculptor would be, of course,

Maillol."[46] Since Osthaus would understand what Behrens was attempting and also was acquainted with the newly renowned French sculptor Aristide Maillol, Behrens asked that Osthaus seek to obtain for exhibition at Mannheim the large female nude shown at the 1906 Sezession exhibition in Berlin and any other works Osthaus or Maillol might find appropriate. Behrens also wished to install works by Bernhard Hoetger, a German artist then working in Paris, since he felt that Hoetger's work participated in the same endeavor as that of Maillol and the design Behrens himself contemplated. He invited further suggestions from Osthaus, but specifically excluded the sculptor George Minne.[47] Finally, Behrens urged haste since the disposition of the space would depend upon the sculptures that were to be exhibited.

Two months later, in a letter to Osthaus of 8 February 1907, Behrens was still most desirous of having works by Maillol as the principal feature of the Mannheim hall, even if these were to be plaster casts. Behrens noted that he was also contacting Hermann Haller and Karl Hofer in Rome and Hoetger in Paris, and expressed interest in works by two artists who apparently did not come to be exhibited in Behrens's room at Mannheim, Marrees [*sic,* Hans von Marées] and Albiker. In a letter of 19 February Behrens also inquired of Osthaus about paintings by Christian Rohlfs.[48]

When Behrens excluded Minne, he rejected the sculptor whose renowned fountain with its tender nude youths was the central feature of the van de Velde-designed main hall of Osthaus's Folkwang Museum. Like Minne and van de Velde, and like Behrens himself, another artist who had received special attention from Osthaus was the Dutch painter Johann Thorn-Prikker. Thorn-Prikker's concern with ornament, with a stylized line, and with such image-making craft techniques as stained glass and intarsia made him one of the artists most sympathetically related to the Jugendstil program. Behrens revealed how much he himself had changed when, in a letter to Osthaus of 26 February 1907, he not only rejected the suggested participation of Thorn-Prikker in the Mannheim exhibition, but did so on the grounds that Thorn-Prikker's works were too hard and too stylized! Behrens wrote: "Last winter I saw a large wall painting by Thorn-Prikker in Krefeld, a painting that was completely worked out in geometric forms. Don't you think that such a painting would form a too strong contrast with the art of Maillol, Hoetger, Haller, and others?"

The room Behrens created at Mannheim is one of the finest interiors of his career (figure 4.15).[49] The long axis terminated in a niche giving a calculated emphasis to the featured work, Maillol's *Méditerranée.* The entire area of the niche was of plain surfaces without any articulation or ornament, as were all the walls up to door height. Thus all the works of art were given a simple, noncompetitive background. Yet, with an elegant articulation of the upper walls and ceiling, Behrens succeeded in giving a formal structure to the entire room—a structure that could also constrain the sublimated yet rich ornament of the coffers and tympana. The large lateral dimension and bold frame of the principal niche continued into the great axial coffers of the ceiling with their geometrical rose ornaments, the principal features of the ceiling plane. Three small squares flanked each of these coffers on either side. Each of these small squares had, in turn, the dimension of two rectangular wall panels below. By this device, the upper corners of the room obtained a harmonious relationship of the three intersecting planes while the articulating black and gold lines still differentiated those planes. Above and behind the *Méditerranée,* Behrens exhibited the large and forceful *Reclining Female Nude* by Hermann Haller, a Swiss artist then working in Rome. At the left in our illustration is a marble *Torso of a Woman* by Hoetger. At the right is a *Bather* by Maillol (both it and the *Méditerranée* were plaster casts). Also exhibited in the room were sculptures by Haller and the Parisian Antoine Bourdelle and paintings by Karl Hofer and the considerably older Christian Rohlfs, who was inspired to inventive new production through his association with Osthaus at Hagen.[50]

The physically and visually disturbing tangencies of niche and frame in the end wall offer the final proof, if proof were needed, that Behrens was still working with a purely abstract, geometrically defined space. The ideality and stylization of space continues, but is now complemented and given meaning by the presence of sculpture chosen for its full

4.15 Behrens. Mannheim,
International Art and Garden
Exhibition. Exhibition hall
and installation (1906–1907).

plasticity and insistent sense of the occupation of space. Just as he ruled out Thorn-Prikker as too stylized, so his failure to include sculpture by Rudolf Bosselt, his colleague at Düsseldorf, demonstrated that Behrens was turning from the relief-oriented stylization of Adolf Hildebrand's powerful influence to a preference for the full-bodied, classicizing forms of Maillol and others. Maillol's *Méditerranée* is generally considered to be the fruition of the first stage of the sculptor's search for these self-contained, reposeful nudes. It had been begun in 1902, the year of his first major exhibition at Vollard in Paris. In 1904, Meier-Graefe dedicated to Maillol a chapter of his *Entwicklungsgeschichte der modernen Kunst*—a multivolume work that concluded with a projection of Behrens as the hope of the future in architecture. The *Méditerranée* was exhibited for the first time at the Salon d'Automne in 1905 and a marble version purchased by a member of the former *Pan* circle, Harry Graf Kessler of Weimar, van de Velde's patron. In 1906, Maillol exhibited at the Sezession exhibition in Berlin. In 1908, the new classical preference was sealed in the trip of Kessler, Maillol, and Hugo von Hofmannsthal to Greece.[51] Behrens and Walter Gropius also planned a trip to Greece shortly after this time.[52]

As a decade earlier, Meier-Graefe is still a critical supporter of Behrens and also a prime source for Behrens's knowledge of new directions in the arts. But Behrens's idea of playing his parcels of continuous space against the emphatically material new sculpture, as well as other new theories, would appear to have been supplied from yet another source. For the Düsseldorf Kunstgewerbeschule, Behrens hired a bright young historian and theoretician of art, Wilhelm Niemeyer, a student of the noted Professor August Schmarsow of Leipzig. Not only was Schmarsow engaged in proportional and geometrical studies of architecture, but he had also just published a work on principles of the study of art, which was terminologically and theoretically provocative for Behrens.[53] To take only one instance, in the conclusion of the book Schmarsow puts emphasis on two seemingly rather obvious principles: that sculpture is a *space-filling* art, while architecture is a *space-creating* art. Understood with some historical awareness, these statements are not as obvious as they seem. The idea of *Gestaltung* and the abstract structuring of space had only just come to the fore in European architecture. In Behrens's own school, the exercises tended to emphasize the search for a similar abstract structure both in objects and in the arts of painting and sculpture. Behrens's exhibition room at Mannheim continues his new exploration of space, but in the exhibited works he turns to the classical theme of the human body as occupier and definer of space.

These new activities were consciously embraced as a renewal of classical principles. A fascinating article by Wilhelm Niemeyer of the same date as the Behrens-Osthaus letters just quoted attests to the seriousness of this new classicism, specifically in the case of Behrens.[54] Niemeyer claims that Behrens is in consonance with their generation's universal new sensibility for Hellenism. Since the time of Schliemann the earth had yielded works that made Greece alive for them.[55] The understanding that Hellas is rooted in the Orient is an instance of how the old classicistic view (ca. 1800) had been replaced by an awareness of the true vitality of antiquity. New experiences sharpened their appreciation of Greece; for example, knowledge of the Japanese woodcut opened their eyes to Greek vase painting. These new experiences and insights gave a deeper conception of history, which was expressed philosophically and poetically in the works of Jakob Burckhardt and Friedrich Nietzsche, and with careful scholarship in the researches of Ulrich Wilamowitz and Adolf Furtwängler.[56] This enlivening of antiquity also led to the "discovery" of what is referred to as "late antiquity" (*Spätantike*). Here Alois Riegl, Josef Strzygowski, and others published their findings on the arts of late antiquity, the Copts, Byzantium, and down to the works of the Cosmati.[57]

According to Niemeyer, such a flowering of new knowledge and deepened sensibility must find its complementary image in current artistic activity. Just as the new architecture of the Italian Renaissance was preceded by a new understanding of antiquity in literature and education, and just as the greatest architect of early nineteenth-century German neoclassicism, Karl Friedrich Schinkel, was preceded by fifty years in the Greek scholarship of Winckelmann, so the architectonic art of Peter Behrens appeared as the immanent, artistically conceived form-manifestation of the scholarly rebirth of antiquity at the turn of the century. Niemeyer continued with a long explication of Behrens's aesthetic of space which had as its fundamental motto: "The spatial structure of Behrens is based on the principle of the absolute clarification of spatial form to mathematical precision."

The Mannheim exhibition room was a well-received triumph of this mathematically clear space and of the new classicism. That one might now preconceive the next step in Behrens's development was demonstrated by one of the admiring visitors in the fall of 1907. Heinrich Wölfflin, the noted Swiss art historian, suggested that Behrens would have his greatest future in architecture if he could add to his eurythmy of line and plane also a cubic beauty such as that which elevates the Palazzo Strozzi in Florence to the status of a classical building.[58]

By the time of Wölfflin's assessment, it was already known that Behrens would be leaving the Kunstgewerbeschule in Düsseldorf to work for the Allgemeine Elektricitäts-Gesellschaft in Berlin, simultaneously marking the end of his self-conducted architectural apprenticeship.[59] In the year after his personal success at the Darmstadt Artists' Colony, Behrens had, in the Turin exhibition, intensified his Zarathustra style only to find that the willful novelty of this manner and all the more florid manifestations of Art Nouveau were fading quickly in the early years of the twentieth century. Consequently, Behrens arrived at his teaching post in Düsseldorf in 1903 without an established manner of design. What he could bring to his administrative position was a presentiment that the way out of the Jugendstil impasse lay in the substitution of a new set of conventions, based largely on an orthogonal geometry, for the old conventions based mainly on a freely curving line. Behrens also brought the ambition and energy to give this presentiment more actuality. His appointments to the faculty at Düsseldorf showed a geographic catholicity; Behrens and Bosselt apart, there was a common denominator in the appointees' interest in stylization through geometry, but inspection reveals that this meant different things to different people. At least in the case of Behrens personally, it was the synthetic structuring vision of the Dutch architect Lauweriks and the emerging notion of *Gestaltung* that triumphed over any merely analytic or ornamental use of geometry. Attention shifted so wholly to the definition and structuring of space that the material aspect of architecture suffered both as form and as technique. In the Mannheim exhibition, Behrens sought to unify the arts, assigning to sculpture the role of material presence. This was a humanistic sculpture that occupied space and gave proportional criteria to the structuring of space, in sharpest contrast to the stylized carving that was captured in the plastic continuum of the vestibule at Turin. Nevertheless, in such projects as the exhibitions at Oldenburg and Mannheim, Behrens created only a graphic skeleton of space. To the degree that these works are successful, it is in marking off and making the viewer aware of a particular region of an infinitely extended metrical space.

In the later teaching of László Moholy-Nagy, the antithesis of abstract space and space-occupying objects is preserved;[60] numerous works by Ludwig Mies van der Rohe are concerted explorations of this antithesis. In the Project for a House with a Court, ca. 1934 (figure 4.16), and in the Project for a Concert Hall of 1942 (figure 4.17), Mies put highly plastic sculptures into metrical spaces. Mies magnified Behrens's spatial conception, but in the Concert Hall project he also reversed Behrens's development in artistic preference: the earlier state of Mies's collage incorporated an image of Maillol's *Méditerranée,* but he later changed it to the Egyptian sculpture shown in our illustration.[61]

Works of this type, whether by Behrens or by Mies, relied heavily on the viewer's awareness of an abstract concept of space and acceptance of the attempt at representing that intellectualization materially. These abstract designs presented neither spaces nor architectural forms as entities of a felt experience. A proper qualification of this statement would be to point out that a few of Mies's works—the Barcelona Pavilion and, to a lesser extent, the concert hall—did participate in that experiential and plastic structuring of space achieved by the de Stijl group in the 1920s.

Behrens, in the period under discussion, and Mies more generally talked about material and architecture but grasped a basically mathematical conception that is carried inadequately by material form; points, lines, and planes cannot be built. The de Stijl artists (and again Mies in his de Stijl-inspired works) talked about lines and planes but allowed the ambiguities of physical assemblies to achieve forms that neither their words nor those of a mathematician can adequately describe.

One of the drives toward a modern form of classicism was the desire to capture an architectural form that could be sensed as well as rationalized, and structured materially as well as formally. Although both the de Stijl group and Le Corbusier were later to demonstrate the limits of his achievement, Behrens felt, as he went off to Berlin, that his Düsseldorf work had fulfilled the desire for a sensible intellectualization of space. He then turned his attention to the physical or material structuring of his designs.

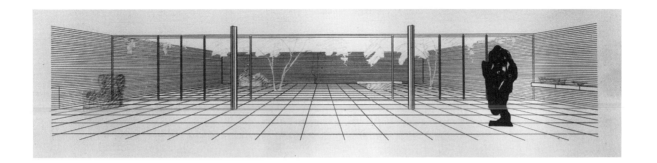

4.16 Ludwig Mies van der Rohe. Project for a house with a court (ca. 1934). Interior perspective.

4.17 Ludwig Mies van der Rohe. Project for a concert hall (1942). Collage, interior perspective.

Postscript

We are fortunate now to have a wealth of detail in several careful studies covering the Düsseldorf period of Behrens's career. This was the subject of a dissertation by Gisela Moeller under Professor Tilmann Buddensieg at Bonn, which, as published, is the definitive study of these years.[62] Moeller examines both the school that Behrens created and the diverse production of this time that centered on Düsseldorf and Hagen. As noted in the text, the importance of Hagen for modern art and architecture in the early years of the century was owing to the patronage of Karl Ernst Osthaus, the subject of a large, excellent monograph by Herta Hesse-Frielinghaus and her colleagues.[63] Behrens's work at the Oldenburg exhibition of 1905 is itself the subject of a detailed monograph.[64]

If, from all the media and types of design in which Behrens engaged, one were to choose the arena other than architecture in which he excelled, it would be in the design of typefaces (figure 4.18). Behrens's modernized version of German *Fraktur,* called *Behrens-Schrift,* was available to publish his celebratory address to Ernst Ludwig at Darmstadt in 1901.[65] Released by the typefounders in 1902, it enjoyed considerable success in the first decade of the century.[66] Behrens continued with the design of type and offered typography courses both in the Düsseldorf school and in his own atelier in Neubabelsberg near Berlin.[67] Working always with the noted typefounders Gebrüder Klingspor (prior to 1906 Rudhard'sche Giesserei) of Offenbach am Main, Behrens released his *Kursiv* in 1908, just after his move to Berlin. His two most successful typefaces were designed immediately after, in the years 1908–1909, but appeared some years apart: the *Antiqua* in 1908 and the *Mediäval* in 1914.[68] The first known use of the *Antiqua* was in the AEG catalog for the German Shipbuilding Exhibition in Berlin in June 1908, for which Behrens also designed the AEG exhibition building and gardens (figure 5.4), but the first book was an edition of the poetry of Michelangelo, published by Eugen Diederichs in 1909.[69]

4.18. Peter Behrens. Four typefaces (1902–1914).

Peter Behrens Behrens-Schrift 1902

Dom Schlechten kann man nie zu wenig und das Gute nie zu oft lefen: schlechte Bücher find intellektuelles Gift, fie verderben den Geift. Um das Gute zu lefen, ift eine Be=

Peter Behrens Behrens-Kursiv 1907

Dom Schlechten kann man nie zu wenig und das Gute nie zu oft lefen: jchlechte Bücher find intellektuelles Gift, fie verderben den Geift. Um das Gute zu lefen, ift eine Bedingung,

Peter Behrens Behrens-Antiqua 1908

Vom Schlechten kann man nie zu wenig und das Gute nie zu oft lefen: fchlechte Bücher find intellektuelles Gift, fie verderben den Geift. Um das Gute zu lefen, ift eine Be~

Peter Behrens Behrens-Mediaeval 1914

Vom Schlechten kann man nie zu wenig und das Gute nie zu oft lefen: fchlechte Bücher find intellektuelles Gift, fie verderben den Geift. Um das Gute zu lefen, ift eine

5
Modern Architecture and Industry, a Cultural Policy of Historical Determinism: Berlin I

Modern industry ruptured ancient relationships among makers, products, and users: owing to the division of labor, a loss of relation between workers and the objects produced, a correlative standardization of the products, and an increasing emphasis on fashion and obsolescence as stimuli to consumption. The Great Exhibition of 1851 in the Crystal Palace in London assembled the machines and products of modern industry in a prefabricated iron and glass building before a popular audience—building and audience themselves being representatives of the same change in productive means. The event occasioned major reassessments of the condition of culture and society in relation to new productive systems and the environment they produced. Although such evaluations need not have hinged on a rejection or even a radical critique of mass production, the immediate consequences of industrialization were sufficiently open to criticism to lend strong support to the Arts and Crafts movement, which, under the leadership of William Morris, attempted to reintroduce craftsmanship as the primary means of cultural production.

It has often been noted that Morris himself was finally forced to realize the inherent impossibility of relying on craft production, with its assumption of the integration of work, production, and society, as the basis for achieving a healthy and equitable social order. It also became clear that the course of industrial production could not be reversed without drastic consequences for a population now reorganized to suit the processes of industrialization. In the end, Morris and his associates could only produce high-quality craft objects, for the most part at luxury prices, within a world dominated by the processes of mass production. At best their work could be valued for achieving an appropriate relation between the character of a product and the process of its production. While this relation might serve as an ideal to be achieved under other modes of production, the Arts and Crafts program could not suggest an alternative organization of production and society.

Where the midcentury Arts and Crafts movement pitted handicraft production and the myth of a preindustrial, organic social harmony against modern technique and the consequent social crises of the industrial revolution, the artistic movements of the late nineteenth century, soon to be known as Art Nouveau, proposed the ideal of a holistic, Nietzschean artistic culture to be set against the advance of a positivist scientific civilization. The new controversial position stemmed from the critique of art and culture rather than from craft production. It confronted not the productive basis of modern civilization but certain characteristics of that civilization and the extension of those traits to intellectual, cultural, and spiritual realms. While the formation of Art Nouveau took place outside the realm of industry, Art Nouveau artists themselves were not programmatically opposed to the use of industrial methods. Henry van de Velde, one of the chief spokesmen of the movement, often argued for the mutual support of art and industry. However, the resistance of these artists to a fragmented, analytic, positivist science (*Wissenschaft*), and their difficulty in imagining either science or technology without these characteristics, divorced Art Nouveau from any productive base and thus led to its early dissolution.

As we have seen, Peter Behrens, when a member of the Darmstadt Artists' Colony, established a typically Art Nouveau and explicitly Nietzschean program for a holistic culture that would be generated by the will of an elite (figures 3.5, 3.9). Yet Behrens's late emergence within Art Nouveau facilitated his shift, notably in his work in Düsseldorf, toward other positions—both theoretical and formal.

In 1907, Behrens left his academic post in Düsseldorf to become the artistic consultant to a large corporation in the electrical industry, the Allgemeine Elektricitäts-Gesellschaft (AEG) in Berlin. He came to control almost every visual manifestation of this corporation, including its product design, graphics, exhibition design, and architecture.[1]

The firm was established in 1883 as the Deutsche Edison Gesellschaft für angewandte Elektricität by Emil Rathenau, a shrewd engineer-businessman who learned of Edison's work at the Philadelphia Exposition of 1876 and later procured the German rights for the Edison patents. The success of the AEG, the related changes in its political and cultural self-awareness, and the emergence of Peter Behrens in this development can all be gauged by comparing AEG participation in three exhibitions.

As a pioneer in power transmission, the AEG arranged an impressive demonstration of this important modern service for the Electrotechnical Exhibition in Frankfurt am Main in 1891. Water power drove a turbine of three hundred horsepower at Lauffen am Neckar, which, in turn, drove an electric generator (figure 5.1). Fifteen thousand volts from this generator were transmitted a record 175 kilometers to Frankfurt, where transformers converted it to light one thousand incandescent lamps and run a one-hundred-horsepower electric motor. Neither the lights nor the motor were the culminating attraction; in accordance with a charming and naive naturalism, the motor drove a pump that lifted water to the top of an artificial hill where a theatrical waterfall spent the electrical energy which, miles away, had been generated by water power (figure 5.2).[2] A quite extraordinary capability for the generation and distribution of large amounts of energy was expended in a poor imitation of nature and with a naive sense of functional symmetry.

5.1 Anon. Lauffen am Neckar, machine house for AEG exhibition, Frankfurt (1891).

5.2 Anon. Frankfurt am Main, Electrotechnical Exhibition, waterfall with water supplied by AEG pumps which had their power source at Lauffen (1891).

Almost equally naive architecturally, the building that housed the equipment at Lauffen was derived from medieval, half-timbered prototypes. At this point the AEG was preoccupied with a popular demonstration of what it could achieve and was little concerned with the expression of its capabilities through artistic form—whether in terms of its equipment, the housing of this equipment, or the image of the corporation.

For the Universal Exposition of 1900 in Paris, the AEG employed a designer to create an artistic setting for its products. While it is clear that by this time the corporation was becoming self-conscious about its production and its relation to art, the pavilion itself was little more than a vulgar combination of Art Nouveau ornament and pseudo-classical forms (figure 5.3). Such a work was as incapable of emulating the dramatic operation of the Frankfurt waterfall as it was of establishing a correspondence between the technical modernism of the AEG and the presumed modernism of its artistic style.

Peter Behrens's first building for the AEG was an exhibition pavilion for the German Shipbuilding Exhibition of 1908 (figure 5.4).[3] Machines stood like sculptures in an austere centralized building modeled on such prototypes as the baptistery of Florence and the imperial chapel at Aachen (figure 5.5). The AEG no longer sought merely to emphasize the utility of its products (certainly not in the form of artificial waterfalls), but rather to exhibit the product itself as an impressive object, indicative of modern industrial potential. Beyond the reification of this utilitarian potential there were cultural and political implications which the AEG increasingly saw as the opportunity and responsibility of the corporation. The 1908 pavilion by Behrens implicitly assumed the necessity of representing industry as a forceful agent within society. Machines became the regalia of power; the

5.3 Unidentified designer. Paris, Universal Exposition, 1900, AEG Pavilion.

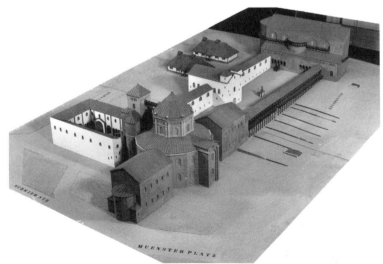

5.4 Peter Behrens. Berlin,
German Shipbuilding
Exhibition, AEG Pavilion
(1908). Exterior.

5.5 Aachen, model of
Carolingian palace complex.

5.6 Berlin, the Kaiser opening the AEG
Pavilion by Behrens at the German
Shipbuilding Exhibition (2 June 1908).

increasingly studied forms adopted for both the machines and the pavilion asserted their political and cultural roles. Significantly, the Kaiser himself opened this pavilion of power and good form (figure 5.6; also illustrated in list of works, no. 49).

A similar formal development occurred in the field of graphics. The AEG passed from elaborate late nineteenth-century job printing[4] to the commissioning of a noted artist as the designer of its graphic image. In 1900 Otto Eckmann adapted his floral and lyrical Jugendstil manner to the design of a corporate logo and decorative borders for changing advertisements. Though these were excellent within their genre, the immediate juxtaposition of Eckmann's designs with images of machine production served only to indicate an aspiration for, rather than the result of, a successful collaboration between art and industry (figure 5.7). The AEG pavilion at Paris and Eckmann's graphics for the AEG may appear as exceptions to the Jugendstil artists' general lack of sympathy for a modern civilization dominated by science and technology, but the contrasts between pavilion and machine and between decorative frame and photographic image of the machine product were so great in these examples that they simply confirmed the exclusion of art from the system of production—confirmed the disjunction of art and industry rather than their union. Beginning in 1907, Behrens created a unified graphic style for the AEG by means of a precise, overt geometrical organization of the surface and the use of antique type-faces (figure 5.8). On occasion, Behrens also reduced the image of the product to two-dimensional graphic terms (figure 5.9).

5.7 Otto Eckmann. AEG
advertisement (1900).

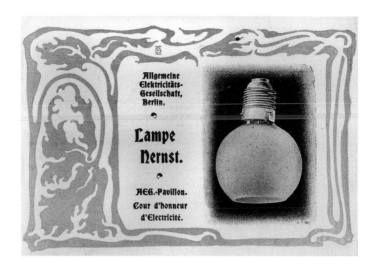

5.8 AEG, development of the corporate logo. Top, Louis
Schmidt (1888). Center left, Franz Schwechten (1896).
Center right, Behrens (1908). Bottom, Behrens (ca. 1912).

5.9 Peter Behrens. AEG advertisement for intensive arc lamps
(1911).

Post-Art Nouveau work, such as that produced by Behrens in Düsseldorf, was more a change in formal convention than a reformulation of the underlying attitude toward industry. Any implication this formal change bore for the union of art and industrial production was ambiguous. Certain conventions, such as the use of the T-square and triangle, the form of a brick, and the geometry of a simple structural bay, suggested that straight linear compositions were more anonymous and comprehensive than curvilinear arrangements. While Behrens and other artists thought of these straight lines in ideal rather than practical terms, figures such as van de Velde argued for the practical function of what he called "wavy lines."[5]

The new convention of the straight line adapted quite well to certain limited problems, as in the case of Behrens's graphics for the AEG. But the same conventions did not go very far in resolving the problem of product design and the structure of material things—objects of use and building. Thus Behrens's past experience and the logic of his new position with the AEG posed problems on several levels. First and foremost, if the relationship of design and product form were to be worked out in terms of industrial production (for the poverty of the handicraft approach was increasingly clear), then a reassessment of such basic attitudes as the artist's antipositivism and mistrust of technology and industry was necessary. More strategically, Behrens had to construct a practice, and an implicit theory, by which a person of artistic talent and interest might contribute to an organizational system whose operational concerns extended from natural resources to the mass marketing of industrial products. Finally, he had the problem of relating design to the productive processes, of discovering a viable relationship between the abstractions of the artist and the material conditions of production. At a more general level, Behrens's employment with the AEG marked a renewal of his search for a functional relationship between art and society—but no longer, as at Darmstadt, through the artists' dictation of a holistic culture. The new search, although equally utopian, entered into a discourse with the existing economic, political, and social conditions.

It is more than incidental that one of the directors of the AEG, Walther Rathenau, the son of its founder and president, shared Behrens's interest in a culture composed of functionally related parts. Both men believed that certain periods of history manifested high levels of culture, that one must work to achieve such a level again, and that modern technology was *not* an inevitable contribution to this goal. Rathenau was one of the last great utopians, composing his positive image from both an evolutionary and a critical understanding of human development. Concerned with the reconstruction of mankind and culture in an industrial society, Rathenau first offered a criticism of his own epoch, his *Zur Kritik der Zeit* (On the Critique of Our Times, 1912).[6] Though renowned as an industrialist in the newly developed fields of electricity, automobiles, and electrochemistry, Rathenau proceeded to analyze the distress and misery of modern man arising under unchecked capitalism, which inevitably led to the mechanization of work, of man, and of culture. In 1913 he wrote *Zur Mechanik des Geistes* (On the Mechanics of the Spirit).

Despite his concern about the mechanization that resulted from industrialism, Rathenau emphasized his belief that such ills could not be removed by abolishing industry. Nineteenth-century dreams of a return to an agrarian and handicraft society, the "garden city idylls of the average architect and art-craftsman" (figure 1.17), were not only impossible in Rathenau's opinion but would condemn great parts of the increased population to death through inefficient production and distribution. While Rathenau did not believe in an inevitable evolutionary progress toward a better world, he argued that the effects of knowledge, technology, and industry could not be rescinded. Human will must enter into the historical process, to guide the way to a better world through the use of technology: "only mechanization itself can lead us beyond mechanization,"[7] to a kingdom of the soul characterized by social consciousness and solidarity, love and creative responsibility. In the event, it would be manifest that it was the spiritual world which needed reconstruction. Rathenau's stated purpose for his book *Von kommenden Dingen* (In Days to Come) was "to show that the spiritual guidance of life and the permeation of the mechanistic order with spirit will transform the blind play of force into a fully conscious and free cosmos, into a cosmos worthy of mankind."[8]

But Rathenau did not mean his call for spiritualization to be a retreat from life:

Every genuine earthly experience must be taken seriously. Faithfulness in sensuous perception and devotion of the spirit lead to the inner comprehension even of everyday occurrences and to the contemptuous rejection of any sipping at the cup of life. If the world be an order, a cosmos, it behooves man to study its interconnections, its laws, and its phenomena; it behooves him to build them up within himself. Plato's, Leonardo's, and Goethe's irruption into the robust world of things was not a mundane aberration but a divine necessity. The poet who, lacking spiritual grasp, despises the present and the future of his world for the sake of artificially selected interests, is not as he fancies a seer, but a purveyor of aesthetic amusement.

What is romance in history? It is sterility. It is incapacity to imagine, still less to shape the yet unknown. . . . Fearing the ugly present and the anxious future, the romantic takes refuge with the dear, good, dead people, and spins out further what he has learned from them. But every big man was a shaper of his own time, a respecter of antiquity and conscious of his inheritance as a grown and capable man may be; not a youth in sheltered tutelage, but a master of the living world, and a herald of the future. "Modernity" is foolish, but antiquarianism is rubbish; life in its vigor is neither new nor antique, but young.[9]

Even before Rathenau wrote of the "big man" engaging the world in order to achieve a true and young culture, Peter Behrens and others were working out this challenge in the arts. In an article of 1908 about Behrens's work for the AEG, the close relationship between means of production and artistic form was recognized.[10] The attempt of William

Morris and his followers to restore an earlier cultural balance through a return to an earlier productive system was specifically criticized on the grounds that such an endeavor could not cope with the basis of modern production—which remained the machine. Behrens repeated this argument and specifically disagreed with a claim made by Muthesius that Morris should be recognized as the founder of the modern movement in arts and crafts. On the contrary, Behrens thought that priority should be given to those who were seeking a new classical art while working in sympathy with modern conditions rather than to the English romantics and their German followers.[11]

Despite Rathenau's and Behrens's acceptance of the modern situation, there remained a traditional, even conservative aspect to the modern society they envisioned. Both men believed there had been a healthy relationship between the methods of production and the social and cultural conditions of certain earlier times—especially classical antiquity, selected periods of the Middle Ages, and Germany of around 1800. The cultural solidarity of those times provided a lesson. It seemed obvious that it was necessary to recreate the orderly, not to say monolithic, organization imagined in the earlier admired epochs.

Rathenau wrote of the big man as not only a shaper of his own time but also "a respecter of antiquity and conscious of his inheritance as a grown and capable man may be." Such a historical consciousness is revealed in Behrens's publications of the Berlin years, which repeatedly deal with the themes of "monumental art" and "art and technology."[12] He saw monumental art, which had become his passion with his projects for the crematorium in Hagen and the Mannheim exhibition hall, as just the opposite of lyrical art. Just as he dissociated himself from the Morris tradition, now he broke with the lyrical in art. What had been so important at Darmstadt and in his relationship with Richard Dehmel and other poets was now relegated to the intimate realms where such art could work its charm on initiated amateurs. Monumental art did not necessarily have to be large (lamps and vases could be monumental while statues as high as houses could be merely decorative); monumentality was distinguished rather in being the expression of what was most important to a people—the source of a people's power or what a people honors. For example, while the church no longer possessed the power and honor of earlier times, death still had its mystery, and consequently a crematorium could sustain monumental art. Furthermore, since monumental art, according to Behrens, was representative of what was most important to a people, it was also the highest expression of the culture of its time (frontispiece); indeed all other art forms, including those of everyday life (figure 6.2), should rely on the touchstones provided by monumental art.[13] But if all art was dependent on monumental art, which was in turn the highest expression of a culture, Behrens needed to ascertain what distinguished, or at least what should distinguish, the monumental art of twentieth-century Western culture.

In 1909, Behrens adopted Houston Stuart Chamberlain's distinction of knowledge, civilization, and culture.[14] Relying on Chamberlain, Behrens constructed his own relationships among these concepts. He viewed civilization as applied knowledge (science and technology). In modern times, knowledge had become essentially analytical and inductive. In contrast, such dominant aspects of culture as the *Weltanschauung* and art were synthetic and deductive.

Chamberlain played these contrasting characteristics into an opposition between civilization and culture. Behrens did not fully agree. Accepting the terminology, the problem, and even the general description of the characteristics of knowledge and art in contemporary society, he argued that knowledge had not always been analytical despite the fact that it was markedly so in his day. He also felt that art in contemporary society was less synthetic than ever before. For Behrens, then, the outcome of this exercise was not that civilization and culture were necessarily opposed, but that the early twentieth century happened to be strongly marked by an analytic, scientific, "civilizational"—that is, noncultural—character.

This analytic character contrasted with the Goethean synthetic spirit that Behrens admired. However, there were, he claimed, clear signs of a return to constructive synthesis in science as well as in art. Behrens's instances of synthesis in science were rather literal; for example, he cited the laboratory synthesis of water from hydrogen and oxygen. In art, there was, he felt, a turn from the materialistic, intellectual analysis of Gottfried Semper and his times to the synthetic, intuitional understanding provided by Alois Riegl and his concept of the *Kunstwollen*.[15] This shift freed the artist from the implicit determinism of a materialist theory of art. In the terms with which Behrens began, a shift was under way from a scientific civilization to a culture in which the will of the artist and the people was dominant.

In 1910, Behrens meshed these abstract thoughts on the development of culture with his involvement in a technological industry.[16] He had claimed that monumental art must be expressive of that which truly moves and grasps a society. He now acknowledged that in his time, technology and material progress brought about by technology had claimed this position. The engineer was the hero of modern times. Nevertheless, Behrens said, technology was still only a material concern—intellectual, and a matter of civilization. The challenge was to synthesize technology and art in order that modern civilization might be elevated to a true culture.

Unfortunately, no one, according to Behrens, was making that synthesis—least of all in industry, where the greatest opportunity lay. The character of the objects produced was determined by a few calculations and the taste of the shop foreman. Architects, charged with the design of industrial buildings, reacted romantically and drew upon a treasury of historical forms—never exploring the formal implications of modern construction. Engineers, on the other hand, gave form to their buildings according to calculations and the conditions of construction. Often the great works of engineering were beautiful (figure 7.19), but according to Behrens this was a pseudo-aesthetic based on the lawfulness of mechanical construction. Such lawfulness was related to that of organic growth in nature, and nature was not culture. Nor could the mere fulfillment of purpose be culture. In contrast, Behrens cited Riegl's theory that the artistic will of an epoch must be accomplished even if it ran counter to material criteria.

Behrens concluded this 1910 statement by outlining the service that men of his persuasion had to provide. As different as art and technology might be, they nevertheless belonged together. Art should no longer be considered a private matter. He wanted no aesthetic that sought its own rules in romantic dreams, but rather an aesthetic "rooted in the laws of surging life." He also did not want a technology that pursued its own ends, but one that was sensible to the artistic will of the time. "Thus German art and technology will work toward a single goal: to the strength [*Macht*] of the German land, which will be recognized by the fact that a rich material life has been ennobled by a spiritually refined form."[17]

In terms of relating artistic form to new modes of production, the AEG had created an unusual opportunity and placed this opportunity in the hands of Behrens. However, on the general level of ideas and policy, Behrens and the AEG were not alone. Already in the nineteenth century a recurrent theme was the claim that excellence of design and production in the crafts—and still more in industry—would be particularly important for Germany.[18] This idea found an especially enthusiastic supporter in the nationalist, liberal politician Friedrich Naumann.[19] The argument ran something like this: Germany is not rich in natural resources and has no great navy or empire (although Naumann was also an enthusiast for achieving both a navy and an empire); consequently it has no cheap source of materials and no ready market for cheap goods. To compete in world commerce, Germany must acknowledge and turn to advantage the fact that it buys material and sells labor and *Kultur.* For volume and economical production, there must be a reliance on machine production; but to overcome the high cost of imported materials and high-quality labor, it must be machine production of high quality, based on good design. The *Kultur* which Germany sells should be the German vernacular of the Machine Age, but this in turn must derive from a machine-oriented people who have been reared in a thoroughly artistic culture. To succeed in satisfying all these conditions would be to assure a high standard of art, an advantageous commercial position, high employment, and elevated working and living conditions.[20]

In 1907, Naumann was instrumental in the founding of an organization, the Deutscher Werkbund, dedicated to the implementation of these ideas. The Werkbund had as its immediate source the artists and the activities of the third Deutsche Kunstgewerbe Ausstellung, which opened in Dresden in May 1906 (figures 2.9, 5.10).[21] The greatest part of the exhibition, under the direction of Fritz Schumacher, was devoted to what was termed *Raumkunst* (interior architecture). Complete rooms, for many different functions, were designed and fabricated in order "to solve each problem not according to an existing formula, but rather in accordance with a formula composed of three concerns: the character of the function which the room serves, the character of the materials used in the room, and the character of the person who created the room."[22] Great stress lay on the

5.10 Dresden, Third German Arts and Crafts Exhibition, 1906, "Ceramic Court" or atrium in Behrens's group of rooms (1905–1906).

"character of the person who created the room." Space in the exhibition was, for the first time, allotted only to the artists who would conceive the designs and oversee their execution. Producers and contractors could be represented in the exhibition only at the request of the artist, rather than vice versa. As further assurance of artistic excellence, the organizers appointed an *Arbeitskommissar* in each of the principal regions of Germany, charged to assure the fulfillment of the general principles of the exhibition. The names of Muthesius, representing Berlin; F. A. O. Kruger of the Münchener Werkstätten for Munich; Bernhard Pankok for Württemberg; Behrens for the Rhineland; Joseph Olbrich for Hesse; and Graf Kessler for Thüringen, indicate the caliber of the administrators who sought to make Dresden 1906 a celebration of a ten-year effort to renew German crafts and architecture. Designers created 131 rooms, largely of a quite elegant character. While these rooms relied on individual production to the designer's specifications, the organizers of the exhibition sought to display high-quality "machine-made" furniture as well. In 1906, the distinction between machine-assisted handwork and elementary industrial production was sufficiently obscure that any attempt to differentiate precisely between craft and industry was difficult—nor is the situation so different today. However, the handsome, simple factory-produced furniture of Karl Schmidt's Dresdener Werkstätten, fabricated to the designs of Richard Riemerschmid (figure 5.11), Bruno Paul, Heinrich Tessenow, and others, became a prominent feature of the exhibition. Naumann visited the Dresden exhibition, discovering in both the person and the production ideas of Karl Schmidt a complement to his own conception of the union of German crafts, industry, and art. In a speech delivered at Dresden, Naumann took the opportunity to advance his ideas. Of particular significance for its relation to the later program of the Werkbund was this: "Many people do not have the money to hire artists, and consequently many wares are going to be mass-produced; for this great problem, the only solution is to infuse mass production with meaning and spirit by artistic means [*künstlerisch zu durchgeistigen*]."23

It is difficult to determine who was the prime mover of the Deutscher Werkbund. Theodor Heuss, who served as the business manager of the Werkbund after World War I and as President of the Federal Republic of Germany from 1949 to 1959, gave principal credit for the founding of the Werkbund to Friedrich Naumann in cooperation with the Dresdener Werkstätten's Karl Schmidt. Heuss also asserted that it was these men who sought out Dr. Wolf Dohrn to be the first manager of the Werkbund.24

5.11 Richard Riemerschmid. Dining room furniture fabricated by the Deutsche Werkstätten für Handwerkskunst, Dresden (ca. 1908).

These claims are something of an oversimplification, since many men were involved in the creation of the institution, and some credence must be given to those who saw Hermann Muthesius as "fathering" the Werkbund.[25] Muthesius's criticism of the low standard of the craft objects produced by established German artisans,[26] his international interests, and his advocacy of new technology while holding the position of Advisor on Applied Arts to the Prussian government brought him under fire from the protective Alliance for German Applied Arts—effectively the extended lobby addressed to Muthesius's governmental position. At a meeting of the Alliance in Düsseldorf in June 1907, Peter Bruckmann, a silverware producer from Heilbronn,[27] Dohrn, an associate of Schmidt at the Dresdener Werkstätten, and the Viennese essayist J. A. Lux sided with Muthesius and withdrew from the meeting and from the Alliance.[28] Fritz Schumacher also came under attack for using public funds while organizing the 1906 Dresden exhibition in such a way as to favor ideological and artistic issues as opposed to immediate economic concerns. The defenders of Muthesius and Schumacher now represented a besieged position that lacked an organization. They claimed that artistic, social, and economic conditions would be improved if there were a considered, artistically conceived relationship between any product and the conditions of its production. This relationship would be different, but no less important, if machine production were involved.

The Dresden exhibition of 1906 provided a focus for many energetic men who shared common ideas and who, after the Muthesius affair, found themselves in need of an official body. Apparently, it was Muthesius who took the initiative in bringing together twelve artists and twelve firms involved in the applied arts.[29] The artists were Peter Behrens (Berlin), Theodor Fischer (Stuttgart), Josef Hoffmann (Vienna), Wilhelm Kreis (Düsseldorf), Max Läuger (Karlsruhe), Adelbert Niemeyer (Munich), Joseph Olbrich (Darmstadt), Bruno Paul (Berlin), Richard Riemerschmid (Munich), J. J. Scharvogel (Darmstadt), Paul Schultze-Naumburg (Saaleck), and Fritz Schumacher (Dresden). The producers were Peter Bruckmann und Söhne, silverware fabricators, Heilbronn; Deutsche (formerly Dresdener) Werkstätten fur Handwerkskunst, Schmidt's furniture factory in Dresden, later in Hellerau; Eugen Diederichs, a publisher in Jena and Leipzig; Gebrüder Klingspor, type founders, Offenbach am Main; Kunstdruckerei Künstlerbund Karlsruhe, printers; Poeschel und Trepte, printers from Leipzig; Saalecker Werkstätten, a firm that dealt mostly in interior furnishings, from Saaleck near Bad Kosen; Vereinigte Werkstätten für Kunst und Handwerk München, interior furnishings and crafts; Theophil Müller's Werkstätten für deutschen Hausrat, household furnishings, Dresden; Wiener Werkstätten, Vienna; Wilhelm und Co., workshop for lighting fixtures and metal work, Munich; and Gottlob Wunderlich, weavers, Waldkirchen i.S.

All of the above received invitations in August 1907 for the founding convention to be held in Munich on 5–6 October 1907. At the celebration of the founding, in the hall of the Vier Jahreszeiten (Four Seasons), Muthesius was to deliver the principal hortatory speech, but found it inadvisable because of his political position. The duty fell to

Schumacher, who was elated and deeply moved when his speech found "a natural echo" in this assembly of "all the German artists allied with the new constructive and decorative endeavors." He emphasized the need to unify the inventive and productive powers:

> The time has come when Germany should cease to look upon the artist as a man who more or less harmlessly follows his inclination, and rather see in him one of the important powers for the ennobling of work, thereby ennobling the entire inner life of the land and making the land victorious in the competition among peoples. For in this competition only those values that cannot be imitated will prove decisive in the turn of events. Everything that can be imitated soon loses its value on the international market; only the qualitative values that spring from the inexpressible inner powers of a harmonious culture are inimitable. And consequently, there exists in aesthetic power also the highest economic value.
>
> After a century devoted to technique and thought, we see the next project which Germany has to fulfill as that of the *reconquest of a harmonious culture.*
>
> In this pioneering work we unite ourselves, not as men who are proud of what they have already achieved, but rather as men who are proud of what they attempt.[30]

At the end of this meeting, at the suggestion of Richard Riemerschmid, the entire assembly, carrying roses, went in procession through the streets of Munich to pay homage to Adolf Hildebrand whose sixtieth birthday it happened to be.[31] While this event is anecdotal, it seems to have sealed an occasion experienced as the triumphant conclusion of years of endeavor, a rededication to a pursuit of the elevated cultural goals these men had previously sought under a now discredited program.

The new program, as expressesd in the articles adopted by the Werkbund, was the following: (1) encouragement of fruitful cooperation among art, industry, and craft for the enhancement of the quality of work; (2) a common position of craftsmen and artists in all the questions that concern their relationship to the state; (3) establishment of a center for professional development and propaganda for the goals of the Werkbund; (4) the obligation of each member to participate in the achievement of excellent work; (5) initiation of action for the increased understanding of quality work; (6) greater influence on the education of the young and above all on training in the crafts; (7) greater influence on trade, on the conditions of bidding, and on the conditions of expertise.[32]

At Munich, and regularly thereafter, Naumann offered inspiring speeches and documents, including the first programmatic booklet of the Werkbund, *Deutsche Gewerbekunst.*[33] Under the managership of Dohrn and later Alfons Paquet and Ernst Jäckh, the Werkbund enjoyed notable growth and success in its programs of "Quality Work," "Infusion of Meaning and Spirit into Work," and "Thorough Forming of All Things."[34]

The conditions of 1907 were even more propitious for the personal contribution of Peter Behrens. Only a few days before Behrens participated in the founding of the Deutscher Werkbund in Munich, he and his family had moved from Düsseldorf to Berlin, where his new duties as artistic advisor to the AEG, the subject of the succeeding chapters, began on the first of October.

In the Turbine Factory (frontispiece) as in other work for the AEG, Behrens learned to work successfully in industry without surrendering his antipositivist position. Even his changing attitude toward technology was not one of acceptance but of accommodation. For Behrens, art and science were still distinct, and art was foremost culturally. But the writings of Alois Riegl persuaded him to accept the lawfulness of art as related not only to certain "constructive [geometric, arithmetic, formal] ideals [as exemplified in the conventions of the buildings of his Düsseldorf period], but also to the epoch in which the art was created, to 'the rhythm of the time.'"[35] This concept of a rhythm of the time, of a zeitgeist, allowed Behrens to submit to science and technology on the level of historical experience without fully accepting them in his ideal understanding of culture. As Behrens might have said, the client's cosmology (in this case, the devotion of modern society to science and technology) is both significant and unavoidable, but it is not central to the creative process. Whereas theorists whom Behrens deprecated as "materialists" (especially Gottfried Semper) accepted material and technical factors as inherent in problems of production and human environment, Riegl's *Kunstwollen* and the concept of zeitgeist acted as filters by means of which an autocratic will could successfully modify material and technical circumstances.

Thus Behrens acknowledged that the most imposing manifestations of his time, those phenomena that established the "rhythm of the time," were the works of modern engineering.[36] The artist, according to Behrens, could not ignore the technological heart of the zeitgeist. At the same time, art could not simply submit to technology, whose currently prevalent role was time-bound. The role of monumental art, upon which all other art forms depended, was to give timeless, lawful, and ideal form to such general but time-bound characteristics of a particular age.[37] Finally, in view of this contemporary need to give artistic form to the accomplishments of technology, modern industry had the opportunity to serve as both the patron and the medium for the establishment of new values of national significance.[38]

Behrens's speech in 1912 at the dedication of his office building for the Mannesmann industry in Düsseldorf (figure 8.35) makes explicit his understanding of architecture in the service of historically determined power.[39] The architect's greatest responsibility was to design the formal building types for those individuals or institutions that provided or represented the political and economic power of their time. For Behrens, modern industry in alliance with central government constituted the prime agency of that power at the beginning of the twentieth century. Its factories and office buildings must then be the architectural touchstones of their age—receiving adequate representational form through the imaginative intersection of architectural convention and new conditions.

Though often highly diluted, Behrens's historical determinism and the consequent character of his practice dominated the main thrust of the modern movement in architecture, and even its attenuations in conventional practice today. For all that his limited position stemmed from the idea of a will to art (*Kunstwollen*) fulfilling its historical destiny, it must be acknowledged that the position defined by Behrens, the AEG, and the Deutscher Werkbund was the first extensive and well-regarded union of art and modern industry. In retrospect, what seems strongest in this position was the mistrust of a narrow, positivistic science and technology. However, the subsequent German assimilation of this positivistic realm, asserting and incorporating it as part of the course of historical necessity, defused both the critical and creative potential of that mistrust. The inherent critique became complicit resignation. The alternative of conceiving a nonpositivistic science (*Wissenschaft,* in the inclusive sense of this German word), one that would have permitted a critical and mutually contributive discourse among art, industry, and society, runs as an aspirational vein throughout this post-Nietzschean epoch, occasionally achieving tentative formulation, as in the writings of Behrens's Belgian colleague Henry van de Velde. A sound construction of the position and the writing of its history are but unrealized projects.

Postscript

The excellent recent literature on Behrens and the AEG is introduced in the postscripts to chapters 6 and 7.

Tilmann Buddensieg and Henning Rogge, in the context of a 1981 exhibition, collected essays on numerous themes relating visual form and technique from the industrialization of the eighteenth century to the present.[40]

In addition to the series of publications by the Werkbund-Archiv (Berlin), the last three decades have seen extensive publication on the Deutscher Werkbund, both in German and English.[41]

6
Industrial Design, a Strategy for Uniting Technology and Art: Berlin II

Early and repeated claims for the innovative role of Peter Behrens in the field of industrial design may serve as an instructive point of departure from which to examine traditional German concepts of the relationship between artistic form and technique. Nikolaus Pevsner most successfully propagandized these claims for Peter Behrens (see figures 6.2, 6.6–8):

> The importance of Germany in the early years of the twentieth century lies altogether in the shift from craft to industrial design and concurrently in the discovery by architects (and engineers) of the aesthetic possibilities of industrial architecture. . . . The most important architect was Peter Behrens, the most important organization the Deutscher Werkbund founded in 1907 and dedicated to the cause of good functional form in the crafts and soon in industry too. Peter Behrens was made consultant to the AEG, the Berlin manufacturers of electrical products, both for these products and for their buildings—a completely new and highly influential job. His tea kettles, his street lamps, his notepaper and invoices, his shop interiors and his large factories have all the same functional directness. Art Nouveau which had been Behrens's own point of departure about 1900 was left leagues behind. The style and the spiritual attitude of the twentieth century had indeed been achieved.[1]

Pevsner remained loath to abandon this position, first expressed in his *Pioneers of the Modern Movement* of 1936, even when he felt compelled to recognize that others did not share his view.[2] An attempt at a better understanding of Behrens's contribution might well start with an examination of his design of an arc lamp (figure 6.2) for the AEG. Though this lamp was his first work in industrial design, it quickly became—and has remained—the touchstone for his reputation as the first industrial designer.[3]

AEG publicity and internal histories misdirect the interpretation of Behrens's role in the origins of industrial design. Two publications illustrate only the ornate "late Victorian" arc lamp (figure 6.1, left) and Behrens's most renowned design (figure 6.2), both produced by the AEG.[4] The former was labeled "aus dem Jahre 1906," the latter dated 1908. Such presentation implied that Behrens, in one fell swoop, swept out nineteenth-century abuses and achieved "the spiritual attitude of the twentieth century." The situation was not that simple; while honoring Behrens's achievement, such comparisons obscure the facts.

The "Victorian" lamp was composed of two basically simple parts: a spherical globe shielding the arc and diffusing its light, and a cylindrical tube housing the regulator and the feed mechanism for the carbon electrodes. The floral decoration was literally "applied art" intended to make the lamp acceptable in rooms with similar decoration. This applied art was supplied by the *Fabrikzeichner* (factory draftsman), one of the predecessors of the industrial designer. According to Arnold Schürer, this lamp was in production in the late nineteenth century and still represented in AEG catalogs after Behrens's arrival.[5] It was always offered not as *the* arc lamp model, but as an alternative to unornamented models. An AEG catalog of 1901 shows a very handsome, unornamented lamp, literally just a sphere and a cylinder with a short cylindrical collar at their juncture.[6] Figure 6.1, right, shows another model available prior to the arrival of Behrens at the AEG. In such a lamp, one recognizes a fundamental, engineered form. One should not imagine either that such form is achieved automatically or that it is the best solution. However, successive AEG catalogs reveal increasing recognition of the problems addressed, mastery of the technology employed, and articulation of these factors in the changing forms of the products.[7]

When Behrens turned to the problem of industrial design, he could accept neither the loose application of ornament nor the simple refinement of "functionally direct" form. Rather, he sought to give such technological products their place within the greater synthesis of *Kultur*:

It is true that the works of engineers are not without a certain beauty. One need only think of the great iron halls, the broad-spanning roofs which definitely give an impression of grandeur. We cannot deny that the simple utilitarian buildings built by engineers, still more their machines, achieve a certain aesthetic impression by means of their often bold and logical construction. This effect is achieved despite the fact that no conception derived according to artistic principles prevailed in these examples and that the aesthetic result is accidental. This phenomenon can be explained in that these works possess a pseudo-aesthetic embodied in a certain lawfulness, that of mechanical construction. This is the lawfulness of organic development which nature also reveals in all her works. But just as nature is not *Kultur*, so the purely human fulfillment of functional and material needs cannot create *Kultur*. Despite all this genuinely enthusiastic recognition of the accomplishments of technology and transport, nothing could be more natural than that the desire for

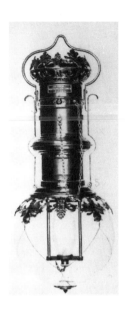

6.1 Arc lamps produced by the AEG, Berlin, prior to Behrens's engagement: left, decorated arc lamp; right, economy arc lamp.

6.2 Peter Behrens. AEG economy arc lamp (1907).

absolute beauty should be awakened in us. Quite naturally we will not believe that from this time on the satisfactions called forth by exactitude and utmost functionalism will take the place of those values that have formerly delighted and elevated us.[8]

For Behrens, then, the engineer's "pseudo-aesthetic" achievement was not art. Far from allowing industrial products to be formed in accordance with the dictates of purpose, material, and technique, he insisted that art was a response to human expectations and psychic pressures. Art must then be free to fulfill itself unhindered by (and perhaps even in contradiction to) material conditions. This was an explicit instance of Behrens's resistance to what he saw as the materialism of Semperian thought and his acceptance, via Riegl, of the dominance of artistic will.[9]

In Behrens's formulation, it was the artist's role to accept the imperatives of technological civilization and then to overcome them in the interest of a holistic culture. In redesigning the arc lamp, he saw his problem as the formulation of an aesthetic that accepted the blunt, prosaic power of the machine, of engineering and industry, but which also raised this power to an electric, economical poetry expressive of a suprapersonal and modern *Kunstwollen*. Behrens's lamp (figure 6.2) did not tamper with the mechanics of the lamp; it was the housing that he reformed.[10] Without apparent coercion, the silhouette of the lamp became simple and harmonious. A strong, central shaft replaced the jointed and molded midsection of the earlier lamp. The absence of these moldings allowed the cap unit of the new lamp to be easily distinguished; the reflector, now shaped in a pair of graceful, repeated curves, was complemented in the similar, reversed curves of the globe below. Even the operable hardware, though still rather flat, asserted itself as a set of bolder stokes in interplay with the massive form of the housing. Beyond the calligraphic elegance of silhouette, this new simplicity suggested that the lamp was made of a few solid parts. The forming of the sheet metal enhanced this effect; rather than expose the sharp edge of this light material, Behrens turned down and gave a bronze facing to each exposed edge, "portraying" the termination of a sturdy material. In contrast to the engineered design (figure 6.1, right), which was perfectly frank in its jointing, assembly, and character of material, Behrens's design was sculptural, almost Egyptian in both its line and weightiness. The engineered lamp was admirably direct, and yet Behrens's design offered, in this instance, the more compelling image of technical efficiency.[11] Wolf Dohrn records the anecdote that salesmen for the AEG were so pleased with the new form of the housing that they requested a similar redesign of the working parts.[12]

Through Behrens, the AEG lamp received a form that provided an aesthetic reformulation of the "new nature" of industrialization, and thus an indirect testimony of the underlying technical efficiency. This comparatively small artistic form drawn from the new nature also implied a new architecture, for Behrens's flowerlike lamp would have been as out of place in a work of raw engineering construction as the florally ornamented lamp had been.[13] Behrens's arc lamp and his AEG Turbine Factory, for example, are complementary designs.

A deeper understanding of Behrens's approach to industrial design and of his opposition to Semper emerges from a consideration of the German concept of *Tektonik*.[14] The late Schinkelesque classicist Karl Bötticher wrote a detailed study of ancient Greek architecture entitled *Die Tektonik der Hellenen*.[15] The motto for his book indicates the immanence of meaning in form to which *Tektonik* was to refer:

Des Körpers Form ist seines Wesens Spiegel!
Durchdringst du sie—löst sich des Räthsels Siegel.[16]

On his first page, Bötticher explained that *Tektonik* referred not just to the activity of making the materially requisite construction that answers to certain needs, but rather to the activity that raises this construction to an art form. That is, every element of a building—a column, for example—has an actual technical function, but this function may not be fully apparent. The functionally adequate must be adapted so as to give expression to its function. The sense of bearing provided by the entasis of Greek columns became the touchstone of this concept of *Tektonik*. Under this interpretation, the Greek temple became a composite of functionally expressive members relying on organic analogies, a kind of mosaic of functions. According to Bötticher, in the Hellenistic tectonic, as in nature, the form of a body was the embodiment or plastic representation of its essence. Form gave to the construction material the expression of its fulfillment of function.[17]

Gottfried Semper shared Bötticher's belief that the Greeks achieved the highest tectonic expression and that this achievement bore a relation to the forms of nature. Semper insisted that "every art form must be the expression of a definite law of the innermost necessity, just as this is certainly the case with natural forms." He also stressed that plans, sections, elevations, and all laws of beauty developed from them were artificial and fell short of the organic tectonic forms of the Greeks, which were not constructed, turned, or cast, but organically developed. He specifically chastised Bötticher for his *Strukturschemen* and his applied symbolic ornament. Rather, in Greek art "the forms in themselves are such as are brought forth when organic energies are thrust into conflict with ponderous matter." Semper drew a lesson from this: "the more the works of our hands appear as though they were the result of a similar conflict between elemental energies and vital energies, the higher these works stand on the ladder of artistic fulfillment."[18]

The book quoted here is Semper's small study of Greek lead shot for slings (figure 6.3), in which he questioned why these missiles should have been almond-shaped. In giving his answer, Semper offers a general study of objects moving in a resistant medium. The book demonstrates his submission of an ancient "industrial" product to a theoretical study conceived to elucidate both timeless artistic problems and production-related concerns such as those of boat or missile design. In his statement of purpose, Semper removes some concern about what might appear to be a simplistic naturalism: "I have been driven to the following study by the desire to demonstrate, by means of a simple example, that the

6.3 Gottfried Semper.
Frontispiece for his *Über die
bleiernen Schleudergeschosse
der Alten* (Frankfurt, 1859).

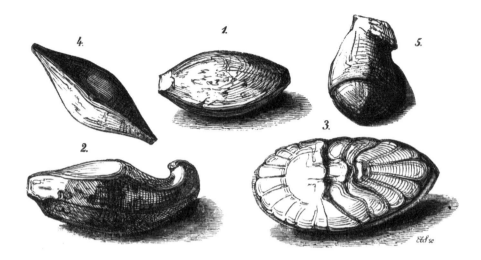

Greeks did not merely observe natural laws and then strive to imitate the forms that resulted from the operation of these laws. Rather, I would like to demonstrate that the Greeks actually researched these laws and out of these laws, independent of all imitation, created their own forms. These new forms relate to those of nature only in the commonality of the underlying natural laws."[19]

As figure 6.4 indicates, Semper's aerodynamic studies satisfied him that the "almond-shaped" missiles of the ancients were the expression of a definite natural law. In the final section (§21), he returns to more conventional aesthetic concerns. Noting that his study of objects moving in a resisting medium revealed that the forms exhibited a "spring-powered resistance" to the straight line, tending to bend into a curve, he remarked that it is such contours and expansions that characterize the Greek tectonic profile in strong differentiation from all other styles of architecture. Finally, he claims not "that the Greeks constructed their forms according to mathematical formulas, which would be absurd in the arts. On the contrary, the Greeks did not merely sense, but clearly recognized a law of nature: in achieving form in objects, extreme limits are observed and energy controls everything."[20]

I am here concerned not to verify the historiographical or scientific adequacy of Semper's study but rather to examine the theoretical insight it offered to his contemporaries. Discovering the form that answered to all the demands of its context (the complexity of the context varying with the problem), Semper asserted a relation between the process of "streamlining" and the form of the Parthenon. Two generations later Le Corbusier wrote:

> The airplane is indubitably one of the products of the most intense selection in the range of modern industry.

The War was an insatiable "client," never satisfied, always demanding better. The orders were to succeed at all costs and death followed a mistake remorselessly. We may then affirm that the airplane mobilized invention, intelligence, and daring: *imagination* and *cold reason*. It is the same spirit that built the Parthenon.

Let us look at things from the point of view of architecture, but in the state of mind of the inventor of airplanes.

The lesson of the airplane is not primarily in the forms it has created, and above all we must learn to see in an airplane not a bird or a dragonfly, but a machine for flying; the lesson of the airplane lies in the logic which governed the enunciation of the problem and which led to its successful realization. When a problem is properly stated, in our epoch, it inevitably finds its solution.

The problem of the house has not yet been stated.[21]

Tektonik was, then, a complex and evolving concept that attempted to establish a relationship between form and technical considerations. According to Bötticher, such a concept was necessary because what was technically functional might not be sensed as

6.4 Semper. Geometrical analytic study of ancient shot for a sling (1859).

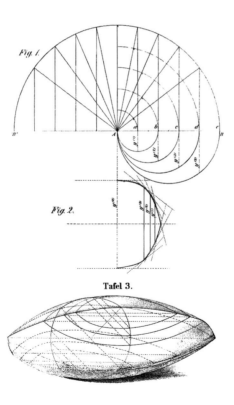

such. This implied the demand that the artist assert himself in giving expression to the function of the object. The artist must be brought in not for an a priori personal sensibility but for the ability to give expression to what was objective in a situation. Semper sought to give a still more reasoned interpretation of good form by demonstrating the necessity of considering all the conditions which the environmental context placed upon the object. *Tektonik* thus received a still more precise functional interpretation.

Such concepts, bringing function to expression through carefully considered form, were overt in much Art Nouveau and Jugendstil work—notably with van de Velde (figures 1.11, 1.21) and Riemerschmid (figure 1.16), but also in early Behrens (the chairs in figure 3.11). The polemics of the time referred to such works as "functionalist." Thinkers as seemingly different as Bötticher and van de Velde were committed to this inferentially functional, organismic world of forms associated with Greek classicism (and Gothic architecture).[22] Semper went on to describe an alternative—an abstract, nonorganic formal world labeled *Stereotomie,* associated with the Renaissance (and Romanesque architecture).

The terms *Tektonik* and *Stereotomie,* as well as the architectures with which they were associated, indicate that these represented, respectively, constructs of articulated elements (elastic skeletal structures, e.g., timber or metal frames) and comparatively inert assemblies (intractable masses, e.g., masonry walls). Successive sections of Semper's principal work, *Der Stil in den technischen und tektonischen Künsten,* are titled "Tektonik" (carpentry) and "Stereotomie" (masonry, etc.).[23] The Greek temple remained the highest form (p. xlii) even though, as a tectonic assembly in stone, it was a heterogeneous combination of the form allied to *Tektonik* and the material allied to *Stereotomie.* The major distinction between the types was that tectonic structures were composed of members; stereotomic assemblies of identical or similar pieces. These pieces all had the same function, the absolutely mechanical one of compression and resistance to compression. In contrast, the members of the tectonic structure (even if executed in stone) were differentiated in their action, in their position in the frame, and consequently "could, by means of art, be brought to life as organisms." In opposition to this functionally expressive and organic quality of the tectonic structure, the stone mass had a lifeless, crystalline mineral quality which built up into totalities of a crystalline or eurhythmic character and which could only be conceived in terms of a regular, closed form.[24]

Behrens's own development reflects a shift from functionally expressive to crystalline form as he passed from his Jugendstil work in Darmstadt (figure 3.7) to the post-Jugendstil work of his Düsseldorf period (figure 2.7). Four years later, beginning work for the AEG in Berlin, he was faced with problems that encouraged a less absolute division between *Tektonik* and *Stereotomie.* His post-Jugendstil preference for *Stereotomie* came into confrontation with the tectonic qualities of metal-framed factory structures. While a new conception of space assisted Behrens in resolving the contradiction between these two structural principles, this understanding held little relevance for the design of industrial objects.

The translation of the ideas behind *Tektonik* into industrial machine construction and machine products had already occurred in Semper's time with the noted mechanical engineer Franz Reuleaux.[25] As the head of the German delegation and a judge in the mechanical section of the Centennial Exhibition at Philadelphia in 1876, Reuleaux wrote periodic letters to the *Nationalzeitung* that caused a great stir in Germany. Reuleaux found that Americans were evolving good form in their machines (figure 6.5), a fact that he both appreciated and found tectonically significant: "Certain details of the steam-engine have been further developed, and [the Americans] are able to give it a truly admirable external finish and appearance. This is a significant sign. For when beauty of form is developed as the object of special care, the difficulties of purely utilitarian design must already have been overcome." Going so far as to refer to German industrial production exhibited at Philadelphia as "billig und schlecht" (cheap and nasty), Reuleaux made a point that anticipates the advocacy of the Deutscher Werkbund around 1910: "German industry must relinquish the principle of competition in price alone and must decide whether to turn instead to competition in quality or value. Nevertheless . . . German industry must adopt machines . . . when bodily effort can thereby be abolished or lightened . . . ; on the other hand, industry must use the intellectual power and the skill of the worker to refine the product, and this to a greater degree the more it approaches art."[26]

Now consider this traditional problem of "good" form and use in relation to Behrens's work for industry. The early nineteenth-century neoclassical architect Bötticher and late nineteenth-century mechanical engineer Reuleaux both accepted that an excellent

6.5 Corliss engines used to supply power for the machine exhibition at the Centennial Exhibition of 1876, Philadelphia.

utilitarian design was not yet necessarily good form. Good form was a further development; it would express the utility of the object, but, as expression, it had as much or more to do with the perception and psyche of the user or viewer as it did with its actual function.

Semper did not hold the mechanically deterministic view that the satisfaction of utilitarian demands insured an ideal form.[27] But his example of the lead shot indicates he would go further than Bötticher or Reuleaux in claiming a symbiosis between utility and good form. We may assume that Bötticher's acknowledgment of good form in a column would be conservative, insisting on the fulfillment of certain traditional expectations. The thrust of Semper's argument suggests that he would be more prepared to alter his understanding and acceptance of conventions in accord with his analysis of the practical problem. Semper's analysis would appeal to Behrens, one might think, since he was willing to work with industry and alter traditional expectations; but we know of Behrens's antagonism toward Semper. Behrens stands in the classical tradition of Bötticher, although his modern, broadly cultural, and more psychological understanding of Hellenism led him to conceive an even weaker bond between good form and technique.

Like Bötticher and Reuleaux, Behrens accepted the excellence of a utilitarian design; to our knowledge, he did nothing to alter the technical design of AEG products. But whereas Bötticher attempted to rationalize the excellence of Hellenic classicism as an assembly of expressed functions, Behrens was persuaded by the more complex psychological and symbolic interpretations that evoked the "spirit of the time" and the collective and individual wills of a civilization and its artists. Consequently, Behrens's own work had other, more abstract sources than functional expression. In his designs for industrially produced objects of domestic use, Behrens was often conservative. Certainly there were predilections based now on tradition, now on ideal geometry, that contributed to the form of the Behrens-AEG electrical heating units (see figure 6.6).[28] These objects suggest more strongly the qualities of Carolingian reliquaries than those of a revolutionary new heating system. In accord with Behrens's design conceptions, many of the details of these objects derived from other sources than a strict analysis of functional expression. Similarly, his electric tea kettles (figure 6.7) relied more on late eighteenth-century *chinoiserie* than on a new functional analysis. Or, to make the point differently, had the handsome Behrens teapots relied for their form on the expression of function, they would not have appeared simultaneously in three different forms and several finishes (including two "machine-hammered" ones).

In domestic or luxury objects, and in domestic or institutional architecture, Behrens was prepared to have established expectations influence the form. Even if electrified, a teapot or a source of warmth in the home had to participate in human expectations beyond functional expression. He stated specifically that manufactured objects that come into close contact with people permit a richer forming, better materials, and ornamentation—though the ornamentation should be economical and "impersonal," as is the case with simple geometric figures.[29]

6.6 Peter Behrens. AEG electric heater (1909).

6.7 Peter Behrens. AEG electric tea kettles (1909).

Only in a secondary sense were the nondomestic arc lamp (figure 6.2) or even the simplest tea kettle (figure 6.7) or electric fan (figure 6.8) more functionally direct than their predecessors (figure 6.1, left; fans with similarly ornamented motor housings were also produced).[30] Both Walther Rathenau of the AEG and Behrens accepted the role of science and technology in modern society with a pessimistic resignation. Where traditional forces were not dominant, Behrens adopted a historicist compulsion to use his artistry to

6.8 Peter Behrens. AEG electric table fan (1908).

create an image of technological efficiency and perfection beyond what the engineered object would have provided. He sought such an image because he believed his place in history compelled him to do so. It is the curious position of an individual human will dominant over material matters but subject to the imagined collective spirit of a people and its history. Thus Behrens was willing to see new forms; but as the theoretical discussion of the preceding chapter suggests, he sought the conventions of a new sensibility that encompassed functional expression rather than seeking reciprocity with it.

Within this context we may return to the question of Behrens's precedence in the field of industrial design. One aspect of industrial design is surely the design of capital goods and major machinery for public works and for industry itself. The turbines and large equipment of the AEG were prominent items in this category, but there is still no hard evidence that Behrens had any more than an indirect influence on the design of these products.[31] That indirect influence stemmed from his well-known designs for mass-produced objects.

If "industrial design" means design of mass-production, mass-distribution goods, certain of the designers for whom precedence might be claimed can be eliminated on the grounds that they were designing for handicraft production or, at most, for machine-augmented handicraft production. In the late nineteenth century, first in England and then on the continent, artists and craftsmen banded together to form workshops where they might produce and market objects meeting their own standards. These workshops were too closely tied to the handicraft tradition to lay claim to an innovative position in design for industry. In 1908, J. A. Lux went so far as to compliment the Wiener Werkstätte as one of the few remaining shops where the worker could devote a labor of love to a single object.[32] At times, much has been made of the "machine furniture" of Bruno Paul or that of Richard Riemerschmid designed for the Deutsche Werkstätten of Hellerau. The Werkstätten published Riemerschmid's designs in a book in which they were at pains to designate themselves as a workshop devoted to careful handwork rather than a factory (figure 5.11).[33]

In point of fact, the Dresden Workshops were quite large and might have some claim to serial production of furniture. However, that claim could be pressed earlier and more convincingly for other industries, such as glass, ceramics, wallpaper, and linoleum. Many Art Nouveau artists, including Behrens, created designs for firms engaged in such manufactures. Sèvres in ceramics, Wedgwood in china, Boulton in iron casting,[34] and the English Arts and Crafts movement[35] provide earlier instances of designers for large-scale production working both within industry and as "consultants."[36] In such industries as ceramics, glass, and weaponry, the existence of "design for industry" must trace back to antiquity. Clearly, there is ample precedent for the design of objects for mass production and mass distribution. The question, then, would seem to be whether the twentieth century, and Behrens in particular, developed an innovative approach that should be distinguished as "industrial design."[37]

One might attempt to distinguish Behrens's contribution by the modernity of the industry for which he worked. But the electrical industry was not totally new in 1907; and the industrial revolution had introduced other technologies, such as steam power, that posed a wide range of industrial design problems. These problems evinced the sometimes functional and sometimes rather loosely conceived design contributions of engineers and *Fabrikzeichner,* as instanced by the AEG arc lamps.

Nor was the scale of mass production of the AEG a distinguishing characteristic. The bentwood furniture manufacture of Michael Thonet was an earlier example of design for large-scale production: an example that also demonstrates a methodology in contrast with Behrens's industrial design. Thonet furniture produced in Boppard in 1836–1840 (figure 6.9) reveals both his new technique and the reminiscences that came to him in his role as his own "factory draftsman." Had Thonet stopped there, he might be viewed as little more than another *Fabrikzeichner;* but in Austria, Thonet and his sons developed their designs until they achieved the still-admired bentwood chairs with wicker seats, one version of which appears in figure 6.10. Through research devoted to their material and technique, and to the more general problems of seating and furniture, the Thonets achieved a variety of seemingly timeless designs. This furniture was made in such numbers (reportedly forty million chairs of the basic style no. 14 between 1859 and 1896) as to clearly establish the Thonets as mass producers.[38]

6.9 Michael Thonet. Bentwood furniture made in Boppard, Germany (1836–1840).

A chair, as a traditional object, contrasts with the technical objects of the electrical industry. But the important difference between Thonet's design and that of Behrens is in method, not in the type of object or scale of production. Generations have now taken pleasure in Thonet chairs, the design, development, and production of which suggest comparison with Semper's idea of *Tektonik*. For Thonet, as for Semper, there was no conception of a technical form that an artist should improve. The fully developed and beautiful form was to be achieved along with the refinement of the material and technique—and this need not imply a deterministic, one-way path from technique to form. According to this conception, it was the oneness of technical and visual excellence that was important, whether the person who achieved it was labeled engineer or artist. Under this interpretation, design for industry was not new with the twentieth century, certainly not with Behrens.

As we have seen repeatedly, Behrens made a clear distinction between technique and art. He influentially diminished the aloofness of early twentieth-century artists to industry; but his acceptance of industry was fatalistic rather than optimistic or wholehearted. Even the best products of the engineer, whether mass-production or capital goods, were eliminated from the canon of good form on the theory that they participated in a pseudo-aesthetic. These products or machines, according to Behrens, had an "organic" lawfulness just as nature does; but just as nature is not yet art, so neither is an "organic" machine yet good design, art, or culture. For Behrens, the work of the engineer is a given of modern Western civilization, but an independent *Kunstwollen* must operate upon it if there is to be a modern Western culture.[39]

It comes as no surprise, then, that one of the early claims for Behrens's contribution to design for industry was based on the dualism of technique and art, the engineer and the artist—and on Behrens's desire to aggregate these parts rather than to conceive of a single creative process. Wolf Dohrn, in speaking of the AEG arc lamps, considered Behrens's method to be a model for the future development of German industry. His lamp designs were the result of a cooperation in which the engineer became half an artist and the artist half an engineer. Behrens was the first, Dohrn said, to put his capability in the service of industry; the AEG had innovated in an exemplary fashion in achieving the cooperation of engineer and artist. It was widely recognized that the AEG had shown the greatest capacity to employ the results of German science for economic benefit, so it was no accident, Dohrn concluded, that this same industry understood how to adapt the artistic capabilities of the time to its economic life.[40]

In summary, Behrens was not the first person to contribute designs (even "good" designs) for the fabrication (even mass production) of products (even peculiarly modern industrial products) by others. Nevertheless, he was the first artist to devote special care to the beauty of form of peculiarly modern industrial products in terms of some larger cultural conception *external to the immediate processes* of production and use. Industry, the machine, and industrial production had to be accepted, for at this point in history they were inevitable. For Behrens, the only remaining opportunity was to bridle this great force of technological civilization under expressive, reductionist artistic forms.[41] The belief advanced by thinkers like Reuleaux—that a process of technical refinement of a particular machine should be accompanied by a refinement of form—was thus in danger of subversion. An alternative belief, rooted in a historical determinist account, that the twentieth century was generally characterized by technical refinement, called for the design of forms that were beautiful, precise, and expressive—forms that were often independent of the machines they housed.

Much, perhaps even the largest part, of what has been known as industrial design in the twentieth century assumes the separateness of technique and art, and the need to give a sympathetic yet independent artistic expression to a technical civilization. The broad acceptance of this particular conception of design for industry may indeed be traced back to Behrens and give him precedence within that interpretation of industrial design.

Before going on to consider Behrens's industrial architecture, it will be well to review the task Behrens and the AEG established for the designer. Behrens was not hired as an engineer with a sensitive eye. He was retained as an artist who could provide the signs of technical perfection through beauty of form, whether this involved a well-formed housing for the electrodes of an arc lamp, a well-formed factory building for a work force which the AEG was proud to say operated almost militaristically, or an elegant letterhead for an intelligent and complex executive staff.

The extensive adoption of Behrens's expressive design by the AEG served to create a corporate image, a precedent for such mid-twentieth-century firms as Olivetti and IBM. IBM in particular used reductionist forms in graphics, industrial design, and architecture to express technological efficiency and to establish an image.[42] It may be the desire for such an "image" that has made Behrens's conception of industrial design dominant. The fruits of an inexorable search for the best solution to each problem (in the manner of the Thonet chair) would relate to one another only in terms of excellence and process; but the application of a dominant artistic will can assure a constant image through a great range of problems (the white plastic boxes of Braun electrical appliances, for example).

In Germany, industrial design is known as *Formgebung* and Peter Behrens is generally acknowledged as the first of these "form-givers." Industrial design may be said to range from product engineering to sales cosmetics. It is significant that Behrens was not engaged to work at either of the poles of this spectrum where engineers or draftsmen had already worked. Behrens was the first *Formgeber* through his exploring of the forms that would signal technical perfection, corporate image, and something still more obscure. Beyond the sign language of technique and corporateness, Behrens was still more interested in finding the symbols, proportions, and constructs that he believed would accord with and reveal the "rhythm of the time." There was also the further, self-imposed demand that this whole endeavor should achieve its "classical" form. Since steel, electricity, rapid transportation, modern industry, and modern enterprise were regarded as the sources of this rhythm, and therefore of the new culture, Behrens's cultural ambitions found support among his employers.

Postscript

Peter Behrens's industrial design for the AEG is now thoroughly documented in the studies of Tilmann Buddensieg and his colleagues, and most fully presented in their book *Industriekultur*.[43]

7

Architecture for Industry, the AEG Factories: Berlin III

During his first years in Berlin, Peter Behrens (figure 7.1) projected the overtly neoclassical house for Dr. Wiegand in Dahlem (figure 8.30) and the equally classicizing and oppressively assertive German Embassy in St. Petersburg (figure 8.45). At the same time he designed the AEG factories in Berlin (frontispiece; figure 7.27) which eventually led Nikolaus Pevsner to extol him as an innovator of "functional directness" in architecture. If such a claim cannot be sustained, there remains a remarkable difference in the manner and degree to which these two groups of buildings rely on historical precedent. This difference is all the more remarkable in that these structures seemingly marked two divergent routes from the highly abstract historical references of Behrens's Düsseldorf period. While at first glance it appears that Behrens adopted a more academic and conventional attitude toward his public and domestic buildings and a more independent and functional one toward his industrial work, it is the purpose of this chapter to reveal basic commonalties in his work of these years.

Ludwig Mies van der Rohe offered a simple explanation for the apparent differences of these two groups of works. Mies argued that Behrens could concern himself with a new expression for industrial buildings because this use-type was largely independent of any strongly held expectations on the part of the clients, the public, or the architectural profession; on the other hand, Mies asserted, at that time no one could conceive of a similar independence for significant public buildings.[1] One correct implication of Mies's observation is that Behrens shared the attitudes that led even progressive architects in those years to employ conventional solutions for such traditional problems as public edifices and private dwellings.[2] The conventions might be explored innovatively, but there was a reliance on convention nonetheless. Behrens's factories are not anomalous in this setting. Within the greater latitude allowed to utilitarian structures, Behrens chose *not* to emphasize that "functional directness" which was already manifest in many engineer-designed factories

(figures 7.17–19); he rather sought to incorporate such works within an established but evolving political and architectural tradition. Behrens sought to bring the factory under the rubric of the embassy, or the temple—not to bring the embassy under the rubric of the factory.

The stance adopted in Behrens's industrial architecture was a resigned acceptance of industrial civilization. The industrial revolution brought new patterns of organization, new personality types, new structural systems, and new materials and techniques of construction. These were rational extensions of earlier stages of human development and had, therefore, to be accepted as elements of a "new nature." For Behrens, the artist's role, as ever, was to exercise a will-to-form in shaping this new nature—the modern condition— into a true culture. He felt there was a spirit and a rhythm to modern times that would find its true expression only through the artist.

In his Düsseldorf period, Behrens was concerned with a formal distinction between spatial definition and the occupation of space. The culmination of this concern was the exhibition hall at Mannheim, an abstract stereotomic space defined by immaterial planes and complemented by plastic sculptures (figure 4.15). However, such an abstract formulation provided little guidance in meeting the physical and material problems of building.

Behrens's first major architectural commission in Berlin, the Turbine Factory of 1909 for the AEG, forced him to recognize and accept certain material considerations. The very large dimensions of the factory, the rugged industrial operations it housed, and its need for durability precluded the use of those ephemeral materials that had been appropriate in the earlier exhibition structures. The Turbine Factory brought about a confrontation between the artist's stereotomic preferences and the tectonic character of the ferro-vitreous wide-span frame. The resolution of this conflict was facilitated by a shift in German architectural theory from emphasis on material form to emphasis on space. Stated differently, the polarity of *Tektonik* and *Stereotomie* was subsumed within an understanding of architecture that emphasized space.[3]

Elaborating on neoclassical theory, Gottfried Semper had contrasted the crystalline, mechanical wholes of *Stereotomie* to the organic, membered structures of *Tektonik*.[4] Coming from a different quarter, Jacob Burckhardt accepted the idea of an organic architecture but claimed this could only result from a fortunate conjunction of naivete and closeness to nature. Burckhardt postulated that there had been only two organic styles, each with its single grand type: the peripteral temple of the Greeks and the multi-aisled Gothic cathedral including its front towers. Any "diversion" from the tectonic norm of the great organic types would cause a transformation into a spatial style (*ein Raumstyl*). "The late Roman style is already close to such a transformation, developing a significant spatial beauty which then lives on to varying degrees in the Byzantine, Romanesque, and Italo-Gothic styles—finally culminating in the Renaissance."[5] As the "diverted" types tend toward planar and cubic compositions, so the space thus created, with an equally assertive cubic quality, comes to have an importance equal to that of the solids. Thus Burckhardt, by contrasting organic styles to spatial styles, honored the great tectonic prototypes but also implied that the organic, tectonic structures were emphatically corporeal and material.[6]

The shift in theoretical dominance from the tectonic conception of architecture to a spatial conception was fixed with August Schmarsow's inaugural lecture at Leipzig in 1893 in which he characterized architecture as, essentially, the former of space (*Raumgestalterin*).[7] The apparent obviousness of this description compelled Schmarsow to engage in a polemic against established positions. He argued that contemporary architectural education, like Semper's theory, sought to construct the essence of a building style in terms of the orders, of the vaulting construction, or even from the crafts of the period. On the contrary, he suggested, an architectonic work is not achieved through the mere assembly of tectonic components. The emphasis must shift from material calculation and the *Formbildung* or *Ausgestaltung* of individual members, to a larger sense of the whole. In architecture, Schmarsow continued, the forming of space is the principle of style formation in all times. He felt that Wölfflin, relying on Semper, was utterly wrong in locating the birthplace of a new style in decoration. Decoration was merely the easiest place to introduce a new feeling for form. Wölfflin also erred in defining architecture as the art of corporeal masses, in that this gave dominance to the material aspect of architecture. In this Wölfflin echoed Burckhardt, whose division of all styles into "organic" and "diverted" left the starting point in the corporeal realm. Furthermore, Schmarsow pointed out, even Semper considered Gothic architecture to be merely constructive, not organic in the sense assigned to Hellenic works.

Understanding architecture as the "former of space" had several results for Schmarsow. The *Tektonik* of the orders, admired by the neoclassicists, was no longer an absolute norm; thus other styles could be more fully appreciated. The search for the spatial conception would be in accord with what Schmarsow considered Aristotle's genuine artistic truth, "The whole precedes the parts." Finally, Schmarsow suggested, the source of such a new holistic spatial conception would be found in the innermost energies of the culture.[8]

Behrens came to be indirectly influenced by Schmarsow's themes of "painterly, optical" perception, holism, and endemic cultural energy, and Schmarsow's acceptance of generally depreciated styles. These themes also lead us to another scholar highly influential on Behrens—Alois Riegl. Although Schmarsow, Riegl, and Behrens were to move away from the internal, "materialistic" criteria of the theory of *Tektonik* toward an understanding that could positively incorporate both tectonic and nontectonic architectural styles, they did not wish to advocate an arbitrary randomness. If the processes of artistic creation could lead to formal results that were polar opposites, then the determining criteria must be external to the creative process. Here Riegl supplied the missing link between the established concept of the zeitgeist and specific artistic acts. This link he termed *Kunstwollen*—the will to art. At the first level, *Kunstwollen* accounted for the artist's control of the creative process *against* the practical dictates of the problem itself. However, to account for the determining criteria behind the unified style of a time, this apparently free will of the artist came to be associated with a collective, goal-oriented, motivating volition shared by the entire culture of which the artist was a part. For Behrens this meant an acceptance of the spirit of the times, which he perceived to involve "an absolute clarification of spatial form to mathematical precision."[9] He regarded this as a metronomic, staccato pulse, as a form of reductionism implicit in modern production and life. There had also to be a recognition of the spirit of the people, of a *deutsche Volksgeist* of clarity and power. For Behrens the great imperative was that these collective, teleological wills be fulfilled—even in battle *against* function, material, and technique.[10]

It is largely due to his avoidance of total or continuous immersion in the industrial situation that Behrens's first works for the AEG (both in architecture and industrial design) were unprecedented in industry; his ideological dictates overcame gratuitous ornamentation and naive engineering functionalism while also undermining the more sophisticated functional theory of *Tektonik.* Behrens was the one to set this precedent in industry, but it must be admitted that there were other theoreticians and artists who might have applied their version of the modern zeitgeist to industry. Ideologically, Behrens is of a school comprised of those who treated *Sachlichkeit* as a symbol of the times, subscribed to a cubic definition of space, and held to a domination of idea over the existential situation. Among those who were similarly committed one could include the more vigorous Viennese who were influenced by Otto Wagner (figure 1.27; but not Adolf Loos); the more radical geometers among the Dutch, e.g., J. L. M. Lauweriks (figures 4.9, 4.14); Hermann Muthesius in his insistence on conventional types, art theorists like Alfred Lichtwark and J. A. Lux; and even political ideologists like Friedrich Naumann.[11]

The most remarkable and well-known example of Behrens's *Kunstwollen,* of his "historicist" form-giving, was the AEG Turbine Factory. The peculiar industrial circumstances surrounding this commission require some discussion. The AEG, founded in 1883, was already a thriving corporation by the early 1890s. In 1896, it began to build its first extensive industrial site on a large terrain on the Humboldthain in northern Berlin. This was the complex Behrens brought to completion before the First World War. The pre-Behrens factories on this site (partly visible in figure 7.3) were nondescript buildings of conventional mixed brick and iron construction with modest amounts of medievalizing ornament. The most exuberant yet characteristic element in this first group was the polychromed and castellated Gothic main gate which still stands at the northeast corner of the site, facing Brunnenstrasse (figure 7.4).[12] However, a more general comparison between the old and the new order may be seen in the (old) Factory for Railway

7.2 Berlin-Moabit, AEG factory site, Hüttenstrasse, aerial view (ca. 1910). Right center: facade of the AEG Turbine Factory by Behrens.

7.3 Berlin-Wedding, AEG Humboldthain (or Brunnen-strasse) factory site, aerial perspective (envisioned state ca. 1912). Three Behrens factories are the U-shaped High Voltage Factory (rear, left), Assembly Hall for Large Machines (left), and New Factory for Railway Equipment (next toward the right). Next along the street in the foreground are the factories built just before Behrens's appointment and modified by him; then the still older buildings of the Berliner Elektricitäts-Werke; finally Behrens's long four-part Small Motors Factory.

7.4 Franz Schwechten. Berlin, AEG factory site, Brunnen-strasse, Main Gate (1896).

7.5 Johann Kraaz (from 1905), with alterations and additions by Behrens (1908). Berlin, AEG Old Factory for Railway Equipment. Court-yard side with tower and modifications by Behrens.

Equipment (Fabrik für Bahnmaterial, figure 7.5). Its building began in 1905 with masonry detailing derived from late medieval north German brickwork. When Behrens arrived, the wing at the left of figure 7.5 was complete, as was most of the wing on the right, including the structural ironwork for the clock and water tower.[13] A study of the facade at right, and especially of the clock tower, reveals how Behrens, unlike his predecessor, was to achieve a broad and simple grandeur in his own derivations from medieval prototypes, such as the Marienwerder and the Marienburg (figures 7.6–7).

Under General Electric patents for the Curtis steam turbine and AEG's own patents from the work of professors Riedler and Stumpf of the Technische Hochschule, Berlin, the AEG had started production of turbines in 1902. After merging with the Union Elektricitätsgesellschaft in 1903, the AEG moved its turbine fabrication to the former Union factory site (figure 7.2, almost 88,000 sq. m.) in the Moabit district of Berlin. Here the first AEG-Curtis turbine was produced in 1904 in an existing 18-by-200-meter iron-framed, clerestory- and skylit shed (near the center of figure 7.2).[14] Large-scale development

7.6 Marienwerder, cathedral and castle with "Dansker" from southwest.

7.7 Marienburg, Mittelschloss, tower and gable of the infirmary.

and production of these turbines began about 1907; soon demand for more and larger turbine construction space was imperative. To that end the AEG commissioned Behrens to design his first factory, the giant turbine fabrication hall sited at the southeast corner of the Moabit factory site at Hutten- and Berlichingenstrasse (figure 7.2, right center; figure 7.8).[15] Designed in 1908–1909, its construction began in the spring of 1909 and the factory was in full operation at the beginning of 1910. Oscar Lasche, an engineer and the director of turbine fabrication for the AEG, specified the physical requirements for the new factory: full utilization of the available site; a main assembly hall of large dimensions; two relatively fast-traveling cranes capable of lifting almost 100 tons together and installed at such a height that the largest machine parts could be carried over machines on the assembly floor; radial cranes at regular points along both sides of the hall; the capability to bring railroad cars directly into the work space; a smaller flanking construction to accommodate storage and secondary manufacturing operations (also equipped with traveling cranes); and the maximum amount of natural light consistent with the strength demanded in a building for such heavy and dynamic utilization.[16]

It is clear that Behrens, completely untrained in engineering and even lacking formal schooling in architecture, a man who had built only small buildings in the most traditional materials and then with a remarkable disregard for practical considerations, was ill prepared for the technical problems of this new work. The need for the talents of an accomplished engineer was obvious, and consequently also the need for Behrens to come to terms with both new building materials and collaborative design. The respected engineer Karl Bernhard became Behrens's collaborator on the Turbine Factory.[17] However, despite Bernhard's expertise, Behrens used the engineer as an agent for his design rather than as a full collaborator, as we shall see.[18] Beyond the forcefulness of his own personality and his intimate connections with the directors of the AEG, the symbolic significance presumed for the Turbine Factory may have helped Behrens achieve this control.

The Turbine Factory was meant to be symbolic in several senses. Elaborate significance was attached to the turbine and to the turbodynamo as impressive sources of modern power. One of the executives of the AEG later wrote that Behrens felt something of what vibrates in the words of the poet Heinrich Lersch:

> *Maschinen rauschen in Heiligen Liedern,*
> *Fabriken sind göttliche Kirchen der Kraft.*[19]

With turbines as the sources of power, the Turbine Factory would stand in a relation to other factories as a great abbey to its priories. The new hall would not only be the most important building on the Moabit site, it was to occupy the southeast corner of the site, oriented to the center of Berlin, and thus would serve as the showfront of the entire factory complex. Executed as it was, this facade became *the* face that the AEG turned to the world, superseding the castellated gate on Brunnenstrasse.

7.8 Peter Behrens. Berlin, AEG Turbine Factory (1908–1909). Rendered perspective, view from the southeast. Signed "Peter Behrens," lower right.

Behrens's design for the Turbine Factory called for a main assembly hall of 207.38 meters along Berlichingenstrasse, although a unit of 127 meters was built in the first phase (figure 7.9). The transverse section (figure 7.10) best reveals Bernhard's structural design: an asymmetrical three-hinged arch with a tie-rod. The impressive mechanical detail above the reinforced concrete foundation on Berlichingenstrasse (figures 7.11–12) is one of the hinges. From this hinge the first, and longer, member of the asymmetrical arch ascends vertically and then arcs, in three facets, into the central hinge at the apex of the main structure (figures 7.10, 7.13). The other, shorter member springs from the highest point of the structure shared by the main and side halls. Tie-rods are attached just above this point; the span is 25.73 meters; a large, continuous skylight about 26 meters above the floor crowns the entire construction The shorter member of the arch and the corresponding part of the longer member have square open latticework cross sections, while the vertical segment of the long member has a solid box section of iron plates. Attached to the interior of this vertical segment is a latticework member that supports one of the tracks for the traveling crane running immediately below the tie-rods. The clearance below the cranes is 14.51 meters; their clear span, 23.64 meters. The asymmetrical arches occur at 9.22-meter centers along the length of the building, with continuous glazing between. At every other arch is located a radial crane cantilevering eight meters (2,000 kilograms capacity at full reach). The side hall included a basement in reinforced concrete and a two-story superstructure of mixed construction.[20] The structure had not only to incorporate large glazed areas for the provision of light to the working surface but also to resist the forces involved in braking heavily loaded cranes moving at the rate of two meters per second.[21] This account of the main physical aspects of the building evokes the scale of the problem and the technology employed. However, as we now expect with Behrens, such technical matters were only means to more ambitious ends.

Behrens was anxious to correlate a number of different concerns. The practical needs outlined by Oscar Lasche dictated a gargantuan scale and a ferrous structure much influenced by these magnitudes.[22] Behrens himself wanted to express the quality, scale, and cultural significance of this "new nature," convinced that such an expression required the formulation of a symbolic structure outside the province of the engineer. He sought to give his architecture a corporeality which it previously lacked but which he now, like most architects before him, thought was necessary even in the housing of a taut structural cage. And he desired to be the prophet of a new classicism destined to reinterpret the energies of contemporary life in terms of eternal verities. This search for corporeality and classical expression was a distinctive point in Behrens's development. The symbolic expression of a "new nature" constituted the challenge of his new position. Less important, but not to be ignored, was the fact that this orchestration played out in Berlin, where Behrens admired but also aimed to rival the work of Germany's most famous neoclassical architects, Karl Friedrich Schinkel and Friedrich Gilly.

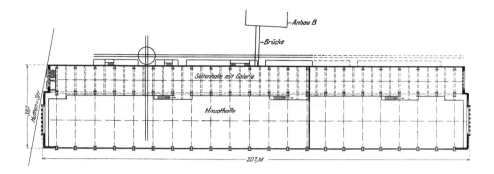

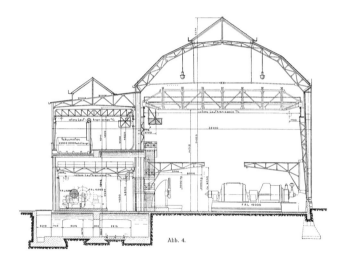

Several of these concerns are notable in a statement made by Behrens upon the completion of the Turbine Factory.[23] The architectonic concept behind the main body of the building, he stated, was to draw the construction together into an emphatic mass of iron rather than allow the iron framing to dematerialize in a dispersed network.[24] This hall should have an enclosed, planar definition emphasizing the architectonic proportions of its space. The principal vertical members were detailed with solid walls in order to give them mass, emphasizing their dual roles as both structural supports and space-definers. The massiveness of these members was all the more important since the building was to be constructed, so far as possible, of iron and glass. Where Behrens felt these materials were architecturally inadequate, carefully executed concrete walls would be used. Behrens maintained an understandable but highly problematic conception of concrete as a plastic material that could easily assume any form desired. In the Turbine Factory, he sought to use concrete as an infill material that would not possess the load-bearing appearance of masonry. Only the iron

7.11 Behrens. AEG Turbine Factory. Berlichingenstrasse side, raking view showing visual massing of the solid bents.

7.12 Behrens. AEG Turbine
Factory. Lower hinge of
three-pinned arch on the
Berlichingenstrasse side.

7.13 Behrens. AEG Turbine Factory. Interior, main hall, view toward front.

members were meant to suggest a supporting function; the windows of the side elevation were inclined along the inner face of the structural members, allowing those members and the beam at the cornice line to stand in strong relief. This entablature-like beam and the gable of the front elevation were to establish, according to Behrens, a corporeality, a body resting on the principal members of the side elevation and on the structural mullions of the window at the front. The iron bands set in the rounded concrete corner elements made horizontal lines which, Behrens felt, provided a distinction between the structural verticals and the more plastic infill. The mullions and glass of the end window were detailed as one large plane in order to suggest its bearing function: all mullions of the same size, the glass in the front plane of these members, and the whole in the plane of the gable.

At the two-story side hall (frontispiece; figure 7.15) the street elevation and four meters of the long side elevation were rendered in concrete so as to accent, according to Behrens, the totally iron and glass construction of the side wall. Since iron and glass lack the volumetric quality of stone, the concrete end walls of both halls were needed to tie the composition together and ensure its desired massiveness. Though the engineer's calculations ensured unity and stability, the eye was seen as requiring its own cues. At the same time, Behrens eschewed sculptural and ornamental decoration as being inappropriate to a factory and inimical to the goal of corporeality.

Behrens could not have been more specific about his rejection of normal factory construction in iron and glass; nor could he have been more frank about his endeavor to bring these materials into the elevated tradition of architecture. In the side elevation on Berlichingenstrasse (figure 7.11), Behrens and Bernhard fulfilled the architect's aims with a minimum of technological compromise: the large scale, industrial materials, and machinelike details are technically appropriate, but also achieve an intensified character. Set on a high pedestal, the functional hinge (figure 7.12) references the more complex engines within. These bases, the solid, boldly revealed uprights, the concealment of the diagonal bracing, and the shadow cast by the trabeation, establish a machine classicism rich in corporeality, in nuance of detail, and in levels of evocative meaning.

On the testimony of Bernhard, the simple iron and glass elevation on the Turbine Factory toward the rear yard (figures 7.14–15) was very different from that on Berlichingenstrasse (figure 7.11). Of course, there are differences inherent in the operation of the two parts of the building itself: two small stories as against one large; an active face

7.14 Karl Bernhard with Peter Behrens. Berlin, AEG Turbine Factory. Side toward the factory grounds.

toward the factory complex in contrast to an inactive face on the street. Beyond these contextual differences were fundamental differences in the design process. Bernhard actually thanked Behrens for accepting, on the courtyard side, what the engineer took to be the direct result of pragmatic considerations.[25]

Bernhard juxtaposed this mildly ironic gratitude with a criticism of Behrens's artistic control of the frontal Huttenstrasse elevation, which needed to be no more than a closure for a series of arches, logically related to the cross section as given by the structural members (figures 7.8, 7.10; compare figures 7.17, 7.33). Asymmetries in the function of the building and in the urban situation led to the use of asymmetric arches, which Behrens concealed in the symmetries of the Huttenstrasse facade. Similarly, the two stories of windows in the Huttenstrasse facade of the lesser side hall mask the irregular conditions of a stairwell and an elevator shaft. In both cases, form and fact are in conflict; the awkward juncture of the side hall against the inclined pylon indicates how independently form was conceived from function.

Something similar can be said of the gable front, which Reyner Banham regarded as displaying the traditionally acceptable formalism of Behrens. Surprised that Behrens did not hold to a normal triangular pediment, Banham offered a technological explanation of the polygonal gable form: the need to gain clearance for the traveling cranes.[26] However, as the section (figure 7.10) indicates, tie-rods forced the cranes to run well below the extra space created by the unusual roof form. Structurally, the spanning portion of the three-hinged arch could have ascended in a straight line from its springing to the crown. According to Bernhard it was Behrens's decision about the facade that predetermined Bernhard's attitude toward the arch. In this case, ideas concerning form and symbolism dictated the physical solution.[27]

Behrens wanted the roof in particular to establish the corporeality of the Turbine Factory.[28] Only by creating a heavy gable, which is not in any way implicit in the asymmetrical arch and tie-rod, could he give the roof the desired weightiness. Behrens's image of the building as a whole, and his desire for a corporate display-facade, required him to move out of the plane of the last arch and establish a new structural system for the facade. The concrete gable, with Behrens's hexagonal logo for the AEG, is borne by a concealed iron truss, the top chord of which coincides with the profile of the arches beyond. This truss had to be supported, and Behrens thus provided his showfront with bearing members that were not just stabilizing mullions or the infill of a plane below a structural arch.

A strange phenomenon may be observed in the completed building. Behrens considered the concrete corners to be infill detailed in such a way as not to compete with the iron structure.[29] Concrete was a rather odd choice for this purpose, for Behrens was creating a building without structural support at the corners—a kind of corner window rendered in concrete! The implication of this would seem to be that he was creating independent facades which required neutral transitions from one to another. The structureless corner was the unexpected and even unexploited consequence of other decisions.[30]

Thus for Behrens the Turbine Factory was clearly a compound of metal supports and concrete infill. Bernhard, on the other hand, was displeased that concrete was used so freely in the Huttenstrasse facade and found it only natural that people interpreted the Turbine Factory as two massive corner piers with a high pediment—or that Oberbaurat Erhard of Vienna misclassified the building as one of reinforced concrete construction.[31] However, these alternative readings of the Turbine Factory are too obvious to encourage the belief that Behrens was unaware of the ambiguities he had established. The unusually weighty, and even classical, character explicitly intended by Behrens in this iron-framed building delighted many contemporaries because it brought this type of utilitarian construction into the architectural tradition.

However, a comparison of the Turbine Factory with a neoclassical portal by Friedrich Gilly yields some notable contrasts (figures 7.15–16).[32] The flanking pylons, the overhanging masses above, and the central void are similarities of the two designs. Yet Gilly was consistent at both a traditional and utilitarian level: solids support or span; voids serve for passage. In the Turbine Factory, the central void did not serve for passage; indeed, its unemphatic framework was the support for the overhanging mass. The factory-temple had no corner columns; the most massive elements of the building, the pylons, were to be read as mere infill. The inherent ambiguities of the factory and its inversion of classical form are consistent with Behrens's will to mark his resigned endorsement of industrial civilization.

Any appraisal of the Turbine Factory as Germany's first monumental iron and glass building[33] may be refuted by citing such precedents as August von Voit's Munich Crystal Palace (Glaspalast, 1854), or the more monumental great circular hall by Friedrich von Thiersch in Frankfurt (Fest- und Ausstellungshalle, 1907–1908), and a number of railway stations, including the impressive structure in Hamburg by the architects Reinhardt and Süssenguth and the engineer Medling (1903–1906).[34] If one chooses to see the Turbine Factory as the "first piece of modern architecture" because it makes "logical use of modern materials such as steel and glass" and "solves a typically modern industrial problem,"[35] or as "frank industrial architecture,"[36] then one is failing to take note of another factory that is even more frank, more logical, of grander scale, and which integrates within it an impressive differentiation of transport systems: namely, the 31-meter-wide Krupp Ninth Mechanical Workshop in Essen, which is a strictly iron-framed building with glass and brick infill (figures 7.17–18).[37] Another example of impressive iron and glass factory buildings is the completely glass-covered slips of the shipyard Friedrich Krupp AG Germaniawerft at Kiel-Gaarden (figure 7.19), built in the years 1898–1902.[38] These Krupp factories serve as precedents for an industrial architecture developed within the conditions of site, use, process, and construction.[39] They were light and spacious, and free of historical reference.[40] On the other hand, it was Behrens's intention to express the essence of powerful contemporary collective institutions. Beyond mere utility, he sought to create the monuments of a culture based on modern industrial power—both physical and corporate power. Behrens's success in this program made his Turbine Factory unprecedented.[41]

7.15 Behrens. AEG Turbine
Factory. Model, view with
factory-side elevation.

Though the Turbine Factory was recognized as a significant pioneering work in the field of modern architecture, a review of Behrens's subsequent industrial work reveals interpolations and variations that produced quite different results. The principal site of these later buildings was the 117,628-square-meter AEG Humboldthain complex in northern Berlin (figure 7.3). Within this complex certain factories had existed before Behrens's arrival. These were concentrated in the central and northern part of the site, separated from Brunnenstrasse by a group of residential buildings. The castellated gate on Brunnenstrasse marked the administrative approach to this complex (figure 7.4; just visible at the far corner of figure 7.3).[42] The railroad and freight approach (at the upper left corner of the perspective) ran parallel to Hussitenstrasse, across Gustav-Meyer-Allee and

---

The AEG Factories

7.17 Essen, Friedrich Krupp
AG, Cast Steel Factory, Ninth
Mechanical Workshop (built
1905, enlarged 1907 and
1910, for large-caliber can-
nons for ships and tanks).
Exterior. Painting by Otto
Bollhagen (1912).

7.18 Essen, Friedrich Krupp
AG, Ninth Mechanical
Workshop. Interior. Color
rendering.

7.19 Kiel-Gaarden, Friedrich Krupp
AG Germaniawerft. Interior of
Covered Slip III (photo ca. 1905).

7.20 Peter Behrens. Berlin,
AEG, project for entrance
gate at the northwest corner
of the Humboldthain site.
Perspective (1909–1911).

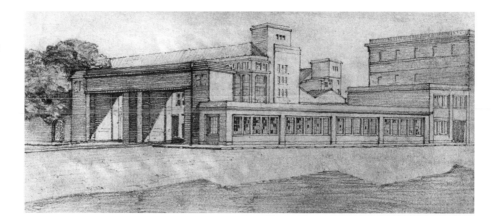

into the site from the northwest. Behrens proposed but never carried out a portal and service building at this point (figure 7.20).[43] Comparatively simple gates and lodges were
later built to Behrens's design. The totally unornamented simple cubic forms of emphatically exposed, hard bluish-red (*Eisenklinker*) brick, characteristic of many of Behrens's
designs, provided a very different introduction to the factory site than the castellated gate
on Brunnenstrasse.

The rail lines continue into the large yard which is the physical and organizational
center of the factory complex. To the north is the first factory built to Behrens's design on
this site, the High Voltage Factory (Hochspannungsfabrik; figure 7.21).[44] Only slightly
later came Behrens's Small Motors Factory facing southeast on Voltastrasse (Klein-
motorenfabrik; figure 7.27).[45]

In contrast to the Turbine Factory, the High Voltage Factory, an assembly plant for
transformers and other equipment for high voltage transmission, presents an irregular silhouette. It consists of interlocking blocks with asymmetrical concessions to the site (figures 7.22–25). The entire surface is clad in brick and tile.[46] The central part of the complex
consists of two large, ferro-vitreous, skylit halls 35 meters in width, 17 meters high, and
just over 100 meters in length. This double hall is flanked by basement services with locker
rooms and multistory working areas that comprise, in ascending order, a 6-meter-high
storage and assembly floor at the main level, four 4-meter-high work floors, and two more
work floors under the roof. At the eastern end (figure 7.25), two regular stories plus a
mansard story literally bridge the wide-span halls below.

At both east and west ends the main halls terminate in greatly simplified temple
fronts in hard steel-blue *Eisenklinker* bricks. However, by far the strongest impression is
made by the multistoried parts with their repetitive bays and prominent access towers.
Continuously open horizontal runs for the assembly lines were attained by the placement
of these towers at the ends or outside the main envelope of the building (or, subject to the
site constraint on the north, in a position that preserved as much of the horizontal conti-

7.21 View from the north-west gate of the AEG Humboldthain factory complex toward the group of factories designed by Behrens: High Voltage Factory in foreground.

nuity as possible). The repetitive bays of the first four floors (figure 7.24) are slightly recessed within a flat brick colonnade. The doubled mullions above give the effect of a frieze.[47] The more emphatic cornice being below rather than above this "frieze," the frieze establishes an ambiguous continuity with the roof rather than with the colonnade—an intentional rupture in classical syntax. In the stair towers (figures 7.24–25), Behrens delighted in working with a broken silhouette, irregular openings for various purposes, and stepped windows for the stair runs.[48]

The picturesque projections of this factory, its irregular western termination in accordance with movement patterns, its overall plan around interlocking courtyards—all these characteristics are reminiscent of the ideas of another architect who fused medieval and academic sensibilities, Camillo Sitte.[49] Speaking of the Humboldthain courtyard, Behrens acknowledged his debt to Sitte:

Now as to the placement of buildings! In this the process of manufacture is paramount. The disposition of trackage will govern building location. By stepping back the buildings, portals and driveways are well accommodated; at the same time liberal loading courts must be provided and thus contact is made with an outstanding principle of city planning. Because of the practical necessity of recession, the group acquires an effective silhouette, and due to the necessary arrangement of courts, a

7.22 Peter Behrens. Berlin,
AEG High Voltage Factory
(1909–1910). Plan.

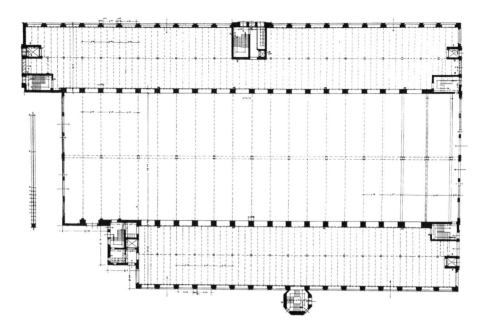

7.23 Behrens. AEG High
Voltage Factory. Section.

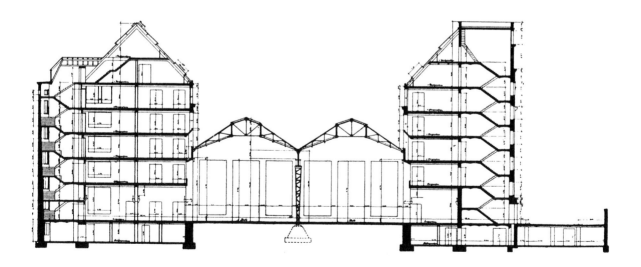

7.24 Behrens. AEG High
Voltage Factory. Model
viewed as from southeast.

7.25 Behrens. AEG High
Voltage Factory. East face
from north.

requirement of that old master of city planning, Camillo Sitte, is complied with. Sitte pronounces plazas enclosed by building units one of the most essential elements in creating artistic effects in city planning. It is only necessary to have had the opportunity for comparison between layouts directed from a purely practical viewpoint by an understanding mind, and those created by chance or time's accretions, granted an equal expenditure in money and equivalent materials, to find an astounding difference in the impression created.[50]

It is characteristic of Behrens that he addressed himself to the understanding mind as well as to practical necessities. For Behrens, this mind worked one way when presenting a street-oriented monument like the Turbine Factory and completely otherwise when creating a factory courtyard interlaced with and surrounded by practical operations.

Behrens's ability to embrace these various conditions was demonstrated in a single building, the Small Motors Factory (figures 7.26–28) of 1910–1913, across the courtyard from the High Voltage Factory.[51] The courtyard side of this later work is articulated by lateral projections and loading courts. The dimensions, the materials, and the detailing are all similar to those of the High Voltage Factory, although a somewhat different inflection is evident in the placement of stairs behind windows that maintain floor lines (figures 7.26, 7.28). The repression of an access element within the whole permitted the simple termination of these wings with strong triangular pediments. This return to the sovereignty of the whole over the parts is emphatic on the opposite, Voltastsrasse elevation (figure 7.27).

7.26 Peter Behrens. Berlin, AEG Small Motors Factory (1910–1913). Plan.

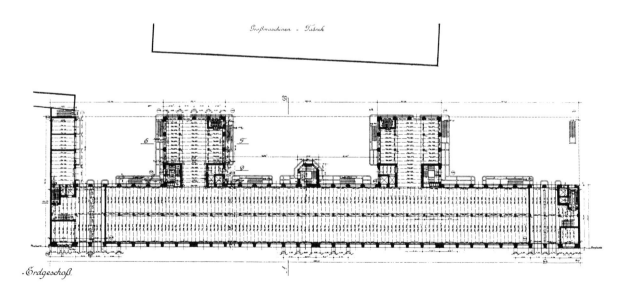

7.27 Behrens. AEG Small
Motors Factory. Street view.

The stance of the Small Motors Factory relative to the street is significantly different from that of the Turbine Factory. The Voltastrasse plant is part of a long wall on a secondary street, not a corner building at a principal point of arrival. The operations housed
did not require spaces of unusual size. This fact, together with the need for relatively
intense utilization of this site, encouraged the construction of a multistory factory (figure
7.27). On the other hand, like the Turbine Factory, the Small Motors Factory presented a
closed and classicizing form to the street; there a frame forming a temple front, here a wall
architecture providing a semi-utilitarian facade. It is an ambiguous wall, its layering of wall
and column reminding one of Roman buildings, although here the columns are revealed
within the wall rather than being superimposed upon it.[52] Emphatic wall segments at the
ends of the facade continue below the cornice line and into square piers that divide the

long front into four segments, each of which contains seven round-faced pier-columns (figure 7.27). Behrens chose an odd number of columns so that a column rather than an intercolumniation would be on center. The asymmetric placement of entrances in the end bays and the central column signified that this was, after all, only a side of a larger factory complex.

Behrens designed and built two other factories on the Humboldthain site: the extension to the Factory for Railway Equipment (Neue Fabrik für Bahnmaterial; figures 7.29–30) and the Assembly Hall for Large Machines (Montagehalle für Grossmaschinen; figures 7.29–32).[53] The latter is especially important for adding a subtle variation to the industrial format Behrens developed for the AEG.[54] The new railway factory and the northwestern thirteen bays of the Assembly Hall were built in the winter of 1911–1912 (the southeastern bays only in the late 1920s). These buildings completed the industrial courtyard Behrens had conceived and executed over the years 1909 to 1913. Figure 7.21 gives the view as one entered through the northwest gate on Gustav-Meyer-Allee. In concept and execution, the New Factory for Railway Equipment was a slightly simplified variant of the Small Motors Factory, displaying a restrained colonnade to Voltastrasse (figure 7.30), a feature which in detail was closer to the courtyard elevation of the Small Motors Factory.

7.28 Behrens. AEG Small Motors Factory. Courtyard side, from northeast.

7.29 Peter Behrens. Berlin, AEG New Factory for Railway Equipment (L-shaped building) and Assembly Hall for Large Machines (clear-span building) (1911–1912) Plan.

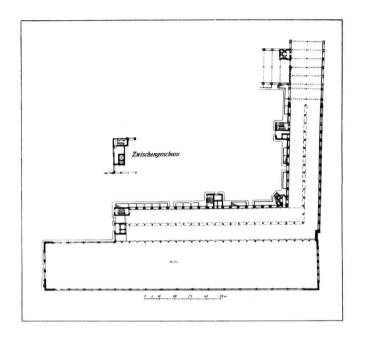

7.30 Behrens. AEG Assembly Hall for Large Machines. Elevations on Hussitenstrasse (below) and end facade on Voltastrasse (above, left). AEG New Factory for Railway Equipment. Elevation on Voltastrasse (above, right). Working drawing (July 1911).

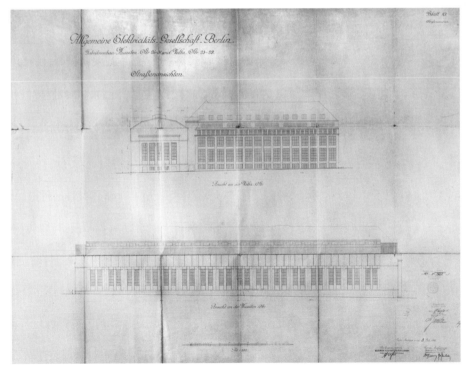

The Assembly Hall for Large Machines is a single large factory space with a 30-meter span (figure 7.31); it presents an imposing end elevation at one corner of the site (figure 7.30). To the northwest, a similar elevation appears, directly confronting the gate on Gustav-Meyer-Allee (figure 7.32). While these elevations invite comparison with the Turbine Factory, the points of arrival which they address do not require a major representative gesture as in the earlier factory—even the northwest gate is mainly for workers and freight. In contrast to the Turbine Factory, the northwest end elevation of the Assembly Hall is also the main point of entry; however, since Behrens would not celebrate mere function, the portal front of the Assembly Hall received a less elaborate form than the closed facade serving as the symbolic point of arrival at the Turbine Factory. The facade of the Assembly Hall, for all its formal impressiveness, is little more than a pragmatic terminal to a repetitive, wide-span structure; and yet this facade, too, should be distinguished

7.32 Behrens. AEG Assembly Hall for Large Machines. Exterior from the northwest.

from one such as that of the slightly later Siemens-Schuckert factory (figure 7.33), which loses nothing of architectural impressiveness for being relentlessly pragmatic.

By the time of the Assembly Hall, Behrens seems to have been confident of integrating his own intentions with practical conditions. Perhaps the clearest indication of this new attitude is his use of iron framing (*Fachwerk,* as in the Siemens factory [figure 7.33]) together with brick infill—a conventional system he had formerly despised both for the linearity of the iron and the apparently insubstantial quality of the brick infill.[55] The principal structural members of the Assembly Hall are three-hinged arches; the cross section of these elements is solid-walled throughout their length (figure 7.31), not just in the principal elevation as in the Turbine Factory. These solid-walled arches contrast sharply with the lightly framed skylights that originally extended from wall to wall. Arches, secondary bents, purlins, diagonal bracing, and glazing bars are here arranged in an easily recognizable hierarchy. The Assembly Hall employed no tie-rods; consequently, the truss structures of the two high traveling cranes were free to operate in the faceted space under the arches.[56]

The result is an interior that is much more comprehensible than that of the Turbine Factory (figure 7.13). The arches are carried on uprights that also support the beams of the crane tracks. In contrast to the superimposed verticals of the Turbine Factory, a single upright provides the critical point in the structure, simultaneously the springing of the arch, longitudinal bracing, and crane track; this element is given a strong and rational articulation both inside and out (figures 7.31–32). On the long facade, between the uprights and below the line of the crane track, a well-defined sequence of brick infill panels imparts a certain weight to the building (figure 7.32). Here Behrens comes close to approximating iron framing and brick infill as conventionally used in factories, though with expected sophistication.

Behrens's express wish for an architectonic embodiment of the "new nature" of technology was seemingly fulfilled in the Assembly Hall, while the arbitrary and ambiguous formulations that led to Bernhard's criticisms of the Turbine Factory were avoided (frontispiece; figure 7.32). Characteristically, Behrens did not terminate the building by glass or

7.33 Hans Hertlein. Berlin, Siemens-Schuckert-Werke (1917).

brick infill within the plane of the last arch. He chose to establish an independent masonry construction at each end. The AEG logo was carved in the depth of the brick wall (figure 7.32), and as this wall turned into the side elevation it remained outside the plane of the brick infill. Behrens's design eliminated two arches and transformed the required end closure into a structurally contributive element. When designed as simply as here, such a termination was a reasonable alternative to a design that employed only framing and infill (figure 7.19). However, the decision to bracket the production processes within these embodying end walls arose from abstract rather than technical reasons.

One of several commissions Behrens received for the German section of the International Exposition in Brussels of 1910 deserves attention here. The hall for the exhibition of German railway equipment (figures 7.34–35) is built of handsomely shaped laminated wood arches. The principal end facade is a series of monumental but simple portals with a light glass infill rising to the directly expressed arch above. While quite unlike the Assembly Hall, these two works show Behrens in his closest approximation to the unity of tectonic form and monumentality.[57]

On his arrival in Berlin, Behrens came to accept contemporary industrial civilization resignedly; nonetheless he saw in it a "new nature" and the source of a "new spirit" which the artist had to master.[58] The more abstract aspect of his new spirit was built on the concept of a strongly interwoven industrial and socio-political organization, as advanced by such men as Walther Rathenau and Friedrich Naumann.[59] For Behrens the new spirit would come into being only through the interaction between the social context *and* the creative man, endowed with both tradition and critical acumen. Behrens believed that industrial civilization had brought about a sensory and perceptual reorganization that implied a new form of environment. The two faces of the AEG Small Motors Factory—the broad sweep of its street elevation and the articulated forms of its court side (figures 7.27–28)—illustrated his "rhythmic principle."[60] This principle held that modern life had altered our perception of the environment. He argued that fast trains transport us so rapidly that the effective image of the city is reduced to a silhouette. Similarly, our rapid passage through the city precludes any consideration of building details. These conditions implied for Behrens an architecture of compact and serene planes that would be easily perceived. Even special details could be handled in a manner harmonious with this intent, he claimed, if one employed broadly conceived elements, contrasted or arranged in repetitive series.[61]

When Behrens visited the United States in 1912, he especially appreciated the accumulation of skyscrapers; these huge particulars, he felt, added up to a massive vertical body, and a tall urban body was necessary if the vastly extended modern city was to have any silhouette.[62] Furthermore, the competitive skyscrapers were striking emblems of the drive of industrial civilization. As a vast, modern entrepreneurial city, Behrens felt Berlin too needed such a silhouette; but his own opportunities for such work were at the scale of the street.[63] If we add to these formulations Behrens's call for a metronomic industrial

7.34 Peter Behrens. Brussels, International Exposition, 1910, German Railway Exhibition Hall. Exterior (1909–1910).

pulse,[64] we have a fairly complete formal program for the street facade of the Small Motors Factory—and a contrast to the Sittesque program of an operational articulation for the courtyard elevation.

In 1913, Walter Gropius, who had left Behrens's studio to build the Fagus Works, provided what he called the "aesthetic scaffolding" for a modern industrial architecture: precisely characterized form, elimination of all that is incidental, clear contrasts, ordering of the elements, identical parts in series, and unity of form and color. While Gropius saw these qualities to be the correlates of the energy and economy of modern life, he also recognized that they were only guidelines, still in need of the fantasy of an artist. In industrial building, he acknowledged his former master Behrens and the AEG as the team that had first successfully embodied these modern characteristics in a factory.[65] But as Gropius also noted, Behrens was inclined to emphasize understanding at the expense of feeling.[66] So Behrens's observations about our altered perceptual, sensory, productive, societal, or political

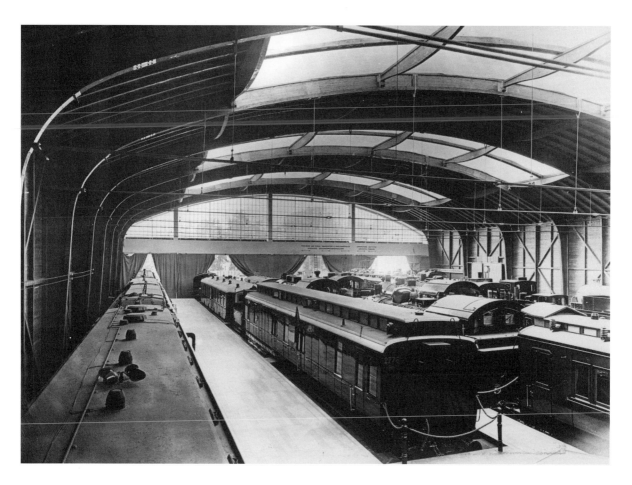

7.35 Behrens. Brussels, German Railway Exhibition Hall. Interior view, toward the front.

conditions remained just that: cool observations. He did not wax enthusiastic, as Le Corbusier would do in 1923 in the pages of *Vers une architecture*.[67] For Behrens "the Engineer's Aesthetic" celebrated by Le Corbusier was finally a false aesthetic. The engineer's calculations were universal, like nature, and neither amounted to culture. For Behrens, the engineer was, alas, the archetypal man of modern civilization. Such a qualified position could hardly serve as the basis for enthusiasm. Instead Behrens continued to endorse the traditional concept of culture. This endorsement permitted him to be critical of modernity and to claim that the artist had the will to reform the modern condition. And yet while one may admire this spirit of critique and reform, in practice Behrens exercised this will in an authoritarian manner, imposing a priori laws rather than allowing conditions to test those laws and lead him to better formulations. Although the Assembly Hall for Large Machines represented a closer correspondence between idea and fact than was evident in the Turbine Factory, this conjunction was like the refinement of a grand theory through the addition of epicycles. The Assembly Hall remained a concretization of an ironic and pessimistic view of modernity. Indeed all of Behrens's AEG factories are cool monuments to the accommodation of giant magnitude, to the representation of the "new nature." Le Corbusier, on the other hand, within his apparent technological determinism, was to discover new opportunities. Eluding the learned detachment and aesthetic distance of Behrens, Le Corbusier presented his idea of the *esprit nouveau* as something to be lived. Behrens, in contrast, chose to complete, to close the serial processes that were present both in the functions and in the structures of his factories. He did not emphasize the environment as a place for human activity, nor architecture as a context for a fuller life. Instead the Turbine Factory was the expression of an ideal vision of a technological civilization related to earlier utopian visions. It was intended as something that ordinary men should live up to, rather than as an occasion for evolving elements of use and enjoyment within a newly conceived and highly operational environment. Behrens sought to render his factories as monuments to an evolving social condition—monuments that were imbued with Spenglerian overtones of both engagement and ominous foreboding.

Postscript

Peter Behrens's architectural work for the AEG is now thoroughly documented in the studies of Tilmann Buddensieg and his colleagues, and most fully presented in their book *Industriekultur*.[68]

8

Expression, Convention, and Convention as Expression: Berlin IV

Among Behrens's works contemporary with the AEG commissions, at least one, the gas-works in Frankfurt am Main, received that ambiguous label "expressionist"; many more have been generally dismissed as classicizing and retrospective, for example the embassy in St. Petersburg.[1] The previous chapter suggests that such perceived disparity among his works is exaggerated in at least one significant respect: the supposedly "frank" industrial buildings were themselves solemnifications of societal organization, just as were the buildings for established institutions—the embassy, for example. The factories, too, possessed both monumental and expressive aspects; a common artistic attitude embraced all of Behrens's work. Nevertheless, there are obvious formal differences among his buildings of the Berlin period. For that matter, a considerable formal range is recognizable just within the factories (frontispiece; fig 7.24). If these buildings were informed by a common artistic attitude, this attitude should be capable of embracing the formal differences.

Rather than explain these formal contrasts as fickle acceptance now of modernity, now of tradition, I suggest that they are central to Behrens's artistic process. Varying results in the work may be explained by the productive competition of convention (medium, tradition, materials, etc.) and personal expression within this process. The balance struck between these elements changed over the course of time and according to various commissions. Finally, Behrens should be recognized for his conflation of these two forces in what may be termed "convention serving as expression."[2]

Behrens constantly engaged such a confrontation of expression and convention. His concern with architecture as evidence of the rhythm or spirit of the time encouraged an expressive approach. His belief that the artist had to give form to that spirit worked in terms of convention (frontispiece), although the artist's expressive or "centrifugal" force could emerge, too (figures 8.3–4).[3]

The balance Behrens struck depended on the characteristics of the commission and on the point in his development (e.g., the expressiveness of the Darmstadt period [figure

8.1 Peter Behrens. Frankfurt-
Osthafen, Main-Gaswerke
(1910–1912). Site plan.

8.2 Behrens. Main-Gaswerke.
Perspective of buildings south
of central yard.

2.5]; the conventions of the Düsseldorf period [figure 2.6]). Within the factories we see a microcosm of such developmental and situational changes. From the Turbine Factory to the later Assembly Hall for Large Machines there was a diminution of the expressive quality. At the Humboldthain site, in accord with the situation, the courtyard elevations were less conventionalized than the street facades.

In the work of the Berlin period other than for the AEG, developmental and situational transformations again present themselves. We need to be aware of the balance of expression and convention in a variety of Behrens's commissions before seeking a more general interpretation of his work. In Berlin, from 1907 to 1914, Behrens received an enormous amount of work from the AEG. He was, nevertheless, a consultant to the AEG rather than one of its staff, and maintained an independent studio on the grounds of his villa in Neubabelsberg, near Potsdam; commissions came from many patrons. It was in this prolific atelier with its wide range of commissions that Walter Gropius (from 1907 or 1908 to March 1910) and Ludwig Mies (from October 1908 to January 1912) were, for lack of a better term, journeymen architects.[4] It was here too that Charles-Edouard Jeanneret (the young Le Corbusier) spent five months of 1910–1911, a critical point in his development.[5] Other members of the atelier also deserve note.[6]

The commissions of this period included the gasworks in Frankfurt am Main; the AEG factories; private houses for an estate near Hagen; a villa for a classical scholar in Berlin-Dahlem; an office building for a large corporation in Düsseldorf; and the German Embassy in St. Petersburg. In these commissions, ranging from utilitarian to representative, Behrens played over a considerable gamut of architectural forms from expressive to conventional.

The robust use of brick and the dramatic contrasting of forms in the Gasworks (Frankfurter Gasgesellschaft, later Main-Gaswerke) in Frankfurt-Osthafen (figures 8.1–7) gave this complex of buildings a prominent place in the early history of expressionist architecture.[7] Reading the site plan of the Gasworks (figure 8.1) clockwise from the lower right (the northwest corner of the site), one finds the director's house and gatehouse, office, bath and canteen building, storehouse and workshop, metering building, apparatus building, towers, ammonia plant, and machine house (the latter four seen from the south in figure 8.2). The furnaces are dispersed about the central void with its coke yard. Here, as in the courtyard of the Humboldthain factories, Behrens confronted an operational space that interacts with, and contributes meaning to, the surrounding buildings. The program does not provide the emphatic centripetal presence of a monumental building, and Behrens adjusted his materials and his formal vocabulary accordingly.

At the Gasworks, as at the Humboldthain factory yard, the material is a dark-red, iron-clinker brick; ornament and overt classical elements, such as columns, are avoided. The magnificently hard and precise brickwork of the base and shaft of the water tower (figures 8.3–5), its lightly framed and stuccoed projecting tank enclosure, and the conical roof and finial again suggest comparison with that late medieval construction beloved by

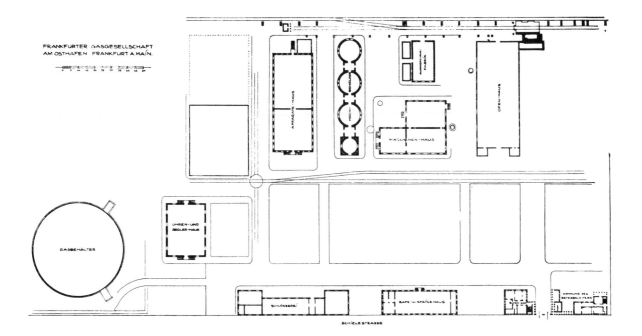

FRANKFURTER GASGESELLSCHAFT
AM OSTHAFEN. FRANKFURT A. MAIN.

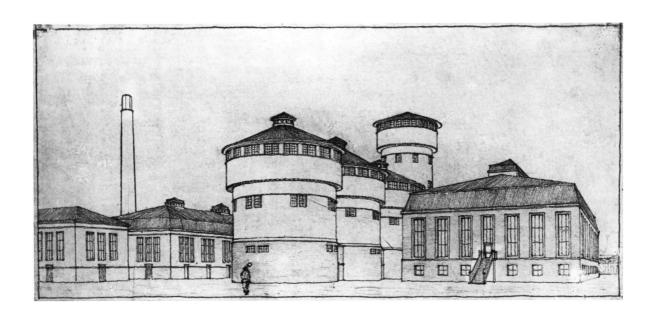

8.4 Behrens. Main-Gaswerke. Water tower.

8.5 Behrens. Main-Gaswerke. Elevation of water and chemical towers.

Friedrich Gilly, the Marienburg (figure 7.7). Typical for the dual medieval and classicizing orientation Behrens employed here, the pendentive-like transformation from the cubic base to the cylindrical shaft has the form, inverted, of a German Romanesque column with *Würfel* capital. The precise geometry is repeated in all the buildings, giving to each element of the complex a wholeness quite different from the continuous organization and the highly complex system of definitions at the Humboldthain site (figures 7.3, 7.28). Here Behrens was working with pure geometric elements that formed a larger organization while maintaining the identity of the units.

This system of planning and the fine detailing with pilaster strips, flat arches, and elegantly shadowed reveals (figures 8.6–7) suggest comparisons to both earlier and later architects: to Gilly and Schinkel as well as to Mies van der Rohe. Gropius wrote, "[Behrens] drew my attention to the stereometric secrets of the medieval mason guilds and to the geometry of the Greek architects. We often went together to see the buildings of Friedrich Schinkel in and around Potsdam, in whom he saw his artistic ancestor."[8] Examples of apt prototypes in Schinkel's work are numerous. His 1835 design for a princely Residenz deployed buildings and spaces on a geometric grid. Schloss Kamenz in Schlesien (1838–1865) was medievalizing in both its masonry and its architectural forms. The large clean-cut windows of the Feilner house in Berlin (1829) reduced the hard brick wall to a series of piers. Schinkel's Militär-Arrestanstalt in Berlin (1817–1818; figure 8.8) is a suggestive model for the Gasworks (figures 8.2, 8.6). Finally, Schinkel's brick detailing itself, in the preceding example or in the lighthouse at Arkona on Rügen (1825–1827; figure 8.9), offered clear precedent for the details of the Gasworks (figure 8.7).[9]

The planning and the brick detailing both suggest the quarter-century-later site development and brick infill of Mies van der Rohe's campus for Illinois Institute of Technology in Chicago. Some of the drawings for the Gasworks date from 1910, most from 1911.[10] The construction period was 1911–1912. Although none of the known drawings bear Mies's name, these were the years he worked in Behrens's studio. It is also in these years that Behrens's buildings employed the negative reveal (figures 8.7, 8.38, 8.40) as a standard detail—a usage that became common in modern architecture, in no small part due to Mies.[11]

Despite the neoclassical borrowings, the Gasworks, with its meticulous brickwork, its references to medieval construction, its bold juxtaposition of forms, and its centrifugal planning, is Behrens's most freely expressive complex. Among his major works, the Humboldthain factories would come next in a series of increasingly greater conventionalism.[12] The Humboldthain factories and the Gasworks, involving spaces for use interacting with built forms, elicited from Behrens some consideration of city-building. In chapter 7 his application of Sittesque principles in the Humboldthain court (figure 7.21) was contrasted with the large scale and simplified forms of buildings as observed in rapid and casual movement through the city (figure 7.27). The idea of simple forms suited to easy perception penetrates the spaces and buildings of the Gasworks. According to Hoeber, and

8.6 Behrens. Main-Gaswerke. Power station, window detail.

8.7 Behrens. Main-Gaswerke. Workshop, window detail.

8.8 Karl Friedrich Schinkel. Berlin, former Militär-Arrestanstalt (1817–1818).

8.9 Karl Friedrich Schinkel. Cape Arkona on the island of Rügen, lighthouse (1825–1827).

consistent with the changes between the factory court and the Gasworks, Behrens came to prefer the city-building ideas of A. E. Brinckmann to those of Sitte.[13] The critical difference was Brinckmann's concern with the form of a city in relation to the typical elements of which it is built; for example, the reciprocity between the typical element and the whole in neoclassical designs of the eighteenth century. In accord with this new respect for the "typical," Behrens, in a series of housing estates, changed from individually conceived asymmetrical housing groups to a greater emphasis on the typical unit.

In 1910 Behrens completed a Catholic Fellowship House in Neuss (figure 8.10) and made a design for a group of middle-class rental houses on the adjoining site.[14] The street-aligned houses enclose a quiet square entered by Sittesque turbine-streets and an asymmetrically placed monument. The "individualistic" method of composition was surprisingly similar to that of the High Voltage Factory. Each corner of the site was considered for its specific role in the cityscape. Vertical elements, passageways, and squares were used for local effect. It was a composition of interlocking volumes in which any series of bays would be transformed for a change of use or, if all else failed, interrupted arbitrarily. In plan there were large, differently shaped apartment blocks, abutting one another in changing manners and frequently requiring lightwells.

Even as Behrens began to explore the use of types, his concern for the whole would not allow him to add identical units one to another in the manner of the eighteenth-century English terraces.[15] He quickly developed an intermediate solution—neither the responsive local composition of the Neuss project (visually responsive, only; individual units were often poorly planned) nor a standard repetitive unit. Behrens conceived what

8.10 Peter Behrens. Neuss, Katholisches Gesellenhaus (1907–1910). Street view.

might be called "standardized clusters"—apartment blocks, or row houses—which preserved some of his concern for silhouette, for the enframement of space, for rhythm. In
1910–1911 he built workers' housing for the AEG on Rathenaustrasse in Hennigsdorf,
near Berlin (figure 8.11) in a configuration he was to explore repeatedly: what could be a
housing block with a continuous street front is recessed at the center to provide a courtyard with gardens front and back.[16] Both the individual apartment and the cluster of
apartments, incorporating some range of choice, were semi-standardized.

The Neuss project could have been conceived only for a specific site. The standardized clusters here under consideration (the first at Hennigsdorf; a rowhouse variant
designed for Merseburg in 1912 [figure 8.12])[17] implicitly could be built on any standardized site; that is, on any street plan—extant or possible—that required no more than
a choice among, and a slight transformation of, standardized clusters. The Merseburg project illustrates this planning technique well.[18]

Surveying the range of Behrens's work from his more expressive to his most conventional buildings, these semi-standardized housing estates occupy an approximately central point. This is implicit in their attempt, just described, to balance standard type against
a sense of place. As might be expected, in this design of rather large-scale housing for
unspecified and changing people who are nonetheless individuals, Behrens strongly asserts
neither individual expression nor the conventions of a standard design. Looking back from
a later time, one can imagine, and wish for, a warmer sense of the individuals who would
inhabit these housing estates; but at least in the case of Merseburg there is a degree of
domestic congeniality unusual in Behrens's production.

The idea of an environment responsive to an individual way of life is not, to understate the case, prominent in Behrens's work; he was too earnest about institutional, social, and cultural considerations. His environments were meant to ennoble, uplift, instruct. The idea of an environment responding to the fleeting needs of individuals would once again be an instance of what he detested most: an undue concession of art to nature.

Select examples of Behrens's residential architecture modify this assessment. The sitting room for the Schede house in Wetter (1904–1905; figure 4.6) and the Obenauer house in Saarbrücken (1905–1908), geometrically conventionalized as they are, create a responsive sense of place. The Schede room succeeds by virtue of its subdued design despite a unique role in the house. On the upper floor of an older, boxlike house, reached at the end of a long passage through the house, the Behrens room breaks through the walls of the box, restoring one to contact with the lovely rolling hills of the Ruhr valley.

8.12 Peter Behrens. Merseburg, workers' housing for the Blancke-Werke (1912).

In the Obenauer house, Behrens's achievement owes much to the difficulties imposed by the steep slope of the site (figure 8.13). The symmetries of his cubic design had to break down (figures 8.14–15); still more importantly, vertical movement through the building invited relations to light, space, and use (figure 8.16–19). Entrance from the street is axial to a point under the terrace, where one shifts to the right, beyond the basic cube of the house, before entering an elegant hall with an asymmetrically placed stair ascending to the main living spaces (figure 8.17). One enters a version of an English living-hall (figures 8.18–19), a place to be, around a fireplace, and the center of circulation for the principal floor and to the bedrooms above, passing a light-filled landing and viewing platform. Figure 8.20 shows the generous dining room with its large, sunny window; at the other end are broad glass doors to the ladies' sitting room and a glass door to the terrace.[19]

Both the Obenauer house and the room of the Schede house are essays, unusual for Behrens, in a post-Jugendstil program of *Sachlichkeit*. In the first years of the century Hermann Muthesius was an important exponent of this call for an architecture that abandoned the willful form-making of Art Nouveau and was based rather on fundamental elements of light, use, construction, sensible materials, and discrete life-style. Precedents were found in the domestic architecture of late nineteenth-century England and, more immediately, in such work as the Heymel apartment in Munich (figure 1.18) and the early work of Adolf Loos.[20] Characteristically, Behrens makes these essays in *Sachlichkeit* within more controlled geometric forms; they are both impressive for the balance of formal elegance and livability.

In the Berlin period, the only approximation to this congenial relation to particular people in a particular place is the modest Goedecke house (figures 8.25–28), the last of three houses by Behrens in Karl Ernst Osthaus's "Villa Colony" above Hagen. Osthaus, Behrens's great, virtually only, patron during the Düsseldorf period, sought to use his industrial wealth to bring avant-garde culture to his native city, Hagen, an industrial center at the hilly eastern fringe of the Ruhr district. As noted in chapter 4, Osthaus's first large endeavor was the founding of a museum devoted to all that was progressive in the fine arts—French, Belgian, and Dutch postimpressionism, for example. Henry van de Velde became the principal architect of the Folkwang Museum; Behrens designed the lecture hall (figure 4.7).

Given the proclivity of these artists and architects to relate life and art, and Osthaus's pleasure in cultural activism, the Folkwang Museum could, however, be no more than a starting point. The small city of Hagen, uphill and downwind from its factories, experienced the transformational, often deleterious effects of nineteenth-century industry: new transit systems, a larger population inadequately accommodated, and air pollution among them. Seeking to set an example, Osthaus obtained eighty acres in Eppenhausen, to the east of the city, above and away from the factory area. Van de Velde designed Osthaus's large villa, Hohenhof (1906–1908). The focus of a new culture and a new urbanism realized within modern industrial civilization, the villa included studios for an entire artists' colony.[21]

8.13 Peter Behrens.
Saarbrücken. Obenauer
house (1905–1907).
Distant view.

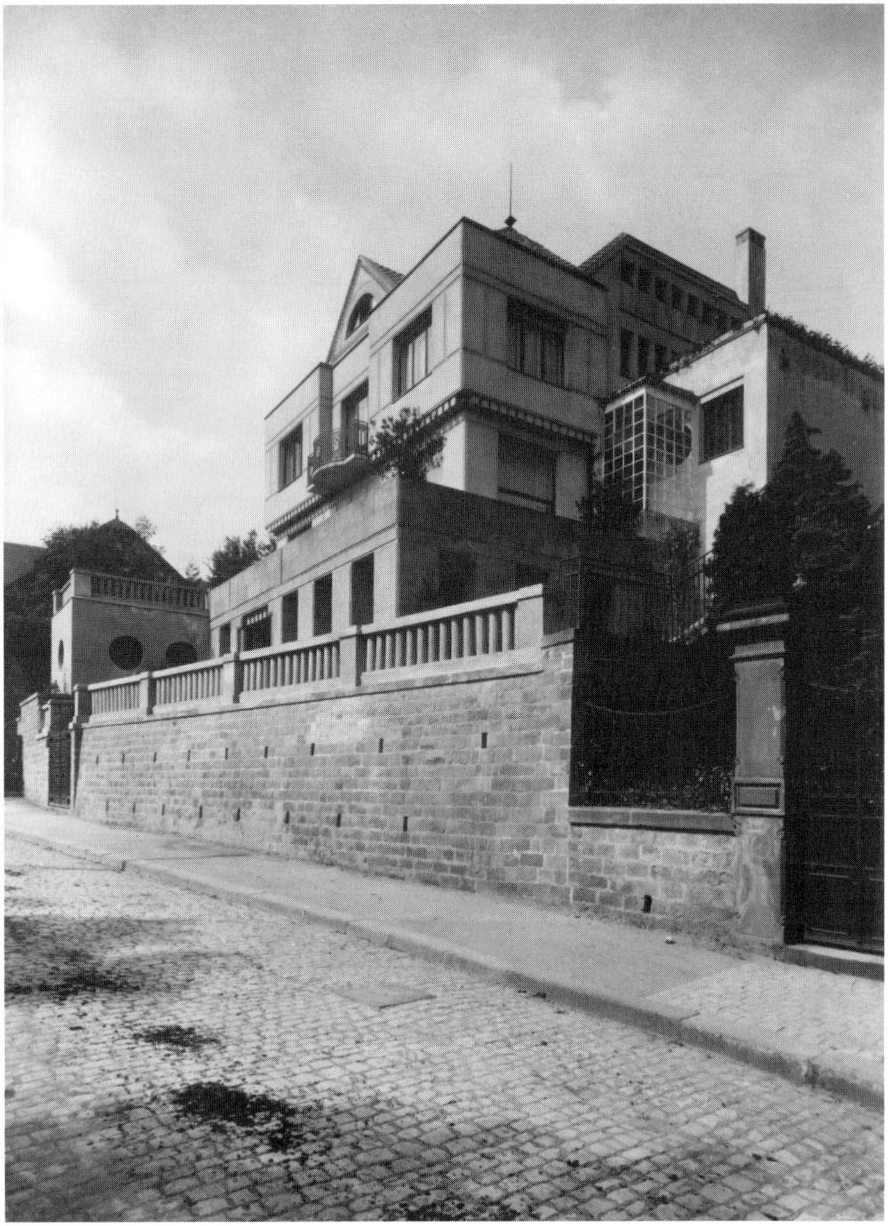

8.14 Behrens. Obenauer house.
Angle view from street.

8.15 Behrens. Obenauer house. Perspective, garden front from left of axis.

8.16 Behrens. Obenauer house. Preliminary plan of principal floor (dining room not as built).

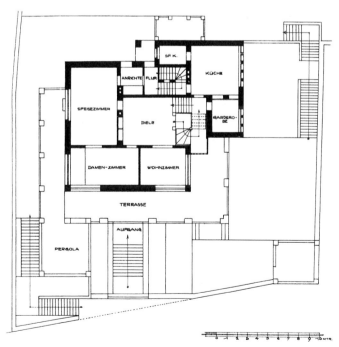

8.17 Behrens. Obenauer house. Vestibule.

8.18 Behrens. Obenauer house. Stair hall toward landing.

8.19 Behrens. Obenauer house. Stair hall toward fireplace.

Outside the gates of Hohenhof, Osthaus and Behrens established a general plan for the whole of the site. Osthaus intended to sell individual residential parcels according to an overall architectural scheme (1906).[22] Specific parts of the site, requiring detailed development, were assigned to van de Velde, Behrens, and J. L. M. Lauweriks.[23] Figure 8.21 is a bird's-eye perspective rendering of Behrens's assigned area. The principal road, Hassleyer Strasse, appears in the lower right corner. A straight street branches off to the left (east). On the axis of this street Behrens proposed a pedimented building to the right of which a passageway led to Osthaus's Hohenhof (indicated only in outline at the top of the sheet). The active public area of Osthaus's colony would have been a Sittesque square dominated by the pedimented building. Still today, though one sees only a wide spot between Hassleyer Strasse and Hohenhof, a sign marks this place as the Goldene Pforte (Golden Gate). A pedestrian cross-axis culminates in a museum building to the northwest and, through an allée of chestnut trees (Unter den Castanien [the drawing is more suggestive of poplar or cypress trees]), in an outdoor theater at the southeast.

Only the street layout, the trees, and some form of outdoor theater were realized; but the area for villas fared somewhat better. At the acute angle formed by the two major streets (near the bottom of the perspective view), Behrens wished to have a building that would make an emphatic pivot. The symmetry, the segmental central motif, and the gardens of the Cuno house (figures 8.21–23) served this purpose. Along Hassleyer Strasse, Behrens proposed three villas disposed symmetrically about a formal garden; only that nearest the Cuno house, the Schroeder house (figure 8.24), was built. The rendering of these two houses in figure 8.21 is quite accurate. The perspective must date, then, from

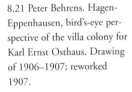

8.21 Peter Behrens. Hagen-Eppenhausen, bird's-eye perspective of the villa colony for Karl Ernst Osthaus. Drawing of 1906–1907; reworked 1907.

8.22 Peter Behrens. Hagen,
Cuno house (1907–1911).
Entry facade.

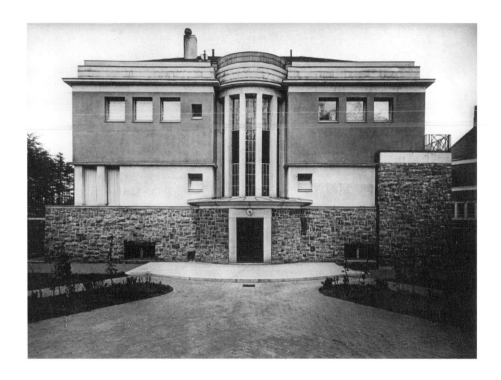

8.23 Behrens. Cuno house.
Plan.

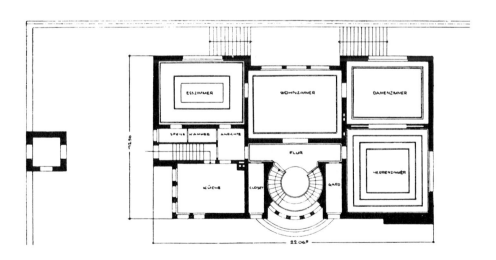

the time of the design of these houses (from 1907) and before the design of the only other executed house, the Goedecke house which, differently oriented, occupies the site of the villa nearest the outdoor theater in figure 8.21.

The house for the dentist, Schroeder (figure 8.24; also illustrated in list of works, no. 39), was built first, and apparently went rather smoothly (1908–1909).[24] Nevertheless, Osthaus later chastised Behrens for "the calamities" at the Schroeder house and the crematorium in Hagen, although Osthaus continued to serve as a faithful intermediary between the architect and the various clients.[25] In the case of the house for Mayor Cuno, Osthaus himself had to act as client.[26] In general, it seems that Behrens's formal sensibilities, his conventions, were so strong, and applied in so a priori a manner, that neither physical nor experiential problems were adequately considered. In the Cuno house, for example, the elegant stair behind the segmental motif of the front facade ascended half a flight to the level of the reception rooms only to arrive in a narrow, unlit interior corridor (figure 8.23). The rooms were boxlike and symmetrically disposed with limited interconnection. Of the four main rooms, none received light from more than one direction, and only one received any light after midday. Three of the four rooms had the same orientation and virtually identical sizes and proportions. The gardens that were visible from these three rooms did not belong to the house. The small terrace at the level of these rooms served only as a landing for two flights of stairs, the sole connection with the gardens at the ends of the house.

There were further physical problems, among them the troublesome setback of the roof (figure 8.22).[27] Its formal purpose would appear to be the union of walls and roof, avoiding the separateness, heavy shadows, and implicit horizontal extension of an over-hanging roof. The setback was one more factor in fusing the whole of the Cuno house into a closed form, of simple silhouette, demonstratively occupying and turning the corner of its site. Even conceding Behrens's concern for strong forms, his subtle but mainly superficial play with asymmetries, and his arguments in favor of architectonic gardens, the residents of such a house may well have wondered if the retreat to the suburbs brought them any real advantages.

That Goedecke fared better was probably to his own credit. The reason for Osthaus's "calamity" letter was to apprise Behrens of what difficulty Osthaus now experienced in finding clients for Behrens's part of the villa colony. Problematic construction must be avoided, especially as Goedecke wanted a small house and office for 40,000 marks. In the same letter, Osthaus reported that, in the interest of completing the initial formal group, he urged Goedecke to take the southwest corner site, opposite Schroeder (figure 8.21).[28] Goedecke himself inclined to the site near the outdoor theater.

Behrens responded while on vacation with Director Paul Jordan of the AEG at Bad Gastein. With remarkable good nature, he agreed with Osthaus about the preferred site and added that he should, for once, produce a truly inexpensive building.[29] Despite the agreement between Osthaus and Behrens, Goedecke obtained what he wanted, as he was to do throughout the process. From letters in the Osthaus-Archiv we know that Goedecke secured the site near the outdoor theater, a small lot to be laid out in accord with the house plan (letter of 1 December 1910). Goedecke retained Behrens's proposed plan to study the siting and the furniture location (5 December 1910). New plans were sent by Behrens at the end of January (2 February 1911); Goedecke was unhappy about the high cost estimates (8 March 1911). Osthaus lowered the land price from 8 to 5 marks per square meter, and chastised Behrens by citing van de Velde's efficiency (3 May 1911). Finally in Berlin, Goedecke and Behrens worked over dimensions, details, and estimates till an agreeable price was reached (12 May 1911). Admittedly these confrontations of the Maecenas, his client, and their architect contain their measure of petty unpleasantry. Nevertheless, in contrast to the neighboring houses, rather well frozen in Behrens's conventions, Goedecke's house emerged as a congenial design.[30] Apparently Behrens, given to abstractions and conventions, profited from the abrasive criticism of a client concerned with specifics.

The exterior of the Goedecke house (figures 8.27–28) is predominantly of stucco. In each elevation are skillful asymmetries, formally and functionally relevant. The narrow entrance elevation (figures 8.26–27) establishes certain continuities and expectations: the brick of the basement extends into the garden wall and, interrupted, resumes in the wall at the right; the form of the overhanging roof repeats to the left. The porch and the stair tower, just visible at the left, fragment the closed form, suggesting movement into and through the house.

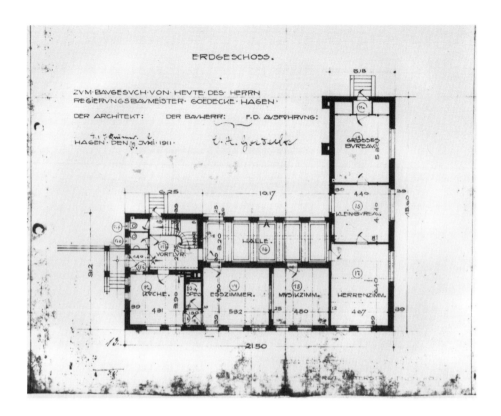

The plan (figure 8.25) is compartmentalized, but has several advances over the sterility of the Cuno house. Every room, on both floors, except for the garden-oriented hall, has exposure to the southeast; the long southerly elevation employs bands of windows (figure 8.26). Corner rooms have double exposure, as does a room in the middle of the narrow office wing. Changes in the proportions of rooms and in light sources give distinctive character to each space. Even the room that lacks southeasterly exposure, the hall–sitting room, receives light at a pleasant and appropriate time, late afternoon. It is in the hall, too, that compartmentalization diminishes; hall, terrace, and garden are at virtually the same level; French doors and large windows provide continuity of vision, movement, and use.

In the garden elevation (figures 8.26, 8.28), typical of those instances where Behrens sought to be responsive to site and use, there is a complex interlocking of volumes reminiscent of the design of the High Voltage Factory. Transformation of the cubic entrance block begins at the stair tower, increasing in the garden-hall arcade and the balcony and airy passageway above. The low office wing embraces the garden, an effect originally enhanced by a pergola running into the garden, parallel to the hall, from the walled recess outside the large office.

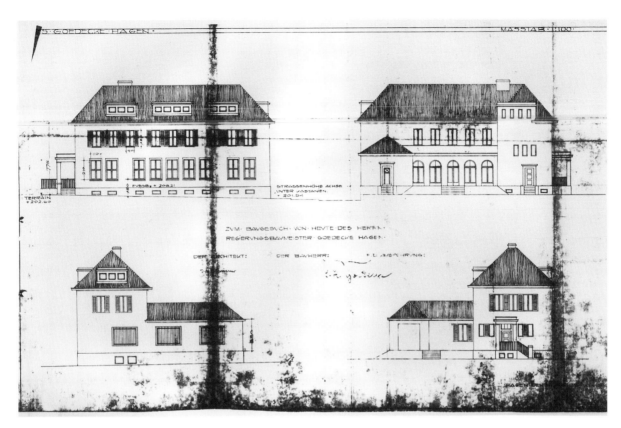

8.26 Behrens. Goedecke
house. Elevations.

8.27 Behrens. Goedecke house. West front.

8.28 Behrens. Goedecke house. Garden front.

This is a rare instance of Behrens designing, within a single building, patterns of changing interaction with the site. His own inclination was toward what he called closed, restful forms. When his commissions were for individual buildings related to imposing organizations, this inclination was intensified and, seemingly, the sources of abrasive criticism were diminished.

Moving from domestic to institutional buildings, consider first the conventionalization evident in the suburban villa Behrens designed for the noted classical scholar and metropolitan figure, Dr. Theodor Wiegand, at Berlin-Dahlem (figures 8.29–33).[31] From the archaic Doric atrium to the tennis tempietto in the garden, there is a masterful, strong but subdued classicism. In the body of the house, inside and out, the classicism reduces to fine

8.29 Peter Behrens. Berlin-Dahlem, Wiegand house (1911–1912). Site and house plan.

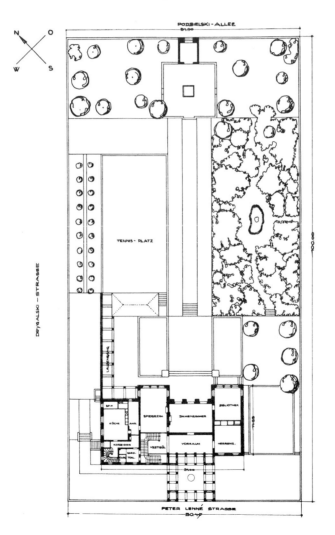

proportions and detail. No doubt formality was appropriate to the situation; it is no surprise that the house serves well today, virtually undisturbed, in institutional use.

Recall that in 1908 Behrens spoke of "monumental art as the highest, the intrinsic expression of the culture of a time. Such an art finds its expression, naturally, in that realm where a people are most accomplished, where they are most intensely engaged, by which they are moved."[32] At the dedication (10 December 1912) of the new offices of the Mannesmannröhren-Werke, in Düsseldorf (figures 8.34–40), before an impressive audience of businessmen, industrialists, and politicians, Behrens elaborated the contemporary significance of his theory of monumental art: "The development of monumental art has always been the expression of a definite group of the powerful interests in an epoch."[33] He reinforced his historical and polemical points by claiming that the monumental art of the Middle Ages owed its existence to the power of the Church, that of the baroque to royalty, that of the time around 1800 to the bourgeoisie. Monumental art of the early twentieth century must stem from the distinctive power establishment of its time: modern industry.

8.31 Behrens. Wiegand
house. Garden and garden
front.

8.32 Behrens. Wiegand
house. Vestibule.

Behrens repeated his dictum that monumentality required "cubic compactness and creation of large forms."[34] However, one must acknowledge that now, abandoning the unmitigated pursuit of pure form of his Düsseldorf period, Behrens could integrate material, functional, and historical concerns within his vision of monumental art for industry. In his dedicatory address, using a gambit common among architects, he claimed that the Mannesmann building derived from an examination of use. This was more than mere rhetoric, however, and there was more than sheer formalism in the building.

Behrens's own account of the design process is worth repeating, for it shows how much his thinking had changed under the impact of the AEG commissions. First pointing out the inadequacy of a building program conceived as a mere list of departments and square footages, he continued:

There are much more important things involved: one must know and comprehend the organic structure of a great administrative body, the functional importance of its different members for each other, and its nervous system, in order to be able to create a healthy body for this complicated organism.

A careful study of this organism disclosed the following vital requirements: the rooms must have the best possible light; direct communication from each room to

8.34 Peter Behrens. Düssel-
dorf, Mannesmannröhren-
Werke, Main Office
Building (1910–1912).
Perspective from northwest.

8.35 Behrens. Mannesmann
offices. View from southwest.

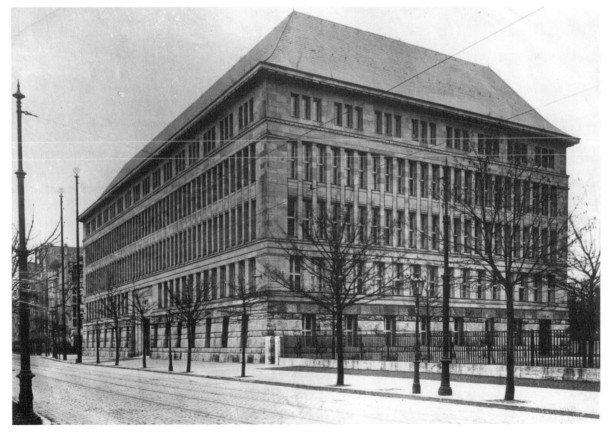

8.36 Behrens. Mannesmann
offices. Plan of ground floor.

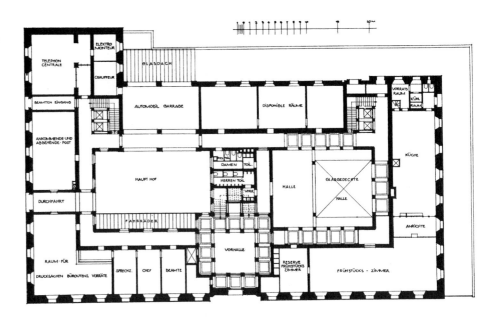

8.37 Behrens. Mannesmann
offices. Plan of basic "cell" of
open plan.

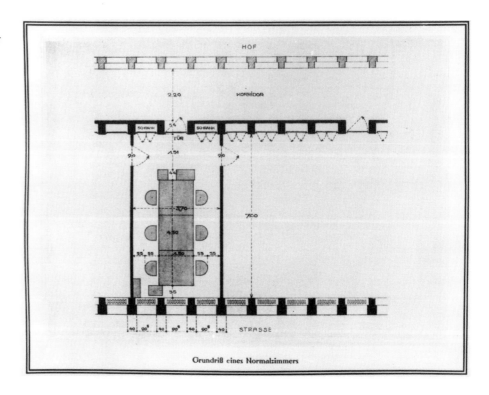

8.38 Behrens. Mannesmann offices. Entrance.

8.39 Behrens. Mannesmann offices. Entrance hall.

8.40 Behrens. Mannesmann offices. Entrance hall, column and beam intersection.

every other one; it must be possible at all times to alter the size of the different rooms, and the whole building must provide the best possible working accommodations.

I shall now explain how I have endeavored to meet these requirements. The different kinds of work done in the various departments made a difference in the size of the separate rooms necessary; in one place a large workroom was required, in another a small office room.

It was developed that the smallest room required was one to contain only one desk, at which six persons could work. This is, in a way of speaking, the unit of the building, the single cell of the whole body [figure 8.37]. Exact measurements were made of the surface of the desk, of the depth of the chair and of the room required to permit one to pass between the chair and the wall. The distance from the windows and the radiators beneath them was determined, as well as the space required for the typewriter tables and tables for letters and documents. In addition, it was found what space was required for an unobstructed passage from door to door and for filing cases. The total gave a minimum but adequate floor area for a normal office room.

The walls of this room established at the same time the method of construction which resulted in an arrangement of piers in which four are at the narrow sides of the room and also, at equal intervals, on the outer wall of the corridor. The spaces beneath the windows accommodated the radiators, and on the opposite side provided room for the filing cases and the entrance door.

This arrangement of piers, which is shown on the plan, greatly increases the utilization of the normal room's space. In addition to that, this arrangement of 40 cm wide columns at comparatively small intervals, had the further advantage of improving the lighting of the room. The windows, situated between the four piers, 90.5 cm wide and reaching to the ceiling, give a lighting surface of approximately 8 sq. m. It is not a matter of indifference whether this surface is cut out of the wall in one unbroken surface, in which case parts of the wall would remain and give dark corners, or whether, as in the case in the arrangement of piers presented, the corners remain light. In the first case the light is centralized and rendered harsh, and produces dense shadows in the room. In the other case—the one before us—it is rendered diffuse by the reflection of walls and ceiling, without any considerable shadows. Thus the room is lighted equally well clear to the opposite wall, despite its comparatively great depth of 7 meters. In other words, not merely the quantity of light but its distribution is also important. This will be the better understood if one compares an intensive lamp with an indirect system in which the light is reflected from all parts of the ceiling and thus gives a very much better light for working.

A third advantage appeared to lie in this arrangement of the piers. As often as I endeavored, in consultation with the directors, to lay out the separate departments in the building, to assign each office of these departments to its most suitable location, just so often it became apparent that, according to whether the momentary condition of business or the future development was considered, a different layout offered still greater advantages. Thus it seemed to me as if the right arrangement for definitely final purposes never could be found. In a talk with the general director of the works it also became obvious that no solution could be found along these lines. Then I said to him: "Even after your administrative building has been erected you will still always be in doubt as to how you are to lay out your departments to fit in with the business conditions at any specified time. Therefore I shall build you a building which is arranged like a big hall in which you can partition off rooms as you like to meet the requirements that may arise at any moment." . . .

For this reason supporting cross walls were not employed in the construction, the whole building being erected on a system of open floors. The walls that now partition off the various large or small rooms are free, soundproof partitions which can be taken out without much trouble or set up in other places.

The open floor system offered advantages not merely for the rooms, but also the corridors. These could be built with the comparatively small width of 2.20 meters, since they are very light because of the long rows of windows due to the arrangement of the piers. Thus they lead around the courts in a gallery-like manner, and create the effect of participating in the breadth and spaciousness of the courts.

The plan [figure 8.36] shows how all the offices lie on the outside of the building and are without exception lighted by the same arrangement of windows. For that reason this building is probably at present writing one of the brightest and best lighted office buildings in existence.[35]

The topics of Behrens's discussion—organization, communications, circulation, dimensional studies, lighting, and accommodations of changing use (he spoke of integrated mechanical systems, too)—remain relevant today. How to accommodate changing use also remains a live issue. Indeed, later architects often endorsed less subtle conceptions of the design process than Behrens. For example, it is significant that the 1925 American translation has Behrens saying "an exact program must be prepared in advance," and going on to say that the program must be more complex than mere square footages. In the original, Behrens said that the Mannesmann "directors had prepared in advance an exact program; but the first plan sketches showed . . . ,"[36] and he went on to describe *not* a system of exact programming, but of complex interaction among program, technical design, and formal matters.

Such systematic interaction may be illustrated with Behrens's use of serial windows for generalized office activity (figures 8.35–37). Concerning the advantages of a continuous band of windows over windows that are holes in walls, Behrens's explanation (more light, but especially better distributed light) is virtually duplicated by Le Corbusier when referring to his strip windows at the Weissenhof Siedlung in 1927.[37] But while the architect devoted to exact programming might take this as a given, both Behrens and Le Corbusier interpreted the distribution of light in relation to other formal, and ultimately philosophical, concerns. Le Corbusier's window was actually continuous (a strip) because it contributed to the fulfillment of a general theory of the free plan and the free facade suspended lightly in front of the structure. Behrens's window was part of a continuous band of windows where the closely spaced solid piers played several important roles: they modulated the light; provided frequent positions for convenient abutting of partitions; and, most importantly for Behrens, established a visual whole more solid than a wall pierced with holes. In his words: "If one views the building not exactly from its axis, but by approaching from any one of its sides, the windows do not have the effect of openings. Instead, the masonry of the piers dominates and produces a satisfactory and uniform façade effect" (figure 8.35).[38]

In contrast to Le Corbusier's generalized extension of the free plan, Behrens's open floor plan was for use when appropriate to function—and even then it had to be brought within conventional formal constraints. Both Behrens and Le Corbusier were aware of, and involved in, the interaction of form and use. Behrens's formal predilections being retrospective, his design process engaged overt historical precedent. In the German publication of his dedicatory address, Behrens showed historical precedents for the Mannesmann building (significantly omitted from the 1925 American edition, which dwelt on Behrens's modernity).[39] Behrens illustrated the Palazzo Strozzi and the Palazzo Riccardi of Florence as classic prototypes for that closed form and grand corporeality which he sought. The horizontal divisions of the Mannesmann facades (figure 8.34–35) into rusticated base, principal floors, and friezelike top floor reveal this influence of the Italian Renaissance. Still more suggestive for the overall form and proportions of the Mannesmann building is the museum in Namur, Belgium (figure 8.41), which Behrens had seen and appreciated for its serene effect. Not mentioned was another Belgian building, the seventeenth-century Curtius House, now Museum, in Liège (figure 8.42). More elegantly detailed than the former market building in Namur, the Maison Curtius has several parallels with Mannesmann: the waterfront site, bands of windows, roof shape, and the towered projection of the wall plane through the roof (as at the rear of the Mannesmann).

Behrens also showed an engraving of the old Hansa trading building in Antwerp and a photograph of a grand, blocky building of 1660 in Hamburg. Both had continuous bands of windows, a detail he saw as establishing "the type" of the office building. Behrens's other historical examples (the city halls of Paderborn and of Ghent) served only to reinforce the idea that there is important and honored precedent for the creation of "types," building forms that witness to their immediate purpose and their societal significance. The Mannesmann building was to accomplish this for the modern industrial office.[40]

At the scale of the city, Behrens envisioned the banks of the Rhine in Düsseldorf lined with buildings of this "type" rather than with the smaller-scale, gabled structures then adjoining the Mannesmann building:

8.41 Namur, Belgium.
Archaeological Museum,
late sixteenth century.

8.42 Liège, Belgium. Curtius
House, ca. 1600–1610.

There can no longer be any doubt that in the large German cities the sanitary and attractive dwelling houses are being steadily forced to the outskirts and the suburbs, and that, starting from the center, the inner city is regularly becoming more and more an exclusive business section. This being the case, it is proper not to regard this too seriously but merely as something that cannot be helped, and then to strive deliberately to attain the character of a proud business city, and to desire that all undertakings in this city be directed toward developing this characteristic to the utmost. A city should be viewed as a united, architectural creation, and nothing more overpowering could be conceived than the accomplishment of a harmonious character and stylistic idea in an entire city.[41]

What is the key to the origin, or to the understanding, of the Mannesmann building? Is it a concept of office lighting, the open floor plan, or the demand for large, closed forms? Is it a concern for historical precedent, the traditional significance of forms, a new scale of events, a formally unified city, a resignation about how life is to be lived in modern industrial cities? It is doubtful that Behrens himself could have told us. As at the end of chapter 7, we are again confronted with Behrens's sense of simultaneous engagement and foreboding. It is beyond question, however, that he understood an artistic process and could now orchestrate a wide range of factors in conceiving a building that is a masterpiece within its own difficult set of concerns. One cannot say where such a process begins; the least one can do is not underestimate its complexity. To Behrens's credit he continually sought a more comprehensive grasp of architectural design within the modern situation.

In 1913–1914, Behrens built a commercial property for Frank und Lehmann in Cologne.[42] The elevation on the side street (figure 8.43) is similar to that of the High Voltage Factory, but more urbane. The windows vary according to location and use; Behrens's interpenetration of wall and roof is here aided by cubic dormers. The symmetry, palazzo-like arrangement of floors, and beautifully detailed and executed stonework bespeak its central location in the city. The facade on the principal street, with fluted pilasters on its slightly projected central area and a complementary unification of the dormers above, goes a step further in the adoption of established conventions.

In this survey starting with Behrens's expressive Gasworks, we finally arrive at his most strenuously conventionalized work, the German Embassy in St. Petersburg.[43] The word "conventional" is used here to refer, within a creative process, to the often inventively employed factors of artistic medium and tradition. When applied to the Embassy, the word easily extends to include another meaning that becomes increasingly relevant in the critique of Behrens's buildings: the evocative power of stylistic motifs made common by repeated use.

In the case of the Embassy, the desire for historically sanctioned stylistic convention might well be assumed to flow from the patronage of the German state rather than from the architect. However, the mutual interest of these parties was recalled by Edmund

Schüler (a member of Hitler's government who claimed to have won for Behrens the 1938 commission to design the unexecuted German Embassy in Washington).[44] Schüler was a member of the Foreign Office in 1911 when money was appropriated for the German Embassy in St. Petersburg. He was also a friend of Wiegand, the classicist whose house was being built by Behrens. After a pilgrimage, as he called it, to Behrens's AEG factories, Schüler was so impressed with this union of a new industrial architecture with Hellenic antiquity that he determined the St. Petersburg Embassy should be by Behrens.

Schüler reports that he went to his own superior and then directly to the secretary of state, Alfred von Kiderlen-Wächter. Within an hour he was authorized to contact Behrens. Behrens soon received the commission, with eight weeks allowed for design and thirteen months for completion. In seven weeks, the design was presented to von Kiderlen. It received his approval, that of the Kaiser, and, with reservations, that of the president of the Bauakademie. Figure 8.45 is from an ozalid print of Behrens's design in the records of the Foreign Office.

The Embassy's strenuous conventionalization is partially explained by the people whose approval the design needed. However, Mies van der Rohe's testimony assures that Behrens was not coerced by the state—that at that time a commission for an embassy could not have been conceived independently of such conventionalism.[45] The state expected such a building to have a worthy character, but the architect shared the expectation. Karl Scheffler wrote of Behrens as "no revolutionary but rather an active conservative," a man who loved ceremony and would gladly have been court architect.[46] Schüler's anecdote of Behrens's playing a prince in order to receive better service on their trips to St. Petersburg adds a desperately needed measure of charm to this situation.

While this discussion indicates Behrens's increasing use of reminiscent stylistic conventions, he continued to hold formal and historicist conventions uppermost: historical motifs were as much subject to his "will to form" as were materials, engineering, use, and all pragmatic considerations. Acknowledging mannerist and neoclassical precedent, a comparison of the Embassy facade with classical prototypes will most readily indicate this supremacy of abstract form and historicist symbolism over stylistic convention in Behrens's work.[47]

8.44 Peter Behrens. St. Petersburg, Russia, German Embassy (1911–1913). Plan of principal floor.

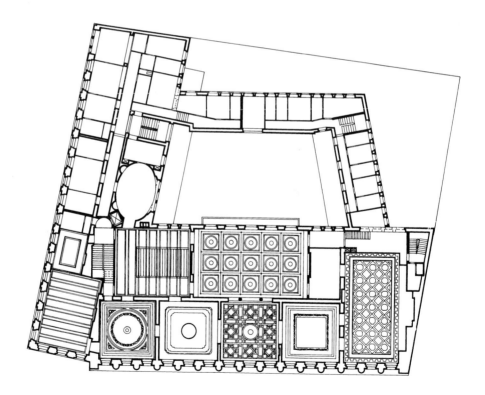

8.45 Behrens. St. Petersburg, German Embassy. Perspective (ca. 1912).

Composed of separate drums, the ancient Doric column was nevertheless crafted and detailed to appear as a single element. Behrens's engaged Doric order (figure 8.46) is overtly detailed to show each stone, smaller than a drum, as similar to the wall elements at either end and in the trabeation above; indeed, the rock face cutting of the columns is cruder than that of the frame. On the other hand, while ancient Greek drums were suppressed in favor of the columnar whole, Greek columns maintained individuality within the ordinance of the temple. Entasis, fluting, a distinctive capital, evident separateness from the stylobate, all served to make the Doric column recognizable in itself as well as adjusted to the whole. It was this distinction of part and simultaneous interdependence of part and whole that underlay the theory of *Tektonik*.[48] This concept is less evident in Behrens's Doric order at St. Petersburg than in the iron arches of the side elevation of the Turbine Factory (frontispiece). Despite Behrens's desired and achieved sense of the whole, the iron arches are identifiable, functioning elements contributing to a larger, framed structure. At St. Petersburg, he countered the characteristic form of the Doric order: beyond the legibility of individual cut stones, there is also the omission of fluting and entasis, the extreme reduction of the capital, and the elongation of the proportions. Finally, his elaborately built-up order is framed in a wall that is part of the same plane. It is a fusion of wall and column, and thus recalls at once Roman prototypes and his own Small Motors Factory for the AEG (figure 7.27).

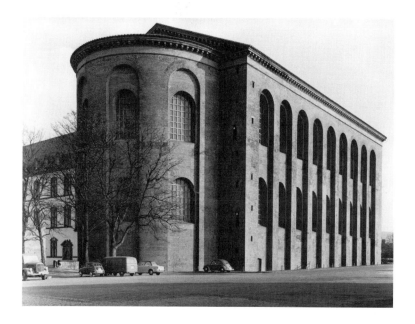

Roman buildings, the Coliseum in Rome, for example, often were of wall and vault construction but with facades of an engaged columnar order. In such instances, the grid of columns and architraves overlays the wall architecture. Whatever criticism may be brought against this Roman practice, it did present a vivacious simulation of a tectonic structure screening the more monolithic structure beyond—quite different from the coerced and ambiguous existence of Behrens's engaged order.

One final comparison is also telling. A Roman structure such as the so-called Basilica at Trier (figure 8.47) used no engaged order. As the building has been known in modern times, there is no question about the integral quality of the entire facade: the entire building exists as a holistic, though perforated, wall architecture. The wall was, however, carved away to a considerable extent, establishing a quality that can be related to Behrens's Small Motors Factory (figure 7.27) and then to the Embassy (figure 8.46). In the Basilica, there is no sense of the suppression of the pier—quite the contrary, it is a monolithic wall architecture giving way to articulation and a less inert system of organization. The piers seem, like a sculpture, to be emerging into life as the excess material is removed: emergent, still becoming. In the Small Motors Factory, and decidedly in the Embassy, Behrens presented ambiguous situations. In the Factory, the piers of a wall architecture developed not in the manner of Gothic shafts but into stillborn columns. To continue the sculptural analogy, there is here an evocation of the pathos induced by Michelangelo's never-to-be-finished Boboli slaves. In the Embassy, the reverse process is suggested: what once were tectonic elements merge into the monolithic whole; there is a chilling ossification of the column that

8.48 Behrens. St. Petersburg,
German Embassy. Facade,
central section.

8.49 Behrens. St. Petersburg, German Embassy. Entrance vestibule with view to courtyard.

8.50 Behrens. St. Petersburg, German Embassy. Throne room.

once had vitality. Schüler, looking back from Nazi times, spoke admiringly of both these facades where ordered thoughts, proud and affirming, march alongside one another. "The need of the time was subordination."[49]

The Embassy represents the assertive employment of both retrospective stylistic convention and that more complex, more interesting conception of convention, the unavoidable role of the artist's medium. But like his Doric order, Behrens's sense of formal convention ossified rather than coming to a life of its own. The ossification increased with the passage of the Berlin years and increasing responsibility to an economic-military-power elite. Behrens's formal conventions were always rather brittle; consideration of the series of buildings leading to the Embassy suggests that he never fully comprehended the potential of the abstract formal aspect of convention. In Behrens's work, not only the Doric column and the stylistic conventions that it represented but also the more abstract formal conventions were all subordinated to a visually expressive role. His factories and institutions alike, conventionalized, centripetal buildings of closed masses, were expressions of resignation in the face of a modern authoritarian, industrial state. Behrens's preliminary design for a communal building in Lübeck (figure 8.51) continues his reduced classicism, if less representationally in this civic role. Yet a subsequent design was the most stolid, monumental design of Behrens's career.[50]

In this treatment of stylistic and formal convention as expression, Behrens was not so different from his neoclassical or even neo-Gothic predecessors. But Schinkel, to whom he is so often indebted, is lyrical by comparison, at once respectful of stylistic conventions like the column and inventive in abstract form. The expressive megalomania of Ledoux and Boullée, who also delighted in clothing industrial buildings and cultural monuments in a classicizing expressionism, is a better analog to all but the most operationally oriented works by Behrens. Effectively, Behrens was seeking an *architecture parlante* for modern times.

Behrens respected the classicists of "the time of Goethe" but knew that, with the passage of a century, his own expression had to be different. It is not too surprising that his Embassy is a still more cold-blooded version of the already rather harsh eclectic classicism of Alfred Messel's AEG Office Building (1905–1906).[51] Looking back from our own time, we owe it to Behrens to recognize that, in those Berlin years, the several impacts of religion and culture and the state were different. He worked in a very different time and at the end of a period. All this is evoked in this account of St. Petersburg in the first days of August 1914:

> Memoirs tell of wildly enthusiastic demonstrations; of processions with flags and icons; of constant cheering and singing of hymns; of the great levée held by the Tsar in the Winter Palace; of the moving response of those present to his brave words about Russia's never laying down her arms until the last invader had been driven from her soil; and of the crowds then kneeling on the square before the palace as the Tsar made his appearance on the balcony. All these things took place, as did also the

Vorläufiger Entwurf zu einem Kaiser-Wilhelm-Volkshause.

8.51 Peter Behrens. Lübeck, Kaiser-Wilhelm-Volkshaus, a cultural center. Preliminary design (1912–1913).

sacking of the German Embassy and the destruction of its art treasures by a ferocious mob, ostensibly motivated by similar sentiments of patriotic fervour.[52]

It was the beginning of World War I and, as it was later to prove, of the Russian Revolution. Under the circumstances, the German Embassy would have been sacked regardless of its appearance; but Behrens could hardly have given the "mob" a more apt symbol to attack.

In the face of the 1914 war, Germans evidenced an exhilaration and a spiritual response that "sprang from something deeper than patriotism"—the release from the intolerable emptiness of bourgeois life in Wilhelmine Germany.[53] Behrens joined in the enthusiasm for the war as a signatory of the so-called "Manifesto of the 93 German Intellectuals," attempting to defend German action—especially the illegal invasion of Belgium—in the face of world opinion.[54] When war ended, however, not only Behrens's Embassy but the world he celebrated had been sacked. It is true that he celebrated that world darkly, resigned to its conflation of modern industrial society with aristocratic German tradition. But the war and its aftermath were a much larger threat to the ancient forms than to Germany's industrialism.

Behrens's position in these years is well summarized by his participation in an important event just prior to the outbreak of war: the Deutscher Werkbund exhibition and convention in Cologne in 1914 and especially the famous debate that arose there between

Hermann Muthesius and Henry van de Velde. The Cologne exhibition, the largest and most comprehensive endeavor of the Deutscher Werkbund, was sited on the right bank of the Rhine, downstream from Deutz. Decreed at the Werkbund convention in Vienna in 1912, the Cologne exhibition was considered a great opportunity to demonstrate the Werkbund's rapid and effective unification of artists, craftsmen, industry, and commerce in the realization of quality products. This achievement included not only artifacts but also graphics, architecture, and city planning. The exhibition was conceived and executed as a demonstration of excellence over this entire range of design activities.[55]

The many facets of the Cologne exhibition would support an extensive study.[56] Behrens's Albertian Festhalle (figure 8.52), the main meeting hall at the exhibition, is so uninventive as to be an offense to its prototypes.[57] More than any other design by Behrens, this hall is allied to the Italian Renaissance; the interior is more familiar in that it is a much larger variant on the interior of the crematorium in Hagen.

With a few notable exceptions—the small Glass Pavilion by Bruno Taut, for example[58]—the conservatism of Behrens's hall is typical of the Cologne exhibition. The obtuse nude males and the compact horses of the sculpture over the portal by Eberhard Encke—the same sculpture as that placed above the St. Petersburg Embassy facade—and the similar motif of Behrens's poster (figure 8.53) display a discomforting conjunction of intended idealization and evident malformation of both natural and artistic form.

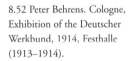

8.52 Peter Behrens. Cologne, Exhibition of the Deutscher Werkbund, 1914, Festhalle (1913–1914).

Later, Walther Rathenau was to describe a position that incorporated both innovation and tradition: "life in its vigor is neither new nor antique, but young."[59] Behrens tried to walk that difficult line, at Frankfurt (figure 8.3) and Berlin (figure 7.21) with considerable success. At Cologne, however, all genuine youthfulness is lost in submission to established formulas; compare the vital youth of Behrens's self-asserting Prometheus of the 1890s (figure 3.2) with the organized Prometheus of 1914 astride the powerful horse of industry (figure 8.53). In the later work, the horse, the man, and even the flame of the torch accept the standard of the frame—are constrained, that is, by convention.

For Behrens there was a continuing but now rather tensionless ambivalence between the individuality of the artist and the dictates of mass, industrial society. The poster maintained a modicum of discomfort, a memory of these tensed forces; Behrens's Festhalle almost wholly suppressed the conflict within a set of accepted conventions.[60] Within the Festhalle, however, the conflict was played out in a dramatic debate. The main protago-

8.53 Peter Behrens. Poster for the Exhibition of the Deutscher Werkbund, Cologne (1914).

nists were Hermann Muthesius and Henry van de Velde; the slogans were, respectively, *Typisierung* and *Individualität*.[61] On 3 July 1914, at the Werkbund convention, Hermann Muthesius was to give a programmatic speech on the future orientation of the Werkbund.[62] The night before, van de Velde received a copy of the ten theses that Muthesius was to issue in his speech. Severely critical of Muthesius's program for the Werkbund, van de Velde prepared ten countertheses and an immediate rebuttal to Muthesius's speech.[63]

Muthesius's first four points are the most important:

1. Architecture, and with it the entire creative activity of the Werkbund, strives toward the development of types [*Typisierung*]. Only in this way can architecture attain again the general significance that it had in times of harmonious culture.

2. Only by means of *Typisierung,* which should be conceived as the result of a salutary concentration [of forces], can a universally valued and sure taste be reattained.

3. An effective dissemination of German arts and crafts in other lands will not develop until a general high level of taste is reached.

4. The world will seek our products only when these evidence a convincing stylistic expression.

To which van de Velde responded:

1. As long as there are artists in the Werkbund and as long as they still have an influence on its destiny, they will protest against every proposal of a canon or *Typisierung.* In his innermost essence, the artist is an ardent individualist, a free spontaneous creator; he will never submit himself to a discipline that forces him to accept a type or canon. He instinctively mistrusts everything that could sterilize his actions and everyone who preaches a rule that could hinder him from exploring his thoughts to their own free ends—a rule that would drive him into a universal form which he can see only as a mask that seeks to make a virtue of a lack of ability.[64]

Van de Velde claimed that the artist was inspired to a new style through his conscious and unconscious submission to suprapersonal currents of the time. For twenty years, many members of the Werkbund had sought, van de Velde continued, the forms and the decorations that would bespeak their epoch; but none of these artists would wish to impose these forms on others as "types." Before a new style would be achieved, further generations must work on what had only been begun. Furthermore, the attractiveness of creative activity would exist only as long as the goal was unachieved; in the moment of achievement the physiognomy of the style would be fixed and the era of imitation and fruitlessness would begin.

No one could mistake van de Velde's defense of the creative role of the artist in the face of a threat that was open to various interpretations. The Werkbund almost shattered on this confrontation—the artists generally siding with van de Velde while other members remained neutral or leaned toward Muthesius.[65] Walter Gropius and Karl Ernst Osthaus planned a confrontation with Muthesius and, if necessary, a secession of the artists from the Werkbund. Muthesius's withdrawal of his ten theses muted the organizational but not the polemical side of this conflict.[66]

All of this would come as no great surprise but for the fact that later historians taught us to associate both Muthesius's *Typisierung* and Gropius's model factory at the Werkbund Exhibition with industrial standardization and the cold, impersonal form supposedly demanded by the twentieth century.[67] Such an interpretation distorts the intentions of both men. Gropius's model factory at Cologne was intensely involved with both tradition and art. Its administration building, factory court, factory, and exhibition pavilion had the plan—and to some degree the form—of the gatehouse, atrium, basilica, and baptistery of an Early Christian church complex (e.g., reconstructions of Old St. Peter's in Rome). Reliefs flanked the main entrance and a sculptural nude reclined outside the "baptistery." Standardization and mechanized production were not uppermost in Gropius's mind; he simply substituted the more articulated and less rigorous Early Christian forms in place of Behrens's temple as the model for a factory.

Muthesius too had broader concerns than industrial standardization; he emphasized architecture in his theses because his *Typisierung* referred mainly to the establishment of certain norms in the interest of a unified formal character in the cityscape. Muthesius's own buildings for the Cologne exhibition relied on a canon of light, flat, planar walls, reduced classical elements, and simple geometrical forms.[68] Although this canon controlled most of the exhibition buildings, this dominant character of Cologne 1914 has been obscured by the renown of the buildings that broke with the norm—Bruno Taut's *Glashaus,* Gropius's factory, and van de Velde's theater.[69] Muthesius's canon and Gropius's exceptional building accord with the opposed polemical camps and shift the meaning of *Typisierung* from industrial standardization to stylistic conventionalism.

In a frankly pro–van de Velde interpretation, Karl Scheffler contrasted the (*Typisierung*) eclectics, theoreticians, and opportunists to the (*Individualität*) free artists and vital talents; the advocates of the *impersonal norm* to the *personal form;* those who seek the economically possible to those who seek an artistic ideal.[70] Although unbalanced, Scheffler's criticism by means of comparisons does remind us of the many theoretical poles that these artists and critics sought to establish. Just in the literature cited here are a series of related pairs of concepts: relative to the object, norm and form; relative to time, tradition and innovation; relative to the artist, convention and expression; relative to the person, understanding and feeling; relative to knowledge, analysis and synthesis; relative to professions, technician and artist; relative to use, practical and beautiful; ontologically, being and becoming.

It may be suggested that Muthesius's advocacy of *Typisierung* set off and continued to arouse violent reactions because it not only polarized the theoretical pairs (a disservice in itself) but also seemed to unite one word from each pair into a set of concepts implying a strict program. Muthesius had long advocated *Sachlichkeit* and an openness to the world of modern engineering and industrial production. By the evidence of the Werkbund exhibition itself, Muthesius also advocated the simple, unified, and conventionalized domestic and urban forms of the eighteenth century and of German neoclassicism. *Typisierung* thus seemed to unite norms, traditions, conventions, intellect, analysis, technique, and functionalism in a formidably conservative program. A sensitive man like van de Velde could only overreact, embracing form, innovation, expression, feeling, synthesis, art, and the beautiful. In the heat of the polemic, most artists could only side with van de Velde.

In the Werkbund discussion, Behrens did not ally himself with either side; or perhaps he allied himself with both sides. If the polarization of the debate was false, however, Behrens was correct in refusing to be categorized as favoring either norm or form. In allying himself with both sides, Behrens was seeking an understanding; he used the word "type" as he himself had used it before, to describe an achievement such as he felt his Mannesmann Office Building (figure 8.35) to be. Behrens prepared his defense of "type" by disclaiming an understanding of what Muthesius meant by *Typisierung.* He assumed there was no intention to impose a canon; rather he thought of the artistic formulation of *types,* an activity he took to be the highest goal of any artistic activity. By type, Behrens meant, for example, what he considered to be the functionally and aesthetically refined and perfected house types of numerous European cities. Shifting to a contemporary problem, Behrens observed that a department store fully expressive of such an enterprise was obviously better architecture than a department store that looked like a castle. Such a formulation of a type, according to Behrens, resulted from the ultimate expression of a personality *and* the mature solution of the problem—a solution free of all secondary characteristics. Behrens concluded that it was in this manner that he understood the important goal of achieving the "typical" in art, and that such an understanding retained the protection of artistic freedom as the most sacred commandment of the Werkbund movement.[71]

From his other writings, one knows that a Hegelian spirit of the times and a spirit of the people is lurking just behind Behrens's statement. Furthermore, the fact that he claimed the necessity of the artist's deep involvement in the formulation of types would not have satisfied those artists who wanted particular solutions to particular problems. Still, Behrens was maintaining a rational position devoid of false polarizations. If the polemical situation had not been so highly charged, his measured and conciliatory statement might have redirected the conflict.

Thinking in terms of dialectical pairs and their polarization is a recurrent problem in German theory of art. E. H. Gombrich's article "Norm and Form" provides examples and warns of the abuse that these polar terms can work—especially on the unwary.[72] An example he does not cite is Karl Scheffler's use of the same rhyming words, *norm* and *form,* in describing the polarization of the Werkbund meeting in 1914. As an advocate of the Germanic or northern spirit, which he believed was most clearly evidenced in the Gothic and in German baroque/rococo, Scheffler supported the *form* pole ("free artist," "personal form," "artistic ideal") against the *norm,* which represented all that was impersonal and uncreative. He even extended the word *norm* to cover industrial standards derived for economic gain.

Gombrich *is* more wary, but even his discussion might give us more pause were it not for the fact that we are studying artists and critics who operated with precisely these theoretical poles. Despite the passage of fifty years, Gombrich's formulation could illuminate the Werkbund debate not only historically but in a direct theoretical confrontation. For Gombrich, *norm* and *form* are a way of dealing with an ingrained aspect of our Western artistic tradition: the confrontation of classical and nonclassical. *Norm* is the classical ideal, an "objective core" of artistic judgment. *Form* is the deviation from the norm for the sake of fidelity to nature. Scheffler would have accepted Gombrich's characterization, though considering it incomplete; but he also would have used it as a basis for polarization (form as antinorm), in contrast to Gombrich's endorsement of what he calls "the principle of sacrifice": the acceptance of norm *and* form. "The principle of sacrifice admits and indeed implies the existence of a multiplicity of values. What is sacrificed is acknowledged to be a value even though it has to yield to another value which commands priority."[73]

Behrens constantly avoided polarization (what Gombrich calls the "principle of exclusion"). Even the highly ordered works of the Düsseldorf period (figures 2.6–12), and the classicizing houses of the Berlin period (figures 8.22, 8.30) incorporate self-conscious asymmetries as foils to the norm. The factories, too, have these asymmetries, and the sacrifices are in these cases more compellingly tied to "natural" problems of materials, site, and use (figures 7.21–28).

Le Corbusier learned this commitment first to form and then to the necessity of sacrificing it. The normative side of this method was learned, or at least reinforced, through Behrens and his Hagen-Düsseldorf connections.[74] Throughout his life, Le Corbusier explored increasingly strong tensions of norm and form. In a significant number of instances (Maisons La Roche-Jeanneret and the Carpenter Center at Harvard, to name only two), both the norm or convention and the form or expression (including use) enhance each other. This synergistic effect was only suggested in the best of Behrens's buildings (figure 7.24). It is also an effect that grows out of the situation Gombrich referred to as the "principle of sacrifice," although his term tends to obscure the potential synergism in the principle.

Now, if Behrens occasionally found a viable middle ground between norm and form, convention and expression, type and individual prior to 1914, and if an artist like Le Corbusier was capable of greatly extending this position after 1914, why was Behrens so ineffectual in the Werkbund debate of 1914? Apparently he had never, for all his devotion, fully grasped the possibility of creatively developing norms and conventions (as Le Corbusier later did). For Behrens, norms and conventions had a strongly retrospective character, carrying with them the powerful associations of their prior uses. As Behrens developed a greater and greater respect for earlier architecture, and as he received commissions from increasingly established institutions, he became more loath to alter existing norms. The worthiness of an institution was not to be expressed anew through an inventive interplay of norm and form (again, as Le Corbusier was to do); increasingly, Behrens felt that the worthiness of the institution was to be expressed by its association with accepted conventions. This is the conflation of "convention as expression" to which the title of this chapter alludes.

Had the situation at Cologne in 1914 been less intensely polarized, and could Behrens have pointed to his strongest works, he might have made an impression. As it was, the debate was being waged in his own canonic Festhalle. Highly unimaginative in its employment of classical norms, the Festhalle demonstrated more clearly than ever before Behrens's reliance on preestablished convention not as a forceful medium but as a style with associational significance.[75]

The polarization at the 1914 Deutscher Werkbund convention was distinctly unfortunate; with the outbreak of World War I, the issue remained unresolved. The polarization continued into the postwar period, giving rise to such extended and questionable conflicts as that which the "functionalist" Pevsner long waged against the "expressionists," and the continuing misunderstanding of the "formalist" Le Corbusier by "pragmatic" critics.

The Interwar Years

After the First World War, Behrens returned to his earlier interest in architectural and artistic education. Modern German culture was still hampered by the divide between an excellent but culturally inadequate technical realm and a confused and imitative architecture. Nevertheless, he continued to consider architecture as the truest image of the essence—of the spiritual character—of an epoch.[1] The revolution of November 1918 and the new government initially dominated by Social Democrats were to be grasped as a new time calling for the cultural expression of a new spirit. The arts of painting and sculpture revealed that a new *Kunstwollen* was arising that would come to be the mirror of this new time.[2] The realization of this *Kunstwollen* and the overcoming of the confused state of architecture could be achieved, Behrens felt, only by a reform of education in the arts.[3] First of all, architecture had to be recognized as an art; students should be selected for their artistic talent and then trained in the arts. Only a student in possession of general artistic capabilities should be introduced to technical subject matter. One must remember that Alberti, Leonardo, Michelangelo, Neumann, and Schinkel were in fact great engineer-architects. Only the modern educational system separated these talents; thus the new school of architecture should include studies in building construction.[4]

The art school of the future should, then, unite the three main fields: architecture, the fine arts, and building technology. Behrens added that every student must work for some time in the workshops of the applied arts section. Finally, other important but secondary subjects should be incorporated in the school: economics and the social sciences, engineering, aesthetics, history, philosophy, and criticism.[5] All this effort was directed to the rehabilitation of architecture and, finally, to the achievement of that high cultural level signaled by the development of a universal art under the leadership of architecture.[6]

With an awareness of Behrens's earlier development, this reform program comes as no surprise. The modern industrial zeitgeist must come to expression. This is achieved through great artists and has its highest expression in architecture. The postwar period is new and therefore calls for some adjustments in expression. Behrens had adjusted this theory to changing conditions before, and these essays of 1919 represent his determination to retain his basic tenets. However, his willingness to deal directly with the technology of modern civilization was soon to falter. An essay of 1920 repeated much of his 1919 essays but gave new emphasis to the importance, especially the ethical importance, of handicrafts in culture and in artistic education. Claiming that the machine had totally destroyed the spiritual in works, he saw the only hope in the reawakening of handicrafts. He entertained the thought that our technical and material civilization was nearing its high point and that an inversion to spiritual and cultural values lay not far in the future.[7] In all this, though making no mention of Walter Gropius or the Bauhaus, Behrens must consciously have supported the April 1919 program of that school, which incorporated Gropius's emphatic call: "Architects, Sculptors, Painters: we must all return to handicrafts!"[8]

The existential conditions of postwar Germany must have been extremely disruptive to have pried a determined personality like Behrens away from his developed position— the position restated in 1919. Apparently the situation in Germany was indeed that intense, for Behrens extended the argument of his 1920 essay, now under the title "The New Romanticism of Handicrafts":

> Quality, in artistic-technical terms, is bound to the *individual object*. The constituent parts of such a piece are chosen by the careful sensibility of the artist; the nerves of the "forming hand" give ever new *living Form* to the piece. *Mechanisms* and mass-produced goods can be "tastefully" influenced; *art*, however, is dependent on the uncontrolled inspiration of the moment, and it relies on the personal fulfillment of the work through the human hand. If the ecstasy of work has transmitted *soul* to the piece, then it is art. It would be good if one no longer spoke of "Art"—if those of us who are involved had the right to call ourselves artisans [*Handwerker*] instead. Our work should again make us proud, should again allow us to participate in what was once the honor of the craft guild [*Handwerks-Ehre*]. I know that our work has been criticized as not participating in the spirit of the time of the automobile and the airplane; that, on the contrary, our work through its strong emphasis on craftsmanship is a *"romantic movement." All right: that's what it ought to be!* We need nothing so much as a little romanticism in order to make our existence more beautiful—indeed, in order to make our life bearable.[9]

This emphasis on work, on the actual productive process, is both new to Behrens's thought and refreshing—but highly romantic indeed. This was the year in which Behrens designed an exhibition building and selected appropriate fellow artist-artisans with whom he carried out an exhibit in what was hoped was the spirit of the medieval cathedral builders: the Dombauhütte for the Gewerbeschau in Munich, 1922 (figures 9.1–3).[10] The name, *Dombauhütte,* refers to the lodge of masons and other artisans gathered for the con-

9.1 Peter Behrens. Munich, Deutsche Gewerbeschau (at the Exhibition Park on the Theresienhöhe), Dombauhütte (1921–1922). Plan.

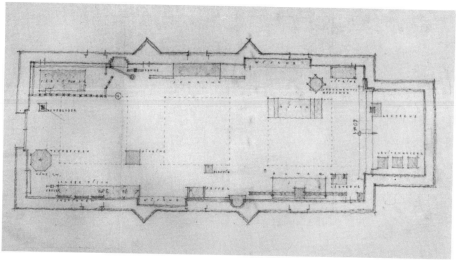

9.2 Behrens. Dombauhütte. Exterior view.

9.3 Behrens. Dombauhütte.
Interior view toward entry.

struction of a medieval cathedral. Behrens's building supported an exhibition, not a guild of workers, but the building itself and its contents directly revealed the commitment to craftsmanship and the unity of the arts under a medievalizing model. As often before, Behrens employed brick. Though I have compared his brick factories with medieval buildings, in the factories Behrens strove for simple, monumental forms, often with sheer surfaces of smooth, hard bricks that forcefully contained these thousands of small building units within a monolithic form. In the Dombauhütte the floor and walls become a rich tapestry of decorative devices, with changes of color not only of bricks and tiles but of the mortar as well. The mastery of the masons was employed in a quite different manner than the anonymous precision of the factories—and all this artistry in a temporary building! The heavy timber construction for the roof of the Dombauhütte was carried out by the firm of Adolf Sommerfeld, the patron of Gropius's heavily crafted log house (Berlin, 1922). Indeed, the representation of a cathedral by Lyonel Feininger on the cover of the early Bauhaus manifesto, the similarities of pedagogical theory, and the battery of craftsmen working under Gropius and Behrens in their respective works indicate how close were the thoughts of the two in the early period of the Weimar Bauhaus. The elaborate woodwork and decorative details of the Bauhaus group in the Sommerfeld house seeks a spiritual unity that, if nominally secular, is nonetheless fully in sympathy with the building craftsmanship and religious art of the Dombauhütte—the painting of the apse, numerous sculptures and religious objects, and the controversial expressionist crucifix by Ludwig Gies, suspended from the roof. Behrens's new sensibility appears also in the presentation drawings from his atelier in the postwar time, even in a simple plan for the Dombauhütte (figure 9.1). Pencil and ink lines are drawn freehand and charcoal enlivens the drawing, as it was to do with great force in perspectives of most of his diverse production in the interwar years.

In an article on the old Werkbund theme of *Qualitätsarbeit,* Behrens concluded that the best artists and art teachers were then anxious to cooperate in mutual tasks with craftsmen.

> And if the ideal which I have announced to you is achieved, we will then have, everywhere, quality workshops in which true art is created. Then we shall no longer need workshops at the schools nor indeed schools of art. Then we will have a master-student relationship like that of the Middle Ages. And that will mean nothing less than that we have again achieved a Culture![11]

Behrens's medievalizing convictions of the early 1920s can be traced to earlier and more general sources. In chapter 3, I quoted the programmatic publisher Eugen Diederichs for his advocacy of the *Neuromantik:* a recognition of two great historical models for German culture, the time of Dürer and that of Goethe. Another Diederichs prospectus of 1915 or 1916 praised the recent publication of Richard Benz, *Die Renaissance: Das Verhängnis der deutschen Kultur* (The Renaissance: The Undoing of German Culture); Diederichs's preferred model had become the time of Dürer.

Combining Benz's ideas with his own, Diederichs labeled the period 1100–1500 "Gotik" and described this as the great national period of the German people and German spirit. But the Peasants' War of the early sixteenth century found no political leader; in the arts, no master came after Dürer; and Luther's translation of the Bible was the last great document of literary creativity in the German language. The Renaissance broke in; the Germans took foreign culture upon themselves; and the "thumbe" German became formal and rationalistic—the dreamer became a thinker and organizer. Now the conditions of the Great War had reestablished, Diederichs believed, the commonality of the German people and their possible existence as a political body. Attention would naturally turn to that medieval closeness which created the beautiful old cities with their fountains, streets, town halls, and cathedrals. Perhaps socialism and its image of the state could come to mean for the German future what the Church and afterlife had meant for the Middle Ages.

What forms the future life of Germany would assume, Diederichs did not claim to know; but the youth of his time sought to be, in their own terms "freideutsch." They were, Diederichs claimed, less acquisitive than the older generation; they did battle against the fragmentation of self; they simplified their lives, strengthened their bodies, and loved that art—especially the folk song—which was adequate to the situation. They strove for character. They sought a bond, Diederichs concluded, with that buried stratum of German life that extended from Master Eckhart to Dürer. Thus Behrens, in the early twenties, was identifying with a medievalizing movement that others had developed.[12]

Beyond a temporary, liturgically oriented work like the Dombauhütte, Behrens pursued these interests in a major corporate building, a work that remains today one of his few widely recognized achievements after the First World War. The facility for the Farbwerke Hoechst, near Frankfurt (figures 9.4–7),[13] employs brick similarly to the Dombauhütte, and the medievalizing craftsmanship of the giant clock would have been at home there too. The Hoechst building is 168 meters long on a site of 4,800 sq. m. Much of it consists of straightforward bays for office and research uses, but the monumental central block of the building provides, at the ground floor, not only a corporate display with an evocative memorial to the war dead (figure 9.6) but, most notably, a great, cathedral-like court rising through the entire height of the building, surrounded by the main circulation (figure 9.7; also illustrated in list of works, no. 141). Incongruously, the brick piers grow larger as they ascend. Evoking the production of this famous dye works, the piers, stained in a spectrum from blues below through reds and oranges to yellow as they near the faceted milk-glass skylights, are dematerialized. Metamorphosed to stalactites, the piers seem almost to hang from an unknown vault.[14]

Reception of the Farbwerke Hoechst has been exceptionally diverse and vehement: immediate shock at the radical romanticism of an architect who had been understood quite otherwise; rejection by Nazi ideologues as decadent; later critical neglect and, more recently, favorable assessments of this well-preserved building. However one evaluates the intent behind the work, it seems evident that the Farbwerke, and the Dombauhütte as

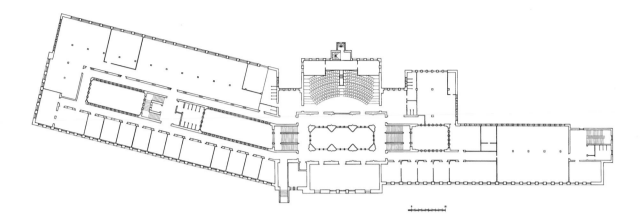

9.4 Peter Behrens. Frankfurt-
Hoechst, Farbwerke Hoechst,
Administration Building
(1920–1924). Plan, first floor.

9.5 Behrens. Farbwerke
Hoechst. Exterior view.

9.6 Behrens. Farbwerke Hoechst. Exhibition room with axial space to memorial at right.

9.7 Behrens. Farbwerke Hoechst. Central hall.

9.8 Peter Behrens. Project
for a mausoleum for Hugo
Stinnes, Mülheim-Ruhr
(1924). Perspective of one
of a number of designs.

well, are remarkably thorough in the fulfillment of their architectural identities and of Behrens's intent: the evocation of a romantic spiritual movement opposed to what was now seen as the materialism and one-sided rationalism of a lost time.

In this mode, Behrens would memorialize the modern industrialist Hugo Stinnes with a mausoleum that, in its several designs, drew on any number of rude early medieval motifs (figure 9.8).[15]

The winter garden designed by Behrens as part of the Austrian pavilion at the 1925 International Exposition of Decorative Arts in Paris (figures 9.9–10), despite its contrasting light steel and glass structure, is fundamentally consistent with Hoechst and the Dombauhütte. The asymmetrical steel structure participates in the decorative handicraft of the glazing patterns; the interior is evocatively expressive, from the shading devices above, through the freely disposed lamps, to the grotto-like stonework of the benches and floor. Here Behrens, rather than dismissing what were seen as modern materials, subverts them within his new romantic vision.[16]

It is no doubt correct to speak of Behrens as setting the agenda for the architectural works that bear his name in the interwar period. However, his ateliers, at various and overlapping times in Berlin, Frankfurt, the Ruhr, and Vienna, included many able assistants. From 1922 to 1928, the most prominent of these was Hans Döllgast (1891–1974), who went on to a significant postwar career in Munich. Döllgast first associated with Behrens in the late stages of the construction of the Dombauhütte and was involved with Hoechst after the initial design. Döllgast was a remarkable draftsman; his large drawings that mixed pen, pencil, crayons, and especially charcoal establish the character of much of the design production under Behrens's name during the 1920s (an example is figure 9.8). At times, as with the Salzburg project to which we next turn, it is generally believed that Döllgast had an almost free hand.[17]

In the years following the Dombauhütte and Hoechst, Behrens received a conventional religious commission, a new college of St. Benedict as an extension of the Benedictine Monastery of St. Peter in Salzburg (1924–1926).[18] In plan, organization, and materials, it accepts the vernacular of the monastery. The windows march in an orderly classical reduction in simple stucco walls above a rusticated stone base (figure 9.11). Off the entry, however, a low hall with a grotesquely giant and contorted carved wooden crucifix (1925), this time by Jakob Adlhart the Younger (1898–?), strongly recalls that of the Dombauhütte (figure 9.12).

The vision of a new unity of craftsmen collectively building a new architecture at one with a true culture, the vision of Gropius's early Bauhaus and of Behrens's contemporary rhetoric and production, could not be sustained. In the years of postwar revival, major endeavors such as large-scale housing provided challenges and creative opportunity. The revival of industry and reawakening interest in the rationalization of building evoked energies even less supported by the craft ideals of the preceding years. Even the more abstruse speculations of the theorists of art and architecture shifted radically with the new avant-gardes of de Stijl and of eastern Europe.

9.9 Peter Behrens. Paris, Exposition
Internationale des Arts Décoratifs et
Industriels Modernes 1925, Austrian
Pavilion, Wintergarden (1924–1925).
Exterior view.

9.10 Behrens. Paris 1925, Austrian
Pavilion, Wintergarden. Interior.

9.11 Peter Behrens and others. Salzburg, College of St. Benedict, an extension of the Abbey of St. Peter (1924–1926). View in the courtyard.

9.12 Behrens and others. Salzburg,
College of St. Benedict. Hall with
crucifix by Jakob Adlhart the
Younger.

Gropius and the Bauhaus struggled in transition, but then achieved a leading position in the new architecture of the 1920s. Behrens struggled. However utopian his thought of 1919, however fleeting the conditions for the realization of his Dombauhütte and Hoechst building, one must see them as impressive, consistently conceived works within the cause they espoused. Bruno Taut's postwar fantasies remained on paper; Gropius's Sommerfeld house is limited in scale and conception. In the mid-twenties, Gropius, Taut, and many other architects of the younger generation moved decisively to new architectural forms in response to social needs and new productive systems. Behrens's attempt to move with his younger colleagues in this emergent architecture was feckless.

For Mr. and Mrs. W. J. Bassett-Lowke, Behrens built a house called New Ways in Northampton in England (figure 9.13).[19] Compact, relatively cubic, and of white stucco, it could be seen, as the *Architectural Review* did in 1926, as introducing to England the continental concept of domestic architecture in concrete. One had only to ignore the fact

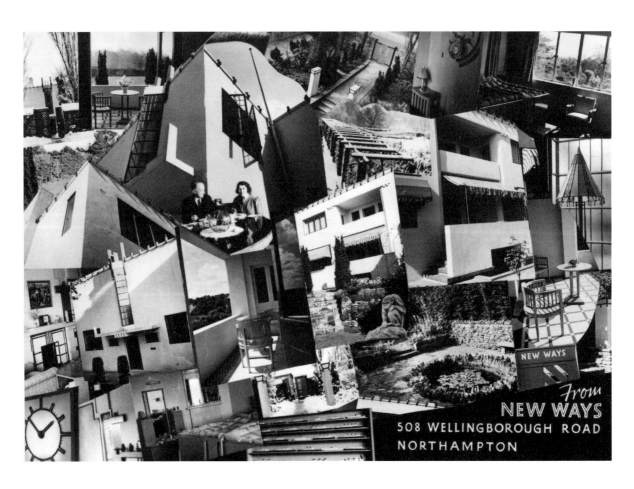

9.13 Peter Behrens. Northampton, England, New Ways, house of W. J. Bassett-Lowke (1923–1926). Photo montage postcard "From New Ways."

9.14 Behrens. New Ways. Interior, perspective in the lounge.

that the house was of brick cavity wall construction (as the *Review* acknowledged), was symmetrically organized and spatially conservative, and had an ornamental skyline and decoration that worked to a crescendo as one moved from outside to the lounge (figure 9.14). The house is a hopeless compromise between Behrens's recent handicraft ambitions and a felt need to move with his ascending younger colleagues.

Given another chance to work in the new idiom of the twenties, now as a partici-pant in the famous 1927 Deutscher Werkbund experimental housing exposition at Weissenhof in Stuttgart, Behrens fared better but stumbled again. We must place this work in context by reviewing his recurrent engagement with the design of housing. In an unre-alized project for a large parcel in Neuss (1910), intended for the middle class, he had essayed Sittesque city-building where street-aligned houses enclosed a quiet square.[20] The 1910–1911 AEG workers' housing in Hennigsdorf (figure 8.11) had initiated what was to become Behrens's type: a housing block with a stepped street front providing courtyards with gardens front and back. At Hennigsdorf this was a three-story block of flats.[21] The executed version of the large AEG housing estate at Berlin-Oberschöneweide (1915) is composed of two-story row houses.[22] The two-story row on Paul-Jordan-Strasse in Hennigsdorf (1918–1919) returns to the device of a set-back entry courtyard for the mix of single- and double-exposure units.[23] This group was a realization of the *Gruppenbau* (cluster building) theory expounded by Behrens and Heinrich de Fries in 1918 (figure

9.15 Peter Behrens
and Heinrich de Fries.
Housing according to
the *Gruppenbauweise*
(method of cluster
building; 1917–1918).
Perspective of one
such type.

9.15).[24] With their clusters of stepped units, the authors claim the advantage of development not only along the street, but also in the depth of the site. They foresee a higher density and reduced infrastructure costs, particularly due to the diminished area of the site given to streets. Although the units often have only a single exposure, the authors succeed in providing a garden for each unit, even if some of these are on the public side of the stepped rows.

In 1920 Behrens designed "Double-garden houses" in which the units of two-story blocks of flats all enjoy double exposure and gardens (figure 9.16; one of the rare drawings from Behrens's own hand).[25] This organization won praise for its viability even in later years.[26] Preparing the way for the Weissenhof project, in the mid-twenties Behrens's concerted new interest was in terrace housing, clusters of flats in which the roofs of lower houses provided terraces for the units above (figure 9.17). These designs mix balconies and ground-level terraces with roof terraces, forming an extension of Behrens's concerns with compact, efficient units and town planning.[27]

The Weissenhof exhibition in Stuttgart is rightly considered one of the key works in the formation of European modern architecture and especially of that set of works that came to be known as the International Style. Under the sponsorship of the Deutscher Werkbund, with Mies van der Rohe as artistic director, this was an exhibition of experimental but permanent houses designed as exemplars by the best-known architects of the emerging generation. Mies designed a steel frame apartment house at the center of the complex; Le Corbusier designed a single and a double house that contributed significantly to the development of the ideas informing his great houses of the late twenties; J. J. P. Oud built a provocative modern transformation of the Dutch row house; and many other architects were represented, including Walter Gropius, Ludwig Hilberseimer, Hans Scharoun, Mart Stam, and Bruno Taut.[28]

9.16 Peter Behrens. Design for *Doppelgärtenhäuser* (Type II: two-story buildings with flats opening to gardens on either side; 1920). Sketch by Behrens.

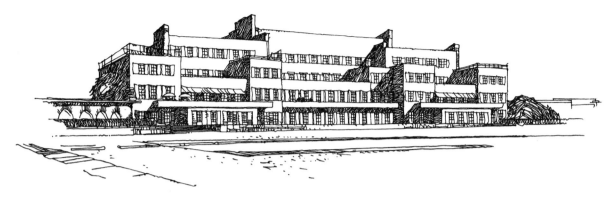

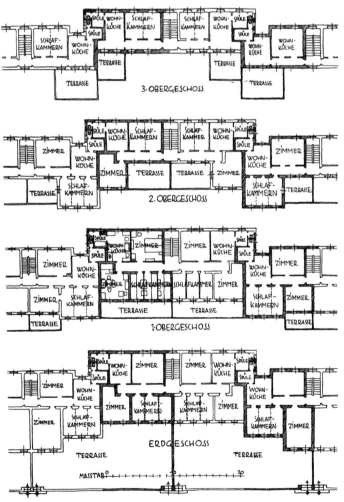

9.17 Peter Behrens. Design
for *Terrassenhäuser* (blocks
of flats with a mixture
of gardens, balconies,
and terraces; ca. 1924).
Perspective and plans.

Behrens and Hans Poelzig were the only architects of the older generation invited to participate in the exhibition. With his record in built and theoretical work in housing, it would seem Behrens was well prepared to provide a significant model of his terrace housing, which was the task he set himself (figures 9.18–19). Cubic in its massing, rendered in sheer planes of stucco, and now without ornament, Behrens's building shares some of the formal traits of most of the Weissenhof units. It was not so important that its complex massing, conventional punched windows, and rather incidental formal moves set it apart from its neighbors and diminished its reception. The intrinsic problems were recognized immediately: there is no coherent concept of circulation; the apartments are so badly organized as to be nonfunctional; and even the terraces are haphazard as to their location and orientation. In the year of the exhibition a critic observed about the four-room apartment at the east of the first floor (figure 9.18, plan C, top) that the small living-dining room had to provide circulation to all rooms of the dwelling; the smallest bedroom provided access to another bedroom, leaving no place for an adult bed; and the end bedroom had three cold walls and a cold ceiling.[29] Behrens provided the very opposite of a convincing model of his own central concerns. Still less was he perceived to have reached the formal and innovative standards of the other Weissenhof architects.

From December 1921 Behrens was professor and leader for the master class for architecture at the Academy in Vienna—the chair once held by Otto Wagner. Almost throughout the twentieth century, the city of Vienna has sustained a major social housing program. We cannot take leave of Behrens's work in housing without noting his part in the design of three large projects (1924–1929): Konstanziagasse 44 in Vienna district XXII, the Winarsky-Hof in Vienna XX (figure 9.20), and the Franz Domes-Hof on the Margaretengürtel in Vienna V.[30]

In two villas of the late twenties, Behrens more successfully adopted the then rapidly evolving modernism of his younger colleagues. The site and program of his villa for Clara Ganz in Kronberg, near Frankfurt (figures 9.21–22), invites comparison with Mies van der Rohe's contemporary Tugendhat house in Brno.[31] In both cases the access street runs along the contours of a hill. Both houses, situated on the downward slope of their streets, present low and relatively closed fronts, and then open to light and generous views over the gardens below. Behrens's villa does not match Mies's open plan, abstraction of space, and rigor of detailing; nor does it compare to the Tugendhat house in its significance in reshaping the discipline of architecture. Yet the Villa Ganz deserves recognition. If its spaces are a sequence of relatively conventional rooms, they are well disposed in relation to one another and to the site. Each major room receives distinctive, sometimes rather exotic, wall coverings or floor materials that intensify the significance of their varied uses. A contemporary admirer was pleased to find this a painterly rather than architectonic architecture and acclaimed Behrens's villa for not falling prey to the "pedantry of *Sachlichkeit*" or giving the impression of a "machine to live in."[32]

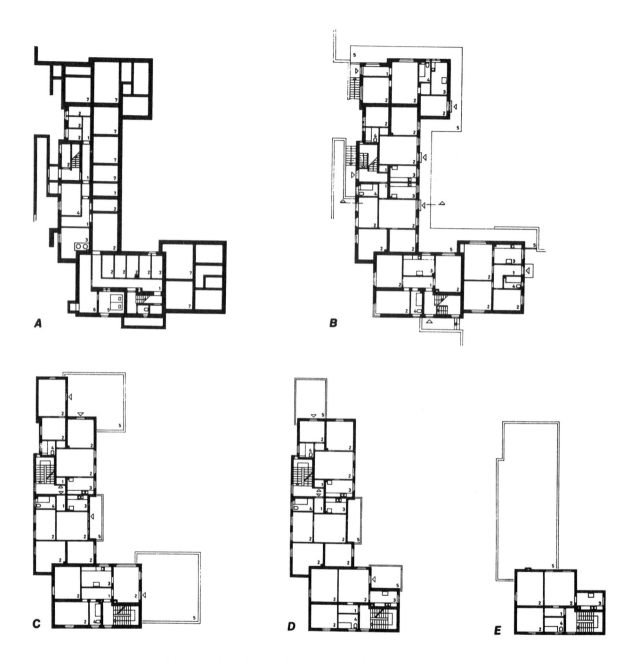

9.18 Peter Behrens. Stuttgart, Weissenhof, Deutscher Werkbund exhibition "Die Wohnung," *Terrassenhaus* (1926–1927). Plans. Key (for all but basement): 1, entrance hall; 2, room; 3, kitchen; 4, bath; 5, terrace.

9.19 Behrens. Weissenhof, *Terrassenhaus.*
View from south; the houses at the right
are by Mart Stam.

9.20 Peter Behrens. Vienna
V, Franz Domes-Hof,
Margaretengürtel 126–134,
social housing (1928–1929).
Street view.

9.21 Peter Behrens. Kronberg
im Taunus, Villa Clara Ganz
(1928–1931). Plans.

SECOND FLOOR

FIRST FLOOR

9.22 Behrens. Villa Clara
Ganz. Villa and garden from
southeast.

Behrens's house for the noted psychologist Kurt Lewin in Berlin is his purest exercise in the white, cubic architecture of the period (figures 9.23–24). A small house with an attached apartment, it offers little opportunity for spatial innovation; it is a compact array of functional rooms. Yet here again the site is used well—a modest urban variant on the closure versus openness of the fronts of the Villa Ganz—and there is an appealing simplicity to the entire house. Indeed, Buddensieg terms it a "true work of art."[33]

9.23 Peter Behrens. Berlin-Zehlendorf, Kurt Lewin house (1929–1930). Plans.

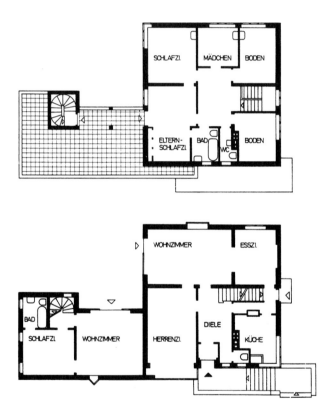

9.24 Behrens. Lewin house.
View from street.

9.25 Peter Behrens. Berlin, competition design for the transformation of Alexander-platz (1928–1929). Model, photographed along the Königstrasse axis, from west to east.

At quite the opposite scale from the suburban villa, Behrens engaged in the 1928–1929 competition for the transformation of the Alexanderplatz in central Berlin (figure 9.25; also illustrated in list of works, no. 194). Though he did not win the competition, he received the commission.[34] Ensuing land speculation precluded the full development of the plan, but Behrens did build two office buildings, named Berolina (figures 9.26–27) and Alexander, on the western part of the site (corresponding to the two buildings in the foreground of the photograph of the model).[35] Both are eight-story concrete frame buildings with restaurants and commercial uses on the first two floors and offices above. Limestone cladding of simple but rather heavy profiles emphasizes the structural frame. Built with American capital, they were perceived as buildings of modern character and construction, bearing an American sensibility in this focal point of the German capital. Heavily damaged and burned out in late Anglo-American bombing raids of the Second World War, they were nonetheless rebuilt by the German Democratic Republic and placed in use by 1950. They remain the distinctive features of Alexanderplatz to the time of this writing.

9.26 Peter Behrens. Berlin, Alexanderplatz, Berolina, a commercial and office building (1929–1931). Night photograph at the corner of Dircksen- and Königstrasse.

9.27 Behrens. Berolina.
Entrance lobby from
Königstrasse.

Behrens's most successful work in the new modern idiom of the prewar years also marked his return to the design of factory buildings. Between 1929 and 1938, together with Alexander Popp, Behrens built the State Tobacco Factory in Linz, Austria.[36] Of the several buildings comprising the factory site, the most distinctive is the Cigarette Fabrication Building (figure 9.28), a 230-meter-long, six-story steel frame construction conforming to the gentle curve of the southern edge of the site. Its long open runs of space for production are directly revealed by the continuous strip windows and unbroken stucco spandrels. Behrens places the columns directly behind the windows, thus, characteristically for him, employing the strip window for expressive effect rather than as an element integrated with a free plan.

Behrens's return to a classicizing, symmetrical monumentality appears already in his 1934 competition design for a Congress, Sport, and Exhibition Hall for Hamburg (figure 9.29), one of four first-prize winners among 175 entrants. After initial hope that the project might be realized, the opportunity was lost. While there had been political intrigue against Behrens for earlier alliances not favored by the National Socialists, the deciding factor seems to have been neither Behrens's personal record nor any qualities of the project itself, but rather Hitler's ambition to make of Hamburg a "Führerstadt" employing works of still grander proportions.[37]

9.28 Peter Behrens and
Alexander Popp. Linz,
State Tobacco Factory
(1929–1938), Cigarette
Fabrication Building
(1930–1932). Exterior
along city street.

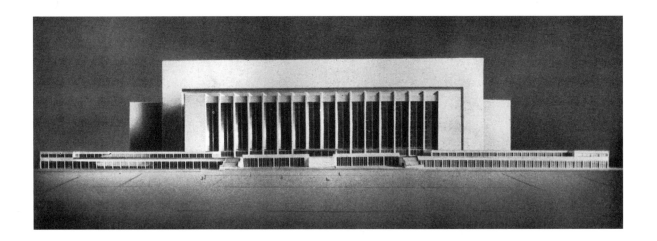

9.29 Peter Behrens and Alexander Popp. Hamburg, competition design for a Congress, Sport, and Exhibition Hall (1934). Main facade.

In 1936 Behrens was called from Vienna to conduct a master class in architecture, in succession to Hans Poelzig, at the Akademie der Künste in Berlin, reportedly with the specific approval of Hitler.[38] Behrens became associated with Hitler's urbanistic dreams for Berlin with the commission for the new headquarters of the AEG (figure 9.30) on Albert Speer's famous planned north-south axis.[39] Speer reported that his selection of Behrens for this commission was resisted by the powerful Alfred Rosenberg, but that his decision was supported by Hitler who admired Behrens's St. Petersburg Embassy.[40] Behrens and the Academy helped his cause by reporting to the Ministry that Behrens had early joined the then illegal Nazi party in Austria on May Day of 1934.[41] The vast AEG building with its marshaled fenestration and detailing, like the project of which it was a part, mercifully was not built. War ensued instead. Behrens, seeking refuge from the cold of his country estate, died in Berlin's Hotel Bristol on 27 February 1940.[42]

9.30 Peter Behrens. Berlin-Tiergarten, design for AEG Main Administration Building on the north-south axis of Albert Speer as part of Hitler's envisioned grand transformation of central Berlin (1938–1939). Photograph of model, the entrance.

Conclusion

The work that established Behrens's renown and sustains his memory was accomplished in a few years before World War I. Despite the intense relation of that work to a new industrial society, for Behrens the time and his work were freighted with doubts. With the collapse of empire and more widespread doubts about the efficacy of modern production and society, Behrens turned in the postwar years to romanticisms of earlier times and of handwork production—work radically different, yet continuous in the still greater infusion of doubt.

Even more than the overtly medieval Dombauhütte in Munich (figures 9.1–3), a room of the following year, a Scholar's Study (Arbeitszimmer eines Gelehrten; figure 10.1), when combined with Behrens's stated position, permits us to infer the complexity of his attitudes.[1] The chairs designed for the study are aggressively hewn. On the desk and along a shelf on one wall lie an extraordinary collection of scientific instruments and other precise objects that contrast startlingly with the furniture. The interior recalls Carpaccio's *St. Augustine in His Study;* the contrasting objects recall Dürer's *Melencolia I* (figure 10.2). As these two comparisons suggest, Behrens walked a line between sensibilities associated with the Middle Ages and those associated with the Renaissance; the attitudes implicit in Behrens's study can be illuminatingly compared with those evidenced in Dürer's engraving. In Panofsky's extraordinary interpretation,[2] this brilliantly executed print interprets melancholy as a passive condition induced by an intense insight into the ironic discontinuities of knowledge and experience. The ignorant putto energetically scribbles in self-condemnation of the active life, but knowledge is immobilized. Much of the supporting symbolism in Dürer's print is built around overt references to architecture and carpentry. Panofsky speaks of the sphere and the (I interpolate "crystalline") stone as emblems of the knowledge behind architecture. In contrast to this ideal knowledge are the incomplete building and the rude wooden ladder. A series of builder's tools ranges from the comparative precision of the compass, scales, and book to the craftsmanly elegance of the carefully shaped plane and the ordinariness of the crooked nails.

10.1 Peter Behrens. Vienna,
Scholar's Study, an exhibit in
the Österreichisches Museum
(1923).

10.2 Albrecht Dürer.
Melencolia I, engraving.

Behrens's room explores a similar range, with an insightful and melancholic effect that is not unworthy of comparison with Dürer. Behrens placed crystals and crystalline materials on the desk and shelf of the study. But the dominant symbol of consummate knowledge, the witness of our "age of electricity," is the glistening, suspended, conical lamp over the desk—as difficult to associate with its built environment as is Dürer's sphere with its. In contrast to the lamp, the purely physical existence of man is most closely associated with the chairs, rough-hewn and plastically shaped. Lamp and chair in Behrens's study, sphere and carpenter's plane in Dürer's engraving, stand in for knowledge and reality, light and substance, abstraction and physical presence.

Between these poles of ideality and materiality, Behrens's study exhibits a range of existential qualities. As with Dürer, there are the comparatively precise instruments and various degrees of craftsmanly architectural abstraction. The desk, with its need for a planar surface and its lesser association with man and greater association with objects, is more hard-edged and abstract than the chairs. The shelf beyond, still more wholly associated with objects, is also still more abstract, partially supported by tensioned wires from the ceiling. The comparatively insubstantial tension force is ironically objectified with medievalizing, wrought-iron wedged turnbuckles. The shelves for books are of a more substantial material and employ interlocking carpentry and simple compressive support. There the unusual variant is the freestanding post beyond: expressively material, indicative of potential growth or expansion, of free sculptural form, useless. Each part of the study is open to multiple interpretations of different kinds; yet both visually and intellectually one senses continuities in this welter of experience. A sufficient wisdom seems also to have forced that intuition of continuities to be questioned—seems to have induced melancholy.

Behrens's turn from "art *and* technique" (the dominant theme in his writings and work after 1907) to "handicraft as the source of art" was a marked shift that should not be underplayed.[3] But there was constancy, too. The "and" of "art and technique" never meant identification. Behrens weighed the proper relation of what he saw as two distinct forms of knowledge. In a building like the Turbine Factory, he actively sought that proper relation, but there was always reservation—a doubt that induced a melancholic attitude toward industrial civilization and a formal expression usually characterized as one of pathos.

On the other hand, even at the Turbine Factory this melancholic attitude was transformed into a celebration of the possible resolution of the problems of knowledge and action. At those times when Behrens attempted a more enthusiastic resolution of these problems—in the Darmstadt period (figure 3.7) or in the main hall of the Farbwerke Hoechst (figure 9.7, perhaps Behrens's finest work of the twenties)—the celebrational character of his work was still more pronounced.[4]

At the time when this celebrational aspect of Behrens's work was least evident (Berlin, 1910), and when reviewing nothing more imposing than Behrens's modestly remodeled house in Neubabelsberg, Robert Breuer still recognized this celebrational quality as central to his work:

Peter Behrens serves sacred expression more than bourgeois livability. He loves the celebrational. As it happens, that pathos for which Behrens has found the classic form in giant iron halls, appears a bit bold, cool, and heavy in dwellings, and especially in interiors. He requires the monumental; little wonder that he seeks to give to his own rooms a priestly and lofty stature.

Peter Behrens is in part a problematic character; the poet often conquers the practical man. Deep in his heart he wills to raise everything, even the everyday, into the crystalline [*gläserne*] atmosphere of that sacred festival house, that temple of mankind, of which he has dreamed and of which he once said: "On the edge of a meadow, atop a mountain, this festival house shall be raised up—so colorfully resplendent, as if it wants to say: 'My walls need no light!' Its columns are wreathed and from seven masts wave long, white banners! At the high gallery, trumpeters stand in glowing robes and sound their measured call far out over the land."[5]

Breuer's commentary points to a constant in Behrens's own work; it also reminds us of the romantic proposals of German architects in the years following World War I. Resplendent festival houses on high mountains, crystal houses as the sacred center of artistic communities, and other wonderful fantasies were again called forth from the dreams of architects—from the members of the Gläserne Kette (1919–1920), for example, including Bruno Taut, Walter Gropius, Hans Scharoun, Max Taut, and Wassily and Hans Luckhardt.[6] In this time Behrens no longer played a distinctly innovative role in architecture; but the Dombauhütte and the Scholar's Study were impressive performances within the new *Handwerk* orientation. The multiple levels of his romanticism of the 1920s made a work such as the study more convincing, and more memorable, than Gropius's *Handwerk* essay at the Sommerfeld (log) house. Recalling Behrens's lamp in the study and his romance of the industrial landscape, one sees his manner in relation to Mies van der Rohe's romance of glass skyscrapers. In addition to the industrial reference, both men shared the contemporary emphasis on quality of materials, excellence of craftsmanship, and a less tangible romantic belief in the unity and truth of the medieval world view.

The strain evoked in Breuer's commentary continued to the end of Behrens's life. His design, from the grand duke's Artists' Colony to the projected AEG headquarters on the Führer's north-south axis in Berlin, was dominantly celebrational. As a celebrant, Behrens often lapsed into an uncritical position, as instanced in his irresolution about an industrial society; his sacrifice of his distinct formal gains for safe conventions in the World War I period; his misconstrued semi–International Style buildings of the late 1920s (New Ways and the Weissenhof Siedlung terrace housing), and his embrace of Nazi policies and expectations in teaching and design in the 1930s.[7]

As celebrational buildings, Behrens's works were often little adapted to the site and other conditions of place and use. It is characteristic that Behrens dreamt of walls that "need no sunlight," while Le Corbusier is famous for his dictum "Architecture is the masterful play of forms in light." Rich materials, color, "modern" materials such as glass, aluminum, and steel—these are central to the celebratory buildings of Otto Wagner, of Behrens, Taut, Gropius, Mies van der Rohe, and most of the German architects of the era. Though the populace were to attend the festivals, in a strange way the buildings were themselves celebratory, without need of sun or people. In contrast, Le Corbusier's short statement implies abstract forms rather than glowing materials, and the necessity of an environment and an observer. Later, his observer was to become an active participant in the architectural environment; a dynamic, interactive role that Behrens's architecture never fully encouraged.

To return, finally, to the allusions generated by Dürer's *Melencolia I:* Behrens had, in his Düsseldorf period, sought an architecture on the model of Dürer's sphere—an attempt at the translation of pure form, pure knowledge into substance. In later years, especially in the Berlin factories, he achieved various, often notable relationships between the ideal and the real, the eternal and the temporal. Every possible resolution, however, was overthrown by Behrens himself or by his understanding of a changing situation. In the *Handwerk* buildings of the early twenties, he developed an architecture on the model of the basic theme of Dürer's engraving: the melancholy induced by an acute awareness of the disparities of knowing and doing. To embody this melancholic recognition was, in itself, a considerable feat; but it remained a limited response, better suited to contemplation than to the useful activity that initiates the problematic process of design. In his buildings and writings, Behrens showed incessant interest in the zeitgeist, in architectural tradition, in relationships to existing political power. Rarely did he go beyond a mechanical sense of function; there was little study of the influence of form upon human use and of human use upon form. Concern for an individual and his or her interaction with the environment was not a prominent aspect of his theory and work. With Behrens, architecture answered to "the Time," not to people.

Behrens's search for architectural form ranged from a program for ideal form to melancholic expression induced by the failure of that idealist program. He never accepted an alternative range of approaches—the definition of form through the interaction of the form with its environment. That alternative is also beautifully evoked by Dürer, in the carpenter's plane (figure 10.2, lower left corner), a tool whose very purpose is to whittle and gouge recalcitrant material into an approximation of a mathematical abstraction. Yet its form could hardly be more lovingly expressive of the materials from which it is made, of the way in which it is made, of its interaction with both the material to be shaped and the hand that shapes. Together, the Werkbund and the Dürerbund exhibited many everyday objects that participate in such a process and such a sensibility.[8] To recognize the absence of this attitude in Behrens contributes to an understanding of his work; to trace the tradition of this attitude of "form through use" would be the beginning of another study.

Notes

Notes to Chapter 1

1. As discussed below, this claim for the Darmstadt exhibition is substantiated by the need for some term like "environmental arts" to designate the comprehensive activities of the Darmstadt colony. A study of Wagner may be initiated with Heinz Geretsegger and Max Peintner, *Otto Wagner* (1964; New York: Rizzoli, 1985). See also J. A. Lux, *Otto Wagner* (Munich: Delphin, 1914), and the references cited in notes 30 and 31 below. On Olbrich, see J. A. Lux, *Josef Maria Olbrich* (Berlin: Wasmuth, 1919); Robert J. Clark, "Joseph Maria Olbrich and Vienna" (Ph.D. diss., Princeton University, 1973); and Peter Haiko, *Joseph Maria Olbrich: Architecture* (New York: Rizzoli, 1988). The definitive study of Hoffmann is Eduard Sekler, *Josef Hoffmann: The Architectural Work* (Princeton: Princeton University Press, 1985).

2. Various related but distinguishable movements in the arts, including Art Nouveau of western Europe and the Secession movements of the Germanic lands (later termed "Jugendstil" in Germany), came to be termed collectively "Art Nouveau" in both English and French literature. The first chapters of this essay deal with certain aspects of Art Nouveau. For more general considerations of these movements, which culminated about 1900, see especially S. T. Madsen, *Sources of Art Nouveau* (New York: Wittenborn, 1955); New York, Museum of Modern Art, *Art Nouveau,* ed. P. Selz and M. Constantine (New York: Museum of Modern Art, 1959); and Robert Schmutzler, *Art Nouveau* (New York: Abrams, 1964). See the Postscript to this chapter.

3. See, for example, Fritz Schumacher, "Die Ausstellung der Darmstädter Künstlerkolonie," *Dekorative Kunst,* 8 (August 1901), 417–431.

   Nikolaus Pevsner's example of Viennese influence on German architecture at the beginning of the twentieth century, namely the supposed influence of Olbrich's Darmstadt Exhibition Halls of 1908 on Behrens's Oldenburg Exhibition Halls of 1905, is an obvious anachronism; Pevsner, *Pioneers of Modern Design,* 3d ed. (Harmondsworth: Penguin, 1960), 203.

4. This attitude had its parallel in, and in turn was encouraged by, Julius Langbehn's enormously popular contemporary aesthetic, cultural, and political program that took Rembrandt as its teacher,

published with the author listed only as "A German": *Rembrandt als Erzieher,* 33d ed. (Leipzig: Hirschfeld, 1891). See also note 3 of chapter 3.

5. Theodor Heuss, *Hans Poelzig* (Tübingen: Wasmuth, 1948), 17; all translations from the German are by the author unless otherwise noted.

6. These attitudes could be further documented with Fritz Schumacher (1869–1947) in Dresden and Theodor Fischer (1862–1938) in Stuttgart and Munich. See Schumacher, *Stufen des Lebens* (Stuttgart: Deutsche Verlags-Anstalt, 1935); H. Karlinger, *Theodor Fischer* (Munich, 1937); and more recently Winfried Nerdinger, *Theodor Fischer: Architekt und Städtebauer 1862–1938* (Berlin: Ernst & Sohn, 1988).

7. Schmutzler, *Art Nouveau,* 191–207. This old polarity is well discussed in Fritz Schmalenbach, *Jugendstil* (Würzburg: Konrad Triltsch, 1935), 26, 65.

8. On Muthesius, see note 29 below. The reference here is to his *Stilarchitektur und Baukunst* (Mülheim a. d. Ruhr: Schimmelpfeng, 1902); trans. S. Anderson, *Style Architecture and Building Art* (Santa Monica: Getty Center, 1994).

9. Henry van de Velde, "Zum Tode Otto Eckmann's," *Zeitschrift für Innendekoration,* 13 (August 1902), 207. On van de Velde, see his own *Geschichte meines Lebens* (Munich: Piper, 1962); and Henry Lenning, *The Art Nouveau* (The Hague: Nijhoff, 1951); A. M. Hammacher, *Le monde de Henry van de Velde* (Antwerp: Fonds Mercator/Paris: Hachette, 1967); and Klaus-Jürgen Sembach, *Henry van de Velde* (New York: Rizzoli, 1989).

10. On Eckmann, see *Otto Eckmann,* 1st *Sonderheft* of the *Berliner Architekturwelt* (Berlin, 1901). The term "floral" was sometimes playfully transformed into *floreal,* apparently a combination of *floral* and *real.*

11. According to the specialist in these matters at Beuron, Br. Wolfgang Keller OSB, the canonic head by Lenz also dates from 1870–1871 (communicated by Fr. Jakobus Kaffanke OSB, 29 January 1998).

12. On Beuron, see Desiderius Lenz, *Zur Ästhetik der Beuroner Schule* (1898; reprint, Beuron: Verlag der Kunstschule, 1927); Ansgar Pöllmann, *Vom Wesen der hieratischen Kunst* (Beuron: Verlag der Kunstschule, 1905); Josef Kreitmaier, *Beuroner Kunst: Eine Ausdrucksform der christlichen Mystik,* 5th ed. (Freiburg im Br.: Herder, 1923); Charles Chassé, "Didier Lenz and the Beuron School of Religious Art," *Oppositions,* no. 21 (Summer 1980), 100–103; and, with numerous color illustrations, Hubert Krins, *Die Kunst der Beuroner Schule: Wie ein Lichtblick vom Himmel* (Beuron: Beuroner Kunstverlag, 1998).

The introduction that Maurice Denis wrote for the 1905 French edition of Lenz's essay (translated by Paul Serusier) is included in Maurice Denis, *Théories 1890–1910: Du symbolisme et de Gauguin vers un nouvel ordre classique* (Paris: Bibliothèque de l'Occident, 1912).

13. Some explanation may be necessary with reference to these terms. "Idealist," in American usage, tends to be related to "ideal" in its normative sense. Here I want to stress the relationship to idea, to abstract thought; I have tried to clarify this by including a second term, "intellectualist."

The derivatives of the word "pathos" are much abused in contemporary usage, but I have been reluctant to change the terms since the words *Pathos* and *pathetisch* were and are used in the relevant

German discussions, and since the proper meaning of "pathetic"—"affecting or exciting emotion"— is appropriate to our context. I have used the somewhat awkward form "patheticist," and occasionally have retained a German form, in an attempt to reduce the irrelevant connotations that would result from the use of "pathetic."

14. Erwin Panofsky, *Idea* (Columbia: University of South Carolina Press, 1968).

15. Van de Velde, *Geschichte meines Lebens,* 40, 63.

16. Quoted by Karl Scheffler, *Die fetten und die mageren Jahre* (Leipzig: P. List, 1946), 11.

17. Van de Velde, *Geschichte meines Lebens,* 115, 109, respectively.

18. August Endell, "Formenschönheit und dekorative Kunst," *Dekorative Kunst,* 1 (November 1897), 75–87; 1 (March 1898), 280; 2 (May 1898), 119–121, 121–25; idem, "Möglichkeit und Ziele einer neuen Architektur," *Deutsche Kunst und Dekoration,* 1 (February 1898), 142–153; idem, "Architektonische Erstlinge," *Dekorative Kunst,* 6 (May 1900), 297–317.

19. Apparently, especially from Robert Vischer, *Das optische Formgefühl* (Leipzig: Credner, 1873); Johannes Volkelt, *Der Symbolbegriff in der neuesten Ästhetik* (Jena, 1876); and Theodor Lipps, *Raumästhetik und geometrisch-optische Täuschungen* (Leipzig: Barth, 1897).

20. Hermann Obrist, *Neue Möglichkeiten in der bildenden Kunst* (Jena: Diederichs, 1903).

21. Konrad Fiedler, "Über den Ursprung der künstlerischen Tätigkeit (1887)," in *Konrad Fiedlers Schriften über Kunst* (Munich: Piper, 1913), 1:183–368. Adolf Hildebrand, *Das Problem der Form in der bildenden Kunst* (Strassburg: Heitz, 1893); see his chapter 6, "Die Form als Funktionsausdruck," for reliance on theories of empathy.

22. Endell, "Möglichkeit," 144.

23. Endell, "Formenschönheit," 122.

24. Endell, "Möglichkeit," 144. In this there is a suggestion, as in Fiedler and Hildebrand, of the influence of the formal musical theory of the Viennese Eduard Hanslick (1825–1904).

25. Ibid., 146.

26. Ibid., 152.

27. Karl Scheffler, "Unsere Traditionen," *Dekorative Kunst,* 6 (August 1900), 436–445.

28. Art historians often use *historicist* to denote a reliance on historical precedent. Since everything fulfills this definition in some sense, I prefer to reserve the words *historicism* and *historicist* for a quite different use, to refer to attitudes which claim that certain events must take place in satisfaction of the forces of history or destiny. See, for example, Karl Popper, *The Poverty of Historicism* (Boston: Beacon, 1957).

29. On Muthesius, see Julius Posener, *Anfänge des Funktionalismus* (Berlin: Ullstein, 1964); Silvano Custoza, Maurizio Vogliazzo, and Julius Posener, *Muthesius* (Milan: Electa, 1981); and Hans Joachim Hubrich, *Hermann Muthesius: Die Schriften zu Architektur, Kunstgewerbe, Industrie in der 'Neuen Bewegung'* (Berlin: Mann, 1981). On events in England, see Madsen, *Sources,* esp. pts. 2 and 3; Hermann Muthesius, *Das englische Haus,* 3 vols. (Berlin, 1904–1905); abbrev. ed. as *The English House* (New York: Rizzoli, 1979); and Stefan Muthesius, *Das englische Vorbild: Eine Studie zu den*

deutschen Reformbewegungen in Architektur, Wohnbau, und Kunstgeschichte im späten 19. Jahrhundert (Munich: Prestel, 1974).

30. Julius Meier-Graefe, "Ein modernes Milieu," *Dekorative Kunst,* 4, no. 7 (April 1901), 249–264. See also Stanford Anderson, "*Sachlichkeit* and Modernity, or Realist Architecture," in Harry Mallgrave, ed., *Otto Wagner: Reflections on the Raiment of Modernity* (Santa Monica: Getty Center, 1993), 322–360.

31. A study of Loos may be initiated with Ludwig Munz and Gustav Künstler, *Adolf Loos* (New York: Praeger, 1964); Benedetto Gravagnuolo, *Adolf Loos: Theory and Works* (New York: Rizzoli, 1982); Burkhardt Rukschcio and Roland Schachel, *Adolf Loos: Leben und Werk* (Salzburg: Residenz Verlag, 1982); Mitchell Schwarzer, "Adolf Loos and Theories of Architecture and the Practical Arts in Nineteenth Century Austria and Germany" (Ph.D. diss., MIT, 1991); and Werner Oechslin, *Stilhülse und Kern: Otto Wagner, Adolf Loos und der evolutionäre Weg zur modernen Architektur* (Zurich: gta; Berlin: Ernst & Sohn, 1994).

32. Pöllmann, *Vom Wesen,* 39.

33. O. J. Bierbaum, *Eine empfindsame Reise im Automobil von Berlin nach Sorrent und zurück an den Rhein* (Buenos Aires: Editorial "El Buen Libro," [1903]).

34. Krefeld, Kaiser-Wilhelm-Museum, *Linie und Form* (Krefeld: Kramer und Baum, 1904).

35. In 1907, when Behrens contributed a major impetus to modern industrial design, he once again veered from his idealist position back toward the patheticists, lending expressiveness to the lines of industrial products. See chapter 6.

36. Emil Pirchan, *Otto Wagner* (Vienna: Bergland, 1956), 13.

37. Pöllmann's *Vom Wesen der hieratischen Kunst* is subtitled *A Foreword to the Exhibition of the School of Art of Beuron in the Vienna Secession.* It was in the late spring of 1905 that the Secession broke into two groups termed *Stilisten* and *Impressionnisten.* See Ludwig Hevesi, *Acht Jahre Sezession* (Vienna: Carl Konegen, 1906), 502–505. I would assess that the Beuron exhibition had significance for Vienna despite this break in the Secession; this is partially substantiated by Hevesi's inclusion of Maurice Denis in a list of honorable *Stilisten* which included Wagner, Hoffmann, and Klimt (*Acht Jahre,* 504). See note 12 above.

38. Pöllmann, *Vom Wesen,* 11.

39. The idea of Behrens's work embodying the contemporary understanding of classical antiquity is developed in chapter 4.

40. Julius Meier-Graefe, *Entwicklungsgeschichte der modernen Kunst,* 3 vols. (Stuttgart: Jul. Hoffmann, 1904): section on van de Velde, II, bk. 5, 666–683; section on Behrens, II, bk. 5, 725–726.

41. Camillo Sitte, *City Planning According to Artistic Principles,* trans. G. R. and C. C. Collins (New York: Random House, 1965). See also George R. and Christiane C. Collins, *Camillo Sitte and the Birth of Modern City Planning* (New York: Random House, 1965).

42. Adolf Loos, *Sämtliche Schriften,* ed. Franz Gluck, 2 vols. (Vienna: Herold, 1962–).

43. Muthesius, *Stilarchitektur und Baukunst;* Otto Wagner, *Moderne Architektur* (Vienna: Schroll, 1896), 4th ed. as *Die Baukunst unserer Zeit* (Vienna: Schroll, 1914).

44. Wagner, *Baukunst,* 31. This program has a distinctly Hegelian ring, an obvious intersection of Hegel's conception that the science of the Idea-developing-in-space (Nature) is geometry and that the science of the Idea-developing-in-time is history. See G. W. F. Hegel, *Reason in History,* trans. R. S. Hartman (New York: Liberal Arts, 1953), xii, 87.

45. Wagner, *Baukunst,* 40–41.

46. See New York, Museum of Modern Art, *Art Nouveau.*

47. Jan Romein, *The Watershed of Two Eras: Europe in 1900* (Middletown, Conn.: Wesleyan University Press, 1978).

48. Hans-Ulrich Simon, *Sezessionismus: Kunstgewerbe in literarischer und bildender Kunst* (Stuttgart: Metzler, 1976).

49. Jost Hermand, *Jugendstil: Ein Forschungsbericht 1918–1964* (Stuttgart: J. B. Metzler, 1965); idem, ed., *Jugendstil* (Darmstadt: Wissenschaftliche Buchgesellschaft, 1971).

50. Gert Selle, *Jugendstil und Kunst-Industrie: Zur Ökonomie und Ästhetik des Kunstgewerbes um 1900* (Ravensburg: Otto Maier, 1974). See also Eckhard Siepmann, ed., *Kunst und Alltag um 1900,* Jahrbuch des Werkbund-Archivs, no. 3 (Lahn-Giessen: Anabas, 1978).

51. Carl E. Schorske, *Fin-de-siècle Vienna: Politics and Culture* (New York: Knopf, 1979).

52. Stanford Anderson, "The Legacy of German Neo-Classicism and Biedermeier: Behrens, Loos, Mies, and Tessenow," *Assemblage,* no. 15 (October 1991), 62–87; idem, "Architecture in a Cultural Field," in Taisto H. Mäkelä and Wallis Miller, eds., *Wars of Classification* (Princeton: Princeton Architectural Press, 1991), 8–35; and idem, "*Sachlichkeit* and Modernity" (see note 30 above).

53. Maria Makela, *The Munich Secession: Art and Artists in Turn-of-the-Century Munich* (Princeton: Princeton University Press, 1990).

Notes to Chapter 2

1. Nikolaus Pevsner, *Pioneers of Modern Design,* 3d ed. (Harmondsworth: Penguin, 1960), 203–204.

2. Henry-Russell Hitchcock, "Peter Behrens," *Encyclopedia of World Art* (New York: McGraw-Hill, 1960), 2: col. 413.

3. J. M. Richards, *An Introduction to Modern Architecture,* 2d ed. (Harmondsworth: Penguin, 1953), 76.

4. Sigfried Giedion, *Space, Time and Architecture,* 2d ed. (Cambridge: Harvard University Press, 1949), 410.

5. Nikolaus Pevsner, "Architecture and the Applied Arts," in Paris, Musée National d'Art Moderne, *The Sources of the XXth Century* (Paris, 1960–1961), 53.

6. Peter Meyer, "Architektur als Ausdruck der Gewalt," *Werk,* 27 (June 1940), 163.

7. Julius Meier-Graefe, "Epigonen," *Dekorative Kunst,* 4 (July 1899), 129–131.

8. Behrens's involvement at Darmstadt will be examined in detail in chapter 3; relevant documentation is given there.

9. Text, music (by Willem de Haan), and description appear in Alexander Koch, ed., *Die Ausstellung der Darmstädter Künstler-Kolonie* (Darmstadt: A. Koch, 1901), 56–87.

10. The noted French chemist Henri Moissan claimed to have achieved this feat in 1893. The claim is disputed, but the theory, which was older than Moissan, was finally demonstrated by F. B. Bunday of General Electric in 1954. See L. W. Marrison, *Crystals, Diamonds and Transistors* (Harmondsworth: Penguin, 1966), 60–62.

11. A similar concern with the idealization of earthly experience occurs in Leonardo: "Thou must show in thy treatise that the earth is a star, like the moon or resembling it, and thus prove the nobility of our world." Freud quotes this in chapter 3 of his *Leonardo,* taking it from Marie Herzfeld, *Leonardo da Vinci,* 2d ed. (Jena: Diederichs, 1906), 141. Both the publisher and the graphic designer (E. R. Weiss) for Herzfeld's book were associated with Behrens in these years. See chapter 4.

12. W[ilhelm] Schäfer, "Ein Dokument deutscher Kunst," *Die Rheinlande,* 1 (June 1901), 39.

13. Peter Behrens, *Ein Dokument deutscher Kunst* (Munich: Bruckmann, 1901).

14. Ludwig, Prince of Hesse and the Rhine, described this lamp in his collection as "a most startling and rather hideous 'Jugendstil' lamp in the shape of a winged figure made of bronze with glass inlay." Letter to the author, 13 June 1963.

15. Friedrich Nietzsche, *Thus Spoke Zarathustra,* trans. R. J. Hollingdale (Harmondsworth: Penguin, 1961), [336].

16. Richard Hamann and Jost Hermand, *Stilkunst um 1900* (Berlin [Ost]: Akademie-Verlag, 1967), 407; Tilmann Buddensieg, "Peter Behrens," in Wolfgang Ribbe and Wolfgang Schäche, eds., *Baumeister. Architekten. Stadtplaner. Biographien zur baulichen Entwicklung Berlins* (Berlin: Historische Kommission zu Berlin/Stapp Verlag, 1987), 344.

17. Georg Fuchs, "La vestibule de la maison de puissance et de beauté," in Alexander Koch, ed., *L'exposition internationale des arts décoratifs modernes à Turin 1902* (Darmstadt: Koch, 1903), 106–115. This work by Koch gives a comprehensive view of the Turin exhibition. Other works treating Behrens's contribution are: F. Minkus, "Die erste internationale Ausstellung für moderne dekorative Kunst in Turin," *Kunst und Kunsthandwerk,* 5 (1902), 402–450; W. Fred, "Die Turiner Ausstellung," *Dekorative Kunst,* 10 (September 1902), 433–482; L. Gmelin, ed., *Erste internationale Ausstellung für moderne dekorative Kunst in Turin* (Munich: Datterer, [1902]); A. Melani, "L'Art Nouveau at Turin," *Architectural Record,* 12 (December 1902), 743–750; L. Nacht[licht], *Turin 1902* (Berlin: E. Wasmuth, n.d.); V. Pica, *L'arte decorativa all'Esposizione di Torino del 1902* (Bergamo, 1903); and Gisela Moeller, *Peter Behrens in Düsseldorf: Die Jahre 1903 bis 1907* (Weinheim: VCH, 1991), 408–411.

18. Marie-Henri Beyle (de Stendhal), *On Love,* trans. H. B. V. (New York: Liveright, 1947), chapter 2 and app. "The Salzburg Bough."

19. Describing Behrens's personality and deportment, Karl Scheffler wrote that he "kam immer etwas senatorenhaft würdig daher [presented himself with dignity, like a senator]," and that self-stylization had become second nature to him. Scheffler, *Die fetten und die mageren Jahre* (Leipzig:

List, 1946), 35. Stendhal's "crystallization" referred to an idealization of an experience in life, but he also referred to this phenomenon in such an abstruse field as mathematics (see *On Love*, 18). A pertinent instance of an artist claiming that "Art is crystallization" was that of Edvard Munch, cited by Frederick Deknatel, *Edvard Munch* (New York: Museum of Modern Art, 1950), 33.

20. See chapter 4.

21. The illustration is taken from Lauweriks, "Architektur," *Ring*, no. 4 (April 1909). See N. H. M. Tummers, *J. L. Mathieu Lauweriks* (Hilversum: G. van Saane, 1968).

22. H. P. Berlage, *Grundlagen und Entwicklung der Architektur* (Rotterdam: Brusse, 1908), 57–58.

23. An important related work is the exhibition room for the Mannheim exhibition of 1907. See chapter 4.

24. Walter Müller-Wulckow, *Bauten der Gemeinschaft aus deutscher Gegenwart* (Königstein: Langewiesche, 1928), 8.

25. Behrens's work in Berlin is the subject of chapters 5–8.

26. Fritz Schumacher, *Selbstgespräche* (Hamburg: Springer, 1949), 220, spoke of Behrens's belief in the mystic power of numbers.

27. Alois Riegl, *Spätrömische Kunstindustrie* (Vienna: Oesterr. archäologisches Institut, 1901).

28. Theodor Heuss, *Hitlers Weg*, 8th ed. (Stuttgart: Deutsche Verlagsgesellschaft, 1932), 23–24.

29. Behrens, "Kunst und Technik," *Elektrotechnische Zeitschrift*, 31 (2 June 1910), 552, also mentions Riegl's theory of *Kunstwollen*—the interest is apparent in the remainder of this chapter.

30. Robert Breuer, "Peter Behrens," *Werkkunst*, 3 (9 February 1908), [145–149].

Notes to Chapter 3

1. Drawn from the essay "The Use and Abuse of History," first published in 1874 in the book known in English as *Thoughts out of Season* (New York: Liberal Arts Press, 1949), 73–85.

2. See, e.g., Henry van de Velde, *Laienpredigten* (Leipzig: Seemann, 1902), 16, where the influence of Nietzsche in the Belgian revolutionary art movement around 1890 is mentioned. Van de Velde designed the Nietzsche-Archiv in Weimar (1903).

3. I am concentrating on Nietzsche as a shorthand notation for the more general situation under discussion. As Nietzsche's writings were becoming common intellectual property, a book appeared that was extraordinarily influential in Germany and especially among artists: *Rembrandt als Erzieher* (Leipzig: Hirschfeld, 1890), written by Julius Langbehn but published anonymously. Though influenced by Nietzsche, Langbehn could hardly compare with his brilliance. Nevertheless, in the decades around 1900 the thought, advocacy, and influence of these two men were confounded. The comparatively shallow and prosaic programmatics of Langbehn, urging the synthesis of an artistic culture that should resolve the antinomy of a lost age of faith and a spiritless age of science, could be more easily and purposively grasped than the writings of Nietzsche. A book of related significance, influenced by Langbehn, urging an artistic education for all German children was Konrad Lange, *Die künstlerische Erziehung der deutschen Jugend* (Darmstadt: Bergstrasser, 1893).

An early enthusiast for feeling and the "heart" as opposed to reason and the mind was Heinrich Pudor, a constant advocate of the movement in the arts discussed here. See his *Die Welt als Musik* (Dresden: Albanus, n.d. [a lecture given in 1891]), and *Kaiser Wilhelm II und Rembrandt als Erzieher,* 2d ed. (Dresden: Damm, 1891).

On the first page of his *Kultur und Kunst* (Jena: Diederichs, 1904), Hermann Muthesius mentions the works of both Langbehn and Lange. He cites the Darmstadt Artists' Colony as an early fruition of these ideas. As late as 1911, Muthesius cited the generative influence of Langbehn's book in an address to the Deutscher Werkbund.

In *Der Weg der Kunst* (Jena: Diederichs, 1904), Albert Dresdner draws upon Nietzsche and Langbehn to put his case against modern science, impressionism, and the corset, and in favor of dance, artistic education, etc. Both of the last-mentioned works were published by Eugen Diederichs, whose prospectuses for his press, in leading from one of his publications to the next, formed not just an essay but a coherent program for cultural reform. Some of his authors might cite Langbehn favorably, but the total program was broader. Diederichs considered himself the leading publisher of what was termed the *Neuromantik.* Under this term were grouped those artists, poets, essayists, historians, and philosophers who sought a comprehensive view of life such as the early nineteenth-century romantics had sought. Goethe was one of the great models, but there were others, and of other eras: e.g., Paracelsus and Dürer. Diederichs felt that an earlier admirable desire for an adequate *Naturphilosophie* had been lost in the materialism, naturalism, and specialization of the later nineteenth century. See Diederichs's program for his press in 1900, quoted near the end of this chapter and documented in note 45 below.

For an excellent consideration of Langbehn and other strongly nationalistic ideologists, see Fritz Stern, *The Politics of Cultural Despair* (Berkeley: University of California Press, 1961).

4. The work of other painters deemed worthy of admiration, such as Van Gogh, Seurat, Emile Bernard, Maurice Denis, and Ferdinand Hodler, became known in Germany only during the course of the movement. The basic conservatism of the German situation is well illustrated by the fact that the publication of a quite unprovocative lithograph by Toulouse-Lautrec in the avant-garde magazine *Pan,* 1 (1895), opp. p. 196, caused an internal crisis that was only resolved by a reformulation of the board of editors.

5. Julius Meier-Graefe, "Peter Behrens," *Dekorative Kunst,* 2 (1898), 70–84. See also Franz Blei, "Peter Behrens—A German Artist," *Studio,* 21 (February 1901), 237–241, color plate of "The Forest"; and Benno Ruettenauer, *Kunst und Handwerk* (Strassburg: Heitz, 1902), 89–93.

6. In *The Birth of Tragedy,* the formulation of an aesthetic metaphysics, Nietzsche extols Prometheus, "the great philanthropist," for his "Titan-like love for man," and suggests that the myth of Prometheus "has the same characteristic significance for the Aryan race that the myth of the fall of man has for the Semitic, that there is a relationship between the two myths like that of a brother and sister." In Nietzsche, *Complete Works,* ed. Oscar Levy (London: Foulis, 1909ff.), 1:35, 40, 77–88.

Prometheus was a popular figure with the poets and artists of the *Neuromantik.* To my knowledge, Behrens's woodcut is not a precise illustration of any literary version of Prometheus. In addition to Nietzsche, however, one might mention Carl Spitteler's epic *Prometheus und Epimetheus* (Aarau: Sauerländer, [1881]), where the imagery is suggestive of some of Behrens's other works. For example, the austere and beautiful goddess whom Prometheus serves in Spitteler's work is suggestive for the meaning of the female figure who dominates the young, nude, sleeping artist in Behrens's decorative painting *Der Traum*. This *Dream* is the painting that held the most prominent position in Behrens's homes in both Darmstadt (figure 3.9) and Neubabelsberg from 1901 through most of his productive career.

7. Behrens's *Victory* was reproduced in color as the key illustration to the special number of *Deutsche Kunst und Dekoration,* 3 (May 1900), on the occasion of the dedication of the artists' studio building at the Artists' Colony (24 March 1900), immediately following the introduction with its excerpt from the address of Behrens to the grand duke, pp. [353–356].

8. "And the Seventh Seal begins:

> *If ever I spread out a still sky above myself and flew with my own wings into my own sky;*
> *if, playing, I have swum into deep light-distance and bird-wisdom came to my freedom;*
> *but thus speaks bird-wisdom: 'Behold, there is no above, no below! Fling yourself about,*
> > *out, back, weightless bird! Sing! speak no more!*
> *'are not all words made for the heavy? Do not all words lie to the light? Sing! speak no*
> > *more!'"*

Thus Spoke Zarathustra, trans. R. J. Hollindale (Harmondsworth: Penguin, 1961), 247. Further, Zarathustra says: "My eagle is awake and, like me, does honor to the sun. With eagle's claws it reaches out for the new light. You are my rightful animals: I love you. But I still lack my rightful men!" (p. 334).

9. Ibid., 102–103.

10. Karl Scheffler, "Das Haus Behrens," *Dekorative Kunst,* 9 (October 1901), 23.

11. Illustrated in *Zeitschrift für Innendekoration,* 10 (1899), 1–8.

12. Alexander Koch, ed., *Die Ausstellung der Darmstädter Künstler-Kolonie* (Darmstadt: Alexander Koch, 1901), 20.

13. The principal publications on Behrens's house are Wilhelm Schaefer, "Das Haus Peter Behrens," *Die Rheinlande,* 1 (August 1901), 27–31, 48–49; Kurt Breysig, "Das Haus Peter Behrens," in Koch, ed., *Die Ausstellung,* 342–347; Scheffler, "Das Haus Behrens"; and W. Fred, "The Artists' Colony at Darmstadt," *Studio,* 24 (October 1901), 430–452. Many of the extensive illustrations of these works are collected in Christian Norberg-Schulz, *Casa Behrens: Darmstadt,* 2d ed. (Rome: Officina, 1986).

Alfred Lichtwark in a letter from Darmstadt dated 14 June 1901 reported that Behrens's house cost 200,000 marks. By comparison, Olbrich's house was expensive at 75,000 marks. *Briefe an die Kommission für die Verwaltung der Kunsthalle,* ed. G. Pauli, 2 vols. (Hamburg: G. Westermann, 1923), 1:456.

14. Otto Stiehl, *Backsteinbauten in Norddeutschland und Dänemark* (Stuttgart: Julius Hoffmann, [1923]), 55 and passim. A specific building that employs a similar network of hard, dark bricks with plaster infill is the fifteenth-century cathedral of Stendal (especially the interior, but certain of the exterior details as well); H. and F. Möbius, *Medieval Churches in Germany* (Berlin: Union Verlag, 1964), pls. 143–144. Fritz Hoeber, *Peter Behrens* (Munich: Müller und Rentsch, 1913), 1, uses the cathedral of Stendal to characterize both the architecture and the personality type of northern Germany; Behrens was very self-consciously a north German.

---

15. The Tyrolean cloister building illustrated in figure 3.8 is from Martin Gerlach and J. A. Lux, *Volkstümliche Kunst* (Vienna: Gerlach und Schenk, 1904), 120. In the same collection, p. 60, see the "Kroneshaus" in Grinzing (the popular wine-producing suburb of Vienna), a house that appears suggestive both in the present case and perhaps even more for Olbrich's houses at Darmstadt. Another group of prominent anonymous houses with high-pitched roofs, ogive-shaped gables, and rows of windows separated only by mullions is illustrated in H. E. von Berlepsch-Valendas, "Toggenbürger Bauernhäuser," *Kunst und Kunsthandwerk,* 9 (1906), 1–23.

16. Karl Scheffler suggested that the music room was like a small temple of Isis. See *Die fetten und die mageren Jahre* (Leipzig: Paul List, 1946), 37.

17. For a general bibliography on the theater in Germany, see Franz Rapp, "Eine Handbibliothek zur deutschen Theatergeschichte," *Monatshefte für deutsche Unterricht* (Madison, Wis.), 34 (1942), 183–191.

18. The theater auditorium had received a significant new configuration through Richard Wagner's demands that every spectator should face directly toward the stage and be able to see into its full depth. This resulted, in the Wagnerian Festspielhaus at Bayreuth (1876), in a theater with a single, fan-shaped bank of seats that looked over an orchestra pit into a deep, framed stage. The modified antique seating arrangement immensely improved simple visual contact and became the prototype of most subsequent theater auditoriums. However, this configuration retained the concept of an illusionistic deep stage behind the picture frame. The gulf between actor and viewer was made even more emphatic as a conscious device for the creation of mystic illusion.

A young Swiss music student turned stage designer, Adolphe Appia, found Wagner's staging instructions to be minimal and the visual aspect of Wagnerian productions to be merely "arbitrary scenic schemes." He considered such staging an ineffectual or even a decidedly disruptive element in what should be the formidable impact of musical drama. Appia first presented his ideas in the small unillustrated volume *La mise en scène du drame wagnérien* (Paris: L. Chailley, 1895). After almost a decade of studies, Appia propounded and illustrated his ideas of theatrical production in *Die Musik und die Inszenierung* (Munich: Bruckmann, 1899), available in English as *Music and the Art of the Theatre* (Coral Gables: University of Miami Press, 1962). Appia wished to achieve a more intense and emotional contact with the audience through a clear exhibition of the movement of the actors, through a stage beheld as space rather than as a picture, and through an environmental and interpretive use of light. In words and pictures, Appia emphasized these factors at the expense of traditional flats, illusionistic painting, and the general elaborateness of the naturalistic stage.

Appia's actors remain on a traditional stage, but they perform on simplified platforms in an evocative light that provides both an envelopment and a heightened awareness of their presence and movements. Despite the creation of an emphatically spatial stage, Appia still speaks of the "pictorial ensemble." The end is still the creation of an illusion, but not an illusion of reality. It is a mystic illusion meant to envelop and transport the spectator.

19. Peter Behrens, "Die Dekoration der Bühne," *Deutsche Kunst und Dekoration,* 6 (May 1900), 401–405. Olbrich, together with Hermann Bahr, was at the same time pursuing a similar interest under the name "Plakatstil." See H. Kindermann, ed., *Kritiken von Hermann Bahr: Theater der Jahrhundertwende* (Vienna: Bauer, 1963), 254–262. Such programs, and specifically that of Behrens, were criticized by Max Martersteig, "Dekorationen," *Die Zukunft,* 32 (1900), 200–208. A sympathetic criticism is offered by Franz Blei, *Die Insel,* 2 (January 1901), 141–144.

20. See penultimate paragraph of note 3 above.

21. Georg Fuchs, "Die Schaubühne—Ein Fest des Lebens," *Wiener Rundschau* (1 September 1899), 483–486. The word *Schaubühne* does translate simply as "stage," but it was also preferred by Fuchs for its evocation of the stage as something to be *seen*.

Georg Fuchs, *Die Schaubühne der Zukunft* (Berlin and Leipzig: Schuster & Loeffler, [1905]), is a definitive statement of what had become the Fuchs-Behrens theater program. Frontispiece and end vignettes in the book are those designed with theater motifs by Behrens and published in his *Deutsche Kunst und Dekoration* article of 1900. The book also includes plans and a longitudinal section of a theater design by Max Littmann—a preliminary design to the Künstlertheater in Munich, about which more below.

22. Fuchs, "Die Schaubühne," 485.

23. Five years older than Behrens, Dehmel fully established his renown in the last five years of the nineteenth century—both through the publication of his books and poetry and through the ensuing legal processes. In a letter of 9 September 1899, Dehmel wrote from Munich to Harry Graf Kessler, a fellow member of the *Pan* editorial staff, requesting generous coverage in *Pan* for Behrens's exhibition at Keller und Reiner in Berlin. Dehmel justified his request with the prediction that Behrens would be the strong leader of "Art for Life" in Germany. Dehmel, *Ausgewählte Briefe* (Berlin: Fischer, 1922), 1: no. 266.

24. Behrens, *Feste des Lebens und der Kunst* (Leipzig: Diederichs, 1900); idem, "Die Lebensmesse von Richard Dehmel als festliches Spiel," *Die Rheinlande,* 1 (January 1901), 28–40. "Eine Lebensmesse—Dichtung für Musik" first appeared in the second edition of Dehmel's book *Erlösungen* (Berlin: Fischer, 1898).

We are certain of Dehmel's participation in these works as well as his acquiesence in their final form. Behrens wrote Dehmel requesting a meeting in what he already considered a joint enterprise ("Darmstadt, 10. Juni 1900," Staats- und Universitäts-Bibliothek, Hamburg, Dehmel Archiv, letter B287). Dehmel's correspondence reveals his identification with Behrens's ideas on the staging of "Lebensmesse" (Dehmel to Gustav Kuhl, 2 February 1901, and to R. de Campagnolle, 27 February 1901; Dehmel, *Ausgewählte Briefe,* 1: nos. 302 and 304, respectively). See also note 48 below.

25. This and other of Behrens's contemporary graphics are illustrated in Tilmann Buddensieg and Gisela Moeller, "Der frühe Behrens," in Nürnberg, Germanisches Nationalmuseum, *Peter Behrens und Nürnberg, Geschmackswandel in Deutschland: Historismus, Jugendstil und die Anfänge der Industrieform,* ed. Peter-Klaus Schuster (Munich: Prestel, 1980), 48–56.

Behrens's pretentious prose is consonant with the character of the enterprise. An adequate translation of this prose would be difficult at best, and might even strain the credulity of the reader.

26. Behrens, "Die Lebensmesse von Richard Dehmel" (1901), 28.

27. Behrens, *Feste,* 19; following material is paraphrased from pp. 19–21.

28. This again suggests Behrens's reliance on ideas about relief propounded in Adolf Hildebrand, *Problem der Form* (Strassburg: Heitz, 1893).

29. Behrens, "Die Lebensmesse von Richard Dehmel" (1901), 29.

30. Ibid.

31. Behrens, *Feste,* 23–24.

32. However, the plans of the Royal Albert Hall in London and the Trocadéro in Paris suggest that the realization of Behrens's scheme was quite conceivable. Behrens appears to have had his attention directed to these buildings, and to certain acoustic principles to which his design conforms, through the convenient *Handbuch der Architektur,* pt. 4, vol. 1, *Die architektonische Composition,* 2d ed. (Darmstadt: Diehl, 1893), 275ff.

33. Behrens, *Feste,* 12–17.

34. The descriptive term I take from Julius Bab, *Richard Dehmel* (Leipzig: Haessel, 1926), 211. Bab's comparative musical image is the last movement of Beethoven's ninth symphony.

35. See chapter 2.

36. Behrens, "Die Lebensmesse von Richard Dehmel" (1901), 40. It was hoped that this theater proposal would be realized as part of the exhibition "Ein Dokument deutscher Kunst" at Darmstadt in 1901. At the last minute it was decided that pressing this program into the atmosphere of a summer exhibition was not possible, and that such an attempt would have resulted in more damage than benefit. Georg Fuchs, "Aus der Vorgeschichte des Künstlertheaters," *Der Spiegel: Blätter für Literatur, Musik und Bühne,* 1 (15 June 1908), 141–150.

37. Scheffler, "Das Haus Behrens," states that Behrens's art and his world view are inseparable. He proceeds to discuss Behrens's natural aristocratic qualities: "He knows nothing of the social compassion that torments so many artists and mars both their lives and their works." Behrens's affinity is not with Tolstoy, Ruskin, and Morris, but rather with Nietzsche. The basic frame of mind is an optimistic egoism in the best sense (pp. 21–22).

An anxious search for a revitalized aristocracy before the threat of a democratic deluge illuminates the motives of the grand duke as well. The Artists' Colony was more a last-minute attempt to fight fire with fire than a wholehearted pursuit of modernity.

Nietzsche, following a warning of the possibility of a despot, wrote (*Zarathustra,* 22):

This, however, is the other danger and my other pity: He who is of the mob remembers back to his grandfather—with his grandfather, however, time stops.

Thus all that is past is handed over: for the mob could one day become master, and all time be drowned in shallow waters.

Therefore, O my brothers, is a new nobility needed: to oppose all mob-rule and all despotism and to write anew upon law-tables the word: "Noble."

For many noblemen are needed, and noblemen of many kinds, *for nobility to exist!* Or, as I once said in a parable: "Precisely this is godliness, that there are gods but no God!"

That Behrens, and therefore also the modern movement, have roots other than Morris has been obvious from the beginning. Complementary to the material discussed here, Friedrich Ahlers-Hestermann, *Stilwende,* 2d ed. (Berlin: Mann, 1956), 79, aptly introduced the term "Zarathustrastil" precisely in connection with his description of the splendor of the music room in Behrens's Darmstadt house (1900–1901)—a room that is a miniature Behrens theater. Behrens emphasized the symbolic importance of the two steps that led into this ceremonial room with its marbles, blue mirrors, gilded ceiling, and prolific crystal symbology.

38. Nietzsche, *Zarathustra,* 325–326.

Julius Bab, in *Richard Dehmel* (Berlin: Gose und Tetzlaff, 1902), 1–2, saw the following verses as the leitmotif of Dehmel's life and poetry:

Und der Mensch will selig werden auf Erden—
weisst Du noch, wie man das machen muss?
[And man wants to find bliss on earth —
do you know how one should do that?]

We seek the harmony of our spirit with the *Urnatur*—reflecting Nietzsche, the overcoming of the little reason of our intellect by the great and powerful reason of our entire bodily existence (*Zarathustra,* 61). Bab uses "Die Lebensmesse" as the most potent example of Dehmel's central theme.

Both Dehmel and Bab were anxious to maintain the independence of Dehmel's thought and poetry from Nietzsche. Bab sees the distinction stemming from the "Germanentum" of Dehmel contrasted to the "slavic-romanisch, humanistisch" spirit of Nietzsche (Bab, *Dehmel,* 12). Nevertheless, Bab writes: "So Dehmel has become the standard-bearer in the progress of a *new Renaissance,* of a new planting of human culture in the colorful ground of this material world; the standard of his art quivers in the zephyr of a new era that more joyfully celebrates the arts, and his bold figure rises head-high above all his comrades. Only one other towers into the same proud heights, he who marches at the head of this host: Zarathustra-Nietzsche" (ibid., 10). See also Nietzsche, *Zarathustra,* 111. A new collection of writings on Nietzsche and the arts is Alexandre Kostka and Irving Wohlfarth, eds., *Nietzsche and "An Architecture of Our Minds"* (Los Angeles: Getty Research Institute, 1999); on Behrens, see especially the essay by Fritz Neumeyer, "Nietzsche and Modern Architecture," 285–309.

39. Behrens criticized Wagnerian staging for its "plastic painting, painted architecture, illustrative music and similar devices which contrive to counterfeit nature or art in an anti-stylistic mixture." Behrens, "Die Lebensmesse von Richard Dehmel" (1901), 28. As these remarks are specifically directed against Bayreuth, it is not clear to what extent Behrens would have pressed his argument against Appia. That he knew Appia's work is certified by E. Bruckmann-Cantacuzène, who published an article in her husband's journal on the necessity for an artistic reform of the theater (*Dekorative Kunst,* 8 [April 1901], 271–288). She writes warmly of Appia's recently published book, and promises to publish Appia designs plus a discussion of Behrens's theater proposals in one of the next numbers. Apparently this second article did not appear; but, considering Behrens's relationship with the Bruckmanns, we can be sure that he learned of Appia's book no later than April 1901—probably much earlier.

40. The first years of the twentieth century saw great activity in inventive theater ideas. (See Rapp, "Handbibliothek zur deutschen Theatergeschichte.") From 1900 to 1903, Gordon Craig developed his highly abstract, virtually cubist stage proposals in London before going to Germany, where he associated with the avant-garde artistic group formed around Harry Graf Kessler in Berlin and Weimar. A series of exhibitions of Craig's theatrical designs made his work famous throughout the German-speaking world. Craig's influential *The Art of the Theater* appeared in 1905 (also as *Die Kunst des Theaters*).

In 1901, Max Reinhardt's small house "Schall und Rauch" opened in Berlin and evolved from cabaret to theater—namely the Kleines Theater, which opened with Frank Wedekind's *Der Erdgeist*

(*The Earth Spirit*) in December 1902. In January 1903, Maxim Gorki's *Nachtasyl* (*Na dyne; The Lower Depths*), a realist play, was staged with fresh fantasy by Richard Vallentin. Financially and popularly, this production may be considered the beginning of the new theater in Germany; it enjoyed 500 performances in two years. Max Reinhardt rose to world renown with his multifarious productions at the Neues Theater and, beginning on 19 October 1905, at the Deutsches Theater in Berlin. There is an extensive bibliography on Reinhardt; *Theatre Research*, 5, no. 3 (1963), is devoted to his career.

The foundation of the Schauspielhaus in Düsseldorf (opened with Friedrich Hebbel's *Judith* in October 1905) by Luise Dumont and Gustav Lindemann already pointed to the post-Jugendstil classical reaction in both its repertoire and its intentions. It embodied a dream of realizing Schiller's *Nationaltheater,* but it continued the search for imaginative theatrical production. Luise Dumont referred to the theater as the "Tempel und Tabernakel des Geistes" and used such phrases as "die Bühne als Höchste Kultstätte." See Kurt Loup, *Schönheit und Freiheit* (Düsseldorf: Stern, 1959), 179. For contemporary comments by the principal, see Luise Dumont, "Das Schauspielhaus in Düsseldorf," *Die Woche* (7 October 1905), 1726–1727. The "Hausordnung" of the theater was printed using the first typeface designed by Behrens (see plate between pp. 88–89 of Loup, *Schönheit*).

Behrens's designs for unexecuted stage sets for Dumont-Lindemann productions of *Hamlet,* Ibsen's *Kronprätendenten,* and Schiller's *Wilhelm Tell* are illustrated and discussed in Gisela Moeller, *Peter Behrens in Düsseldorf: Die Jahre 1903 bis 1907* (Weinheim: VCH, 1991), 398–404.

One of the major stage designers for the Schauspielhaus was Eduard Sturm, who, according to information supplied by Dr. Walter Kordt of Düsseldorf, emphatically declared himself a "Behrens-Schüler." For six illustrations of Sturm stage designs see *Das Schauspielhaus Düsseldorf: Ein Vierteljahrhundert deutscher Bühnenkunst* (Düsseldorf: Freihochschulbund, 1930).

In 1907, Karl Scheffler wrote a lengthy article summing up the rapidly changed situation of the theater: "Bühnenkunst," *Kunst und Künstler,* 5 (March 1907), 217–244. His dominant theme was an appreciation of Max Reinhardt. Scheffler gave Behrens the opportunity to express his theater ideas; the details remain the same as in 1900. Significantly, however, Behrens's presentation is now strictly descriptive of the physical proposals for a relief-like stage—there is none of the pompous prose and none of the philosophical and sociological scaffolding.

While Behrens was engrossed in teaching and in the beginnings of his architectural career at Düsseldorf, Georg Fuchs continued to pursue the ideas of stage and society that evolved from the Darmstadt time. In 1905 Fuchs propagandized the relief stage in *Die Schaubühne der Zukunft,* a work that contained two plans and a section by Max Littmann for a proposed theater with the prescribed shallow stage. In 1906, in the series Flugblätter für künstlerischer Kultur, no. 6, Fuchs described the role of dance for a culture in which the whole of life is given form: Fuchs, *Der Tanz* (Stuttgart: Strecker & Schröder, 1906).

At this time, under the patronage of Rupprecht, Prinz von Bayern, Fuchs, together with the stage designer Fritz Erler and the architect Max Littmann, created the Künstlertheater (Artists' Theater) in Munich (1907–1908). Littmann was an important theater architect of the time; he built both the Prinzregententheater and the Schauspielhaus in Munich at the turn of the century. See G. J. Wolf, *Max Littmann, 1862–1931* (Munich: Knorr & Hirth, 1931). The Künstlertheater (destroyed in World War II) opened with a production of Goethe's *Faust* on 17 May 1908. The theater was set above the Theresienwiese on a site in the exhibition park; along the paths that led the Bavarian nobility to the festival performance were rows of torches. The building was rectangular in plan and had a modified, broad, and simple proscenium opening. In other details, the theater reflected many of Behrens's principles. The direct view of the audience, the broad forestage reaching almost to the front seats, the slight terracing of the comparatively shallow stage (approximately 13 by 33 feet), the segmental background against which the actors appeared either in relief or in silhouette (the background was here formed by one of four interchangeable, differently colored cycloramas) are all familiar. The economy of sets and costuming approximates the demands of Behrens. Even the restrained and geometric architectural decoration of the building seems to derive from Behrens's work of the Düsseldorf period. Fuchs indeed became the active advocate of the "relief stage" and the social principles associated with it at Darmstadt. Nonetheless, the architect Max Littmann, in *Das Münchner Künstlertheater* (Munich: Werner, 1908), does not mention Behrens as he evokes extensive precedents in antiquity, the Orient, and throughout the nineteenth century with such figures as Goethe, Schinkel, and Semper.

To judge from the descriptions of the Künstlertheater production of *Faust*, it was mainly the evocative use of light that separated this staging from Behrens and related it to the main trends of twentieth-century stagecraft. For an evaluation of this "first symbolist production of *Faust*," see M. Gorelik, *New Theatres for Old* (New York: Dobson, 1948), 175–188. Gorelik also notes the importance of the theater building (p. 289) and gives a brief account of Fuchs's monarchist political activities.

Gordon Craig's visit to the Künstlertheater in 1908 made him an ecstatic enthusiast of all aspects of this theater project. See Craig, *On the Art of the Theater*, 2d ed. (London: Heinemann, 1911), the first of the two letters to John Semar.

An incisive study of the Künstlertheater and its influence is Walter Grohmann, *Das Münchner Künstlertheater in der Bewegung der Szenen und Theaterreform* (Berlin: Gesellschaft für Theatergeschichte, 1935), with 77 illustrations. See also Lenz Prüttig, *Die Revolution des Theaters: Studien über Georg Fuchs* (Munich: Kitzinger, 1971).

Further: Fuchs, "Aus der Vorgeschichte des Künstlertheaters"; Fuchs, *Die Revolution des Theaters* (Munich and Leipzig: G. Müller, 1909), in English as *Revolution in the Theatre*, "condensed and adapted" by C. C. Kuhn (Ithaca: Cornell University Press, 1959); Gertrude Rudloff-Hille in Helmut Seling, ed., *Jugendstil: Der Weg ins 20. Jahrhundert* (Heidelberg and Munich: Keyser, 1959), 397ff.

W. F. Storck reviews what he sees as the first important exhibition of modern theater art (Mannheim, 1913) in "Die neue Bühnenbildkunst," *Dekorative Kunst,* 16 (1913), 297–312. Appia, Craig, and Behrens are seen as the principal initiators of the movement.

41. Georg Fuchs repeatedly emphasized the importance of visual factors; the goal of theater, as he saw it, was to achieve artistic effects, not literary effects. Theater should not be a "Schankstätte für Literatur"; on the contrary, we should have theater that is nothing else but "Theater: l'art pour l'art, le théâtre pour le théâtre" (Fuchs, "Aus der Vorgeschichte des Künstlertheaters," 147).

Behrens's friend, the poet and essayist Otto Julius Bierbaum, described the *Neuromantik* theater which both he and Behrens sought in this way: "We envision as the ideal a juxtaposition of the arts in which none of them holds a position of superiority." O. J. Bierbaum, *Die vernarrte Prinzess: Ein Fabelspiel in drei Bildern, mit einer Vorrede über das musikalische Bühnenspiel* (Munich: Langen, 1904), xx.

On 28 December 1901, Bierbaum opened his Trianon-Theater in Berlin, an attempt at lyric theater that did not survive the opening night. It may have been a symbolic as well as a physical fact that one of the elements contributing to the Trianon fiasco was the punctuation of the verses of "the little Muse" by the rumbling of elevated trains. Bierbaum presents the evening's program and makes his excuses in *Die Insel,* 3 (January 1902), 119ff.

In his article of 1907, Scheffler spoke of the danger of loss of hierarchy among the arts and placed the blame on Gordon Craig, who personified in stagecraft what Scheffler felt were the recognized dangers of the English cult of arts and crafts. Scheffler protests that for Craig the word is one with movement, line, color, and rhythm. "If this attitude wins the day, then the reform of the stage must necessarily end in superficial theatricalism" (Scheffler, "Bühnenkunst," 220–221). Scheffler's summary treatment of Craig is inadequate; I present it only because his argument points up a relevant problem in a context that would have been known to Behrens.

42. The first two scenes of *Diogenes* were written in 1896 and published in *Pan,* 4 (December 1896), 223–232. Scenes 3, 4, and 5 were written at the same time; the first scene was reworked in 1898. Never completed, the work was published in its fragmentary state (Berlin: Fischer, 1905). The work was a free adaptation of *Diogenes* by Felix Pyat (Paris and Leipzig, 1846).

43. For contemporary descriptions and criticisms of this production, see: Ernst Schur, "Peter Behrens und die Reform der Bühne," *Kunstgewerbeblatt,* n.s. 22 (December 1910), 41–44; *Leipziger Tageblatt* (30 June 1909), 10–11; Theodor Lessing, "Welt und Wissen," *Hannoverscher Kurier* (7 July 1909); idem, in *Düsseldorfer Generalanzeiger* (17 July 1909); idem, in *Die Schaubühne,* 5 (August 1909), 145–151; Wilhelm Schäfer, in *Die Rheinlande,* 9 (August 1909), 265–281; A. Jolles, in *Die neue Rundschau,* 20 (August 1909), 1227–1229. According to Jolles, the presentation did not fulfill the potential of either the drama or the stage theory. See also Kraft-Eike Wrede, *Karl Ernst Osthaus und das Theater: Peter Behrens' Inszenierung des 'Diogenes' von Otto Erich Hartleben für die Hagener Sommerschauspiele (1909)* (Hagen: Karl Ernst Osthaus Museum, 1984). With particular reference to Osthaus, but also with a facsimile of the Behrens-designed announcement for the *Diogenes* production, see Walter Erben, "Karl Ernst Osthaus, Lebensweg und Gedankengut," §5, in Herta Hesse-Frielinghaus et al., *Karl Ernst Osthaus—Leben und Werk* (Recklinghausen: Bongers, 1971), 59–65.

44. For the "dramatic" achievement of sheer recitation see the commentary on Karl Kraus's Theatre of Poetry (in Vienna, first decade of the twentieth century) in Erich Heller, *The Disinherited Mind* (New York: Farrar, Straus and Cudahy, 1957), 242–243.

As indicated in Behrens's interesting final statement on theater ("Über die Kunst auf der Bühne," *Frankfurter Zeitung* [20 March 1910], 1–3; now translated by Howard Fitzpatrick as "On the Art of the Stage," *Perspecta,* no. 26 [1990], 137–142, with an introduction by Stanford Anderson, 135–136), he had come to respect what could be achieved in recitation or in rehearsal. He insisted, however, that verse should be recited as verse, and with proper gestures; soon he was at the position discussed in the text: a desire for an architectonic structure of the several arts culminating in the unified rhythm of a production that did justice to the poetic word. Movement and gesture on a relief stage remained Behrens's principal theme.

Behrens cited the admirable work of Jacques Dalcroze and his students in eurhythmics. It was at this time that Heinrich Tessenow designed and built a theater and associated school and residential complex for Dalcroze. This institution was the elevated communal cultural center of Hellerau near Dresden, a garden city created and sustained by Karl Schmidt's Deutsche Werkstätten für Handwerkskunst—important contributors to the development of the Deutscher Werkbund. See Hans-Jürgen Sarfert, *Hellerau: Die Gartenstadt und Künstlerkolonie* (Dresden: Hellerau-Verlag, 1995).

45. *Eugen Diederichs: Leben und Werk,* ed. Lulu von Strauss und Torney-Diederichs (Jena: Diederichs, 1936), 52–53. Also quoted in Eugen Diederichs, *Aus meinem Leben,* 2d ed. (Leipzig: F. Mainer, 1938), 27–28. A long series of statements by Diederichs and a full bibliography, edited by Walther Oschilewski, appeared as a *Beilage* after p. 32 in *Imprimatur,* 9 (1940). See also the latter part of note 3 above.

46. Nietzsche, "The Use and Abuse of History," 77.

47. Stanford Anderson, "Peter Behrens's Highest *Kultursymbol,* the Theater," *Perspecta,* no. 26 (1990), 103–134.

48. Based on her 1969 dissertation for the Institut für Theaterwissenschaft in Vienna, Jutta Boehe published "Theater und Jugendstil—Feste des Lebens und der Kunst," in G. Bott, ed., *Von Morris zum Bauhaus* (Hanau: Peters, 1977), 143–158. Elisabeth Motz, "Pathos und Pose: Peter Behrens' Theaterreform," in Hans-Georg Pfeifer, ed., *Peter Behrens: "Wer aber will sagen, was Schönheit sei?" Grafik, Produktgestaltung, Architektur* (Düsseldorf: Beton-Verlag, 1990), 38–51. See also M. A. Keller, "Richard Dehmel–Peter Behrens: Kunst und Theater um 1900" (thesis, University of Venice, 1980); Manfred Brauneck, *Theater im 20. Jahrhundert: Programmschriften, Stilperioden, Reformmodelle* (Reinbek: Rowohlt, 1982).

49. See sources cited in note 5.

50. An insight into Behrens's paintings and woodcuts, and into the difficulties of an inquiry, is to be found in Norbert Werner, "Peter Behrens: Die Kunst des Könnens und die Kunst des Schönen," in Pfeifer, ed., *Peter Behrens,* 24–37. Catalog entries for some woodcuts appear in Buddensieg and Moeller, "Der frühe Behrens," 48–49. *The Kiss* was an original woodcut insert in *Pan,* 4, no. 2 (September 1898); there is an accessible color reproduction in New York, Museum of Modern Art, *Art Nouveau* (New York: Museum of Modern Art, 1959), frontispiece.

51. Nürnberg, Germanisches Nationalmuseum, *Peter Behrens und Nürnberg,* cited in note 25 above.

52. Buddensieg extols the asymmetrical planning of Behrens's house, seeing it as a precedent for Le Corbusier and Mies van der Rohe; see Brussels, Palais des Beaux-Arts, *Jugendstil* (Brussels: Europalia 77, 1977), 30. A good review of the critical literature is Tilmann Buddensieg, "Das Wohnhaus als Kultbau: Zum Darmstädter Haus von Behrens," in Nürnberg, Germanisches Museum, *Behrens und Nürnberg,* 37–47. See also note 13 above and Guglielmo Bilancioni, *Il primo Behrens: Origini del moderno in architettura* (Florence: Sansoni, 1981).

53. Ellen Spickernagel, "Unerwünschte Tätigkeit: Die Hausfrau und Wohnungsform der Neuzeit," *Kritische Berichte,* 20, no. 4 (1992), 80–96.

Notes to Chapter 4

1. A magazine such as the Dutch *Bouw- en Sierkunst* combines a concern for most of these categories with its interest in contemporary developments. In the specific case of Behrens, similar interests are illustrated in his work and the criticism it received: Julius Meier-Graefe, "Peter Behrens, Düsseldorf," *Dekorative Kunst,* 8 (July 1905), 381–390; Wilhelm Niemeyer, "Peter Behrens und die Raumästhetik seiner Kunst," *Dekorative Kunst,* 10 (January 1907), 131–186, who also mentions the example of Cosmati work, 142; Max Creutz, "Das Krematorium von Peter Behrens in Hagen in Westfalen,"

Kunstgewerbeblatt, n.s. 20 (December 1908), 41–48. In September 1906, the card that Behrens chose to send from Florence to Karl Ernst Osthaus illustrated a work by Giotto (Hagen, Osthaus-Archiv, Ordner 3, "Künstler und Gelehrten. 1905–06"), the greatest "primitive" of the Italian Renaissance.

2. The preference for *Sachlichkeit* and against Jugendstil emerges over the period April-September 1901 in *Dekorative Kunst;* the promise of this new orientation was borne by the Schröder interiors mentioned and illustrated in chapter 1 (figure 1.18). The relevance of the Viennese magazine *Höhe Warte* was also mentioned in chapter 1. The following title speaks for itself: Hermann Muthesius, "Kunstgewerbe, Jugendstil und bürgerliche Kunst," *Rheinlande,* 4 (October 1903), 53–61. J. A. Lux, *Der Geschmack im Alltag* (Dresden: Kühtmann, 1908), was a popular book that directed a simplified taste against the excesses of the late nineteenth century, including Jugendstil excesses. For my later development of the issue of *Sachlichkeit,* see Stanford Anderson, "*Sachlichkeit* and Modernity, or Realist Architecture," in Harry Mallgrave, ed., *Otto Wagner: Reflections on the Raiment of Modernity* (Santa Monica: Getty Center, 1993), 322–360.

3. Lux, *Geschmack,* 126–129; Alfred Meyer, *Eisenbauten: Ihre Geschichte und Ästhetik* (Esslingen: P. Neff, 1907); and Hermann Muthesius, "Kunst und Maschine," *Dekorative Kunst,* 5 (January 1902), 141–147, serve as examples. The last-mentioned comments on the efficiency and modernity of the bicycle.

4. Even more than in the other instances listed, a concern with medieval brick architecture at this time cannot be strictly distinguished from earlier such interests. However, we do find Olbrich, in the Hochzeitsturm at Darmstadt (1907), abandoning his sheer plaster surfaces and floral ornament in favor of substantial forms in brick. See Gustav Adolf Platz, *Die Baukunst der neuesten Zeit* (Berlin: Propyläen, 1927), 567. Hans Poelzig, whose work in brick is distinctly innovative, begins to emerge at this time; ibid., 569–580. Karl Scheffler, *Moderne Baukunst* (Berlin: Bard, 1907), opp. p. 24, illustrates an apartment house in Berlin by Dinklage and Paulus. The overall form is responsive to its use and its situation on an urban street, but it employs the detail and hard edges of north German brickwork. Scheffler's point is that a more individual and studied vocabulary, whatever its intrinsic excellence, is inappropriate for such urban social problems as the modern apartment house. Fritz Schumacher, himself an architect of significance, asserted the importance of H. P. Berlage for German architecture of this time, in *Strömungen in deutscher Baukunst seit 1800,* 2d ed. (Cologne: Seemann, 1955), 118.

5. Schumacher, *Strömungen,* 139, cites the following works as significant examples of a scientific awareness of form prior to World War I: Heinrich Wölfflin, *Prolegomena zu einer Psychologie der Architektur;* Theodor Lipps, *Psychologie des Schönen und der Kunst;* and Wilhelm Worringer, *Abstraktion und Einfühlung.*

6. Platz, *Die Baukunst,* 89–90, cites only Riegl as a theoretician who, around 1900, offered a new and influential alternative to what was recognized as the mechanistic dynamics of Semper's theories. Niemeyer, "Behrens und die Raumästhetik," 142, assures us that Behrens and the Düsseldorf school were interested in Riegl and many others who contributed to a more vital understanding of antiquity. Fritz Hoeber, *Peter Behrens* (Munich: Müller und Rentsch, 1913), 219, characterizes Behrens as being opposed to Semper and in favor of Riegl's teleological understanding of artistic processes. See also Margaret Iversen, *Alois Riegl: Art History and Theory* (Cambridge: MIT Press, 1993).

7. See the sources cited in chapter 3, note 45.

8. Again, Muthesius is the central figure; see the sources cited in chapter 1, note 29.

9. American architecture was quite well known in Germany following the Chicago Exposition of 1893; see, e.g., Wilhelm Bode, "Moderne Kunst in den Vereinigten Staaten von Amerika: Eindrücke von einem Besuche der Weltausstellung zu Chicago. II. Die Architektur und Kunsthandwerk," *Kunstgewerbeblatt,* n.s. 5, nos. 7–8 (April, May 1894), 113–121, 137–146. A large collection of plates was compiled by Paul Graef, *Neubauten in Nordamerika* (Berlin: Becker, 1897ff.), with a foreword by K. Hinckeldeyn that put special stress on the excellence of American domestic architecture. Scheffler, *Moderne Baukunst,* 64–82, illustrates and comments favorably on both English and American houses.

10. Neither a science nor a mysticism of an underlying geometry was new. We have seen this sort of interest in connection with the Beuron school, and such theories could be traced among much more important artists and philosophers right back to antiquity. The point is simply that the artists of concern here, and especially Behrens, became much more involved in such theory and practice after Jugendstil collapsed.

11. Rudolf Steiner, quoted in P. M. Allen's introduction to Steiner, *Friedrich Nietzsche* (Englewood, N.J.: Steiner Publ., [1960]), 18–19.

12. H. Board, "Die Kunstgewerbeschule zu Düsseldorf," *Dekorative Kunst,* 7 (August 1904), 409–432.

13. In March 1901, the director of the Bayerisches Gewerbemuseum in Nürnberg, Oberbaurat Theodor von Kramer, proposed that the museum sponsor a master's course in the applied arts in order that the developed handicraft workers of Nürnberg might profit from and participate in the new activities in the arts and crafts. His proposal was well received by the administration of the museum and by the craftsmen. Behrens agreed to teach the first course (October–November 1901). Sixteen persons from many different crafts worked six days per week on designs or actual works that Behrens guided and criticized. The success of the course was sufficient that Max Abel, in December 1901, opened a special shop, Nürnberger Handwerkskunst, selling only objects produced by the craftsmen of Nürnberg and of design and quality approved by the museum. Behrens designed the shop interior and was also charged with a second master's course with 25 participants (January–February 1902).

Paul Johannes Rée, librarian of the museum, explained the rationale behind these courses. Second-rate artists and craftsmen who had won the popular label "Jugendstil" quickly undermined genuine modern art. This vulgarization profited only the unprincipled producer and the half-trained artists turned out by the extant schools. The Nürnberg program proposed a "return" to development out of the workshop, where those with inadequate artistic talent would remain craftsmen while the true artist would emerge in possession of sound technique.

Contemporary reports indicate that Behrens did not present exemplars, nor did he enter directly into the work of the participants. Nevertheless his current "Zarathustra style" is marked in the Nürnberg production; see figs. 112a-b in Nürnberg, Germanisches Nationalmuseum, *Peter Behrens und Nürnberg, Geschmackswandel in Deutschland: Historismus, Jugendstil und die Anfänge der Industrieform,* ed. Peter-Klaus Schuster (Munich: Prestel, 1980). The critic Dr. Friedrich Carstanjen saw in this a healthy sign that the Nürnberg craftsmen were working through the form conception of a master rather than seeking a premature individual style. However, in order to stress the principles of modernism rather than its personal idiosyncrasies, the museum did change instructors for the third course, held in March-April 1903 under Richard Riemerschmid of Munich. In both 1902 and 1903, the museum exhibited work from the master's courses.

Although rather local in its impact, the Nürnberg program did pioneer work in the educational principle of training new masters through direct involvement with craft technique under the formal tutelage of avant-garde artists devoted to a new plastic vision. Nürnberg also pioneered in seeking to inform the public of this new work through exhibitions and especially through its quality-controlled marketing enterprise.

This description of the Nürnberg master's courses is drawn from the following works: Friedrich Carstanjen, "Kunstgewerbliche Meisterkurse in Nürnberg," *Dekorative Kunst,* 9 (March 1902), 227–232; idem, "Nürnberger Handwerkskunst," *Dekorative Kunst,* 10 (June 1902), 321–336; Nürnberg, Bayerisches Gewerbemuseum, *Bericht für das Jahr 1901* (Nürnberg, [1902]), 45–48 and ill. passim; idem, *Bericht für das Jahr 1902* (Nürnberg, [1903]), 35 and ill. opp. pp. 50, 52, 54; idem, *Bericht für das Jahr 1903* (Nürnberg, [1904]), 57, ill. passim; the publication of a lecture given in 1902 by P. J. Rée, "Kunstgewerbliche Zeit und Streitfragen," ibid., 61ff.; E. W. Bredt, "Nürnberg und die neue Handwerkskunst," *Kunst und Handwerk,* 54 (1903–1904), 297–308. See also note 62 below.

14. W[ilhelm] Schaefer, "Moderner Stil," *Rheinlande,* 2 (June 1902), 48, 51–53.

15. This sweeping criticism directed against science in art, rather than a criticism of a particular kind of knowledge in art, could be especially venomous as long as the new artists were buoyed by an unquestioned enthusiasm. The criticism and the situation that supported it are illustrated in Alfred Lichtwark's report on a visit with Behrens at Darmstadt in May 1900. The eminent director of the Kunsthalle in Hamburg recounted that Behrens had, before coming to Darmstadt, sought a position in his native Hamburg, only to be refused. Having been much impressed by Behrens, Lichtwark lamented that Hamburg had a mathematician as the director of its Gewerbeschule. In *Briefe an die Kommission für die Verwaltung der Kunsthalle,* ed. G. Pauli (Hamburg: G. Westermann, 1923), 405.

16. *Kunst für Alle,* 18 (1 February 1903), 215. Unlike the schools at Berlin and Breslau, which were administered and largely supported by the Ministry of Education, the Düsseldorf school had its corresponding ties with the Ministry of Commerce and Trade. In the winter semester of 1902–1903, just prior to Behrens's arrival, the school had 49 beginning students, 114 students who had entered into the specialized courses, and 141 evening students. The faculty in Behrens's first year numbered sixteen. Financial support was basically municipal, although the state contributed 30,000 marks annually. Statistics from W. Lexis, ed., *Das Unterrichtswesen im Deutschen Reich* (Berlin: Asher, 1904), 4:86–87. The calling of Behrens to Düsseldorf by the Berlin Ministry came in the era of the creative Düsseldorf Mayor Wilhelm Marx, supposedly under the encouragement of the architect Hermann von Endt. This and the gradual separation from the faculty of the Behrens circle under the new director, Wilhelm Kreis, and the listing of some of the students of the Behrens period appear in Walter Kordt, "Die Kunstgewerbeschule von Peter Behrens in Düsseldorf (1903–1908)," *Die Heimat,* nos. 4–6 (April-June 1963), 81–85, 114–120, 137–139. See also Walter Gebhardt, "Anklang und Nachklang: Peter Behrens und Düsseldorf," in Hans-Georg Pfeifer, ed., *Peter Behrens:*

"Wer aber will sagen, was Schönheit sei?" Grafik, Produktgestaltung, Architektur (Düsseldorf: Beton-Verlag, 1990), 122–137; and Wilhelm Busch, *Bauten der 20er Jahre an Rhein und Ruhr* (Cologne: Bachem, 1993), 16–23.

17. W. Schaefer, "Die neue Kunstgewerbeschule in Düsseldorf," *Rheinlande,* 4 (October 1903), 62–63. Schaefer imagined a more radical program than that which came about.

18. Persons definitely on the faculty of the Kunstgewerbeschule of Düsseldorf in the year 1903–1904: Director and class in architecture, Peter Behrens (Darmstadt); introductory drawing class, architect Johann Hermanns; preparatory class A, Josef Bruckmüller (Vienna); preparatory class B and class in architectural drawing, Max Benirschke (Vienna); class in figural and ornamental sculpture, Rudolf Bosselt (Darmstadt); class in two-dimensional design and course in graphics, Fritz Hellmuth Ehmcke (Steglitz); class in two-dimensional design, painter Julius de Praetere (Krefeld); art historian, Dr. Wilhelm Niemeyer; class in animal studies, painter Professor Friedrich Neuhaus; class in plant studies, painter W. Sprengel; class in studies of the nude, painter L. Heupel-Siegen; class in decorative painting, painter Ignaz Wagner; class in metalworking, Julius Peyerimhoff; class in bookbinding, Schulz; library, painter A. Hochreiter. Information from Board, "Kunstgewerbeschule," 409–432, which is the source also for most of the information in the text concerning the first year of Behrens's directorship.

19. On German participation in the St. Louis fair, see [Leo Nachtlicht, comp.], St. Louis, Louisiana Purchase Exposition 1904, Imperial German Commission, *Descriptive Catalogue of the German Arts and Crafts at the Universal Exposition, St. Louis 1904* (n.p.: Th. Lewald, 1904); Leo Nachtlicht, *Deutsches Kunstgewerbe: St. Louis 1904* (Berlin: Wasmuth, [1904]); Max Creutz, "Amerika und die Weltausstellung in St. Louis 1904," *Dekorative Kunst,* 7 (September 1904), 449–486; and Gisela Moeller, *Peter Behrens in Düsseldorf: Die Jahre 1903 bis 1907* (Weinheim: VCH, 1991), 419–423.

According to a letter of 13 February 1962 from Dr. Patas of the Kunstmuseum in Düsseldorf, Behrens's reading room was destroyed during World War II.

20. Board, "Kunstgewerbeschule," passim.

21. Ibid., 429–432.

22. On the *Vorkurse* of Johannes Itten and of László Moholy-Nagy and Josef Albers at the Bauhaus, see H. M. Wingler, *The Bauhaus* (Cambridge: MIT Press, 1969), 280–293.

23. H. P. Berlage, *Grundlagen und Entwicklung der Architektur* (Rotterdam: Brusse, [1908]).

24. Adolf Meyer (1881–1929) was a member of Behrens's atelier in Berlin, as was Walter Gropius. When Gropius left the atelier in 1910, Meyer went with him (from a conversation with Gropius, Cambridge, Mass., 6 February 1964). See Ulrich Thieme and Felix Becker, eds., *Allgemeines Lexicon der bildenden Künstler: Von der Antike bis zur Gegenwart,* 37 vols. (Leipzig: W. Engelmann, 1907ff.), 24:461.

25. Berlage, *Grundlagen,* student designs and discussion, 56–60.

26. Meier-Graefe, "Behrens, Düsseldorf," 381–390. Also Lichtwark, *Briefe,* 2:324–327; Krefeld, Kaiser Wilhelm Museum, *Masssystem und Raumkunst: Das Werk des Architekten Pädagogen und Raumgestalters J. L. M. Lauweriks* (Krefeld: Kaiser Wilhelm Museum, 1987).

27. Mentioned above, but see also Hoeber, *Peter Behrens,* 37.

28. Illustrations of Haus Schede in Meier-Graefe, "Behrens, Düsseldorf," 409–412. I am much obliged to both Frau Dr. Hesse-Frielinghaus and the owner of Haus Schede, Herr Harkort, for the opportunity to visit this well-preserved room in 1962. The house also contains other furniture by Behrens and van de Velde. Moeller, *Behrens in Düsseldorf,* 427–430.

29. Karl Ernst Osthaus, "Peter Behrens," *Kunst und Künstler,* 6, no. 3 (December 1907), 118, 120–121; Hoeber, *Peter Behrens,* 66–80; Herta Hesse-Frielinghaus et al., *Karl Ernst Osthaus—Leben und Werk* (Recklinghausen: Bongers, 1971), 50–51; Moeller, *Behrens in Düsseldorf,* 437–438.

30. Conversation with Gropius, Cambridge, 6 February 1964; with Mies van der Rohe, Chicago, 27 June 1961.

One may also note that Le Corbusier, probably during his time in Behrens's studio, became aware of Lauweriks's work, as is witnessed in his *Le Modulor* (Boulogne: Editions de l'architecture d'aujourd'hui, 1950; and London: Faber & Faber, 1954), 26. Le Corbusier recalls that at age 23, in designing a villa, he felt his need for "the rule that orders, that connects all things. . . . Great disquiet, much searching, many questions. Then he remembered [Le Corbusier speaking of himself in the third person] how once, on a voyage of discovery, as he was looking over a modern villa in Bremen, the gardener there had said to him: 'This stuff, you see, that's complicated, all these twiddly bits, curves, angles, calculations, it's all very learned.' The villa belonged to someone called Thorn Brick(?), a Dutchman (about 1909)." Le Corbusier immediately continues about his discovery of the controlling geometric lines in historic buildings and his first vision of the application of this principle to practice, finally culminating, of course, in the Modulor. The "Dutchman" of whom Le Corbusier speaks was Johann Thorn-Prikker, a painter who was a member of Karl Ernst Osthaus's artists' colony at Hagen in Westfalen (not Bremen) from 1910 to 1919. His strange and complicated villa was designed according to geometrical principles by a fellow member of the colony, Lauweriks, who left the Düsseldorf Kunstgewerbeschule in 1909. The house is illustrated in A. Behne, "Holländische Baukunst in der Gegenwart," *Wasmuths Monatshefte für Baukunst,* 6 (1921–1922), 13. Lauweriks's interest in the golden section and in the idea of a rectangle which, being halved, still possesses the same proportion as the original rectangle would seem to be especially suggestive for Le Corbusier's development of the Modulor. See Lauweriks, *Holzarbeit* (Leipzig and Berlin: Teubner, n.d. [latest 1909]), 5–8. Le Corbusier's visit to Hagen is documented in a letter from Behrens's office in Berlin to Osthaus dated 6 October 1911 (Osthaus-Archiv, Hagen).

31. Lauweriks, *Holzarbeit,* passim.

32. See Peter Vöge, *The Complete Rietveld Furniture* (Rotterdam: 010 publishers, 1993).

33. See, for example, Marcel Breuer's armchair of 1924, illustrated in Alfred Barr, *De Stijl* (New York: Museum of Modern Art, 1961), fig. 13.

34. On the school, see Board, "Kunstgewerbeschule," 417–422. A more sophisticated presentation, with emphasis on Behrens's "mathematical harmony," is Niemeyer, "Behrens und die Raumästhetik," 143–150. On de Stijl, see H. L. C. Jaffé, *Die Gruppe 'de stijl'* (Amsterdam: Meulenhoff, n.d.), 13–15.

35. Nancy J. Troy, *The De Stijl Environment* (Cambridge: MIT Press, 1983).

36. Hoeber, *Peter Behrens,* 28; Moeller, *Behrens in Düsseldorf,* 424–425.

37. See chapter 8; and Moeller, *Behrens in Düsseldorf,* 438–440.

38. H. L. C. Jaffé, *de Stijl. 1917–1931* (London: Tiranti, [1956]).

39. So much so that he was deprecatively referred to as "Lattenpitter."

40. The best photographic presentation of these pavilions is Otto Krebs, "Die architektonische Anlage der Nordwestdeutschen Kunstausstellung in Oldenburg von Peter Behrens," *Dekorative Kunst,* 9 (November 1905), 77–88. Hoeber, *Peter Behrens,* 34–39, gives a detailed analysis of Behrens's geometric schema (emphatically not an arithmetic schema, for the reliance on number and one-dimensional measure is a modern error, Behrens thought). Hoeber, 35, illustrates a system of parallel diagonal lines that determine the critical points in the facade of the Kunsthalle—the same type of system we saw with Berlage. And see Moeller, *Behrens in Düsseldorf,* 432–437.

The discipline of an architectonic geometry in the Oldenburg pavilions is also illustrated by their relation to the forms of Palladio's villas. Recalling also the formal garden at Oldenburg and the two small pitched-roof pavilions at the entrance to the garden, compare the *Quattro libri* plans and elevations of the Villa Godi and Villa Thiene (Cicogna). The continuity and parallelism of gable lines through different blocks is also a typically Palladian interest.

Fritz Wichert, "Luftschiffahrt und Architektur," *Frankfurter Zeitung* (21 March 1909), saw Behrens's straight lines, simplicity, and lack of decoration as contributing to a sense of weightlessness; the buildings rest upon the ground rather than growing out of it. To Wichert, Behrens anticipated the appropriate architectural form for the age that conquered gravity and thus achieved a new sense of speed and distance.

The Oldenburg pavilions were so antigravitational and so geometrically perfect that Alfred Lichtwark was led to complain that the water did not run off the terraces. However, Lichtwark was a great admirer and gave what is surely the best brief summary of Behrens's intentions: "Er geht auf Urformen zurück und will nur mit gestalteten Raum wirken [He goes back to archetypes and wants to create an effect only with formally organized space]." Lichtwark, *Briefe,* 137–140 (letter of 10 June 1904). This note serves well as an illustration of the willingness—desire, perhaps—of Behrens and his admirers to range freely over the future and the past in the development and explication of their work. The present received less attention.

41. Meier-Graefe, "Behrens, Düsseldorf," 383–390.

42. Admittedly these terms were not used in a narrow sense (see chapter 1), but they did not encourage a conception of architecture as complex as the problems it faced.

43. Meier-Graefe, "Behrens, Düsseldorf," 381–384.

44. J. L. M. Lauweriks, "Architektur," *Ring,* no. 4 (April 1909). Behrens's project for an Art Exhibition Building in Cologne of 1905 shows how close he was to Lauweriks in the early Düsseldorf years. See the color plate in Meier-Graefe, "Behrens, Düsseldorf," opp. p. 408.

Also in 1909, Lauweriks figured prominently in the Ausstellung für christliche Kunst in Düsseldorf. He was caught in the petrification of his own system. Benirschke showed a design for a church with freestanding bell tower that used Lauweriks's system somewhat more inventively. Meanwhile, Behrens had gone on to incorporate many other factors into his work. The Düsseldorf show also displayed Egyptianizing work from the school of Beuron and especially featured Beuronesque church interiors by the noted Viennese artist Koloman Moser (windows for Otto Wagner's church at Steinhof and first-prize designs for the interior of the Church of the Holy Ghost,

Düsseldorf). See Max Schmid, "Baukunst und Innendekoration auf der Ausstellung für christliche Kunst in Düsseldorf 1909," *Moderne Bauformen,* 8 (1909), 385–456.

45. Meier-Graefe, "Behrens, Düsseldorf," 381–382.

46. This letter, and those that follow in this discussion, are preserved in the Osthaus-Archiv in the Karl Ernst Osthaus Museum in Hagen. For much kind assistance, I am indebted to Frau Dr. Herta Hesse-Frielinghaus, then Director of the Museum, and her assistant, then succeeding Director, Anna-Christa Funk-Jones. This aid was of special importance due to the scarcity of documentary material on Behrens and because Osthaus was directly or indirectly involved in almost all of Behrens's commissions during the Düsseldorf period. What Ernst Ludwig, the grand duke of Hesse, offered in one grand program, Osthaus sustained over a period of years until Behrens achieved undeniable international renown. See Herta Hesse-Frielinghaus, "Karl Ernst Osthaus," *Westfälische Lebensbilder,* n.d., 145–162. Some of the documentation is presented in idem, *Peter Behrens und Karl Ernst Osthaus* (Hagen: Karl Ernst Osthaus Museum, 1966), and idem et al., *Karl Ernst Osthaus—Leben und Werk.*

47. George Minne (1866–1941), Belgian sculptor whose work was admired and collected by Osthaus.

48. Hermann Haller (1880–1950), Swiss painter and sculptor; see the catalog for the memorial exhibition, Zurich, Kunsthaus (1951).

Karl Hofer (1878–1955), German painter; see Hofer, *Aus Leben und Kunst* (Berlin: Rembrandt Verlag, 1952).

Bernhard Hoetger (1874–1949), German sculptor and architect; see Albert Theile, *Bernhard Hoetger* (Bremen: Angelsachsenverlag, 1930).

Hans von Marées (1837–1887), German painter, mainly active in Italy; see Julius Meier-Graefe, *Hans von Marées* (Munich: Piper, 1909–1910).

Karl Albiker (1878–1961), German sculptor; see B. E. Werner, *Die deutsche Plastik der Gegenwart* (Berlin: Rembrandt Verlag, 1940), 40ff.

Christian Rohlfs (1849–1938), German painter; see Paul Vogt, *Christian Rohlfs* (Cologne: Seemann, 1956).

49. On the Mannheim exhibition: Mannheim, Jubiläums-Ausstellung Mannheim 1907, *Offizieller Katalog der Kunst-Ausstellung* (Mannheim, 1907); Felix Poppenberg, "Mannheimer Ausstellungsregie," *Werkkunst,* 2 (30 June 1907), 309–314; Karl Kölitz, "Die Mannheimer Internationale Kunstausstellung," *Die Kunst für Alle,* 22 (1 August 1907), 500–509 (with ills. of exhibited works by Bourdelle, Hoetger, and Maillol); and now Moeller, *Behrens in Düsseldorf,* 494–496.

Behrens's work at the III. Deutsche Kunstgewerbe Ausstellung in Dresden, 1906, is also relevant to the present discussion. See chapter 5.

50. The works exhibited in Behrens's room at Mannheim, according to the official catalog cited in the preceding note (objects not noted as in private collections were presumably still in the possession of the artists):

Sculpture
Antoine Bourdelle (Paris), *Pallas Athene* (plaster, private coll.) [cat. 36a; Kölitz, "Mannheimer Internationale Kunstausstellung," ill. p. 504]; *Die Sphinx* (plaster, private coll.) [cat. 36b].

Hermann Haller (Rome), *Gehendes Mädchen* (bronze, private coll.) [cat. 116]; *Weiblicher Halbakt* (terra cotta, private coll.) [cat. 117]; *Weibliche Büste* (terra cotta, private coll.) [cat. 118]; *Weibliche Büste* (terra cotta) [cat. 119]; *Sitzendes Mädchen* (terra cotta) [cat. 120].

Bernhard Hoetger (Paris), *Torso einer Frau* (marble) [cat. 127b; Kölitz, ill. p. 505]; *Betende Frau* (plaster) [cat. 127d]; *Eva* (wood and bronze) [cat. 127e]; *Stehende Holzfigur* [cat. 127f].

Aristide Maillol (Paris), *Frauenstatue* [or *Bather,* 1900] (plaster, private coll.) [cat. 173c; Kölitz, ill. p. 509]; *Sitzende Frau* [or *Méditerranée,* 1902–1905] (plaster, private coll.) [cat. 173d].

Painting

Hermann Haller (Rome), *Liegendes Weib* (casein) [cat. 399].

Karl Hofer (Rome), *Zwei Frauen sich umarmend* (oil, private coll.) [cat. 458]; *Zwei Frauen mit Fels* (oil, private coll.) [cat. 459]; *Zwei weibliche Figuren am Meer* (oil) [cat. 460].

Christian Rohlfs (Hagen), *Obstgarten* (oil) [cat. 669a]; *Baumgruppe* (oil) [cat. 669b].

Marées and Albiker were thus not included. The reference to Gauguin in Poppenberg, "Mannheimer Ausstellungsregie," is apparently erroneous, though Gauguin was exhibited in a room designed by Joseph Olbrich.

51. The information on Maillol in the preceding text may be found in Waldemar George, *Aristide Maillol et l'âme de la sculpture* (Neuchâtel: Ides et Calendes, 1964), 222–223.

52. Gropius reported this to me in a conversation (Cambridge, 6 February 1964). Although they had tickets, the press of new work forced them to cancel their trip.

53. August Schmarsow, *Grundbegriffe der Kunstwissenschaft* (Leipzig and Berlin: Teubner, 1905). Schmarsow conceived of architecture as the "former of space" in 1893; see chapter 7, note 7, below.

54. Niemeyer, "Behrens und die Raumästhetik," 131–176. Parts cited here are from 141ff.

55. Heinrich Schliemann (1822–1890), who, after amassing a fortune in business, devoted himself to the quest for Troy and other Homeric sites. In 1871, he began excavations at his own expense at Hissarlik in Turkey, claiming to discover the site of Troy. He continued with other important excavations. See his works and those of his assistant, Wilhelm Dörpfeld.

56. Ulrich von Wilamowitz-Möllendorff (1848–1931), noted classical scholar, professor at German universities from 1876 to 1922.

Adolf Furtwängler (1835–1907), German archaeologist, wrote important works on Greek sculpture (1893), ancient gems (1900), and Greek vase painting (1900–1904).

57. Alois Riegl (1858–1905), Viennese art historian, the author of a work on late Roman crafts, *Die spätrömische Kunstindustrie* (Vienna, 1901), which has had a continuing large influence on both historiography and the theory of art. See note 6 above.

Josef Strzygowski (1862–1941), Viennese art historian, chiefly concerned with demonstrating that the origins of late antique and early medieval art lie in the Near East rather than in Rome (*Orient oder Rom,* Leipzig: Hinrichs'sche Buchhandlung, 1901).

58. Cited in Hoeber, *Peter Behrens,* 72.

59. A brief statement by Behrens on the school is contained in *Kunst und Künstler,* 5 (February 1907), 207. A report on the exhibition of student work in the Kunsthalle in Düsseldorf is published in the *Generalanzeiger für Düsseldorf und Umgebung* (31 March 1907). An appreciation of Behrens's

work in Düsseldorf is given in the *Düsseldorfer Zeitung* (3 August 1907). See also Kordt, "Kunstgewerbeschule"; Moeller, *Behrens in Düsseldorf,* 1–163.

60. The four main sections of Moholy's *The New Vision,* 4th ed. (New York: Wittenborn, 1947; orig. *Von Material zu Architektur,* Munich: A. Langen, 1928), are: "I. Preliminaries; II. The material (surface treatment, painting); III. Volume (sculpture); and IV. Space (architecture). "Sculpture is the best form—the original form—for taking possession of volume" (42).

61. The earlier state is illustrated in Arthur Drexler, *Ludwig Mies van der Rohe* (New York: Braziller, 1960), pl. 61. Drexler dates that version to 1942, the date currently assigned by the Museum of Modern Art.

62. Moeller, *Behrens in Düsseldorf,* cited in note 19 above. This work is supplemented by a study of Behrens's craft works in these years: Moeller, "Peter Behrens in Düsseldorf: Kat. 442–63," in Nürnberg, Germanisches Nationalmuseum, *Behrens und Nürnberg,* 262–285. See also the series of exhibition catalogs *Der Westdeutsche Impuls 1900–1914: Kunst und Umweltgestaltung im Industriegebiet* (Essen: Bacht, 1984).

63. Hesse-Frielinghaus et al., *Karl Ernst Osthaus—Leben und Werk.*

64. Kurt Asche, *Peter Behrens und die Oldenburger Ausstellung 1905: Entwürfe—Bauten—Gebrauchsgraphik* (Berlin: Gebr. Mann, 1992).

65. Behrens, *Ein Dokument Deutscher Kunst: Die Ausstellung der Künstler-Kolonie in Darmstadt. Zur Feier der Eröffnung 15. Mai 1901* (Offenbach: Rudhard'sche Giesserei, [1901]).

66. The fundamental documents for all the typefaces are the sample books offered by the type-founders, the Rudhard'sche Giesserei for *Behrens-Schrift* and the successor firm Gebrüder Klingspor for all others. An early study of modern typographic design, itself set in *Behrens-Schrift,* is Rudolf Kautzsch, ed., *Die neue Buchkunst: Studien im In- und Ausland* (Weimar: Gesellschaft der Bibliophilen, 1902 [1903]), with a chapter on Behrens by Haupt, 188–200. *Behrens-Schrift* provided the culminating illustration to a publication prepared for the 1904 St. Louis world's fair: Gustav Kühl, *On the Psychology of Writing* (Offenbach: Rudhard'sche Giesserei, 1904 [also in a German edition]).

67. On Düsseldorf, Roswitha Riegger-Baurmann, "Schrift im Jugendstil in Deutschland," in Jost Hermand, ed., *Jugendstil* (Darmstadt: Wissenschaftliche Buchgesellschaft, 1971), 209–257; Anna Simons, "Der staatliche Schriftkursus in Neubabelsberg," *Kunstgewerbeblatt,* n.s. 21, no. 6 (March 1910), 101–113.

68. Fritz Hoeber, *Die Behrens-Mediaeval* (Offenbach: Gebr. Klingspor, n.d. [1914]); F. Meyer-Schönbrunn, *Peter Behrens,* Monographien deutscher Reklamekünstler, no. 5 (Hagen and Dortmund: Ruhfus, 1913); Hans Loubier, *Die neue deutsche Buchkunst* (Stuttgart: Krais, 1921), 18–49; Julius Rodenberg, *In der Schmiede der Schrift: Karl Klingspor und sein Werk* (Berlin: Büchergilde, 1940), 45–51 on Behrens; Georg Kurt Schauer, *Deutsche Buchkunst 1890 bis 1960,* 2 vols. (Hamburg: Maximilian-Gesellschaft, 1963), 1: passim.

69. Michelangelo Buonarroti, *Dichtungen,* trans. Heinrich Nelson (Jena: Diederichs, 1909). Among numerous books set in Behrens's *Antiqua* is Fritz Hoeber's monograph on Behrens (1913).

Notes to Chapter 5

1. The exact circumstances of Behrens's employment by the AEG are not clear; most of the AEG archive was lost in the war. One often sees the president of the AEG, Emil Rathenau, credited with hiring Behrens; but equally often the credit goes to Baurat Paul Jordan, the manager of the AEG's huge Humboldthain factory complex and a member of the board of directors of the corporation. Paul Joseph Cremers, *Peter Behrens: Sein Werk von 1909 bis zur Gegenwart* (Essen: Baedeker, 1928), 6, asserts that the credit goes to Jordan, not Rathenau.

The industrial designer Arnold Schürer (see chapter 6, note 5), who worked for the AEG for some years and studied the industrial design of Behrens, was not able to discover the exact conditions of Behrens's employment. In conversation, Schürer suggested the following: It would appear that the friendship of Jordan and Behrens begins sufficiently early that it probably was Jordan who initiated the matter by introducing Behrens to Rathenau. Since Rathenau was known as an open person, and since Behrens came to have the AEG position, the two men must have entered into a good relationship. This is indicated all the more by the fact that only Rathenau could have given Behrens so much power and enabled him to work in divisions of the AEG that were outside Jordan's jurisdiction.

One should note, however, that as early as the 1890s, Emil Rathenau's son Walther (1867–1922) and Behrens shared a number of common friends in the arts—especially in the *Pan* circle. Walther, himself a highly influential director of the AEG, may have introduced Behrens to his father, though Walther Rathenau's published letters and essays give no clarification of the matter. The city of Berlin, Walther Rathenau, and Behrens's future were already juxtaposed by Julius Meier-Graefe, *Entwicklungsgeschichte der modernen Kunst* (Stuttgart: J. Hoffman, 1904), 725.

There is a sizable literature on the AEG; see especially: Conrad Matschoss, "Die geschichtliche Entwicklung der AEG in den ersten 25 Jahren ihres Bestehens," *Beiträge zur Geschichte der Technik und Industrie. Jahrbuch des Vereins deutscher Ingenieure,* 1 (1909), 53–82; Karl Wilhelm, *Die AEG* (Berlin: Widder, 1931); a 1933 manuscript published as *50 Jahre AEG* (Berlin: AEG, 1956); *75 Jahre AEG* (Berlin and Frankfurt: AEG, 1958); Helmut Lindner, "Die Entwicklung der Elektrotechnik im 19. Jahrhundert am Beispiel der Firmen Siemens & Halske und AEG," in Berlin, Technische Universität, *Berlin: Von der Residenzstadt zur Industriemetropole,* 3 vols. (Berlin: Technische Universität Berlin, 1981), 1:212–221; and Henning Rogge, *Fabrikwelt um die Jahrhundertwende am Beispiel der AEG Maschinenfabrik in Berlin-Wedding* (Cologne: DuMont, 1983), chapter 2, "Entstehung und Expansion einer Elektrofirma."

On Emil Rathenau, see the biography by Felix Pinner (Leipzig: Akademische Verlag, 1918); Lindner, "Die Entwicklung"; and Manfred Pohl, *Emil Rathenau und die AEG* (Mainz: Hase & Koehler, 1988).

On Behrens's move from Düsseldorf to Berlin, see F. H. Ehmcke, in the *Frankfurter Zeitung* (23 August 1907; reprinted in his *Persönliches und Sachliches* [Berlin: Reckendorf, 1928], 5ff.); Ernst Schur, "Peter Behrens und Berlin," *Dekorative Kunst,* 11 (October 1907), 48; Robert Breuer, "Peter Behrens," *Werkkunst,* 3 (9 February 1908), 145–149; and Tilmann Buddensieg with Henning Rogge et al., *Industriekultur: Peter Behrens und die AEG 1907–1914* (Berlin: Gebr. Mann, 1979), passim.

2. Data from Berlin, AEG, *50 Jahre AEG,* 263–264. Artificial waterfalls were an established technique in exhibits of power transmission, first used by Hippolyte Fontaine for the Gramme exhibit at the Vienna Exhibition of 1873 (three-quarter-mile transmission) and again by Marcel Deprez at

the Munich Exposition of 1882 (57 km). See W. James Kind, "The Development of Electrical Technology in the 19th Century: 3. The Early Arc Light and Generator," *United States National Museum Bulletin,* no. 228 (Washington: Smithsonian Institution, 1962), 385–390.

3. Anton Jaumann, "Neues von Peter Behrens," *Deutsche Kunst und Dekoration,* 12, no. 6 (March 1909), 343–361; Buddensieg with Rogge et al., *Industriekultur,* A1–8.

4. Such printing relied heavily on historical precedent (figure 5.8); an example at a large scale is provided by the stained glass window installed behind the pump at the 1891 Frankfurt exhibition discussed above. The window spelled out the name of the AEG in an ornamental nineteenth-century antique typeface enclosed in a band-and-strapwork frame based on German Renaissance models (*Dr. Felix Deutsch zum 70. Geburtstag* [Berlin: AEG, 1928], 23).

5. As demonstrated in the thesis of the exhibition "Linie und Form." See figures 1.21–22 above and Krefeld, Kaiser-Wilhelm-Museum, *Linie und Form* (Krefeld: Kramer und Baum, 1904).

6. Major works by Walther Rathenau: *Reflexionen* (Leipzig: Hirzel, 1908); *Zur Kritik der Zeit* (Berlin: Fischer, 1912); *Zur Mechanik des Geistes* (Berlin: Fischer, 1913); *Von kommenden Dingen* (Berlin: Fischer, 1917; trans. as *In Days to Come,* New York: Knopf, 1921); *Die neue Gesellschaft* (Berlin: Fischer, 1921; trans. as *The New Society,* New York: Harcourt, Brace, 1921).

On the man, see the biography by Graf Harry Kessler, *Walther Rathenau* (Berlin: Klemm, 1928; New York: Harcourt, Brace, 1930); James Joll, *Three Intellectuals in Politics* (New York: Pantheon, 1961); Fred L. Polak, *The Image of the Future,* 2 vols. (New York: Oceana, 1961), 1:341ff.; Ernst Schulin, *Walther Rathenau: Repräsentant, Kritiker und Opfer seiner Zeit* (Göttingen: Musterschmidt, 1979); and note 1 above.

Arnheim, in Robert Musil's *The Man without Qualities* (originally published 1930), can only be modeled on Walther Rathenau. That interpretation is at least a pleasurable and enlightening way to observe critically the issues raised by the protagonists of the present essay.

7. Quoted in Kessler, *Walther Rathenau,* 107. The same idea appears at the beginning of Frank Lloyd Wright's remarkable lecture given in Chicago in 1901, "The Art and Craft of the Machine" (printed in full for the first time in Edgar Kaufmann and Ben Raeburn, eds., *Frank Lloyd Wright: Writings and Buildings* [New York: Meridian, 1960], 55–83). Many of Wright's proposals, for example the need for artists to work with manufacturers, are highly suggestive of the concerns of Behrens, Rathenau, and members of the Deutscher Werkbund around 1907; but I know of no evidence for their awareness of Wright's lecture. See Joseph Siry, "Frank Lloyd Wright's 'The Art and Craft of the Machine': Text and Context," in Martha Pollak, ed., *The Education of the Architect: Historiography, Urbanism, and the Growth of Architectural Knowledge* (Cambridge: MIT Press, 1997), 3–36.

8. Rathenau, *In Days to Come,* 44.

9. Ibid., 16.

10. Carl Widmer, "Handwerk und Maschinenarbeit," *Kunstgewerbeblatt,* n.s. 20 (December 1908), 49–51.

11. Behrens, in *Volkswirtschaftliche Blätter,* 9 (27 August 1910), 265–266.

12. In addition to the article cited in the preceding note, Behrens also wrote: "Was ist monumentale Kunst," *Kunstgewerbeblatt,* n.s. 20 (December 1908), 46, 48; a contribution to "Die Zukunft unserer

Kultur," *Frankfurter Zeitung* (14 April 1909), 1–2; "Professor Peter Behrens über Ästhetik in der Industrie," *AEG-Zeitung*, 11 (June 1909), 5–8; "Kunst und Technik," *Elektrotechnische Zeitschrift*, 31 (2 June 1910), 552–555, also published in *Der Industriebau*, 1 (15 August 1910), 176–180, and (15 September 1910), suppl. lxxxi–lxxxv; "Kunst und Technik," *Werkkunst*, 6 (1910–1911), 124–125, 131–133; "The Aesthetics of Industrial Buildings," *Scientific American Supplement*, 76 (23 August 1913), 120–121; and especially "Über den Zusammenhang des baukünstlerischen Schaffens mit der Technik," in Berlin, Kongress für Ästhetik und allgemeine Kunstwissenschaft 1913, *Bericht* (Stuttgart, 1914), 251–265.

13. Behrens's concept of monumental art is reconstructed from A. Lindner, "Peter Behrens in Hamburg," *Neue Hamburger Zeitung* (9 April 1908), and Behrens, "Was ist monumentale Kunst," *Kunstgewerbeblatt* (1908).

14. Based on Behrens, "Die Zukunft unserer Kultur" (1909).

15. Gottfried Semper, *Der Stil in den technischen und tektonischen Künsten oder Praktische Aesthetik*, 2 vols. (1860, 1863; 2d ed., Munich: F. Bruckmann, 1878–1889). Alois Riegl, *Spätrömische Kunstindustrie* (Vienna: Oesterr. archäologischen Institut, 1901).

16. Based on a lecture given by Behrens at the eighteenth annual convention of the Verband Deutscher Elektrotechniker in Braunschweig, 26–27 May 1910. See Behrens, "Kunst und Technik," *Elektrotechnische Zeitschrift* (1910).

17. Ibid., 555.

18. E.g., Julius Lessing, "Neue Wege," *Kunstgewerbeblatt*, n.s. 6 (October 1894), 1–5; idem, "Das Kunstgewerbe als Beruf," *Volkswirtschaftliche Zeitfragen*, no. 97 (Berlin: L. Simon, 1891).

19. Here I correct my political terminology according to the criticism of Matthew Jefferies, *Politics and Culture in Wilhelmine Germany: The Case of Industrial Architecture* (Oxford and Washington: Berg, 1995), 150.

20. Friedrich Naumann, "Kunst im Zeitalter der Maschine," *Kunstwart*, 17 (July 1904), 317–327.

21. The two earlier exhibitions were in Munich in 1876 and 1888 and thus part of that understanding of handicraft against which the artists of the late 1890s rebelled. The decision to sponsor a third national crafts exhibition was made by the Dresdener Kunstgewerbeverein in the spring of 1904. See *Die Raumkunst in Dresden 1906* (Berlin: Wasmuth, n.d.); Ernst Schur, "Die Raumkunst in Dresden 1906," *Rheinlande*, 6 (1906), 56–82; Gisela Moeller, *Peter Behrens in Düsseldorf: Die Jahre 1903 bis 1907* (Weinheim: VCH, 1991), 463–485.

22. A statement from the catalog of the exhibition, quoted in H. Rodewald, "Die III. deutsche Kunstgewerbeausstellung Dresden 1906 und ihre soziale Bedeutung," *Monatsschrift für christliche Sozialreform*, 29 (1907), 22–23, 156–180.

23. Friedrich Naumann, *Kunst und Industrie* (Berlin, n.d.); also published in *Kunstwart*, 20 (October-November 1906), 66–83, 128–131. The first yearbook of the Deutscher Werkbund bore the title *Die Durchgeistigung der deutschen Arbeit* (Jena: Diederichs, 1912).

On the Dresden exhibition, see the previous footnotes and *Kunstgewerbeblatt*, n.s. 17 (June-September 1906), passim; Fritz Schumacher, *Stufen des Lebens*, 3d ed. (Stuttgart: DVA, 1949),

312ff.; idem, in *Kunstwart,* 19 (July-August 1906), 347–349, 396–400, 458–462; Eugen Kalkschmidt, in *Deutschland,* 5 (October 1906), 50–63; Moeller, *Behrens in Düsseldorf,* 463–488.

24. Theodor Heuss, *Friedrich Naumann* (Stuttgart and Berlin: DVA, 1937), 296–300; idem, "Notizen und Exkurse zur Geschichte des Deutschen Werkbundes," in Hans Eckstein, ed., *50 Jahre Deutscher Werkbund* (Berlin and Frankfurt: Metzner, 1958), 19ff., where Heuss also notes that the archive of the Werkbund was lost in a bombing raid on Berlin in World War II. The Werkbund-Archiv is a postwar foundation in Berlin. To its first *Jahrbuch* of 1972, Sebastian Müller contributed "Zur Vorgeschichte und Gründungsgeschichte des Deutschen Werkbundes," 23–53. Jefferies, *Politics and Culture,* 146, notes that it was Heuss who recommended Dohrn for his position.

25. Reyner Banham, *Theory and Design in the First Machine Age* (London: Architectural Press, 1960), 68; Karl Scheffler, *Die fetten und die mageren Jahre* (Leipzig and Munich: List, 1946), 42. As early as 1902, Scheffler suggested that the prostituted industries be opposed by the unification of craftsmen into their own industries, a proposal that bore some resemblance to the approximately contemporary "workshops" of Vienna, Munich, Dresden, etc. See *Dekorative Kunst,* 10 (July 1902), 381. Schumacher, *Stufen des Lebens,* 329–330, seems to share the credit for the Werkbund idea with Schmidt, Dohrn, and Muthesius.

26. Hermann Muthesius, "Die Bedeutung des Kunstgewerbes," *Dekorative Kunst,* 10 (February 1907), 177–192.

27. Friedrich Naumann was elected to the Reichstag from the city of Heilbronn from 1907 to 1918, not coincidentally the native city of Heuss.

28. Heuss, *Naumann,* 297; Eckstein, *50 Jahre Werkbund,* 8.

29. Schumacher, *Stufen des Lebens,* 330.

30. Schumacher's speech is published in part in *Die Form,* 7 (November 1932), 329–331. See also Schumacher, *Stufen des Lebens,* 329–331, 523–524; Peter Bruckmann, "Die Gründung des Deutschen Werkbundes 6. Oktober 1907," *Die Form,* 7, no. 10 (1932), 297–299.

31. Schumacher, *Stufen des Lebens,* 331.

32. E. Frölicher, "Der deutsche Werkbund," *Monatsschrift für christliche Sozialreform,* 36 (1914), 20.

33. Friedrich Naumann, *Deutsche Gewerbekunst: Eine Arbeit über die Organisation des deutschen Werkbundes* (Berlin: "Hilfe," 1908).

34. "Qualitäts-Arbeit," "Durchgeistigung der Arbeit," and "Durchformung aller Dinge." On the Deutscher Werkbund, see: Eckstein, *50 Jahre Werkbund;* Theodor Heuss, *Was ist Qualität?* (Tübingen and Stuttgart: Wunderlich, 1951); Peter Bruckmann et al., special number on the founding of the Werkbund, *Die Form,* 7 (October 1932), 297ff.; Walter Riezler, *Die Kulturarbeit des Deutschen Werkbundes* (Munich: Bruckmann, 1916); Hermann Muthesius, "Der Werkbundgedanke: Seine Grundlagen," *Deutsche Politik,* 1 (3 March 1916), 459–467. See also the *Jahrbücher* of the Werkbund, published 1912ff.; and see the sources cited in note 41 below.

For a critical assessment of the Werkbund from an interesting source, see Adolf Loos, "Die Überflussigen," *März,* 2 (August 1908), 185–187. Loos argues that artists should be free of applied work and, perhaps even more important, that practical objects should be free of the artist's "cultural" intrusion.

35. Behrens, as quoted in Lindner, "Peter Behrens in Hamburg," 2.

36. Behrens, "The Aesthetics of Industrial Buildings" (1913), 120, a brief version of Behrens's thoughts on "art and technology," poorly translated.

37. Lindner, "Peter Behrens in Hamburg," 1.

38. Behrens, "The Aesthetics of Industrial Buildings," 121.

39. Düsseldorf, Mannesmannröhren-Werke, *Zur Erinnerung an die Einweihung des Verwaltungsgebäudes der Mannesmannröhren-Werke in Düsseldorf 10. Dezember 1912* (Düsseldorf: Mannesmann, 1913), 70–85; Behrens's address at the dedication appeared also as "Administration Buildings for Industrial Plants," *American Architect,* 128 (26 August 1925), 167–184.

40. Tilmann Buddensieg and Henning Rogge, eds., *Die nützlichen Künste: Gestaltende Technik und bildende Kunst seit der Industriellen Revolution* (Berlin: Quadriga, 1981)

41. Sebastian Müller, *Kunst und Industrie: Ideologie und Organisation des Funktionalismus in der Architektur* (Munich: Hanser, 1974); Gert Selle, *Jugendstil und Kunst-Industrie: Zur Ökonomie und Ästhetik des Kunstgewerbes um 1900* (Ravensburg: Otto Maier, 1974); W. F. Haug, *Warenästhetik: Beiträge zur Diskussion, Weiterentwicklung und Vermittlung ihrer Kritik* (Frankfurt: Suhrkamp, 1975); Munich, Die Neue Sammlung, *Zwischen Kunst und Industrie: Der Deutsche Werkbund* (Munich: Die Neue Sammlung, 1975); Joan Campbell, *The German Werkbund: The Politics of Reform in the Applied Arts* (Princeton: Princeton University Press, 1978); Lucius Burckhardt, ed., *The Werkbund: History and Ideology 1907–1933* (Woodbury, N.Y.: Barron's, 1980); Kurt Junghanns, *Der Deutsche Werkbund: Sein erstes Jahrzehnt* (Berlin [GDR]: Henschel, 1982); Stanford Anderson, "Peter Behrens, Friedrich Naumann, and the Werkbund: Ideology in *Industriekultur,*" in Roberto Behar, ed., *The Architecture of Politics: 1910–1940* (Miami Beach and Genoa: Wolfsonian Foundation, 1995), 8–21; Jefferies, *Politics and Culture,* chapter 3, "'From Sofa Cushions to Town Planning': The German Werkbund," and passim; Mark Jarzombek, "The Discourses of a Bourgeois Utopia, 1904–1908, and the Founding of the Werkbund," in Françoise Forster-Hahn, ed., *Imagining Modern German Culture: 1889–1910* (Washington: National Gallery of Art, 1996), 126–145; and especially Frederick J. Schwartz, *The Werkbund: Design Theory and Mass Culture before the First World War* (New Haven: Yale University Press, 1996).

Notes to Chapter 6

1. Nikolaus Pevsner in Paris, Musée National d'Art Moderne, *The Sources of the XXth Century* (Paris: Musée National d'Art Moderne, 1960), 53.

2. Nikolaus Pevsner, "Architecture in Our Time," *The Listener,* 76 (29 December 1966), 953–955, and 77 (5 January 1967), 7–9.

3. Two works assigning this priority to Behrens are: Gillo Dorfles, *Il disegno industriale e la sua estetica* (Bologna: Cappelli, 1963), 74; Otto Bartning, "Zur Eröffnung der Austellung Peter Behrens," mimeograph accompanying exhibition (Darmstadt, Institut für neue technische Form, 14 September 1957). This exhibition showed certain AEG products wrongly attributed to Behrens, including a simple chromed electric iron and a simple tall electric kettle. Well attuned to the sym-

pathies of later viewers, these works enhanced the reputation of Behrens without clarifying his actual contribution.

Most works on the AEG, on Behrens, and on the history of modern architecture give some attention to Behrens's work in industrial design. See notes to chapter 5 above, and: Karl Scheffler, "Kunst und Industrie," *Kunst und Künstler,* 6 (July 1908), 430–434; Wolf Dohrn, "Das Vorbild der AEG," *März,* 3 (3 September 1909), 361–382; Artur Fürst, "Blech, Beton und Kunst," in *Die Wunder um uns* (Berlin: Vita, 1911), 186–198, figs. 74–82; Eugen Kalkschmidt, "Deutsches Kunstgewerbe und der Weltmarkt," *Dekorative Kunst,* 19 (July 1911), 465–480; C.-E. Jeanneret [Le Corbusier], *Etude sur le mouvement d'art décoratif en Allemagne* (La Chaux-de-Fonds: Haefeli, 1912); Hermann Lanzke, "Industrielle Formgestaltung und Formentwicklung," *AEG Informations Mappe 99* (Berlin: AEG, 1954); Rudolf Villiger, *Industrielle Formgestaltung* (Winterthur: Keller, 1957); mimeograph transcripts of speeches by Ludwig Prinz von Hessen und bei Rhein, Otto Bartning, and Hermann Lanzke at the opening of the AEG-organized exhibition "Peter Behrens: 50 Jahre Formgebung in der Industrie" (Darmstadt, Institut für neue technische Form, 14 September 1957); Hermann Lanzke, *Peter Behrens: 50 Jahre Gestaltung in der Industrie* (Berlin: AEG, 1958); Bernhard Siepen, "Peter Behrens: 50 Jahre Formgebung in der Industrie," *Die Innenarchitektur,* 5 (April 1958), 669–680. On AEG arc lamps, see Tilmann Buddensieg with Henning Rogge et al., *Industriekultur: Peter Behrens und die AEG 1907–1914* (Berlin: Gebr. Mann, 1979), P16–35; subsequently cited as Buddensieg. See also important later literature cited in the postscript to this chapter.

4. Lanzke, "Industrielle Formgestaltung," 1; Lanzke, *Peter Behrens,* 2. The same incomplete comparison also appears in early publications; e.g., Dohrn, "Das Vorbild der AEG," 362–363. Even the recent extensive work of Buddensieg chooses an intermediate model (comparable to figure 6.1b, right), the cap and reflector of which allow a comparison more favorable to the evaluation of Behrens's innovations (Buddensieg, 51, figs. 39, 40).

5. The industrial designer Arnold Schürer while in the employ of the AEG researched the design development of AEG products. See his *Der Einfluss produktbestimmender Faktoren auf die Gestaltung* (Bielefeld: the author, 1969).

6. Berlin, AEG, *Elektrische Kraftübertragung und Kraftverteilung,* 3d ed. (Berlin: AEG, 1901), 327.

7. It is this phenomenon that Schürer studied in great detail. To give one general example, Schürer demonstrated that increasing understanding and improvement of materials, productive technology, and electrical and mechanical technology contributed to a progressive miniaturization and formal simplification of the products of the electrical industry.

8. From a speech delivered by Behrens at the eighteenth annual convention of the Verband Deutscher Elektrotechniker in Braunschweig in 1910, published as "Kunst und Technik," *Elektrotechnische Zeitschrift,* 31 (2 June 1910), 552–555.

9. Ibid., 553.

10. This design was published September 1907 in *Mitteilungen der Berliner Elektricitätswerke,* 3 (1907), 130. From January 1907 the cover of this journal used a design by Behrens. Thus Behrens completed graphic and industrial design commissions for the AEG before he assumed his new position in Berlin.

11. Concerning this lamp, Behrens said that the housing had an "aesthetic requirement; it should remove from the viewer's sight the naked, barren electrodes and conceal these in what should preferably be a pleasant form"; quoted in "Die A.E.G.-Sparbogenlampe in modernem Kleide," *Mitteilungen der Berliner Elektricitätswerke,* 4 (March 1908), 41, 43–44. This statement hardly constitutes an endorsement of new functional forms; Behrens's attitude stands as testimony to Reyner Banham's assessment that "the 'Machine Aesthetic' of the pioneering masters of the Modern Movement was thus selective and classicizing . . . and it came nowhere near an acceptance of machines on their own terms or for their own sakes" ("Machine Aesthetic," *Architectural Review,* 117 [April 1955], 224–228).

12. Dohrn, "Das Vorbild der AEG," 371. Fritz Mannheimer, "Arbeiten von Professor Peter Behrens für die AEG," *Der Industriebau,* 2 (15 June 1911), 124, claims that the AEG invested 200,000 marks in the design and models of Behrens's arc lamp designs, but that this was recovered in one year's production savings and increased sales.

13. The flowerlike quality of the lamp is worth noting, since the early volumes of almost all Art Nouveau periodicals presented designs for domestic electric lamps that predictably took flower forms. This lyrical form is something of a throwback for Behrens at this time (note his own early lamp, figure 2.4); it again illustrates the distance between Behrens's *Kunstwollen* and a "machine aesthetic."

14. Fritz Schmalenbach, "Jugendstil und Neue Sachlichkeit," *Kunsthistorische Studien* (1937; Basel: the author, 1941), 9–21, is suggestive for this discussion, though he is not directly concerned with Behrens.

15. Karl Bötticher, *Die Tektonik der Hellenen,* 3 vols. (Potsdam: F. Riegel, 1852). Hermann Muthesius, "Die ästhetische Ausbildung der Ingenieurbauten," *Zeitschrift des Vereins deutscher Ingenieure,* 53 (31 July 1909), 1211–1217, refers to Bötticher and his tradition (1213).

16. *The form of the body is the mirror of its essence!*
    Master it and the seal of the riddle is broken.

17. Bötticher, *Die Tektonik,* 6.

18. Gottfried Semper, *Über die bleiernen Schleudergeschosse der Alten und über zweckmässige Gestaltung der Wurfkörper im Allgemeinen* (Frankfurt: Verlag für Kunst und Wissenschaft, 1859), 1–5.

19. Ibid., 6.

20. Ibid., 59–60. The Harvard University Library copy of Semper's work on ancient lead shot presents an engaging anecdote. Inside the front cover is written: "The first pages of this curious treatise are of importance. Semper was a man of genius, and his remarks on aesthetics, on the use of sections, ground plans, and outlines, and on the fundamental principles of Greek art are admirable. C[harles] E[liot] Norton. 1880."

21. Le Corbusier, *Towards a New Architecture* (1923; London: Architectural Press, 1946), 191–192. Le Corbusier also speaks of the necessity of a standard for perfection; this he illustrates with photos and discussion of the Parthenon and a 1921 Delage automobile (p. 125). A similar linkage, but with characteristic irony about the modern situation, had already been made by Walther Rathenau, *Auf dem Fechtboden des Geistes* (Wiesbaden: Greif, 1953), 39: "an automobile is more important to him [the modern worker] than the Parthenon."

22. Because "organic" so often modifies "architecture" to mean different things, I use the rather awkward form "organismic" to mean "like, or resembling, an organism." Bötticher tended to see this in the individual building elements, and the Greek temple became a "mosaic of functionally expressive elements." Van de Velde had a stronger sense for continuities and the organism-like quality of the whole, characteristics that were associated with Gothic and baroque-rococo architecture. Organism, the ideas behind *Tektonik,* energy, Gothic and rococo precedent—all these and more are associated with one another, with a "Germanic essence," and with van de Velde in Karl Scheffler, "Henry van de Velde," *Zukunft,* 33 (1900), 465–467.

23. Gottfried Semper, *Der Stil in den technischen und tektonischen Künsten oder Praktische Aesthetik,* 2 vols. (1860, 1863; 2d ed., Munich: Bruckmann, 1878–1879), 1:9 (a full discussion of Semper would include his two other principal categories—*textile Kunst* and *keramische Kunst*) and pts. 7–10.

24. Ibid., 2:341–342. Gustav Adolf Platz, *Die Baukunst der neuesten Zeit* (Berlin: Propyläen, 1927), 132–134, continues Semper's division of architectural constructs—*Tektonik* referring to membered structures and now including iron and steel; *Stereotomie* referring to wall structures, now including concrete.

25. Franz Reuleaux (1829–1905), though especially noted for his inventive studies in kinematics and machine construction, was a man of broad scientific and cultural interests. He and Semper were colleagues at the Polytechnic in Zurich (Semper, 1853–1871; Reuleaux 1856–ca. 1866). On Reuleaux, see Hans Zopke, "Professor Franz Reuleaux," *Cassier's Magazine,* 2, no. 2 (December 1896), 133–139. The implications of Reuleaux's statements pass far beyond the naive early nineteenth-century conceptions of propriety in machine design exemplified by Samuel Clegg, *Architecture of Machinery* (London: Weale, 1842), which concerns itself with such matters as the choice of the proper antique order for the static superstructure of a machine. The moving parts of machines were rarely forced into traditional forms (though Arnold Schürer drew my attention to a charming Doric piston for a steam engine in the Deutsches Museum, Munich), but only slowly, and through such thinkers as Reuleaux, were machines fully recognized as dynamic mechanisms for the transformation of energy and therefore in need of a new and dynamic form language. The competition between traditional architectural forms and "dynamic" forms is a recurrent theme. Walter Gropius's Adler automobile of 1930 is still a static architectural concept in contrast to R. Buckminster Fuller's ground taxiing unit of 1933 (which curiously resembles Semper's aerodynamic shot in figure 6.4). On the Gropius-Fuller comparison, see Reyner Banham, *Theory and Design in the First Machine Age* (London: Architectural Press, 1960), 304.

26. From Franz Reuleaux, *Briefe aus Philadelphia* (Braunschweig: Vieweg, 1877), trans. in Friedrich Klemm, *A History of Western Technology* (New York: Scribner, 1959), 326–27. Sigfried Giedion, *Space, Time and Architecture* (Cambridge: Harvard Univ. Press, 1941), mentions Reuleaux's favorable impression of American tools at Philadelphia. For Reuleaux's understanding of a technological civilization, see his *Technology and Civilization* (Washington, D.C.: GPO, 1891).

27. Semper, *Der Stil,* 1:6–8.

28. Buddensieg, P113–132.

29. Behrens, "Kunst und Technik," *Elektrotechnische Zeitschrift* (1910), 554–555.

30. On AEG fans and humidifiers, see Buddensieg, P37–89; tea kettles, P133–141; clocks, P99–112.

31. An exception to this statement is the AEG diesel-electric railroad passenger car attributed to Behrens by W. Franz, "Peter Behrens als Ingenieur-Architekt," *Dekorative Kunst,* 20 (February 1917), 150–151. Sabine Bohle in Buddensieg, 198–203, dates this design to 1914–1915 and provides details.

32. J. A. Lux, *Das neue Kunstgewerbe in Deutschland* (Leipzig: Klinkhardt und Biermann, 1908), 248.

33. Dresden, Deutsche Werkstätten für Handwerkskunst, *Handgearbeitete Möbel* (Dresden: Deutsche Werkstätten, ca. 1908).

34. F. D. Klingender, *Art and the Industrial Revolution* (London: Carrington, 1947), chapter 3.

35. Nikolaus Pevsner, *Pioneers of Modern Design,* 3d ed. (London: Penguin, 1960), 26, gives special emphasis to Lewis F. Day (1845–1910) and John D. Sedding (1837–1891). In a personal communication, Edgar Kaufmann, Jr., emphasized the somewhat earlier A. W. N. Pugin (1812–1852) and Sir Henry Cole (1808–1882). See also Sigfried Giedion, *Mechanization Takes Command* (New York: Oxford, 1948).

36. Christopher Dresser (1834–1904) was such a consultant to various producers of objects for domestic use. That position is applauded and termed "commercial designer" in "The Work of Christopher Dresser," *International Studio,* 6 (November 1898), 104–114. The same article refers depreciatively to the—presumably poor—designers within industry as "trade designers"; the term is apparently the English equivalent of *Fabrikzeichner.*

37. M. Armengaud, *The Practical Draughtsman's Book of Industrial Design* (New York: Stringer & Townsend, n.d.), indicates that mid-nineteenth-century use of the term "industrial design" meant what we call "mechanical drafting"—in both cases including some understanding of the technical problems involved.

38. On the Thonet industry, see *Michael Thonet* (Vienna: n.p., 1896), and the exhibition catalog Hans H. Buchwald, *Form from Process: The Thonet Chair* (Cambridge: Harvard University, Carpenter Center, 1967), which supplies a more modest figure on the production of model no. 14: thirty million chairs between 1859 and 1920. See also Karl Mang, ed., *Das Haus Thonet* (Frankenberg and Eder: Gebr. Thonet AG, 1969); and Alexander von Vegesack, *Michael Thonet: Leben und Werk* (Munich: Bangert, 1987).

39. See Behrens's discussion of the engineer's pseudo-aesthetic in the text quoted at note 8 above, and the illustrations of AEG arc lamps (figures 6.1–2).

40. Dohrn, "Das Vorbild der AEG," 372. The alliance of art and industry represented by the Behrens-AEG enterprise was recognized in the United States through a series of exhibitions in Newark, St. Louis, Chicago, Indianapolis, Cincinnati, and Pittsburgh: "Modern German Applied Arts," *Art and Progress,* 3 (May 1912), 583–587. This traveling exhibition was prepared by Karl Ernst Osthaus and the Deutsches Museum für Kunst in Handel und Gewerbe, which operated out of the Folkwang Museum in Hagen. Edgar Kaufmann informed me that photos and documentation of this exhibition still exist at Newark.

41. Behrens, "Professor Peter Behrens über Ästhetik in der Industrie," *AEG-Zeitung,* 11 (June 1909), 5–8, states that the "aesthetic improvement" of industrially produced utilitarian objects must rely upon simplification and good proportions.

42. This image is now well documented and illustrated in Buddensieg. Corporate image is the aspect of Behrens's AEG work emphasized by Günter Drebusch, *Industriearchitektur* (Munich: Heyne, 1976), 158–160.

43. Buddensieg with Rogge et al., *Industriekultur* (cited in note 3 above); second printing with minor corrections, 1981; third printing, unchanged, 1990; in English as *Industriekultur: Peter Behrens and the AEG 1907–1914,* trans. Iain Boyd Whyte (Cambridge: MIT Press, 1984). See especially the essay by Rogge and the catalog on products (P1–141) by Karin Wilhelm. Also Stanislaus von Moos, "Die Erneuerung," *Werk,* 54 (April 1967), 211–215; Gert Selle, *Jugendstil und Kunst-Industrie: Zur Ökonomie und Ästhetik des Kunstgewerbes um 1900* (Ravensburg: Otto Maier, 1974); Klaus-Jürgen Sembach, "Auf der Suche nach der Physiognomie des industriellen Zeitalters," in Nürnberg, Germanisches Nationalmuseum, *Peter Behrens und Nürnberg, Geschmackswandel in Deutschland: Historismus, Jugendstil und die Anfänge der Industrieform,* ed. Peter-Klaus Schuster (Munich: Prestel, 1980), 23–28; John Heskett, *Design in Germany: 1870–1918* (London: Trefoil Books, 1986), 137–150; Tilmann Buddensieg, "Von der Industriemythologie zur 'Kunst in der Produktion': Peter Behrens und die AEG," in Vittorio Magnago Lampugnani and Romana Schneider, eds., *Moderne Architektur in Deutschland 1900 bis 1950: Reform und Tradition* (Stuttgart: Hatje, 1992), 78–103. A rare author in dismissing the claims for Behrens as the originator of industrial design is Herwin Schaefer, who sees Behrens's work as comparable to that of others and tainted by the decorative arts: *Nineteenth-Century Modern: The Functional Tradition in Victorian Design* (New York and Washington: Praeger, 1970), 188–191.

Notes to Chapter 7

1. From a conversation with Mies van der Rohe in his Chicago office, 27 June 1961. This assessment of the situation in Germany prior to the First World War is corroborated by Theodor Heuss, *Hans Poelzig* (Tübingen: Wasmuth, 1948), 31. Heuss cited Poelzig's Werdermühle of 1906 as an example of the simplicity allowed to utilitarian buildings. But, of course, the lack of preconceptions about the form of industrial buildings didn't necessarily imply a reductionist attitude. *Dekorative Kunst,* 7 (January 1901), 148, gave an exemplary presentation to a design, in limited competition, for a power station by Schilling und Gräbner of Dresden; this was an overwrought Secessionist temple complete with atlantes and at least thirty-four ornamented chimneys belching Art Nouveau smoke.

2. See chapter 8.

3. Iron construction, architecture as the forming of space, the concepts of *Tektonik* and *Stereotomie,* and prospects for architecture appeared as key topics in Julius Lessing's introduction to Alfred G. Meyer, *Eisenbauten: Ihre Geschichte und Aesthetik* (Esslingen: Neff, 1907).

4. Gottfried Semper, *Der Stil in den technischen und tektonischen Künsten,* 2 vols., 2d ed. (Munich: Brinckmann, 1878–1889), 341–342.

5. Jacob Burckhardt, *Geschichte der Renaissance in Italien,* 3d ed. (Stuttgart: Neff, 1891), §32:46 and §61:113–115.

6. It is now difficult to think of Gothic architecture in other than *spatial* terms. In view of the fact that "the orders" had long been the touchstone of classical architecture, however, and that the nineteenth century treated Gothic architecture first as "pointed" and then as "ribbed," it is easier to comprehend the categorization of such buildings as "material." The planes of Renaissance architecture seemed, by comparison, inert and primarily descriptive of the space enclosed. See also Paul Frankl, *The Gothic* (Princeton: Princeton University Press, 1960), 606–608. In 1904, Alois Riegl still spoke of membered structures as distracting the observer from the "pure appreciation of free space"; quoted in Frankl, 637.

7. August Schmarsow, *Das Wesen der architektonischen Schöpfung* (Leipzig: Hiersemann, 1894); translated as "The Essence of Architectural Creation," in Harry F. Mallgrave and Eleftherios Ikonomou, eds., *Empathy, Form, and Space* (Santa Monica: Getty Center, 1994), 281–297.

8. August Schmarsow, "Zur Frage nach dem Malerischen," in *Beiträge zur Aesthetik der bildenden Künste* (Leipzig: Hirzel, 1896), 1:14–24.

9. Wilhelm Niemeyer, "Peter Behrens und die Raumästhetik seiner Kunst," *Dekorative Kunst,* 10 (January 1907), 131–186. See chapter 4 above.

10. Another documentation of Behrens's independence from functional and technical factors was provided by Karl Ernst Osthaus, "Ein Fabrikbau von Peter Behrens," *Frankfurter Zeitung* (10 February 1910): "Among the modernists, Behrens has long been almost alone in the view that one can find no creative basis for artistic form in function and technique. It is largely owing to Behrens that we today know how to grasp optical and rhythmic values independently of questions of style." It is important to remain aware of the distinction between such ideas and the concept of new forms evolving from a considered engagement with the given situation. The formal *expectation* of the adherents of these two methods may, at times, be similar. However, those devoted to the artist's formalization of the collective will see to it that their formal expectations are fulfilled. Those devoted to the exploration of a problem are prepared to have the dynamics of that situation alter, transform, or even destroy their formal expectations.

Behrens and those of his persuasion triumphed over those who were most open to the problematic situation, despite the appearance of clear and compelling articulations of the "situationist" position earlier than the zeitgeist formulations. Consider the following example. The first director of the Kunstgewerbemuseum in Berlin, Julius Lessing, who like Franz Reuleaux had been favorably impressed by the simple American products at the Philadelphia exposition of 1876, published an insightful article, "Neue Wege," *Kunstgewerbeblatt,* n.s. 6 (October 1894), 1–5. Lessing had an understanding of late nineteenth-century eclecticism but was more concerned to point the way beyond historical allusion. He wanted his contemporaries to see iron girders as they saw Greek columns; to look for inspiration in railroad stations and the Paris exposition of 1889 (Eiffel Tower; Halle des Machines) rather than in the sham edifices of Chicago's exposition of 1893; to recognize that new lighting techniques and doorbells implied new art forms. He again praised American furniture and hardware exhibited at Chicago, claiming they were so clearly developed from the materials and techniques involved that they exceeded the calculations of reason and gave to the eye "that joy we call beauty." Lessing insisted that those who saw the machine as an enemy could not be helped. "Whether we like it or not, our work must be staked out on the ground of the practical life of our time and must create those forms which bespeak our needs, our technique, and our material. If in this way we achieve a form of beauty in the sense of our scientific age, this form will not appear like the pious beauty of the Gothic or the luxurious beauty of the Renaissance, but rather as the perhaps somewhat austere beauty of the end of the nineteenth century—and that is all that one can ask of us." See also Lessing, "Das Kunstgewerbe als Beruf," *Volkswirtschaftliche Zeitfragen,* no. 97 (Berlin: L. Simon, 1891).

11. See Otto Wagner, *Moderne Architektur* (Vienna: Spiehagen und Schurich, 1897); Hermann Muthesius, "Kunst und Maschine," *Dekorative Kunst,* 9 (January 1902), 141–147; Friedrich Naumann, "Kunst im Zeitalter der Maschine," *Kunstwart,* 17 (July 1904), 317–327; J. L. M. Lauweriks, "Architektur," *Ring,* no. 4 (April 1909).

12. The reliance of contemporary architects on accepted styles for factory buildings may be seen in C. Z., "Fabrikarchitektur," *Architektonische Rundschau,* 26 (1910), 65–82, pls. 57–64. The respectable, but not unusual, early stages of the AEG's factory construction can be seen in: Berlin, AEG, *Elektrischer Einzelantrieb in den Maschinenbauwerkstätten der A.E.G.* (Berlin: AEG, 1899). This book also gives a good impression of contemporary AEG machinery and of the graphics (conventional job printing; see chapter 5) employed by the firm immediately before its flirtation with Jugendstil. Just as the AEG had, before Behrens's arrival, turned to a noted graphic artist, Otto Eckmann (chapter 5), so too they had commissioned Berlin's most renowned architect of that time, Alfred Messel, for the design of a central office building on the Friedrich-Karl-Ufer in Berlin (1905–1906). But this was an office building, not a factory, and of a sober, classicizing manner. In fact, this building should be recognized as a precedent for Behrens's general development, but not for his immediate contribution to the industrial architecture of the AEG.

13. The commencement in 1905–1906 is recorded in [Berlin, AEG], *Ansichten aus den Fabriken Brunnenstrasse* (Berlin: AEG, n.d. [ca. 1913–1914]). Fritz Hoeber, *Peter Behrens* (Munich: Müller und Rentsch, 1913), 136, records the state at the time of Behrens's redesign (1908). The AEG-Archiv photograph for figure 7.5 is dated 30 June 1909. This work thus constitutes Behrens's first, limited contact with industrial architecture; see Tilmann Buddensieg with Henning Rogge et al., *Industriekultur: Peter Behrens und die AEG 1907–1914* (Berlin: Gebr. Mann, 1979), A49–51; in English as *Industriekultur: Peter Behrens and the AEG 1907–1914,* trans. Iain Boyd Whyte (Cambridge: MIT Press, 1984), where the corresponding catalog numbers are A51–53. (This work is cited below as Buddensieg; where the catalog numbering differs in the MIT Press edition, the latter is given following the numbering of the original, German edition.) The Turbine Factory remains Behrens's first major work for the AEG. Its only other predecessors are the AEG pavilion for the Deutsche Schiffbauausstellung of 1908 in Berlin (figure 5.4) and a small AEG exhibition pavilion of 1907 illustrated without credit in *Mitteilungen der Berliner Elektricitätswerke,* 3 (September 1907), 131 (see Buddensieg, A9). Both pavilions have characteristics closely allied with the work of Behrens's Düsseldorf period.

14. In the same year, a complete 100-horsepower, direct-current AEG turbodynamo system of handsome construction won wide popular attention at the same Düsseldorf exhibition where Peter Behrens built a garden and restaurant. Hermann Muthesius, in "Die ästhetische Ausbildung der

Ingenieurbauten," *Zeitschrift des Vereines deutscher Ingenieure,* 53 (31 July 1909), 1212, cited the 1904 Düsseldorf exhibition as the point when the modern movement in arts and crafts recognized the beauty of the machine—an appreciation shared by the press.

15. Much of this information comes from Berlin, AEG, *25 Jahre AEG-Dampfturbinen* (Berlin: AEG, 1928), 1–27, 96–101.

16. This and most of the factual information about the executed building is taken from articles by the engineer of the building, Karl Bernhard: "Die neue Halle für Turbinenfabrik der Allgemeinen Elektricitäts-Gesellschaft in Berlin," *Zeitschrift des Vereines deutscher Ingenieure,* 55 (30 September 1911), 1625–1631, and (7 October 1911), 1673–1682; idem, "Die neue Halle für Turbinenfabrik der Allgemeinen Elektricitäts-Gesellschaft in Berlin," *Zentralblatt der Bauverwaltung,* 30 (15 January 1910), 25–29. West of the well-known Turbine Factory, Behrens built at the same time a small, handsome, and meticulously detailed power station in brick; see Hoeber, *Peter Behrens,* 114; Buddensieg, A13–16.

17. Works by Bernhard are illustrated in Deutscher Werkbund, *Jahrbuch 1914* (Jena: Diederichs, 1914), pl. 42.

18. In Behrens's article "Kunst und Technik," *Elektrotechnische Zeitschrift,* 31 (2 June 1910), 552–555, he recognized the need to use new building materials such as iron but also continued his argument that no style could be achieved through material conditions alone. He drew the conclusion that artists and engineers must collaborate—even referring to them as equals—but it was "good artistic form" that the buildings had to possess. His belief in the supremacy of the artist was not heavily disguised from the audience of technicians he was addressing.

19. Literally, "Machines roar in sacred songs/Factories are godly churches of power." Quoted in Hermann Lanzke, *Peter Behrens: 50 Jahre Gestaltung in der Industrie* (Berlin: AEG, 1958), 5. Osthaus, "Ein Fabrikbau," found the Turbine Factory to be perfected "like a Doric temple." Such religious imagery contrasts interestingly with, is perhaps an overcompensation for, the recurrent nineteenth-century conflation of industrial and infernal imagery. See "The Age of Despair" in Francis D. Klingender, *Art and the Industrial Revolution* (London: Carrington, 1947). In 1905 Henry Adams (in *The Education of Henry Adams*) saw 1900 as the end of the Age of the Virgin and the beginning of the Age of the Dynamo.

20. The span of this side hall is 12.93 meters on center. The two traveling cranes for the ground level of this side hall had a capacity of 40,000 kilograms each and a clearance between supports of 11.44 meters; at the upper level, the cranes were designed for 10,000 kilograms each.

21. At the time of its completion, the Turbine Factory was Berlin's largest ferrous construction. For details, see Bernhard, "Die neue Halle," 1625–1631, 1673–1681.

22. Just as Behrens participated in the transformation of factory imagery from the infernal to the divine (see note 19), so also he participated in an inversion of values related to the gigantism of modern industrial buildings. Hoeber, *Peter Behrens,* 165, pointed out that if Viollet-le-Duc thought that scale and proportion were based on the dimensions of man, then Behrens's industrial buildings were created for an industrial race of vastly increased power. For Viollet-le-Duc man was the measure of his environment; for Behrens, the industrial environment was the measure of Man. There is in this

an inversion of the dependent-independent relationship and a shift from man the individual to Man as a race. Again the decision to deflect or rebut the criticism of industrial civilization led to over-compensation.

23. Behrens, "Die Turbinenhalle der Allgemeine Elektricitäts-Gesellschaft zu Berlin," in Düsseldorf, Rheinischer Verein für Denkmalpflege, *Mitteilungen,* 4 (March 1910), 26–29. See also the version of this article in *Deutsche Technikerzeitung,* 27 (12 February 1910), 87–90. There is an extensive and continuous literature on the Turbine Factory; see Buddensieg, A17–32.

24. Muthesius, "Die ästhetische Ausbildung," 1213, traced back to Semper a common opinion that iron construction tended toward dematerialization and was thus antithetical to the essential materiality of architecture. Praising the Eiffel Tower, Muthesius sought to expand the architects' range of aesthetic appreciation to include the transparencies of iron frameworks. Anticipating Muthesius's position, Friedrich Naumann spoke of a new style that must have "iron bones" (1896) and repeatedly praised the Eiffel Tower. See Naumann, *Ausstellungsbriefe* (Berlin: Der "Hilfe," 1909), 31, 73, 103–109. Typically, Behrens sought to give the new material sufficient visual weight to bring it into conformity with a traditional aesthetic; accordingly, he condemned the Eiffel Tower for its lack of corporeality: Behrens, "Kunst und Technik," *Elektrotechnische Zeitschrift* (1910).

25. Bernhard, "Die neue Halle," 1630. Fritz Neumeyer, *The Artless Word: Mies van der Rohe on the Building Art* (Cambridge: MIT Press, 1991), 354 n. 40, reports a personal communication from Sergius Ruegenberg that Mies in the 1920s "proudly recounted that he had contributed to the window design on the long western side of the Turbine Factory." Tilmann Buddensieg, "Architektur als freie Kunst," in Bernhard Buderath, ed., *Peter Behrens: Umbautes Licht* (Munich: Prestel, 1990), 67, arrives at counting this factory elevation as an early work of Mies, as does Mechthild Heuser, "Die Fenster zum Hof: Die Turbinenhalle, Behrens und Mies van der Rohe," in Hans-Georg Pfeifer, ed., *Peter Behrens: "Wer aber will sagen, was Schönheit sei?" Grafik, Produktgestaltung, Architektur* (Düsseldorf: Beton-Verlag, 1990), 115–116. I am disinclined to believe more than the observation reported by Ruegenberg. There is the unequivocal claim of the engineer Bernhard, cited at the beginning of this note, that he had free reign to design this elevation. In my conversation with Mies in his Chicago office (27 June 1961), his response to the question of what buildings he had worked on in Behrens's atelier included the Small Motors Factory and the Large Machine Assembly Hall, but not the Turbine Factory. When I asked if persons such as he and Gropius could make original contributions within the atelier, he said "No," that Behrens had very definite ideas and his workers learned them. "We were more Behrens-like than Behrens himself." See chapter 8, note 4.

26. Reyner Banham, *Theory and Design in the First Machine Age* (London: Architectural Press, 1960), 83.

27. Bernhard, "Die neue Halle," 1628. On the multiple symbolisms of pylon, temple, crystal, and machine parts, see also chapters 1–3.

28. Behrens, "Die Turbinenhalle" (1910), 26.

29. Ibid. Inspection does reveal light iron framing and diagonal bracing at the inner surface of the concrete pylons.

30. The same situation arose with the famous corner window of the Fagus Works by Walter Gropius.

Using glass as the neutral transition from one elevation to the other avoided the ambiguous sense of support evident in the Turbine Factory. But like Behrens, Gropius arrived at this arrangement through visual explorations. "I liked it that way. Only later did I realize that there was structural logic to it as well." Gropius made this comment to me (Cambridge, 6 February 1964) in order to emphasize the importance of intuition and feeling in the creative process. In his later works, too, Gropius explored the visual character of materials—in the Fagus Works a transparent material—not new conceptions of space. Like Behrens, he was not, as Frank Lloyd Wright, concerned with "destroying the box." On Gropius and transparency, see Colin Rowe and Robert Slutzky, "Transparency: Literal and Phenomenal," *Perspecta,* no. 8 (1964), 45–54; reprinted in Rowe, *The Mathematics of the Ideal Villa and Other Essays* (Cambridge: MIT Press, 1976), 159–183.

31. Bernhard, "Die neue Halle," 1629. Without mistaking the structural elements of the factory, Walter Müller-Wulckow, *Bauten der Arbeit und des Verkehrs aus Deutscher Gegenwart* (Königstein and Leipzig: Langewiesche, 1925), 24, found its expressive force to be in the concrete pylons and gable.

32. Behrens's relation to the classicism of 1800 becomes still more evident in the works discussed in chapter 8 (see figures 8.30, 8.45). One may note here that, according to Harry Graf Kessler, *Walther Rathenau* (New York: Harcourt, Brace, 1930), 135, Friedrich Gilly was the favorite architect of Walther Rathenau. Rathenau bought a country seat which, though Kessler implies its design by Friedrich Gilly, was designed by Friedrich's father David (1798). Hermann Schmitz, *Berliner Baumeister vom Ausgang des achtzehnten Jahrhunderts,* 2d ed. (Berlin: Wasmuth, 1925), 330, pl. 206, illustrates the elegantly simple facade of Freienwalde (five two-storied bays controlled by flat giant pilasters) and credits Rathenau as one of the first and most ardent admirers of the classicizing architecture of 1800.

33. "Peter Behrens," *Allgemeines Lexikon der bildenden Kunst des XX. Jahrhundert,* ed. H. Vollmer (Leipzig: Seemann, 1953), 1:157–158.

34. The Frankfurt and Hamburg buildings are illustrated in Gustav Adolf Platz, *Die Baukunst der neuesten Zeit* (Berlin: Propyläen, 1927), 187–188.

35. J. M. Richards, *An Introduction to Modern Architecture,* 2d ed. (Harmondsworth: Penguin, 1953), 76.

36. H. R. Hitchcock, "Peter Behrens," *Encyclopedia of World Art* (New York: McGraw-Hill, 1959ff.), 2: col. 413.

37. This factory and Krupp's Eleventh Cannon Workshop were built over a period of a few years beginning in 1906. Exterior illustrated in Essen, Krupp, *Fried. Krupp Aktiengesellschaft* (Essen: Krupp, 1927), 10; and W. Berdrow, *Alfred Krupp und sein Geschlecht* (Berlin: Krupp, 1937), 205. Interior of both shops illustrated in D. Baedeker, *Alfred Krupp und die Entwicklung der Gussstahlfabrik zu Essen,* 2d ed. (Essen: Baedeker, 1912), pls. after 278. Dates and statistics from Essen, Krupp, *Fried. Krupp Aktiengesellschaft,* 34, and in Essen, Krupp, *Krupp: A Century's History of the Krupp Works 1812–1912* (Essen: Krupp, ca. 1912), 323–324.

38. Essen, Krupp, *Fried. Krupp Aktiengesellschaft: Statistical Data* (Essen: Krupp, 1907), 87–93.

39. The best of such factories are architectural parallels to the process-oriented design of Thonet chairs discussed in chapter 6. Such works break down the simplistic notion of technical solutions

plus aesthetics—a notion that stood behind much of the (often slightly ornamented) factory architecture around 1900. For example, the advice given in one handbook: "Considerations about the architectonic organization of the whole take only a second place. Only after the functional form has been established in all its parts may one reflect on how this functional form is to be brought into relation with the most suitable aesthetic form." Wilhelm Rebber, *Fabrikanlagen,* 2d enl. ed. (1888; Leipzig: Voigt, 1901), 94.

40. Most industrial cities in the United States could also provide examples.

41. In a formulation such as Rebber's (see note 39), the aesthetic characteristics were superimposed on the functional form. The situational approach was capable of drawing these together, but could not claim to generate forms that were immediately applicable, or stylistically appropriate, to other new situations. As a third formulation, Behrens conceived of technical and artistic forms as separate, and sought to control the utilitarian aspect by his artistic form. He felt that modern times required the artistic form to be related to the conditions of industrial civilization, but believed forms could be generated that were general to the time and applicable in various situations. That is, he sought the formal basis for a contemporary style, as recognized in Karl Scheffler's commentary on the AEG factories in the *Vossische Zeitung* (Berlin, 26 September 1912): "One would, with praise, stress the eminent cultural sensibility of the AEG, which can be of the greatest significance for the future in as much as its architectonic products allow one to glimpse the nuclei of a new, modern, international architecture—the seed of a new 'style.'" Intimations of an International Style!

42. For this reason, the complex was also referred to as the "factories at Brunnenstrasse," although none of the factories fronted directly on that street. See Berlin, AEG, *Elektrischer Einzelantrieb;* idem, *Ansichten,* a picture book; and idem, *Führer durch die Fabriken Brunnenstrasse* (Berlin: AEG, 1929), a guidebook. Artur Fürst, *Emil Rathenau* (Berlin: Vita, 1915), reports the following contemporary statistics: area of site, 117,628 sq. m.; floor area, 211,130 sq. m.; 14,000 workers.

43. A variant design appears in Hoeber, *Peter Behrens,* fig. 164 (see Buddensieg, A74/A76, who illustrates other designs as well: A72–86/A74–88). The pairs of windows in the street front of the pylons were shifted to the side elevations, thus preserving the massive portal from any reference to human scale. The four-story building at the far right was an existing building which, along with all the residential buildings facing on Hussitenstrasse, was later demolished for Behrens's Assembly Hall for Large Machines.

44. Franz Mannheimer, "Arbeiten von Professor Peter Behrens für die AEG," *Der Industriebau,* 2 (15 June 1911), 127, records completion of this factory in the summer of 1910. All the factories on the site still exist.

45. The two small buildings to the southwest of the Small Motors Factory on Voltastrasse were earlier constructions, part of the Berliner Elektricitäts-Werke (BEW). The BEW was the electric utility corporation for Berlin. The AEG was commissioned to administer and develop this utility company, with control reverting to the municipality in 1915. See Fürst, *Emil Rathenau.*

46. Hoeber, *Peter Behrens,* 58, rightly considers Behrens's unpremiated competition design for the Tietz Department Store in Düsseldorf (1906; competition won and building executed by Joseph Olbrich) as a precedent for the High Voltage Factory. Behrens's department store design was singular in his oeuvre until the High Voltage Factory. Distinctive in these two buildings are the wholly

masonry exteriors; exterior detailing of a simple classicizing character which unifies the repetitive bays; clear articulation of stairs and elevators in plan and in external detailing; and skylines broken by elements that indicate separate uses below. The factual information on the High Voltage Factory is from Mannheimer, "Arbeiten von Behrens," 121–140; see Buddensieg A52–81/A54–83.

47. Neither of the bay dimensions of these facades was set by the structure immediately behind the facades. The beams in these assembly line floors run perpendicular to the facade, at the third points of the large bays established by the main assembly halls (figure 7.22). These smaller floors were probably framed in this way in order to maintain a constant beam size (with no deep girders) over the assembly lines.

48. In their material (red brick) and their form and detail, these towers are reminiscent of the late medieval brickwork celebrated a century earlier by the eminent classicist Friedrich Gilly. See, e.g., figure 7.6 and Alfred Rietdorf, *Gilly: Wiedergeburt der Architektur* (Berlin: Hans von Hugo, 1943), 32–33.

49. Camillo Sitte, *City Planning According to Artistic Principles,* trans. George R. and Christiane C. Collins (New York: Random House, 1965); and George R. and Christiane C. Collins, *Camillo Sitte and the Birth of Modern City Planning* (New York: Random House, 1965).

50. Behrens, "Seeking Aesthetic Worth in Industrial Buildings," *American Architect,* 128 (5 December 1925), 476. The German version appeared as "Werbende künstlerische Werte im Fabrikbau," *Das Plakat,* 11 (June 1920), 269–283.

51. On the Small Motors Factory, see Mannheimer, "Arbeiten von Behrens," 121–140; Buddensieg A81–104/A83–105. Construction of this long building began at the southwestern end in 1910; by the summer of 1911 construction terminated at the tenth bay on the street side. By the fall of 1912 over half of the 196-meter-long building was completed (Hoeber, *Peter Behrens,* 140). Berlin, AEG, *Ansichten,* pl. 4, gives the completion date as 1913.

52. This comparison is more fully discussed in chapter 8 with reference to the German Embassy in St. Petersburg.

53. Constructionally related, these factories are usually discussed together: Hoeber, *Peter Behrens,* 144–150; idem, "Die neuen Bauten von Peter Behrens für die AEG," *Kunst und Künstler,* 11 (1913), 262–266; Berlin, AEG, *Ansichten,* pls. 1, 5–8; Franz Mannheimer, "AEG-Bauten," in Deutscher Werkbund, *Jahrbuch 1913* (Jena: Diederichs, 1913), 33–42 and pls. 2, 4; "Grossmaschinenhalle der AEG in der Hussitenstrasse in Berlin," *Der Industriebau,* 6 (15 September 1915), 411–412; Buddensieg, A112–137.

54. Mention should be made of other industrial or commercial works by Behrens for the AEG, although they do not give rise to significantly different discussion. These include the no longer extant AEG retail appliance shops in Berlin (in Königgrätzer and Potsdamer streets; 1910): Hoeber, *Peter Behrens,* 155–163; Buddensieg P2–9. At the Turbine Factory site in Berlin was the Munitionsfabrik (1916; Buddensieg A38–42). Little is known about the factory for the AEG in Riga, Latvia (1913): Paul Joseph Cremers, *Peter Behrens: Sein Werk von 1909 bis zur Gegenwart* (Essen: Baedeker, 1928), 25; Buddensieg A137/A138. At Hennigsdorf near Berlin, another significant but lower-density AEG industrial site, were the Porcelain Factory (1910–1911; illustrated in list of works, no. 65a), Oil Cloth and Paint factories (1911), the Locomotive Factory (1913), and the Aircraft Production Halls (1914–1915; illustrated in list of works, no. 112); on these, see "Einige

Neubauten von Professor Peter Behrens, Berlin," *Der Industriebau,* 6 (15 August 1915), 396–399; Buddensieg A138–151/A139–153. In Berlin-Oberschöneweide is the factory originally for the Nationale Automobil AG (1915–1916); damaged during World War II, under the GDR it was the VEB Werk für Fernmeldeelektronik. See Cremers, *Peter Behrens,* pls. 45–47; Werner Hegemann, *Façades of Buildings* (London: Benn, 1929), 228, fig. 450; Buddensieg A152–160/A154–162. Further works include a showroom in the AEG's old Apparatefabrik (Deutscher Werkbund, *Jahrbuch 1913,* pl. 80), and the AEG exhibition pavilion in Brussels (1916): Buddensieg A11–12.

55. Interesting examples of this type of construction are illustrated in Munich, Die Neue Sammlung, *Industriebauten 1830–1930* (Munich: Die Neue Sammlung, 1967).

56. As noted above, this was not the case at the Turbine Factory despite its high-shouldered, faceted arches. At the Assembly Hall the space was available, but Behrens diminished the "shouldering" by eliminating two "facets." Again Behrens's form depends on his volition rather than on technical considerations, although the basis of his willed form here may be something as modest as sympathy with neighboring gable forms (see figures 7.5, 7.32).

57. Franz Mannheimer, "Die deutschen Hallen der Brüsseler Weltausstellung [I]," *Der Industriebau,* 1, no. 9 (15 September 1910), 193–207, continued by Hermann Kügler, 207–216; Gottfried Stoffers, ed., *Deutschland in Brüssel 1910: Die Deutsche Abteilung der Weltausstellung* (Cologne: M. DuMont Schauberg, 1910).

58. "It is precisely the inner organism of a building that serves industrial purposes which must be clearly retained and which must come to be the origin of a new beauty that bespeaks the spirit of our time. Everything great that will be created in life is the result not of a scrupulous professionalism, but rather of the energy of a great and strong personality." Behrens, "Kunst und Technik," *Elektrotechnische Zeitschrift* (1910), 554.

59. See chapters 5 and 6; and Stanford Anderson, "Peter Behrens, Friedrich Naumann, and the Werkbund: Ideology in *Industriekultur,*" in Roberto Behar, ed., *The Architecture of Politics: 1910–1940* (Miami Beach and Genoa: Wolfsonian Foundation, 1995), 8–21.

60. This discussion is based on Behrens, "Kunst und Technik," *Elektrotechnische Zeitschrift* (1910). See also Peter Behrens, "Kunst und Technik," *Werkkunst,* 6 (1910–1911), 132; idem, "Über den Zusammenhang des baukünstlerischen Schaffens mit der Technik," in Berlin, Kongress für Ästhetik und allgemeine Kunstwissenschaft 1913, *Bericht* (Stuttgart: Enke, 1914), 251–265; idem, "Einfluss von Zeit- und Raumausnutzung auf moderne Formentwicklung," in Deutscher Werkbund, *Jahrbuch 1914,* 7–10.

61. Max Creutz, in "Das Krematorium von Peter Behrens in Hagen in Westfalen," *Kunstgewerbeblatt,* n.s. 20 (December 1908), 41–48, referred to Behrens's reliance on what he called the "Prinzip der unendlichen Musterung."

62. Adolf Behne, "Romantiker, Pathetiker und Logiker im modernen Industriebau," *Preussiche Jahrbücher,* 154 (October 1913), 172.

63. Peter Behrens, "Zustimmung der Städtebauer," in *Berlins dritte Dimension: Offener Brief an Herrn Oberbürgermeister Wermuth* (Berlin, 1913), 9–11 (from a public letter originally published in the *Berliner Morgenpost,* 27 November 1912):

There is no longer any doubt that Berlin will increasingly be a new city of business. Therefore, rather than suffering this inevitability with a lighter or heavier heart, nothing could be more correct than that one purposefully aspire to this character and that all measures which are taken in the interest of the city seek fully to realize this character. Characterization—the creating of a type—is for every art, and not least for architecture, the most important moment in the whole of form-making [*Gestaltung*]. One can imagine nothing more imposing than the realization of a unified character and stylistic idea for an entire city.

. . . In the aesthetic realm—and quite generally—what made the greatest impression on me in America was without question precisely the giant office buildings. These office buildings, in their bold construction, carry the seed of a new architecture.

Nevertheless, one cannot be convinced of the correctness of this building principle solely by the impression that one allows to work upon oneself; but rather this conviction must also be supported by an aesthetic consideration. A city should still, in an urbanistic sense, be comprehended as a contained architectural image. A metropolis that spreads out incomprehensibly will not, in a spatial-aesthetic sense, be helped by a considered layout of squares. Similarly the effect of a church tower will fail to affect the total image of an excessively flat, spreading city: such a horizontally extended plan needs corporeality, which will only be found in the joining of compact vertical masses.

Behrens's image of these compact vertical masses appeared as the cover image of a special issue of *Das Plakat* (June 1920); see Stanford Anderson, "Modern Architecture and Industry: Peter Behrens and the AEG Factories," *Oppositions,* no. 23 (Winter 1981), fig. 39.

64. Hoeber, *Peter Behrens,* 216, refers to Behrens's uniform repetition of a coordinated type with the resultant infinite movement of the factory facades, in contrast to the rhythmic intensification toward the center of a Renaissance facade.

65. Walter Gropius, "Die Entwicklung moderner Industriebaukunst," in Deutscher Werkbund, *Jahrbuch 1913,* 17–22.

66. Gropius, *Apollo in der Demokratie* (Mainz and Berlin: Florian Kupferberg, 1967), 125.

67. Le Corbusier, *Towards a New Architecture,* trans. Frederick Etchells (1923; New York: Praeger, 1946), 16.

68. See the final note of chapter 6. In Buddensieg, see especially his essay and the catalog on architecture (A1–213/A1–212) by Henning Rogge. See also Hans-Joachim Kadatz, *Peter Behrens: Architekt—Maler—Graphiker und Formgestalter 1868–1940* (Leipzig: E. A. Seemann, 1977); Alan Windsor, *Peter Behrens: Architect and Designer* (New York: Whitney, 1981); and Pfeifer, ed., *Peter Behrens: "Wer aber will sagen, was Schönheit sei?"*

Notes to Chapter 8

1. This comment on the general dismissal of Behrens's more classicizing buildings was correct at the time of writing (1968), but the situation was also changing in just those years. Philip Johnson and Robert Stern hung a small exhibition of photographs of Behrens for, as I recall, the Modern Architecture Symposium at Columbia University in May 1964. In comments to viewers, they

showed greatest enthusiasm for the St. Petersburg Embassy, and then for the cognate AEG Small Motors Factory. This text attempts an even-handed critical assessment, but comes down closer to the negative criticism of the Embassy.

2. The terms "convention" and "expression" were chosen for their relevant usage by E. H. Gombrich, "Freud's Aesthetics," *Encounter,* 26 (January 1966), 30–40. Gombrich, a product of the scholarly milieu that emphasized such distinctions (see his *Norm and Form* [London: Phaidon, 1966]), here explores the general significance of an exchange between Freud and the *diseuse* Yvette Guilbert.

By "expression," Gombrich refers to the artist's projection of personal feeling, speaking also of the "centrifugal force" in art. Projection of the psyche is a quality easily associated with the famous *diseuse.* However, in her exchange with Freud, Guilbert insisted that her artistry relied not on personal projection but on the artist's medium, style, and tradition—what Gombrich terms "convention" and the "centripetal force" in art.

Freud maintained his emphasis on the centrifugal or expressive qualities in Guilbert's stage art, as one might expect. However, Gombrich places Freud's position in a general nineteenth-century German context that traces back to Goethe—a major strain of German *Bildung* that sought the discovery of the spiritual message behind or within human expressions.

Surely adherence to convention or expression is never black or white, but there are recognizable, significant differences of degree. Gombrich's point, and Freud's too, he claims, is that both the centrifugal and the centripetal forces act to shape the art that we admire. In such manner, an artist avoids the dual pitfalls of mere expression and mere convention. We may recognize the "idealist-patheticist" confrontation described in chapter 1 above as an instance of the general phenomenon.

3. Fritz Hoeber, *Peter Behrens* (Munich: Müller und Rentsch, 1913), 179, in praising Behrens's German Embassy and explaining why he deserved such an imperial commission, argued that the Secessionists of 1900 had changed. His description and terminology parallel our expressive/conventional conceptualization: ". . . dass sich allmählich eine Umgestaltung dieser neuesten Architektur aus dem Exzentrischen in's Konzentrishe, aus einer individualisierenden Romantik in's Klassische und Typische vollzogen hatte [. . . that gradually a transformation of the most recent architecture has come to pass: from the eccentric to the concentric, from the individualistic romantic to the classic and typical]."

4. Walter Gropius, "Una testimonianza diretta," *Casabella,* no. 240 (June 1960), 3, gives the 1907 date for his arrival. Max Hertwig claims to have entered Behrens's atelier in February 1908 and puts Gropius's entry as June 1908, asserting that Gropius claimed too early a date and too large a role (Stressig, in Herta Hesse-Frielinghaus et al., *Karl Ernst Osthaus—Leben und Werk* [Recklinghausen: A. Bongers, 1971], 504 n. 6). Tilmann Buddensieg, "Neue Dokumente zur Baugeschichte der Fabriken am Humboldthain," in M. Sperlich and H. Borsch-Supan, eds., *Festschrift für Margarethe Kühn* (Munich and Berlin: Deutscher Kunstverlag, 1975), 280–282, accepts Hertwig's date for Gropius's entry and on this basis argues that Gropius could not have participated in the Turbine Factory and High Voltage Factory; though Buddensieg's own design dates—see Tilmann Buddensieg with Henning Rogge et al., *Industriekultur: Peter Behrens und die AEG 1907–1914* (Berlin: Gebr. Mann, 1979), A17–32—do not preclude Gropius's participation, and furthermore Buddensieg assigns Mies, who entered the atelier later, a (disputed) role in the Turbine Factory (see chapter 7, note 25). On Gropius's departure, see note 27 below.

On Mies, see Arthur Drexler, *Ludwig Mies van der Rohe* (New York: Braziller, 1960), 10–13. In a conversation with the present author in Chicago, 27 June 1961, Mies stated that he left Behrens's office for a short time, apparently to work on the Perls house, Zehlendorf, in 1911. Wolf Tegethoff, "Ludwig Mies van der Rohe," in Wolfgang Ribbe and Wolfgang Schäche, eds., *Baumeister. Architekten. Stadtplaner. Biographien zur baulichen Entwicklung Berlins* (Berlin: Historische Kommission zu Berlin/Stapp Verlag, 1987), 473, notes this break, putting Mies's return at early 1911 and final departure at January 1912.

Arthur Korn, "55 Years in the Modern Movement," *Arena,* 81 (April 1966), 264, claimed that Mies, at age 17 in 1903, worked for Behrens (that would have been in Düsseldorf); we need stronger evidence for this assertion.

5. Stanislaus von Moos, "Standard und Elite: Le Corbusier, die Industrie und 'Esprit Nouveau'," in Tilmann Buddensieg and Henning Rogge, eds., *Die nützlichen Künste* (Berlin: Quadriga, 1981), 310.

6. Other well-known members of Behrens's pre–World War I atelier:

Paul Thiersch (1879–1928), according to a conversation with Mies van der Rohe (Chicago, 27 June 1961), was an important assistant in Behrens's office (Thieme-Becker places him in Behrens's Düsseldorf studio in 1906). Thiersch went to the Berlin studio of Bruno Paul, there inducing Mies to become an assistant to Behrens. Thiersch, whom Mies credited as a "good architect," had thus left Behrens by 1908. See Klaus-Jürgen Sembach et al., *1910. Halbzeit der Moderne: van de Velde, Behrens, Hoffmann und die Andere* (Stuttgart: Hatje, 1992), 142–145.

Jean Krämer (1886–1943) was characterized by Gropius as a "right-hand man" in the studio, capable adjutant of Behrens or even of Gropius (conversation in Cambridge, 6 February 1964). His name appears regularly in the Behrens-Osthaus correspondence (Hagen, Karl Ernst Osthaus Museum, Osthaus-Archiv, Ordner "Behrens, von April 1910") from 13 June 1907 in Düsseldorf to 12 April 1911 in Berlin, mainly in connection with the Goedecke house and other works in Hagen. Tilmann Buddensieg, "Architektur als freie Kunst," in Bernhard Buderath, ed., *Peter Behrens: Umbautes Licht* (Munich: Prestel, 1990), 68–69, posits that Krämer played a role in the design of the Farbwerke Hoechst as late as 1920. See also Max Osborn, *Jean Krämer Architekt* (1927; reprint Berlin: Gebr. Mann, 1996).

Adolf Meyer (1881–1929), a student at the Kunstgewerbeschule in Düsseldorf during Behrens's directorship, came to Berlin with Behrens in 1907. Meyer left with Gropius, and the two men shared credit for the Fagus Factory in Alfeld and later works; see also chapter 4. Jane Fiske McCullough (now Thompson) and Kenneth Kaiser kindly provided four photographs preserved in Adolf Meyer's notebook (p. 9) in the Bauhaus-Archiv, Berlin. Taken at or near Behrens's Neubabelsberg studio, each photo shows Adolf Meyer and up to seven other persons. Ms. Thompson showed the photos to Gropius, who stated that the photos do not show Mies, Jeanneret, or himself and thus probably antedate their presence in the office (which means that the photos could only be from late summer 1907). Tilmann Buddensieg, however, in "Industriekultur: l'oeuvre de Peter Behrens," *Architecture d'aujourd'hui,* no. 208 (April 1980), dates the best-known of the photos to March 1910 and recognizes Gropius, Meyer, Krämer, Mies, Peter Grossman, and Le Corbusier. Gropius's identification of Meyer agrees; otherwise he recognized only the furthest figure, as Max Hertwig.

Max Hertwig (1881–?) was a student under Behrens at Düsseldorf; in two of the photographs just mentioned, a man assuming dominant positions within the groups was identified by Gropius as

Hertwig. By his own statement, he entered Behrens's atelier in February 1908 (Stressig, in Hesse-Frielinghaus et al., *Karl Ernst Osthaus,* 504 n. 6).

Carl Fieger (1893–1960) joined Behrens's atelier in 1911 as a designer of interiors. The Bauhaus-Archiv preserves some of Fieger's drawings for furniture and interiors of the St. Petersburg Embassy. The Archiv published a pamphlet "Carl Fieger" (1962).

Heinrich de Fries (1887–1938) was said to have been a colleague of Behrens for the AEG in 1916–1918 (Gustav Adolf Platz, *Die Baukunst der neuesten Zeit* [Berlin: Propyläen, 1927], 555). For his collaborative work on housing, see chapter 9 below.

7. Reyner Banham, *Theory and Design in the First Machine Age* (London: Architectural Press, 1960), 69; Vittorio Gregotti, "Peter Behrens," *Casabella,* no. 240 (June 1960), 5–8, 16–17; idem, "L'architettura dell'espressionismo," *Casabella,* no. 254 (August 1961), 24–50; Dennis Sharp, *Modern Architecture and Expressionism* (New York: Braziller, 1967), 36. More complete descriptions of the Gasworks are in Hoeber, *Peter Behrens,* 162–166; W. Müller-Wulkow [*sic*], "Bauten in Frankfurter Osthafen," *Der Industriebau,* 8 (15 March 1917), 33–44; Tilmann Buddensieg, "Documenti di architettura: Il Gaswerk di Peter Behrens," *Casabella,* 46, no. 479 (April 1982). The Gasworks is of mixed construction, with bearing masonry, wood or iron framing, and reinforced concrete used as specific problems suggested.

8. Gropius, "A Testimonial," *Casabella,* no. 240 (June 1960), suppl. p. v.

9. The Feilner house and the Militär-Arrestanstalt appear as figs. 83 and 86 in August Grisebach, *Carl Friedrich Schinkel* (Leipzig: Insel, 1924). The other three Schinkel works mentioned are illustrated in Hermann Beenken, *Schöpferische Bauideen der deutschen Romantik* (Mainz: Matthias-Grünewald-Verlag, 1952), figs. 47, 90, and 66, respectively.

10. Examined in 1962 in the offices of the Main-Gaswerke, on the site.

11. As is well known, this detail also refers back to Schinkel, especially the rear corners of the Altes Museum in Berlin (see Grisebach, *Schinkel,* fig. 47). See also note 33 below.

On the street front of the Gasworks (northward on Schielestrasse) is another detail worth noting: a type of color coding in the brick. The street front of the director's house is of a hard yellow brick except for dark brick forming slablike capitals on the square piers. In the office building (which includes engineers' residences) the dark iron clinkers are used as a base and a panel farther up, but the yellow brick still predominates. The ratio is reversed for the canteen building for the workmen. Finally, still along Schielestrasse, the workshop is all of clinkers, like the other industrial buildings. Different-colored bricks were thus used for local contrast of form and color and to key the transition from domestic use to industrial operations.

Related brickwork appears in the Fagus Factory of Gropius and Meyer and again in the Graduate Center at Harvard by Gropius and the Architects Collaborative after World War II. According to information transmitted to me by Jane Fiske McCullough (now Thompson; letter of 12 July 1966), Gropius expressed displeasure with the Gasworks and did not recall having worked on it. The dates would also seem to preclude his participation, but, of the drawings preserved in offices on the site in Frankfurt, that with the plan and sections for the *Apparaten-Anlage* (apparatus building) is marked "Gez[eichnet] 14. II. [1911] W. GR." Yet another, with the plan and elevations for the *Uhren- und Regler-Haus* (metering building; also called the compressor house), is marked "20.1.11 E.D.

[Damm]; 17.2.11 Gr." Unless there was a new draftsman in the office whose initials were W. GR., it would seem that Gropius was involved in the project and in Behrens's office (again?) in the latter part of February 1911. Buddensieg, "Documenti di architettura," 38, reads my "W. GR" as "W. BR" and associates it with the name "Brendel" which he finds on another sheet, but about whom nothing is known (including first initial). Buddensieg does not mention the second notation of "Gr" referenced above. The matter is uncertain; however, when Gropius left Behrens's atelier in March 1910, his first office was also in Neubabelsberg. Is it inconceivable that less than a year later Gropius could have been enlisted to help in the extremely busy Behrens atelier?

Mies, too, denied participation in the Gasworks (Chicago conversation, 27 June 1961), saying he thought Adolf Meyer had worked on it. According to the reports that Meyer, with Gropius, left in 1910 (see note 6 above), this too is problematic. It may be significant that it is Behrens's reputedly most expressionist work that draws these disclaimers. Buddensieg, "Documenti di architettura," 38, also denies, for chronological reasons, the possibility of Mies's involvement in the Gasworks. I have no reason to implicate Mies, but all the drawings in Frankfurt are dated within the time Mies was associated with Behrens.

12. Two factories not for the AEG and thus not discussed in chapter 7 should be mentioned here: the office and factory group for the T-Z-Gitterwerk in Berlin-Tempelhof (1911–1912): Hoeber, *Peter Behrens,* 169–180; and a group of industrial buildings for the Hannoversche Waggonfabrik, Hannover-Linden (ca. 1917; illustrated in list of works, no. 122b). Partially destroyed during World War II, in 1962 it was partially occupied by Hanomag: Paul Joseph Cremers, *Peter Behrens: Sein Werk von 1909 bis zur Gegenwart* (Essen: Baedeker, 1928), pls. 48, 71; Walter Müller-Wulckow, "Bauten für die Hannoversche Waggonfabrik," *Der Industriebau,* 10 (15 June 1919), 77–85, and (15 July 1919), 98–106.

13. Hoeber, *Peter Behrens,* 84, refers to A. E. Brinckmann, *Deutsche Stadtbaukunst in der Vergangenheit* (Frankfurt: Keller, 1911) and idem, *Platz und Monument* (Berlin: Wasmuth, 1908).

14. Not built, the project is illustrated in Hoeber, *Peter Behrens,* 82–87, who cites the influence of A. E. Brinckmann rather than Sitte.

On the Katholisches Gesellenhaus, see *Festschrift zur Einweihung des Katholischen Gesellenhauses zu Neuss* (Neuss, 1910). The house was rebuilt, but with significant changes, after partial destruction in World War II; see Gisela Moeller, *Peter Behrens in Düsseldorf: Die Jahre 1903 bis 1907* (Weinheim: VCH, 1991), 499–504. For both projects, see Elmar Siepe, "Das Gesellenhaus und eine städtebauliche Studie von Peter Behrens in Neuss," *Neusser Jahrbuch* (1961), 9–18.

15. To the contrary, P. Morton Shand, "Scenario for a Human Drama," part 2, *Architectural Review,* 76 (August 1934), 40, stated that "the spark which vitalized Behrens (though he would probably deny this) came, perhaps unconsciously, from Adolf Loos; and Loos's direct inspiration—again as I see it—came from those rows of late 18th century plain brick boxes that still form whole quarters of London." Shand's commentary appears to be part of that 1930s misunderstanding of the Germans' concept of "standardization," and an exaggeration of Behrens's devotion to industrial production.

16. See Hoeber, *Peter Behrens,* 150–155; "Arbeiterhäuser bei den AEG-Fabriken in Henningsdorf [*sic*]," *Der Industriebau,* 4 (15 April 1915), 332–333. Fritz Neumeyer, "Der Werkwohnungsbau der Industrie in Berlin und seine Entwicklung im 19. und frühen 20. Jahrhundert" (Ph.D. diss., Technische Universität Berlin, 1978), 208–227, figs. 89–96; Buddensieg with Rogge et al., *Industriekultur,* A183–189/A184–190; Richard Pommer and Christian F. Otto, *Weissenhof 1927 and*

the Modern Movement in Architecture (Chicago: University of Chicago Press, 1991), 74, 89–90, 242 (n. 46). See discussion of Behrens's *Gruppenbauweise* in chapter 9.

According to a letter from [East] Berlin, Arbeitsstelle für Kunstgeschichte, 30 August 1963, both the factories and housing by Behrens at Hennigsdorf still existed. Chiara Negri and Raffaela Neri, "Behrens e Berlino: L'architettura per l'industria," Domus Itinerario no. 86, *Domus,* 745 (January 1993), 5, however, report that all the factories were lost in World War II, except that for oil cloth and a partially rebuilt porcelain factory.

Another surviving Behrens building of this time is the boathouse for the Elektra Rowing Club, Berlin-Oberschöneweide (1911–1912; illustrated in list of works, no. 83), originally a club for AEG employees. See Robert Breuer, "Das Bootshaus der Rudergesellschaft 'Elektra'," *Wasmuths Monatshefte für Baukunst,* 2 (1915–1916), 220–230.

17. Design for a factory and residential quarter for the C. W. Julius Blancke-Werke in Merseburg an der Saale (unbuilt): Hoeber, *Peter Behrens,* 203–214.

18. In 1908, Behrens commented on the garden city movement stemming from Ebenezer Howard, in "Die Gartenstadtbewegung," *Berliner Tageblatt* (5 March 1908). While he wished to maintain some relation to the site conditions, Behrens's main point was to advocate compact groups of houses as against the dispersed building manner of the garden city.

19. The plan of the house in figure 8.16 shows the dining room as proposed by Behrens. A marked-up plan showing the improved layout, apparently according to the client's wishes, appears in Moeller, *Behrens in Düsseldorf,* fig. 131. The door between the dining room and central hall was made a single leaf and aligned with the new door to the terrace; the remainder of the wall between the rooms was closed, yielding the fireplace wall in the hall.

Although in the possession of the state and under historic preservation, the interiors of the Obenauer house are considerably altered. See Robert Breuer, "Peter Behrens," *Werkkunst,* 3 (9 February 1908), [145–149]; Hoeber, *Peter Behrens,* 39–46; Dieter Heinz, "Haus Obenauer, Trillerweg 42," *Saarheimat,* 9 (1965), 233–238; and esp. Moeller, 242–290, 438–440. Werner and Ursula Hempel kindly provided me with copies of drawings and contemporary photographs; Anne-Catrin Schultz served as a generous intermediary.

20. On *Sachlichkeit,* see Stanford Anderson, "*Sachlichkeit* and Modernity, or Realist Architecture," in Harry Mallgrave, ed., *Otto Wagner: Reflections on the Raiment of Modernity* (Santa Monica: Getty Center, 1993), 322–360; and idem, introd. and trans. of Hermann Muthesius, *Stilarchitektur und Baukunst* (Santa Monica: Getty Center, 1994).

21. Artists-in-residence eventually included the Dutch painter and craftsman Johann Thorn-Prikker, the Dutch architect J. L. M. Lauweriks (formerly with Behrens in Düsseldorf), and an artist whom Behrens increasingly admired, Christian Rohlfs: see Anselma Heine, "Karl Ernst Osthaus und sein Werk," *Frankfurter Zeitung* (7 July 1912). Jeanneret (the young Le Corbusier) visited the colony, as is documented by a letter from Behrens's office to Osthaus (Hagen, Karl Ernst Osthaus Museum, Osthaus-Archiv, letter of 6 October 1911). See also discussion of Le Corbusier and Lauweriks above, chapter 4; and Stressig, in Hesse-Frielinghaus et al., *Karl Ernst Osthaus,* 385–511.

22. Karl Ernst Osthaus, "Lebenslauf," in his *Grundzüge der Stilentwicklung* (Ph.D. diss., Würzburg, 1918), iv–v. A letter from Behrens to Osthaus dated 16 October 1906 (Osthaus-Archiv), records transmittal of a site plan. Also see Stressig, in Hesse-Frielinghaus et al., *Karl Ernst Osthaus,* 412–415.

23. Hoeber, *Peter Behrens*, 83, lists the Viennese Josef Hoffmann and not Lauweriks. However, there are no houses on the site by Hoffmann while there are Lauweriks houses, thus sustaining Osthaus's own account which speaks of eleven houses by Lauweriks (Osthaus, "Lebenslauf," v). Stressig, in Hesse-Frielinghaus et al., *Karl Ernst Osthaus*, 440–447, discusses Hoffmann's unrealized work for Hohenhagen.

24. The house was destroyed in World War II. Eleven original drawings (plans, sections, elevations), ink on linen, signed by Schroeder and Behrens, dated 30 September 1908, were in the Bauordnungsamt, Hagen, in 1962. The Osthaus-Behrens correspondence in the Osthaus-Archiv includes only tangential reference to the construction of the Schroeder house in a letter from Behrens dated 13 November 1909 (according to the sequence of letters, the correct date is 13 October). Stressig, in Hesse-Frielinghaus et al., *Karl Ernst Osthaus*, 416–417.

Alfred Lichtwark, *Briefe an die Kommission für die Verwaltung der Kunsthalle,* ed. G. Pauli (Hamburg: Westermann, 1923), 324–327, in a letter of 8 October 1910, from Hagen, says the first villa by Behrens cost 40,000 marks rather than the projected 30,000 marks. In contrast, he claims that a ten-room house by Lauweriks cost 18,000 marks rather than a projected 22,000 marks.

25. Osthaus-Archiv, letter from Osthaus to Behrens, 15 September 1910. See ensuing discussion on the Schroeder house. Mention of the crematorium refers to the fact that the marble revetment was coming loose; it was replaced with stucco in 1910.

26. Herta Hesse-Frielinghaus, *Peter Behrens und Karl Ernst Osthaus* (Hagen: Karl Ernst Osthaus Museum, 1966), 13, documented by many letters of 1908–1911 in the Osthaus-Archiv. The house still exists, but the interior retains little of its original character. Eleven ozalid prints (plans, sections, elevations), signed by Osthaus and Behrens on 25 August 1909, were in the Bauordnungsamt, Hagen, in 1962. All the drawings are dated in May 1909. Stressig, in Hesse-Frielinghaus et al., *Karl Ernst Osthaus,* 417–419.

27. In the "calamities" letter cited above, Osthaus referred to Behrens's curious detail, used in both the Cuno and Schroeder houses, of a slight setback from lower wall planes to higher ones, and again at the roof. It had been difficult, and at best expensive, to construct and maintain these junctures in a waterproof manner. Correspondence in July-August 1910, also in the Osthaus-Archiv, indicates that the main circular stair of the Cuno house was sagging. A drawing of the revised condition (August 1910) is in the archive and illustrated in Hesse-Frielinghaus, *Peter Behrens und Karl Ernst Osthaus,* 13.

Already in March 1910, with particular reference to the Cuno house, Walter Gropius wrote to Osthaus that, due to intensifying differences with Behrens, he often had to do things contrary to his own knowledge and volition. On 5 March, Gropius had notified Behrens that he could not work with him any longer (idem; Osthaus-Archiv P89).

28. Osthaus-Archiv, Osthaus to Behrens, 15 September 1910.

29. Osthaus-Archiv, 20 September 1910: "Ich bin auch ganz damit einverstanden einmal einen wirklich billigen Bau herzustellen."

30. The house still exists in good condition, though divided into apartments. Frau Else Bechem was a most gracious hostess in making the house and gardens available to me. Seven ozalid prints (plans, sections, elevations), signed by Goedecke and Jean Krämer (as agent for Behrens) on 10 July 1911, were in the Bauordungsamt, Hagen, in 1962. Krämer was often in Hagen, sometimes with Walter Gropius, as Behrens's representative for the three villas and for the refinishing of the crematorium. Stressig, in Hesse-Frielinghaus et al., *Karl Ernst Osthaus,* 420.

31. The house is in good condition, occupied by the Deutsches Archaeologisches Institut. I thank Dr. Hans Jessen for the opportunity to examine the house in a leisurely manner. Robert Breuer, "Das Haus Wiegand in Dahlem bei Berlin," *Innendekoration,* 24 (November 1913), 431–450, referred to Behrens as a "seer of form," conquering over the pettiness of life. Also Fritz Stahl, "Landhaus Wiegand in Dahlem," *Wasmuths Monatshefte,* 3 (1918–1919), 265–285; and especially Wolfram Hoepfner and Fritz Neumeyer, *Das Haus Wiegand von Peter Behrens in Berlin-Dahlem: Baugeschichte und Kunstgegenstände eines herrschaftlichen Wohnhauses* (Mainz: Philipp von Zabern, 1979).

32. From a lecture at the Hamburger Kunstgewerbeverein on 8 April 1908. Partially published as: Behrens, "Was ist monumentale Kunst?" *Kunstgewerbeblatt,* n.s. 20 (December 1908), 46, 48. See the discussion of monumental art in chapter 5 above.

33. Düsseldorf, Mannesmannröhren-Werke, *Zur Erinnerung an die Einweihung des Verwaltungsgebäudes der Mannesmannröhren-Werke in Düsseldorf. 10. Dezember 1912* (Düsseldorf: Mannesmann, 1913), 85. Behrens's address was later published as "Administration Buildings for Industrial Plants," *American Architect,* 128 (26 August 1925), 167–184. This album and its American translation (p. 172) supply some information on materials: structural members were mainly iron, clad in two types of limestone; reinforced concrete was used occasionally (as for the glazed roof of the smallest court); the roof was slate; the entrance and main stair were of Untersburg marble. This entrance (figures 8.39–40) shows extraordinary reticence and precision in the detailing of its reticulated framing. Once again the negative reveal is important in maintaining clear distinctions between elements. Henry-Russell Hitchcock wrote, in a letter of 12 December 1962, that Paul Schneider-Esleben claimed Mies van der Rohe detailed this hall and stair. In the 1930s the building was extended, in a simplified manner, around the site limits; though this extension was intended by Behrens, he did not design it. See also W. Franz, "Peter Behrens als Ingenieur-Architekt," *Dekorative Kunst,* 20 (February 1917), 145–158; Brigitte Schlüter, "Verwaltungsbauten der Rheinisch-Westfälischen Stahlindustrie 1900–1930" (Ph.D. diss., University of Bonn, 1991), 129–166.

34. Behrens, "Administration Buildings" (1925), 173.

35. Ibid., 167–169.

36. Ibid., 167, and Düsseldorf, Mannesmannröhren-Werke, *Zur Erinnerung,* 70, respectively.

37. Le Corbusier in Deutscher Werkbund, *Bau und Wohnung* (Stuttgart: Fr. Wedekind, 1927), 28.

38. Behrens, "Administration Buildings" (1925), 173.

39. Düsseldorf, Mannesmannröhren-Werke, *Zur Erinnerung,* 84, 87–99. The various addresses in this album suggest that the provision of some historical pedigree was a conciliatory gesture toward the Düsseldorf public; but the prototypes are far too apt to be mere propaganda.

40. Behrens himself extended the "type" in his administration headquarters for the Continental Rubber Company in Hannover (begun 1912, enclosed by 1914 and used as a military warehouse in World War I; restoration and completion 1919–1920; heavily damaged in World War II; restored again with somewhat simpler interiors: Cremers, *Peter Behrens,* pls. 42–47, and here at list of works, no. 92).

41. Behrens, "Administration Buildings" (1925), 173–174.

42. Mentioned in Cremers, *Peter Behrens,* 164; Prof. Dr. August Hoff, Cologne, an acquaintance of Behrens in the 1920s and 1930s, kindly directed me to this little-known building.

43. See K. Sch[effler], "Das neue Haus der deutschen Botschaft in St. Petersburg," *Kunst und Künstler,* 11 (May 1913), 414–424; Walter C. Behrendt, "Die deutsche Botschaft in Petersburg," *Die Zukunft,* 21 (24 May 1913), 259–265; Karl Schaefer, "Kaiserl. Deutsche Botschaft in St. Petersburg," *Deutsche Kunst und Dekoration,* 16, no. 10 (July 1913), 260–292; idem, "Das Gebäude der Kaiserlich Deutschen Botschaft in St. Petersburg," *Der Profanbau* (1914), 309–348; Julius Posener, *Berlin auf dem Wege zu einer neuen Architektur: Das Zeitalter Wilhelms II 1890–1918* (Munich: Prestel, 1979), 369–381; Tilmann Buddensieg, "Die Kaiserlich Deutsche Botschaft in Petersburg von Peter Behrens," in Martin Warnke, ed., *Politische Architektur in Europa vom Mittelalter bis heute—Repräsentation und Gemeinschaft* (Cologne: Dumont, 1984), 374–398; and Georg Krawietz, *Peter Behrens im Dritten Reich* (Weimar: Verlag und Datenbank für Geistes-wissenschaften, 1995), 75–81.

44. Edmund Schüler, "Peter Behrens," *Die Kunst im Deutschen Reich* (Ausgabe B: *Die Baukunst*), 4 (April 1940), 65–66.

45. Conversation in Chicago, 27 June 1961. In this same meeting, Mies stated that, while he had been out of the office during the design of the Embassy, on returning he served as the supervisor of the project and made several trips to St. Petersburg. Mies's success in bringing the bids into line, after Behrens had failed, made Behrens angry. Later, when Mies went to receive the structurally complete building from the contractor, he spoke of Behrens's plans for the interiors. Overheard by a journalist, Mies's account of Behrens's plans appeared in the press before reaching German officials. Behrens was still more angry, so Mies quit the office (1912).

Mies continued that he had also been involved with Behrens's design for the Kröller-Müller villa and private gallery near The Hague (illustrated in list of works, no. 79). On leaving Behrens's office, Mies wrote to Mrs. Kröller, explaining his departure and wishing her well. The Kröllers had been dissatisfied with Behrens's design, and now proposed that Mies work with H. P. Berlage. This led to separate designs by Berlage and Mies. Berlage's design was chosen, but World War I interrupted work. After the war, the Kröller property was threatened by urban growth and their collection had grown; they then planned and executed their great park and Kröller-Müller Museum (by van de Velde) near Otterlo.

46. Karl Scheffler, *Die fetten und die mageren Jahre* (Munich: Paul List, 1946), 39 (written 1933–1934).

47. Behrens appreciated Alfred Messel's saying "What the nude is for the sculptor, the Greek column is for the architect." In Behrens, "Alfred Messel: Ein Nachruf," *Frankfurter Zeitung* (6 April 1909).

48. See chapter 6.

49. Schüler, "Peter Behrens," 65–66. Certain Nazi buildings had formal similarities to Behrens's Embassy, notably the Haus der Kunst in Munich.

50. The Lübeck Kaiser-Wilhelm-Volkshaus remained unbuilt. The announcement of its founding by Senator Possehl on 9 March 1913 appeared in the *Vaterstädtische Blätter* (Lübeck, 16 March 1913), 93–94, with the preliminary design by Behrens. However, a limited competition was later

arranged; invited competitors were Behrens, Theodor Fischer, Hermann Billing, Max Littmann, and a local architect, the winner with a Gothic design, Erich Blunck (who had shared the Schinkel Prize with Poelzig in 1898). Behrens's design was vast and neoclassical, reminiscent of design around 1800 (see *Kunst und Künstler,* 12 [1913–1914], 246). His work won the ardent support of Arthur Moeller van den Bruck, "Der Kaiser und die architektonische Tradition," *Die Tat,* 5 (September 1913), 595–601, which in turn touched off a running debate in the *Lübeckische Blätter.* After World War I, Moeller van den Bruck translated his conservative criticism into more political form and became what Fritz Stern (*The Politics of Cultural Despair* [Garden City, N.Y.: Doubleday, 1965], 231) called "the leading figure of the conservative revolution," author of *Das Dritte Reich* (1922). For local bibliography on the Lübeck affair, I am indebted to Dr. Fritz Schmalenbach. See also Fritz Hellwag, "Lübeck," *Kunstgewerbeblatt,* n.s. 25 (1914), 56–58.

See also Behrens's contemporary, classicizing design for an exhibition hall, illustrated in *Der Industriebau,* 6 (1915), 381–382.

51. Recall Behrens's appreciative essay on Messel, *Frankfurter Zeitung* (6 April 1909).

52. George F. Kennan, "1914: What Happened in Russia," *The Listener* (9 July 1964), 47.

53. See Stern, *The Politics of Cultural Despair,* 256ff., writing of Moeller van den Bruck but employing statements of Thomas Mann as evidence.

54. See R. H. Lutz, *Fall of the German Empire 1914–1918,* 2 vols. (Palo Alto: Stanford University Press, 1932), 1:74–85. Among the signatories: Wilhelm von Bode, Justus Brinkmann, Richard Dehmel, Gerhardt Hauptmann, Adolf von Hildebrand, Max Klinger, Max Liebermann, Bruno Paul, Max Planck, Hans Thoma, and Theodor Wiegand.

In a letter to, and preserved in, the Akademie der Künste, Berlin, of 23 March 1939, Behrens reported: "Während des Krieges habe ich jedoch mehrfach freiwillig Zuge zum IX. Armeekorps zum General von Scheffer an die Ostfront begleitet und erhielt vom Kaiser die persönliche Erlaubnis, während der Mobilmachung wieder Uniform mit Rucksicht auf diesen Anlass zu tragen [Repeatedly during the war I voluntarily accompanied General von Scheffer to the Ninth Army on the eastern front and for this reason received the Kaiser's personal permission to again wear the uniform during the mobilization]."

55. A preliminary report and site plan appeared as "Die Deutsche Werkbundausstellung Köln 1914," *Zentralblatt der Bauverwaltung,* 33 (24 December 1913), 711–712.

56. The bibliography on the exhibition runs into hundreds of items; two major items are *Deutscher Werkbund, Deutsche Werkbund-Ausstellung Köln 1914: Offizieller Katalog* (Cologne and Berlin: R. Mosse, [1914]), and idem, *Jahrbuch 1915: Deutsche Form im Kriegsjahr* (Munich: Bruckmann, 1915). Angelika Thiekötter gives a general discussion of the exhibition, with attention to Behrens's Festhalle, in Cologne, Kölnischer Kunstverein, *Die Deutsche Werkbund-Ausstellung, Cöln 1914* (Cologne: Kölnischer Kunstverein, 1984), 60–113 and 160–162. See also chapter 5, note 41 above; and Stanford Anderson, "Deutscher Werkbund—the 1914 Debate: Hermann Muthesius versus Henry van de Velde," in B. Farmer and H. Louw, eds., *Companion to Contemporary Architectural Thought* (London and New York: Routledge, 1993), 462–467.

57. The reference, of course, is to the facade with its superimposed temple and triumphal arch motifs. Compare Alberti's S. Andrea, Mantua, and the discussion by Rudolf Wittkower, in *Architectural Principles in the Age of Humanism* (New York: Random House, 1965), 47ff.

58. Werkbund, *Jahrbuch 1915*, pls. 77–82. See Rosemarie Haag Bletter, "The Interpretation of the Glass Dream: Expressionist Architecture and the History of the Crystal Metaphor," *Journal of the Society of Architectural Historians*, 40 (March 1981), 20–43.

59. Walther Rathenau, *In Days to Come* (New York: Knopf, 1921), p. 16. See the discussion of Rathenau in chapter 5.

60. Strangely, the Festhalle at Cologne is a throwback to the templelike facade in a vignette that Behrens designed to head his first essay, "Die Dekoration der Bühne," *Deutsche Kunst und Dekoration*, 6 (May 1900), 401. Similarly, the name he gave his 1900 theater was *Festhaus* (*Rheinlande*, 1 [January 1901], 29).

61. Deutscher Werkbund, *Jahrbuch 1912* (Jena: Diederichs, 1912), 27–28 (the first yearbook), reports similar formulations as early as the 1911 convention: Cornelius Gurlitt asserted that alongside the Werkbund's well-stated program for *Qualität* must come a concern for *Form*—and thus the question "Typus oder Individualität." Osthaus responded with an insistence that the *Typ* be artistically controlled.

62. "Die Werkbundarbeit der Zukunft," reprinted in part in Julius Posener, *Anfänge des Funktionalismus: Von Arts and Crafts zum Deutschen Werkbund* (Berlin: Ullstein, 1964), 199–204. Posener's brief commentaries are written in support of Muthesius's position.

63. Henry van de Velde provided his account of the confrontation with Muthesius in his *Geschichte meines Lebens,* ed. Hans Curjel (Munich: R. Piper, 1962), 360ff.

64. Translated from the theses of Muthesius and van de Velde published in Posener, *Anfänge*, 205–207; also in Ulrich Conrads, ed., *Programme und Manifeste zur Architektur des 20. Jahrhunderts* (Berlin: Ullstein, 1964), 25–27; trans. as *Programs and Manifestoes on 20th-Century Architecture* (Cambridge: MIT Press, 1970), 28–29. My interpolation "[of forces]" in Muthesius's second thesis is borrowed, for its seemingly accurate clarification of the original, from Nikolaus Pevsner, *Pioneers of Modern Design* (Harmondsworth: Penguin, 1960), 37.

65. Van de Velde, *Geschichte meines Lebens,* 360ff., was able to claim the support of Hermann Obrist, August Endell, Bruno Taut, Karl Ernst Osthaus, and Robert Breuer as well as Gropius. The statements of these men and others are included in Posener, *Anfänge,* 208–221.

66. Gropius, in conversation with the present author, Cambridge, 6 February 1964, pictured himself as the *enfant terrible* of the 1914 Werkbund affair. He had seen the plea for "type" as bad in itself and evidence of a lack of artistic and creative feeling on the part of Muthesius; he therefore led the campaign against Muthesius. Gropius stated that he had also been offended by Behrens's Festhalle.

In a personal communication of 4 October 1966, Kenneth Kaiser informed me of a voluminous correspondence (July-August 1917; preserved in the Osthaus-Archiv, Hagen) in which Gropius and Osthaus planned their secession. Muthesius's withdrawal of his theses is partially published in Posener, *Anfänge,* 222. See Stressig, in Hesse-Frielinghaus et al., *Karl Ernst Osthaus,* 466–469.

67. Pevsner, *Pioneers of Modern Design,* 36–37, explained the Muthesius–van de Velde conflict as one of a progressive, industrially inspired standardization pitted against a fervent individualism. Later, he indicated that the success of Gropius's Fagus Werke and the Cologne model factory demonstrated that "the architect, to represent this century of ours, must be colder, cold to keep in command of

mechanized production, cold to design for the satisfaction of anonymous clients" (p. 214). An examination of the model factory suggests that Gropius, if anything, was rebelling against the cold, mechanical quality of Behrens's Turbine Factory.

Banham, *Theory and Design in the First Machine Age,* 78, though aware of Muthesius's distinctly nonindustrial architecture for the Cologne exhibition, also considered Muthesius to have been concerned with standardization and mechanization; he interpreted van de Velde's polemic and his theater for the Cologne exhibition as "a spirited rearguard action by an outgoing type of designer."

68. Kenneth Kaiser, in an unpublished study of 1965, described the canon and rightly insisted on this shift in the interpretation of *Typisierung.*

69. Fritz Stahl, "Die Architektur der Werkbund-Ausstellung," *Wasmuths Monatshefte für Baukunst,* 1 (1914–1915), 153–204, already emphasized these buildings.

70. Karl Scheffler, "Über die Auseinandersetzung im Deutschen Werkbund" (1915), reprinted in Posener, *Anfänge,* 225.

71. Posener, *Anfänge,* 208.

72. Gombrich, *Norm and Form,* 81–98. Also see note 2 above.

73. Ibid., 97.

74. See chapter 4 and Richard Klapheck, *Neue Baukunst in den Rheinlanden* (Düsseldorf: L. Schwann, [1928]), 16–24.

75. During World War I, several of the combatant nations strove to propagandize their cultural accomplishments in neutral Switzerland. Behrens was charged with the organization of a Deutscher Werkbund exhibition that was shown at the Gewerbemuseum, Basel (March-April 1917), and then at the Winterthur Museum (May-June 1917). For its showing in Bern, Behrens designed a classicizing demountable wooden exhibition building (see Cremers, *Peter Behrens,* pls. 139–141). While no author is cited for the text of the catalog, Deutscher Werkbund, *Ausstellung auf dem Kirchenfeldplatz, Bern, 1917* (n.p., 1917), it is by Behrens, restating his resolution of the *Typisierung-Individualität* debate. See Fritz Hellwag, "Die Deutsche Werkbund-Ausstellung in Bern," *Innendekoration,* 29 (May 1918), 155–162.

Also during the First World War, Behrens finished second to German Bestelmeyer in a competition for a German-Turkish Friendship House in Constantinople (1916); see Deutscher Werkbund and Deutsch-Türkischen Vereinigung, *Das Haus der Freundschaft in Konstantinopel,* with introduction by Theodor Heuss (Munich: Bruckmann, 1918).

Notes to Chapter 9

1. Peter Behrens, "Reform der künstlerischen Erziehung," in Berlin, Zentrale für Heimatdienst, *Der Geist der neuen Volksgemeinschaft: Denkschrift für das deutsche Volk* (Berlin: Fischer, 1919), 93–106.

2. Peter Behrens, "Wiederaufbau der deutschen Baukunst," *Westdeutsche Wochenschrift für Politik,* 1 (1919), 214–218. Behrens was not specific as to which painting and sculpture incorporated the new *Kunstwollen;* a bow to France indicates that he included at least some postimpressionist work, perhaps even cubism.

3. Behrens, "Reform der künstlerischen Erziehung" (1919), 95.

4. Ibid., 98–99; Behrens also lampooned the modern educational separation by suggesting how peculiar "Dr. ing. Michelangelo" sounds. Shortly before, W. Franz wrote of "Peter Behrens als Ingenieur-Architekt," *Dekorative Kunst,* 20 (February 1917), 145–148. In 1922 Behrens accepted his own honorary doctorate of technology (Dr. tech. ehrenhalber) from the Deutsche Technische Hochschule in Prague; see *Zentralblatt der Bauverwaltung,* 42 (24 June 1922), 311–312.

5. Behrens, "Reform der künstlerischen Erziehung" (1919), 102–103.

6. Behrens, "Wiederaufbau der deutschen Baukunst" (1919), 216.

7. Peter Behrens, "Das Ethos und die Umlagerung der künstlerischen Probleme," in *Der Leuchter: Weltanschauung und Lebensgestaltung. Jahrbuch der Schule der Weisheit,* ed. Graf Hermann Keyserling (Darmstadt: Reichl, [1920]), 336. Reflecting on cultural work prior to World War I, and certainly implicating his own work, Behrens observed: "Monumental art: aesthetic imperialism" (p. 324).

8. Walter Gropius, "Programm des Staatlichen Bauhauses Weimar" (April 1919), trans. in Ulrich Conrads, ed., *Programs and Manifestos on 20th-Century Architecture* (Cambridge: MIT Press, 1970), 49–53.

9. Peter Behrens, "Die neue Handwerks-Romantik," *Innendekoration,* 33 (October 1922), 341. Industrial design as a matter of good taste supplied by an artist was part of a positive assessment of the Behrens-AEG relationship from the outset: J. A. Lux, *Das neue Kunstgewerbe in Deutschland* (Leipzig: Klinkhardt und Biermann, 1908), 242–246.

Behrens was anticipated by his former apprentice, Walter Gropius. In 1919, the year in which Behrens's reform statement emphasized the union of architecture with the strengths of the fine arts and engineering (and with *Kunstgewerbe* as an adjunct study), Gropius was uniting Weimar's school of fine arts and van de Velde's Kunstgewerbeschule in a new school, the Staatliches Bauhaus, under the aegis of *Handwerk.* Gropius called for the return of all architects, painters, and sculptors to handicraft (*Handwerk*). Art should not be conceived as a calling, for the artist is merely an artisan, fortuitously elevated. By the grace of heaven, in rare moments of illumination, beyond the power of man's will, art blossoms forth unconsciously from the work of the artisan's hand. The source of all creative forming is in the practical competency of the artisan. The program of the Bauhaus (see preceding note) stated that the school was to be the servant of the workshop and would one day be absorbed into the workshop.

10. Peter Behrens, "Die Dombauhütte: Aus der Eröffnungsrede von Peter Behrens," *Deutsche Kunst und Dekoration,* 26 (January 1923), 220–230; Paul Joseph Cremers, *Peter Behrens: Sein Werk von 1909 bis zur Gegenwart* (Essen: Baedeker, 1928), 20, pls. 83–88; Tilmann Buddensieg, "Architektur als freie Kunst," in Bernhard Buderath, ed., *Peter Behrens: Umbautes Licht* (Munich: Prestel, 1990), 70–81.

11. Peter Behrens, "Qualitätsarbeit," *Deutsche Zeitung für Spanien,* 7, no. 149 (1922), 3.

12. Another member of the Werkbund circle, like Behrens and Diederichs, was Ferdinand Avenarius who, in 1902, founded the Dürerbund in Dresden, "a rapidly growing society that sought to advise the government, the public, and business on esthetic problems, in a general effort to combine utility with beauty. It became an effective lobby for cultural excellence." Fritz Stern, *The Politics of Cultural Despair* (Garden City, N.Y.: Doubleday, 1965), 221.

13. Walter Schürmeyer, "Das technische Betriebsgebäude der Farbenindustrie-A.-G., Hoechst a. M.," *Deutsche Bauzeitung,* 60, nos. 33 and 34 (24 and 28 April 1926), 273–277, 281–284, pl. 33; Cremers, *Peter Behrens,* 15–17, pls. II, 2–10; Shepard Vogelgesang, "Peter Behrens, Architect and Teacher," *Architectural Forum,* 52 (May 1930), 716–718; Günter Drebusch, *Industriearchitektur* (Munich: W. Heyne, 1976), 165–168; and especially Buderath, ed., *Peter Behrens.*

14. For the Gutehofnungshütte, Behrens built an administration building and two warehouses of reinforced concrete construction in Oberhausen (1920–1925; illustrated in list of works, no. 140b). The complex is related to the Farbwerke Hoechst in time and in fine brick construction, but programmatically and architecturally it is a more workaday group. Rather than a medievalizing and handicraft orientation, at Oberhausen one can detect affinities with contemporary Dutch architecture and even, at considerable remove, with Frank Lloyd Wright. See Cremers, *Peter Behrens,* 17–18, pls. III, 11–23; Roland Günter, *Beiträge zur rheinischen Kunstgeschichte und Denkmalspflege* (Düsseldorf: Rheinland, 1970), 365–382; Buddensieg, "Architektur als freie Kunst," 63–64; Brigitte Schlüter, "Verwaltungsbauten der Rheinisch-Westfälischen Stahlindustrie 1900–1930" (Ph.D. diss., University of Bonn, 1991).

15. Designs for the Stinnes mausoleum in Mülheim-Ruhr appear in Cremers, *Peter Behrens,* pl. 91, and Paolo Portoghesi, "Disegni di Peter Behrens, 1922–1929," *Controspazio,* 2 (January-February 1970), 18–19. Other designs were in the possession of Hans Döllgast in 1961; still others are in the Pfalzgalerie, Kaiserslautern.

16. Paris, Exposition internationale des arts décoratifs et industriels modernes, 1925, *L'Autriche à l'Exposition internationale des arts décoratifs et industriels modernes. Paris 1925* (Vienna: Commission Exécutive, 1925), 11–28, pl. after p. 60; Cremers, *Peter Behrens,* pls. 144–146.

17. In a publication of the Technische Universität München, *Hans Döllgast* (Munich: Callwey, 1987), 247, Winfried Nerdinger notes Döllgast's extensive design freedom, but that he signed drawings only for the Salzburg project. The most extensive discussion of Döllgast's role in design and especially in the production of the most notable drawings from Behrens's office in the 1920s is by Buddensieg, "Architektur als freie Kunst," 58–83.

18. In addition to the just-mentioned significant role of Döllgast in this building, according to Michael Hartig, "Der Studienkollegbau zu St. Peter in Salzburg," *Die christliche Kunst,* 24 (May 1928), 234–240, the city architect Franz Wagner drew the basic scheme to which Behrens "gave the artistic character." See also J. A. Lux, "Salzburgs steinerne Sprache," *Deutsche Bauhütte,* 30 (8 September 1926), 256–257; Cremers, *Peter Behrens,* 22–23, pls. 92–99; "Zehn Jahre Architektur um Prof. Behrens," special number of *Österreichische Kunst,* 3 (November 1932), 19, and commentary by Carl Moll, 34–35; Ernst Hanisch, "St. Peter in der Zwischenkriegszeit," in Heinz Dopsch and Roswitha Juffinger, eds., *St. Peter in Salzburg: Die älteste Kloster im deutschen Sprachraum* (Salzburg: Salzburger Landesregierung, 1982), 216–220; Norbert Mayr, *Peter Behrens 1868–1940: Entwürfe und Werke für Salzburg und Oldenburg. Teil II: Salzburg* (Salzburg: Salzburger Museum Carolino Augusteum, 1994).

19. The closing date of 1926 is later than is usually given in the literature. This is, however, the date over the entrance to the house. Also, a letter of Behrens to Bassett-Lowke, 7 August 1926 (with Mrs. Bassett-Lowke in 1963), sends thanks for photographs of the finished house, and on the basis of

these makes suggestions for interior changes. See "'New Ways': The House of W. J. Bassett-Lowke, Esq., Northampton," *Architectural Review,* 60 (November 1926), 175–189 and plates; Cremers, *Peter Behrens,* pls. 108–112.

20. See chapter 8, note 14, and corresponding discussion in the text.

21. See chapter 8, note 16.

22. Fritz Neumeyer, "Der Werkwohnungsbau der Industrie in Berlin und seine Entwicklung im 19. und frühen 20. Jahrhundert" (Ph.D. diss., Technische Universität Berlin, 1978), 227–243, figs. 97–116; Tilmann Buddensieg with Henning Rogge et al., *Industriekultur: Peter Behrens und die AEG 1907–1914* (Berlin: Gebr. Mann, 1979), A196–210; in English as *Industriekultur: Peter Behrens and the AEG 1907–1914,* trans. Iain Boyd Whyte (Cambridge: MIT Press, 1984), where the corresponding catalog numbers are A197–209; Karl-Heinz Hüter, *Architektur in Berlin 1900–1933* (Dresden and Stuttgart: Kohlhammer, 1988), 252–253. Cremers, *Peter Behrens,* pl. 130, illustrates the wartime housing designed by Behrens for Hennigsdorf (1917).

23. Peter Behrens, "Die Gruppenbauweise," *Wasmuths Monatshefte für Baukunst,* 4 (1919–1920), 122–127; Neumeyer, "Der Werkwohnungsbau der Industrie in Berlin," 244–255, figs. 117–119; Buddensieg A211–213/A210–212.

24. Peter Behrens and Heinrich de Fries, *Vom sparsamen Bauen: Ein Beitrag zur Siedlungsfrage* (Berlin: Bauwelt, 1918). The book received a thorough critique by Dr.-Ing. Weishaupt, "Das Wesen der neuen 'Gruppenbauweise'," *Deutsche Bauzeitung,* 53 (6 September–18 October 1919), 430–432, 433–434, 439–440, 450–455, and 498–502.

25. Peter Behrens, "Doppelgärtenhäuser," *Die Volkswohnung: Zeitschrift für Wohnungsbau und Siedlungswesen,* 2 (24 January 1920), 23–28; Cremers, *Peter Behrens,* 27–28, pls. 133–135.

26. P. Morton Shand, "Scenario for a Human Drama," part 3, *Architectural Review,* 76 (September 1934), 86; Erich Göldner, "Gedanken zur Industrialisierung des Wohnungsbaues von Peter Behrens," *Baukunst und Werkform,* 8 (1955), 308–310.

27. The first prominent publication of this and closely related designs was by Behrens in 1927 as part of his exposition of his Weissenhof building ("Terrassen am Hause," in Deutscher Werkbund, *Bau und Wohnung* [Stuttgart: Fr. Wedekind, 1927], 16–25). Behrens gives no date for the unbuilt designs. A year later, Cremers published the illustrated design and a charcoal rendering of a similar project, giving the date of 1920, which Behrens scholars have followed since. Karin Kirsch, *The Weissenhofsiedlung: Experimental Housing Built for the Deutscher Werkbund, Stuttgart, 1927* (New York: Rizzoli, 1989), 176–185, gives the date as 1926. However, a different charcoal rendering of the same building (with soft corners, giving a Santa Fe pueblo effect) was published in *Kunstblatt* (1924), 104. The underlying design of all these renderings is so similar that they must all be part of one design effort. It would be unlike Behrens to fail to publish his designs for four years, especially when in the period 1920–1924 he was advancing other housing projects. Consequently I suggest a date of ca. 1924 for these projects. See also Shand and Göldner in the preceding note, who approve of these designs also.

28. On the Weissenhof exhibition, including Behrens's apartment building, see Deutscher Werkbund, *Die Wohnung* (the official catalog of the exhibition; Stuttgart, 1927); idem, *Bau und*

Wohnung; Heinz and Bodo Rasch, *Wie bauen? Bau und Einrichtung der Werkbundsiedlung am Weissenhof in Stuttgart 1927* (Stuttgart: Wedekind, 1927); Edgar Wedepohl, "Die Weissenhof-Siedlung der Werkbund-Ausstellung 'Die Wohnung', Stuttgart 1927," *Wasmuths Monatshefte für Baukunst,* 11 (October 1927), 391–402; Jürgen Joedicke, *Weissenhofsiedlung Stuttgart* (Stuttgart: Krämer, 1989 [in English and German]); Kirsch, *The Weissenhofsiedlung;* and especially Richard Pommer and Christian F. Otto, *Weissenhof 1927 and the Modern Movement in Architecture* (Chicago: University of Chicago Press, 1991).

29. Konrad Nonn, "Unabänderliches im Kleinwohnungsbau," *Wasmuths Monatshefte für Baukunst,* 11 (October 1927), 407. In 1938, Nonn was passing information to Hitler, using Behrens's Dombauhütte as evidence against the selection of Behrens for the commission for the AEG administration building on Speer's Nord-Süd axis (see below, and Alan Windsor, *Peter Behrens: Architect and Designer* [New York: Whitney Library of Design, 1981], 156–158).

30. Peter Behrens, "Die Gemeinde Wien als Bauherrin," *Bauwelt,* 19 (11 October 1928), 976–980; Cremers, *Peter Behrens,* 30–31, pls. 122–125. General works on social housing of "Red Vienna": Karl Mang and Eva Mang-Frimmel, *Kommunaler Wohnbau in Wien: Aufbruch 1923–1934 Ausstrahlung,* 2d ed. (Vienna: Stadt Wien, 1978); Manfredo Tafuri, ed., *Vienna rossa: La politica residenziale nella Vienna socialista, 1919–1933* (Milan: Electa, 1980), on Behrens, 49ff., and A. Passeri, 178–189, 184–185. Now also see Eve Blau, *The Architecture of Red Vienna, 1919–1934* (Cambridge: MIT Press, 1999).

31. Wolf Tegethoff, *Mies van der Rohe: The Villas and Country Houses* (New York: Museum of Modern Art, 1985), §11.

32. H. K. Zimmermann, "Ein Landsitz am Taunus erbaut von Prof. Peter Behrens, Berlin," *Deutsche Kunst und Dekoration,* 35 (April 1932), 32–40. By September 1934 the villa stood empty, as Ganz had fled Germany (Shand, "Scenario for a Human Drama," part 3, 83–86). In November 1934 the villa was damaged in the infamous Kristallnacht; some days later Nazis set fire to it (Alan Windsor, "Letters from Peter Behrens to P. Morton Shand, 1932–1938," *Architectural History,* 37 [1994], 174, relying on a personal communication from Georg Krawietz, 12 August 1993). At least as late as 1975, the villa was in a ruinous state; it was subsequently restored, though with significant alterations. On the villa: Max Eisler, "Peter Behrens: Landhaus einer Dame im Taunus," *Moderne Bauformen,* 31 (March 1932), 117–132; Otto Riedrich, "Neue Arbeiten von Peter Behrens," *Baugilde,* 14 (1932), 765–780; P. Morton Shand, "A Villa in the Taunus Mountains by Professor Peter Behrens," *Architectural Review,* 72 (October 1932), 121–123; and Tilmann Buddensieg, "Peter Behrens," in Wolfgang Ribbe and Wolfgang Schäche, eds., *Baumeister. Architekten. Stadtplaner. Biographien zur baulichen Entwicklung Berlins* (Berlin: Historische Kommission zu Berlin/Stapp Verlag, 1987), 355.

33. Tilmann Buddensieg, gen. ed., *Berlin 1900–1933: Architecture and Design. Architektur und Design* (New York: Cooper-Hewitt/Berlin: Gebr. Mann, 1987), 24. Contemporary voices: Peter Behrens, "Ein Landhaus in Schlachtensee," *die neue linie* (November 1932), 16ff., and Riedrich, "Neue Arbeiten von Peter Behrens," 770–788.

34. The winner was the team of the Luckhardt brothers and Alfons Anker; Mies van der Rohe's

design was much admired. Martin Wagner, "Das Formproblem eines Weltstadtplatzes: Wettbewerb der Verkehrs-A.G. für die Umbauung des Alexanderplatzes," *Das neue Berlin*, 1 (1929), 33–39, gives the background and provides Stadtbaurat Wagner's seven requirements for an "organically formed 'Weltstadtplatz'." Paul Westheim, "Umgestaltung des Alexanderplatzes," *Bauwelt*, 20 (1929), 312–316, gives an assessment of the entries, unfavorable to Behrens.

35. Peter Behrens, "Die neuen Hochhäuser am Alexanderplatz in Berlin," *Der Bauingenieur*, 13 (1 January 1932), 10–12. There is a detailed historical survey in Waltraud Volk, *Berlin, Hauptstadt der DDR: Historische Strassen und Plätze heute*, 2d rev. ed. (Berlin: Verlag für Bauwesen, 1972), 203–253. See also Kaiserslautern, Pfalzgalerie, *Peter Behrens: Berlin Alexanderplatz. Pläne, Zeichnungen und Photographien zum Wettbewerb und der Bebauung 1929–1932* (Kaiserslautern: Pfalzgalerie, 1993).

36. "Peter Behrens—Alexander Popp," *Bau- und Werkkunst* (September 1930), 273–281; Baron Salvator von Friedel, ed., *Die Neubauten und Betriebseinrichtungen der Tabakfabrik in Linz* (Salzburg: Kiesel, [1936]).

37. The National Socialist aspect of this competition is revealed in Gerhard Langmaack, "Unser Massenschicksal und der Weg der Baukunst: Eine kritische Untersuchung an dem Wettbewerb für eine Kongress-, Sport- und Ausstellungshalle in Hamburg," *Die Baugilde*, 16 (1934), 511–535. It would seem that Behrens's design conforms adequately to these demands, but Buddensieg reports that Behrens did not receive this commission in his native city because he was denounced as a cultural Bolshevist and the architect of Jewish industrial internationalism (Buddensieg, "Peter Behrens," in Ribbe and Schäche, 357). The loss of the project in the greater dreams of Hitler is argued in Georg Krawietz, *Peter Behrens im Dritten Reich* (Weimar: Verlag und Datenbank für Geisteswissenschaften, 1995), 25–33, 143.

38. This claim is made by the officers of the Academy in requesting of the Reich's Ministry of Science and Education a two-year extension of Behrens's teaching contract (letter of 20 January 1939, Handakte von Peter Behrens, Akademie der Künste, Berlin).

39. H. Wolff, "Der Neubau des Hauptverwaltungsgebäudes der AEG in Berlin," *Die Kunst im Dritten Reich* (Ausgabe B: *Die Baukunst*), 3 (October 1939), 447–454; Buddensieg with Rogge et al., *Industriekultur*, A170–183/A171–174; Krawietz, *Peter Behrens im Dritten Reich*, 99–133.

40. Albert Speer, *Inside the Third Reich* (New York: Macmillan, 1970), 144–145.

41. Letter from the Berlin Academy to Behrens and his response, in which he claims never to have joined any party but the NSDAP in Austria "(was dortseits ja bereits bekannt ist)" (letters of 18 and 23 March 1939, Handakte von Peter Behrens, Akademie der Künste, Berlin). Already in 1932 Behrens, for politically opportune reasons, had separated from his Jewish mistress of many years, Else Oppler-Legband, whom he had first met as a student in his Nürnberg master's course of 1901 (Buddensieg, "Peter Behrens," in Ribbe and Schäche, 356). For an extended study and more sanguine view of Behrens under the Third Reich, see Krawietz, *Peter Behrens im Dritten Reich*.

42. Obituaries: Theodor Heuss, *Die Hilfe*, 46, no. 5 (1940), 74–76; and Edmund Schüler, *Die Kunst im deutschen Reich* (Ausgabe B: *Die Baukunst*), 4 (April 1940), 65–66.

Notes to the Conclusion

1. "Arbeitszimmer eines Gelehrten," an exhibition interior for the Österreichisches Museum in Vienna (1923); see Paul Joseph Cremers, *Peter Behrens: Sein Werk von 1909 bis zur Gegenwart* (Essen: Baedeker, 1928), pls. 147–148.

2. Erwin Panofsky, *The Life and Art of Albrecht Dürer* (Princeton: Princeton University Press, 1955), 156–181; Dürer's St. *Jerome* and *Melencolia I* appear as figs. 208, 209.

3. See chapter 9.

4. The rich composite of Behrens's *Romantik* included not only the elements that have been mentioned but also the "true" romanticism of the time of Goethe (not the degraded romanticism of the later nineteenth century), the industrial landscape of the Ruhr, and the contemporary architectural work of the "Amsterdam school" (the carefully crafted brick architecture of J. M. van der Meij, Michael de Klerk, and others, including Behrens's old associate J. L. M. Lauweriks). Behrens posed his advocacy of this Dutch expressionist school in specific contrast to the "classicizing, type-forming" work of J. J. P. Oud and the Rotterdam school. The work of the Amsterdam architects was in accord with Behrens's claim that the concept of a total art was rooted in the impression of mastery provided by a complete absorption in the material and a genuine craftsmanly devotion to the task ("Peter Behrens über neue Ziele," *Hellweg,* 4 [1924], 872, which also notes that Behrens was then the chairman of the Verein für Deutsches Kunstgewerbe).

5. Robert Breuer, "Häuser, die Künstler sich bauten," *Über Land und Meer,* 105 (November 1910), 195–197.

6. See Leverkusen, Museum Leverkusen, *Die gläserne Kette* (n.p., 1963); Bruno Taut, *Alpine Architektur* (Hagen: Folkwang-Verlag, 1919); Rosemarie Haag Bletter, "The Interpretation of the Glass Dream: Expressionist Architecture and the History of the Crystal Metaphor," *Journal of the Society of Architectural Historians,* 40 (March 1981), 20–43.

7. See the materials cited in chapter 9, notes 38, 41.

8. See Dürerbund-Werkbund Genossenschaft, *Deutsche Warenbuch,* with an introduction by Ferdinand Avenarius (n.p.: ca. 1916).

Project names are in **bold.** Locations are in bold if the work was built.

Moeller's 1991 book on Behrens's Düsseldorf period (1903–1907) includes a catalog of works of that period. In the list below, "Moeller" followed by a number [in brackets] refers to her catalog number.

Buddensieg's 1979 book on Behrens's AEG work (1907 to World War I) includes an architectural catalog compiled by Henning Rogge. "Bu" followed by a number [in brackets] refers to Rogge's catalog. Where the MIT Press edition numbering is different, this is given in second position.

N.B. References to both these catalogs also constitute major bibliographic references which are not repeated in the lists of literature.

Moeller includes extensive bibliographic references for each work, but since her work is less readily available in the English-language world, I provide select references for the buildings and projects she catalogs, along with references published since her work.

Rogge's catalog in Buddensieg also has extensive references and is available in the MIT Press edition. I provide a still more select set of references here, along with references published since their work.

Behrens's works not cataloged by Moeller or Rogge receive fuller bibliographic references. In all cases, author-date citations refer to items in part 3 of the bibliography below; references to writings by Behrens refer to the chronological list in part 2 of the bibliography.

Finally, it should be noted that Behrens began as an artist, moving on to graphic and then craft work before launching his autodidact career as an architect. There is no extensive single work on Behrens's early career. The most helpful start is the catalog of the exhibition "Peter Behrens und Nürnberg" from the Germanisches Nationalmuseum in Nürnberg (1980). See also the catalog of AEG graphics in Buddensieg, compiled by Gabriele Heidecker. On Behrens's work in typography, see the Postscript to chapter 4 above. Behrens's groundbreaking work in industrial design (see chapter 6 above) was predominantly for the AEG, and is cataloged by Karin Wilhelm in the "Products" section of Buddensieg.

1. Idea-project; Munich or Darmstadt?
Design for a **Gallery of Modern Art** (Galerie
    moderner Kunst)
1900

Deutsche Kunst und Dekoration, 6 (May 1900),
    403–404

2. Darmstadt, Mathildenhöhe, Künstler-
    Kolonie
Project for a **Theater for the Artists' Colony**
1900

Behrens, "Die 'Lebensmesse' von Richard
Dehmel," 1901
A. Koch 1901, 313–318
Scheffler 1901, 30ff., and 1907b
Fuchs 1909, 197–199
Breuer 1912b, 6, 9
Hoeber 1913, 216–218
Hamann and Hermand 1967, 403
Anderson 1968, chap. 3
Anderson 1969, 74f.
Simon 1976, 150–153
Posener 1979, 434–441
Buddensieg in Nürnberg 1980, 40–41
Keller 1980
Windsor 1981, 27–37
Anderson 1990, 121–125
Dal Co 1990, 191–197
See chapter 3 (and figures 3.13–14) here

3. **Darmstadt, Mathildenhöhe, Künstler-
    Kolonie,** Alexandraweg
Behrens house (Haus Behrens)
1900–1901

Meier-Graefe 1900
Behrens, "Über Ausstellungen," 1900
[Darmstadt, Künstler-Kolonie] 1901
Behrens, *Haus Peter Behrens,* [May 1901]
Graul 1901, 49–50
Schäfer 1901 and 1901b
F. Schumacher 1901, 426–431
Vossische Zeitung (7 June 1901)
Generalanzeiger für Düsseldorf (19 June 1901)
Norddeutsche Allgemeine Zeitung (22 June 1901)

Fuchs 1901
Scheffler 1901
Meier-Graefe 1901
Fred 1901 and 1901b
A. Koch 1901, 94, 98, 128, 328, 329–392 (Breysig
    essay and accompanying figs., also in Breysig
    1902)
Breysig 1902 (also in A. Koch 1901)
A. Hofmann 1902, part I
Meier-Graefe 1902 and 1902b
Ruettenauer 1902
Meier-Graefe 1904, Engl. ed. 2:324
Heyck [1907?], 1:418, 420, pls. 31, 51
Lux 1908, 45, and 1908c, 174
Breuer 1912b
Hoeber 1913, 9–19
Scheffler 1913, 161
Hegemann 1925, 7, 9f.
Platz 1927, 21–22, fig. 259t
Klapheck 1928, 15
Siedler 1928, 763
Vogelgesang 1930, 715–716
Posener 1934, 8
Ahlers-Hestermann 1941, 87
Madsen 1955, 64ff., 420, 425ff.
Hennig-Schefold 1967, 7
Anderson 1968, chap. 3
Anderson 1969, 74
Bott in Wietek 1976, 155–159
Darmstadt 1976:
    W. Hofmann, 1:27, fig. 5
    Huber in vol. 5
    Sperlich, 5:167
Simon 1976, 137–172, 230
Anderson 1977, 54, 56
Buddensieg in Brussels, Palais 1977, 30
Kadatz 1977, fig. 29
Karlsruhe 1978, 59–61
Romein 1978, 568, 571
Anderson 1980, 85–87
Buddensieg in Nürnberg 1980, 37–47
Bilancioni 1981
Windsor 1981, 14–26
Brauneck 1982, 73
Cramer 1984, 63, 94–98, 103
Krause 1984, 82–86

Norberg-Schulz 1986
Heskett 1986, 52–53
Moeller in Internationaler Kongress 1986, 78
Gräf in Dyroff 1988, 89
Anderson 1990, 111–116
Dal Co 1990, 190–193
Werner in Pfeifer 1990, 32–37
Anderson 1991, 64, 76
Anderson 1991c, 17–19, 28
Neumeyer 1991, 48–50
Sembach et al. 1992, 15
Spickernagel 1992, 86–88
Anderson 1993, 328–330
Anderson 1995, 10–13
Baird 1995, 40ff.
Schwartz 1996, 93–95
See chapter 3 (and figures 3.6–7, 3.9–12) here

4. Nürnberg
Shop interior for Nürnberger Handwerkskunst [Moeller 1]
October-December 1901

Nürnberg, Gewerbemuseum, *Jahresbericht* (1902)
Buddensieg in Ribbe and Schäche 1987, 358
Pfeifer 1990, cat. 64, 155

5. Düsseldorf, Industrie- und Gewerbe-Ausstellung 1902
Stall for the Krefelder Vereins für Bucharbeit [Moeller 2]
1901–1902

6. Turin, Italy, International Exposition of Decorative Arts 1902, German Section

6a. **Hamburg Vestibule** (Hamburger Vorhalle der Macht und der Schönheit) [Moeller 3.1]
1901–1902

Fuchs 1902, 1–20
Fuchs in A. Koch 1902 (same as Fuchs 1902)
Fred 1902, 438
Dehmel 1922, letter 355 to Behrens (18 October 1902)
Nacht. [1902], pl. 7
Meier-Graefe 1904, Engl. ed. 2:324
Pudor 1905, 21
Hoeber 1913, 20–22
Hamann and Hermand 1967, 407
Anderson 1968, chap. 2
Windsor 1981, 50–53
See chapter 2 (and figure 2.5) here

6b. **Room for the publisher Alexander Koch designed as a man's study** (Herren-arbeitszimmer) [Moeller 3.2]
1902

See preceding entry

6c. **Living room (Hessisches Zimmer), produced by Ludwig Alter** [Moeller 3.3]
1902

See preceding entry

7. Lindau, Schachener Strasse 53
Ladies' sitting room (Damenzimmer), library, and dining room for the Villa Wacker [Moeller 4]
1901–1902

Fuchs 1902
Hoeber 1913, 22–23
Kaiserslautern 1966, fig. 59
Windsor 1981, 52
Speidel in Pfeifer 1990, 91

8. Berlin, Wertheim Department Store, Exhibition of Modern Dwelling Interiors 1902 (Gesamtanlage moderne Wohn-räume) [Moeller 5]
Dining room
Fall 1902

Osborn 1903
Hoeber 1913, 21–23
Buddensieg in Ribbe and Schäche 1987, 345
Buddensieg 1987, 27
Schönberger in Buddensieg 1987, 89–94

9. **Bremen, IX. Internationaler Kongress gegen den Alkoholismus** (Ninth International Congress against Alcoholism), April 1903
Dining room
1902

Moeller 1991, 171–172

10. **Darmstadt**
Study for the Darmstadt publisher Alexander Koch (Arbeitszimmer; furniture by Henry van de Velde and from Behrens's Turin Exhibition study)
1902–1903?

Le Corbusier 1967, 211
Selle 1974, 111
Selle in Siepmann 1978, 73

11. **Düsseldorf, Behrens's apartment in the Kunstgewerbeschule**
Dining room [Moeller 7]
January-April 1903

Schäfer 1903, 57–59
Jaumann 1909, 356–357

12. Design for a **Small Summer House** (Kleines Sommerhaus) [Moeller 6]
Summer 1903

Haenel 1906, 106–109; with Behrens's own description
Hoeber 1913, 22–24

13. **St. Louis, USA, Louisiana Purchase Exposition 1904, Varied Industries Building**
13a. **Reading room** (for Düsseldorf City Library)
Subsequently **Düsseldorf, Kunstgewerbemuseum**, Friedrichsplatz
City Library Reading Room [Moeller 8]
1903–1904; installed in Düsseldorf, 1906

Nachtlicht 1904b, 13, 76–77
Creutz 1904, 466–468, 473
Muthesius 1904, 212–213
Heitmann 1905, 24–27
Hoeber 1913, 30–32
Kaiserslautern 1966, cat. 131
Hamann and Hermand 1967, 407
Anderson 1968, chap. 4
Kadatz 1977, 39, fig. 30
See chapter 4 (and figure 4.3) here

13b. **Anteroom** (Room 44a, b) executed by Ludwig Alter, incorporating furniture exhibited as the Hessisches Zimmer, Turin exposition, 1902
1904

Nachtlicht 1904b, 13
Creutz 1904, 468, 470
Heitmann 1905, 26–27
Moeller in Nürnberg 1980, 266
The endpapers of the present volume simulate the type of Behrens wall covering used in this and other rooms in his early works

14. **Dresden, Ausstellungspalast**, exhibition of the Dresdener Werkstätten für Handwerkskunst, 1903–1904
Dining room [Moeller 9]
Summer-Fall 1903

Haenel 1904, 154–155
Singer 1904, 55, 58
Waentig 1909, 3
Hoeber 1913, 32
Lancaster 1952, 309
Le Corbusier 1967, 212

15. **Düsseldorf, Internationale Kunst- und grosse Gartenbauausstellung** (International Art and Garden Exhibition) **1904**

15a. **Formal garden** [Moeller 39]

15b. **Alcohol-free restaurant Jungbrunnen** [Moeller 10]
1903–1904

[Behrens] in Düsseldorf 1904
Osborn 1904, 433, 501–504
Lichtwark 1923, 2:105–106
S[chäfer] 1904
Schneider 1905, 246–250
Meier-Graefe 1905, 390–405
O. Bernhard 1905, 25–40
Osthaus 1907, 123
Muthesius 1907, 229
Behrens, "Der moderne Garten," 1911
Hoeber 1913, 26–30
Windsor 1981, 53–58
Moeller in Internationaler Kongress 1986, 79, fig. 50
Buddensieg in Ribbe and Schäche 1987, 346
Busch 1993, 21, figs. 2–4

15c. **Room installation for Internationale Vasenausstellung** (International Vase Exhibition) [Moeller 11]
February-May 1904

16. **Hamburg, Haus Dr. jur. Wolf Mannhardt,** Blumenstrasse 15
Dr. Mannhardt's study (Herrenzimmer) [Moeller 12]
1904

Meier-Graefe 1905, 413–416
Hoeber 1913, 30ff.
Windsor 1981, 60

17. **Hagen,** Bahnhofstrasse 51
Living room and dining room for Dr. med. H. Deetjens [Moeller 13]
1904

Muthesius 1907, 93

18. Cologne, Exposition of Art, 1905
Design for the **exposition grounds with a main building** [Moeller 16]
September-October 1904

Meier-Graefe 1905, 406–408, color pl.

19. **Wetter an der Ruhr, Haus Schede**
Salon [Moeller 14]
1904–1905

Meier-Graefe 1905, 409–412
Muthesius 1907, 91
Hoeber 1913, 32, 34
Platz 1927, fig. 258
Müller-Wulckow 1930, 6
Platz 1933, 25, 115, fig. 207
Shand 1934, 84
Hesse-Frielinghaus 1966, 5
Anderson 1968, chap. 4
Posener 1979, 223–224
Buddensieg in Nürnberg 1980, 45–47
Moeller in Nürnberg 1980
Moeller in Internationaler Kongress 1986, 78–79, fig. 49
Buddensieg in Ribbe and Schäche 1987, 346
Speidel in Pfeifer 1990, 82–88
See chapter 4 (and figure 4.6) here

20. **Hamburg, Firma Wm. Klöpper,** Rödingsmarkt
Interiors, especially the private office of the director (Privatkontor) [Moeller 15]
1904–1905

Hoeber 1913, 31–32
Windsor 1981, 60

21. **Oldenburg, Nordwestdeutsche Kunstausstellung 1905** (Northwest German Art Exhibition, June-October 1905) [Oldenburger Landesausstellung 1905]
Buildings [Moeller 17]; **gardens** [Moeller 39]
1904–1905

General literature
A. Koch 1905
K. Schaefer 1905
Schaefen [*sic;* K. Schaefer] 1905b, 428–429
Hoeber 1913, 33–39
Lichtwark 1923, 2:137–140
Siedler 1928, 763
Hamann and Hermand 1967, 407
Anderson 1968, chap. 2
Windsor 1981, 60–62
Asche 1992
See chapter 2 here

21a. **Kunsthalle** [Moeller 17.1] and

21b. **Forecourt with a music pavilion** [Moeller 17.4] **as a festival place** (Festplatzanlage mit Kunsthalle, on the Dobengelände)

See general literature above
Platz 1927, 27, 145–150
Anderson 1968, chap. 2
Buddensieg in Ribbe and Schäche 1987, 346–347
Pfeifer 1990, cat. 109, 158
Neumeyer 1991, 54–55
Asche 1992
See chapter 2 (and figures 2.5–8) here; the endpapers simulate the type of printed fabric used as wall covering and upholstery in the Reading Room of the Kunsthalle

21c. **Pavilion for the Delmenhorster Lino-leumfabrik Anker-Marke** [Moeller 17.2]

See general literature above
Hoeber 1913, 34–39
Asche 1992
Burke 1992, 28
Jefferies 1995, 244–255

21d. **Pavilion for the Th. Rogge Zigarrenfabrik** [Moeller 17.3]

See general literature above
Hoeber 1913, 34–39
Asche 1992

21e. **Formal garden (sculpture garden) with fountain and light wood frame pergo-las** (Lattenpergolen) [Moeller 39]

See general literature above
K. Schaefer 1905, 20–21
Muthesius 1907, 230–231
Hoeber 1913, 34ff.
Platz 1927, 32, fig. 320
Buddensieg in Ribbe and Schäche 1987, 347
Asche 1992

22. **Hagen, Folkwang Museum** (now the Karl Ernst Osthaus Museum)
Lecture Hall (Vortragssaal) [Moeller 18] 1904–1905

Osthaus 1907, 118–121
Lux 1908, 43–46
Schäfer 1909, 265
Hagen, Museum Folkwang, *Katalog. Band I,* 1912
Hoeber 1913, 66–70
Hesse-Frielinghaus 1966, 4
Hamann and Hermand 1967, 528
Anderson 1968, chap. 4
Hesse-Frielinghaus et al. 1971, 50–51
Windsor 1981, 58–60
See chapter 4 (and figure 4.7) here

23. **Cologne, Flora, Deutsche Kunstausstel-lung** (German Art Exhibition) **1906**

23a. First design for **Tonhaus (recital hall)** [Moeller 21.1] **and garden** [Moeller 40.1]
April-August 1905

Schäfer 1905
Windsor 1981, 65–68
Mai in *Westdeutsche Impuls* (Cologne, 1984), 34–36

23b. **Tonhaus** [Moeller 21.2] **and garden** [Moeller 40.2]
1905–1906

Schäfer 1905
Köln. Katalog 1906
Köln 1906
Schur 1906b
Niemeyer 1907, 149ff., 164–165
Scheffler 1907, pl. opp. 96
Sutter 1907, 32–34
Lux 1908, 45, and 1908c, 173
Hoeber 1913, 53–57
Hamann and Hermand 1967, 409
Hesse-Frielinghaus et al. 1971, 175
Mai in *Westdeutsche Impuls* (Cologne, 1984), 34–36
Buddensieg in Ribbe and Schäche 1987, 347
Pfeifer 1990, cat. 110, 158

No. 23b. Tonhaus, entrance seen over water garden.

No. 23b. Tonhaus, interior.

24. **Saarbrücken,** Trillerweg 42
Gustav Obenauer house [Moeller 19]
1905–1907; Obenauer's library designed
    and built at the upper floor, 1910

Scheffler 1907b
Osthaus 1907
Breuer 1908, 146–147
Haenel and Tscharmann 1908, 67–68, 139–140
Lux 1908, 40
Hoeber 1913, 39–46
Shand 1934, 84
Heinz 1965
Anderson 1968, chaps. 4, 8
Buddensieg in Nürnberg 1980, 45–46
Windsor 1981, 63–65
Asche 1982, 85
Moeller in Internationaler Kongress 1986, 79, fig. 51
Buddensieg in Ribbe and Schäche 1987, 346
Speidel in Pfeifer 1990, 92–93
See chapters 4 and 8 (and figures 8.13–20) here

25. **Berlin, Wertheim Department Store,**
    Exhibition of Modern Dwelling
    Interiors (Moderne Wohnräume) **1905**
    [Moeller 20]
Spring 1905

25a. **Bedroom** (Schlafzimmer) and

25b. **Living room** (Wohnzimmer)

Stoeving 1905
Högg 1905, 661–666
Hoeber 1913, 39f.
Moeller in Nürnberg 1980, 266–267
Schönberger in Buddensieg 1987, 95

26. Hagen
Design of a **Small Milk Stand**
    (Milchhäuschen) [Moeller 26]
Fall 1905

Hesse-Frielinghaus 1966, 6
Kadatz 1977, 39

27. Düsseldorf, Kunstgewerbeschule,
    Burgplatz 1
Wall decoration for the stairwell [Moeller 28]
1905

28. **Hagen, Delstern**

28a. **Crematorium** [Moeller 22.1]

28b. Design for the associated **columbarium,
    cemetery plan, and mortuary**
    (Kolumbarium, Friedhofsanlage und
    Leichenhalle) [Moeller 22.2–4]
1905–1908; exterior marble replaced with
    stucco, 1911–1912

Köln 1906
Scheffler 1907b, 274–275
Osthaus 1908
Creutz [and Behrens] 1908
Jaumann 1909
Schäfer 1909, 267–269
Klopfer 1909
Behne 1911
Le Corbusier 1912
Hoeber 1913, 62–67
Deutscher Werkbund 1914b, 63
Klopfer 1919, 36, fig. 5
Platz 1927, 27, 68, figs. 268–269
Müller-Wulckow 1928b, 8, 103f., 107
Scheffler 1948, 38
Weber 1961, 23
Hesse-Frielinghaus 1966, 7–10, 18
Hamann and Hermand 1967, 139, 407
Anderson 1968, chap. 2
Erben in Hesse-Frielinghaus et al. 1971, 52
Stressig in Hesse-Frielinghaus et al. 1971, 357–360
Tummers 1972, 52–53
Windsor 1981, 65–68
Buddensieg in Ribbe and Schäche 1987, 347
Pehnt 1989, 72–75
Pfeifer 1990, cat. 111–112, 159
Neumeyer 1991, 51–53
Sembach et al. 1992, 15, 72–73
Busch 1993, 21
See chapter 2 (and figures 2.10–12, 2.15) here

29. **Dresden, III. deutsche Kunstgewerbe-
    Ausstellung** (Third German Arts and
    Crafts Exhibition), Summer 1906
**Marble hall, music salon, ceramic atrium, and
    reception room** (Raumgruppe:
    Marmordiele, Musiksaal, keramischer
    Hof, und Empfangszimmer) [Moeller
    23]
1905–1906

General literature
Dresden, *Die Raumkunst* 1906
Schur 1906, 68–72
Schumacher 1907, 205–228
Niemeyer 1907
Hoeber 1913, 46–52
Windsor 1981, 68–70

29a. **Marble hall** [Moeller 23.1]

Lehnert 1909, 610
Kadatz 1977, fig. 37

29b. **Music salon** [Moeller 23.2]

Scheffler 1907, opp. 120
Lehnert 1907, 12
Klapheck 1928, 17–19
Hamann and Hermand 1967, 407–409
Neumeyer 1984, 58

29c. **Atrium** (Ceramic Court) [Moeller 23.3]

Kadatz 1977, fig. 35
Koch in Speer 1978, 146
See chapter 5 (and figure 5.10) here

29d. **Reception room** [Moeller 23.4]

Kadatz 1977, fig. 36
Moeller in Nürnberg 1980, 266–267
Müller, in *Westdeutsche Impuls* (Cologne, 1984), 267

30. **Dresden, III. deutsche Kunstgewerbe-
    Ausstellung** (Third German Arts and
    Crafts Exhibition), Summer 1906
**Exhibition Pavilion of the Delmenhorster
    Linoleumfabrik Anker-Marke** [Moeller
    24]
1905–1906

Schur 1906, 68
Niemeyer 1907, 152ff.
Hoeber 1913, 52–54
Platz 1927, 27, fig. 265
Herrmann [1933] 1977, 2:81
Hamann and Hermand 1967, 409
Anderson 1968, chap. 2
Kadatz 1977, 40, fig. 34
Asche 1988, 114–145
Busch 1993, 21
Jefferies 1995, 244–255
See chapter 2 (and figure 2.9) here

31. **Hagen,** Elberfelderstrasse 35
Josef Klein, later Becker, **Wallpaper Shop**
    (Tapetenfirma) [Moeller 25]
1905–1907

Osthaus 1913, 66, pl. 94r
Hoeber 1913, 66–70
Hesse-Frielinghaus 1966, 6
Windsor 1981, 70

No. 31.

32. **Berlin, Nationalgalerie, Deutsche
    Jahrhundertausstellung 1906**
    (Exhibition of German Art 1775–1875)
Design (Raumgestaltung) **of the exhibition
    space** [Moeller 27]
1905–1906

*Ausstellung deutscher Kunst aus der Zeit von
    1775–1875* [off. cat.], 2d ed. (Munich:
    Bruckmann, 1906)

Scheffler 1906, 95
Hoeber 1913, 40f.
Leppien in Hamburg, Kunsthalle 1987, 138–144

33. **Essen, interior design firm Isidor Scherbel
    & Co.,** Limbecker Strasse 104
Facade renovation (Fassadenumbau des
    Wohnungseinrichtungsgeschäftes I.
    Scherbel & Comp.) [Moeller 29]
1905–1906

Hoeber 1913, 41–42, 69
Kordt 1963, 119
Buddensieg in Ribbe and Schäche 1987, 359

34. Hagen, Wehringhausen, Lange Strasse
Two designs (basilical and octagonal central
    plan) for a **Protestant church** (Paulus-
    Kirche) [Moeller 30]

34a. **Basilical design; "first variant"** [Moeller
    30.1]
March–August 1906

D. Koch 1907
Lux 1908c
Kadatz 1977, fig. 32

34b. **Central plan (octagonal) design; "second
    variant"** [Moeller 30.2]
October 1906–February 1907

Scheffler 1907b, 275
Osthaus 1907, 121–123
Lux 1908, 46
Lux 1908c
Hoeber 1913, 59–63
Hesse-Frielinghaus 1966, 11–12
Fahrner 1970, 27
Erben in Hesse-Frielinghaus et al. 1971, 51–52
Kadatz 1977, fig. 33
Windsor 1981, 71–72
Pfeifer 1990, cat. 113, 159

35. Düsseldorf, Königsallee
Competition design for the **Tietz Department
    Store** (Warenhaus Tietz) [Moeller 31]
Fall 1906

No. 38. View across the theater, with performers of the Düsseldorf Schauspielhaus and spectators (Grossherzog and Grossherzogin of Baden and members of the court).

No. 39. View in living room.

39. **Hagen, Eppenhausen, Hohenhagen,** Hassleyer Strasse
Schroeder house (see no. 36 above)
1907–1909

Schäfer 1909, 269–270
Anon. 1911 (*Architektur des XX. Jahrhunderts*)
Hoeber 1913, 88–91
Platz 1927, 28, figs. 259, 266
Müller-Wulckow 1928, 13, 119
Weber 1961, 23
Hesse-Frielinghaus 1966, 15–16
Anderson 1968, chap. 8
Stressig in Hesse-Frielinghaus et al. 1971, 413–417
Windsor 1981, 108–109
Windsor 1981b, 170–172
Westdeutsche Impuls (Hagen, 1984), suppl. vol., 42
Pfeifer 1990, 159, cat. 114
See chapter 8 (and figures 8.21, 8.24) here

40. **Hagen, Eppenhausen, Hohenhagen,** Hassleyer Strasse
Cuno house (see no. 36 above)
1907–1911

40a. **Unbuilt project**

Anon. 1911 (*Architektur des XX. Jahrhunderts*), 40
Windsor 1981, 107

40b. **Built project**

Schäfer 1909, 268–270
Osthaus 1912
Hoeber 1913, 91–93
Platz 1927, 28, figs. 266–267
Müller-Wulckow 1928, 13, 119
Weber 1961, 23
Kaiserslautern 1966, cat. 142b, fig. 74b
Hesse-Frielinghaus 1966, 13
Anderson 1968, chap. 8
Stressig in Hesse-Frielinghaus et al. 1971, 413–419
Kadatz 1977, fig. 31
Windsor 1981, 109–113
Windsor 1981b, 170–172
Westdeutsche Impuls (Hagen, 1984), suppl. vol., 42
Neumeyer in Buddensieg 1987, 56
Pfeifer 1990, 159, cat. 115
Sembach et al. 1992, 16, 139
Jefferies 1995, 272
See chapter 8 (and figures 8.21–24) here

41. Düsseldorf, Deutsch-Nationalen
    Kunstausstellung (German-National
    Art Exhibition) **1907**
**Room with exhibition of works of the
    Kunstgewerbeschule, Düsseldorf**
    (Sammlungsraum) [Moeller 34]
early 1907

Hoeber 1913, 73f.
Moeller in Nürnberg 1980, 266.

42. **Neuss am Rhein,** Sternstrasse 62
Catholic Workers' Hostel (Katholisches
    Gesellenhaus) [Moeller 35]
1907–1910

Scheffler 1907b, 274
Osthaus 1907, 116–117
Lux 1908, 46, and 1908c
Neuss 1910, 11–23
D. 1911, 7, 9
Hoeber 1913, 94–105
Neuss 1952
Siepe 1961, 9–14
Hesse-Frielinghaus 1966, 18
Kadatz 1977, figs. 38–39
Windsor 1981, 116–117
Buddensieg in Ribbe and Schäche 1987, 347
See chapter 8 (and figure 8.10) here

43. **Berlin, Allgemeine Ausstellung von
    Erfindungen der Klein-Industrie**
    (General Exhibition of Inventions of
    Light Industry), Summer 1907
AEG-Pavilion [Moeller 36; Bu A9]
Spring-Summer 1907

Mitteilungen der Berliner-Elektrizitätswerke, 3
    (September 1907), 130f., 135

44. **Berlin, Internationale Automobil-
    Ausstellung** (International Automobile
    Exhibition)

**Exhibition stand of the Neue Automobil-
    Gesellschaft** (NAG) [Moeller 37; Bu
    A10]
Fall 1907

Mitteilungen der Berliner-Elektrizitätswerke, 4
    (February 1908), 19, 21

45. **Neubabelsberg bei Potsdam**
**Garden and remodeling of Behrens's rented
    house,** Haus Erdmannshof
1907–1908

Jaumann 1909
Breuer 1910
Behrens, "Moderne Garten," 1911
Scheffler 1911
Klein 1912
Buddensieg in Ribbe and Schäche 1987, 348

46. Bookholzberg bei Gruppenbühren in
    Oldenburg (Ganderkesee-
    Bookholzberg/Kreis Delmenhorst)
Design for a Bismarck Monument (Bismarck-
    Denkmal)
1907–1908

Creutz 1908, 41
K. Schaefer 1908
Hoeber 1913, 92–96
Aschenbeck 1990
Asche 1992, 287–319
Jefferies 1995, 257

47. **Fürstenwalde an der Spree, Power Station**
    (Kraftwerk Fürstenwalde)
**Intervention in the architectural detail and
    ornament of the power station**
1908

R. Rose, *Deutsche Bauhütte,* 14, no. 19 (1910),
    162–163
G. Siegel, *AEG-Zeitung,* 12 (March 1910), 1ff.
Wilhelm in Buddensieg et al. 1979, 141–143; Engl.
    ed. 138–141
Buddensieg in Ribbe and Schäche 1987, 349

48. **Berlin** NW 40, AEG-Verwaltungsgebäude
    (AEG Administration Building),
    Friedrich-Karl-Ufer 2–4; Alfred Messel,
    architect
Exhibition of AEG products [Bu P10–12];
    possibly by Behrens
1908

Mitteilungen der Berliner-Elektrizitätswerke, 4 (July
    1908), 105–110

49. **Berlin-Charlottenburg,** Ausstellungs-
    gelände am Zoo (Exhibition Grounds at
    Zoo), **Deutsche Schiffbauausstellung**
    (German Shipbuilding Exhibition),
    June-September 1908
AEG-Pavilion and Garden, Auguste-Viktoria-
    Platz [Bu A1–8]
1908

Berlin, AEG, *Deutsche Schiffbauausstellung 1908*
    (Berlin, 1908)
Mitteilungen der Berliner-Elektrizitätswerke, 4 (August
    1908), 114–119

No. 49. Night view of garden
trellis and lighting.

Jaumann 1909
Behne 1911
Hoeber 1913, 108
Weber 1961, 23
Hamann and Hermand 1967, 409
Anderson 1968, chap. 5
Anderson 1969, 76ff.
Berlin, Architekten- und Ingenieur-Verein, 9 (1971),
    19, 30
Anderson 1977, 57–58
Windsor 1981, 83–85
Anderson 1991, 68–71
Sembach et al. 1992, 25
Negri 1993, [2]
Anderson 1995, 19
Baird 1995, 40ff.
See chapter 5 (and figures 5.4, 5.6) here

50. **Berlin-Wedding, AEG factories on the
    Humboldthain,** Voltastrasse, Old
    Factory for Railway Equipment (Alte
    Fabrik für Bahnmaterialen); Johann
    Kraaz, architect, 1905ff. [Bu A43–44]
Changes to design of unexecuted parts (tower
    and west wing on the courtyard side)
    [Bu A44a–48/A45–50]
May 1908–April 1909 (construction of parts
    altered by Behrens)

Buddensieg 1975, 277–279
Posener 1979, 388, 392
Windsor 1981, 85–86
Negri 1993, [3]
See chapter 7 (and figure 7.5) here

51. **Berlin-Moabit, AEG Turbine Factory
    complex**
Powerhouse (Kraftzentrale) [Bu A13–16]
June 1908–April 1909

Lasche 1909 (technical information and images, but
    some of the latter give architectural informa-
    tion)
Hoeber 1913, 116
Negri 1993, [2]

52. Berlin-Moabit, AEG Turbine Factory complex, Huttenstrasse, corner of Berlichingenstrasse

AEG Turbine Factory, Assembly Hall
(Turbinenfabrik, Montagehalle); Karl Bernhard, engineer [Bu A17–32]
Fall 1908–October 1909

Dohrn 1909, 369
Behrens, "Neuzeitliche Industriebauten," 1910
Behrens, "Kunst und Technik," 1910
K. Bernhard 1910
Breuer 1910
Dohrn 1910
Kalkschmidt 1910, 28–29
Lasche 1910
Mannheimer 1910
Osthaus 1910 and 1910b
Stoffers 1910, 292
Lasche 1911, 1198–1201
K. Bernhard 1911
Mannheimer 1911b
Worringer 1911, 500
K. Bernhard 1912, 1230–1231
Gropius 1912
Le Corbusier 1912, 43–44
Hoeber 1913, 108–116
Mannheimer 1913, 36, 40
Scheffler 1913, 158–159
Breuer 1913b, 205
de Fries 1916
Franz 1917
Mendelsohn [1919] 1930, 16
Behne 1920, 274–276
de Fries 1920–1921, 127–128
Franz 1923, 55–61
Müller-Wulckow 1925, 24
Behne [1926] 1964, 27–32; Engl. ed. 105–109, 116, 124
Platz 1927, 28–29, 99–100, fig. 262
Behrens, "Zur Ästhetik des Fabrikbaus," 1929, 129–130
Hirschberg 1929, 38–40
Vogelgesang 1930, 716–717
Herrmann [1933] 1977, 79–84
Posener 1934, 8–9
Shand 1934, 39–42
P. Meyer 1940
Sedlmayr [1948] 1958, 54–56
Bauch [1959] in Hermand 1971, 269–270, pl. 41
Weber 1961, 23–25
Hamann and Hermand 1967, 409, 529–531
Hennig-Schefold 1967, 7–9
Anderson 1968, chap. 7
Anderson 1969, 72f.
Kinser 1969, 28, 91
Berlin, Architekten- und Ingenieur-Verein, 9 (1971), 50–52, 98
Buddensieg 1975, 280–282
Drebusch 1976, 161–164
Kadatz 1977, fig. 41
Romein 1978, 571–572
Posener 1979, 396, 494, 498, 510, 564–571, 596–600
Peschken in Burckhardt 1980, 35–48
Berlin, Technische Universität 1981, 1:423–427, 2:122–123
Buddensieg in Buddensieg and Rogge 1981, 63–64
Windsor 1981, 87–94
Henn 1983, 73ff.
Posener in *Westdeutsche Impuls* (Cologne, 1984), 16
Asche 1986, 364–365
Buddensieg in Ribbe and Schäche 1987, 351
Buddensieg 1987, 34, 146–155
Neumeyer in Buddensieg 1987, 35–40
Posener in Kleihues 1987, cat. V43, 149–150, 307
Hüter 1988, 241–245
Plischke 1989, 53
Dal Co 1990, 231, 235–237
Gebhardt in Pfeifer 1990, 100–101
Heuser in Pfeifer 1990
Pfeifer 1990, cat. 116–117, p. 159
Anderson 1991, 70–71
Anderson 1991b, 29–31
Buddensieg 1992, 72ff.
Sembach et al. 1992, 16–17, 83
Anderson 1993, 343–347
Negri 1993, [2]
Jefferies 1995, 126–131, 242–243
Schwartz 1996, 3–4, 56–58, 181–183, 187–188, 197, 204–205
See chapter 7 (and frontispiece and figures 7.2, 7.8–15) here

53. Berlin-Wedding, AEG factories on the Humboldthain, Brunnenstrasse 107a, Administration Building and Large Machine Factory
New design for the old AEG roof garden [Bu A105–106/A106–107]
1908–1909

Buddensieg 1975, 279, 299

54. Berlin, A. Wertheim Department Store, Exhibition of Modern Dwelling Interiors
Living room
Spring 1909

Hoeber 1913, 129

55. Düsseldorf, Ausstellung für christliche Kunst (Exhibition of Christian Art), Summer 1909
Behrens Room (Sonderraum Behrens; room with Behrens's ornament and exhibition)
Spring 1909

Düsseldorf, Ausstellung für christliche Kunst, *Katalog* (Düsseldorf, 1909)
Schmid 1909, 386, 415
Hesse-Frielinghaus 1966, 15
Hesse-Frielinghaus et al. 1971, 201
Kocks in *Westdeutsche Impuls* (Cologne, 1984), 293
Westdeutsche Impuls (Düsseldorf, 1984), 27–28

56. Hagen, Parkhaus-Saal, Hagener Sommer-Schauspiele
Relief stage (Reliefbühne) **for Behrens's production of O. E. Hartleben's** *Diogenes,* 22 June 1909
June 1909

Anderson 1968, chap. 3
Erben in Hesse-Frielinghaus et al. 1971, 60ff.
Anderson 1990, 127–130
See chapter 3 (and figure 3.15) here

57. Berlin, Reichstag; Paul Wallot, architect
Facade inscription: "Dem deutschen Volke"
1909 (designed); 1917 (installed)

P[aulsen] 1930, 987
Raack 1978
Windsor 1981, 43
Buddensieg in Ribbe and Schäche 1987, 360
Burke 1992, 29

58. Berlin-Moabit, AEG Turbine Factory, Old Assembly Hall (Turbinenfabrik, Alte Montagehalle), existing factory; architect unknown
North and east facades simplified and given large glass areas; possibly by Behrens
ca. 1909–1910

Lasche (1911) commends the high level of natural light in Behrens's Turbine Factory (no. 52 above) and cites it as the model for the architectural reworking of the north and east facades of the Old Assembly Hall. No architect is credited, but Lasche also illustrates Behrens's new factory without credit; conceivably this renovation was by Behrens.

Lasche 1911, 1199–1200, fig. 7 (north facade)

59. Berlin-Wedding, AEG factories on the Humboldthain
High Voltage Factory (AEG Hochspannungsfabrik; or **Factory for Transformers, Resistors, and High Voltage Equipment** [Fabrik für Transformatoren, Widerstände und Hochspannungsmaterial]) [Bu A52–71/A54–73]
1909–1910

Osthaus 1910b
Breuer 1910
Mannheimer 1911
K. Bernhard 1912, 1188–1189
Kalkschmidt 1913
Mannheimer 1913
Hoeber 1913, 136–142
Hoeber 1913b, 263–265

Scheffler 1913, 159
Behrens, "Werbende künstlerische Werte," 1920,
    271ff.
Hegemann 1925, 2, 6, 15
Müller-Wulckow 1925, 27–28
Platz 1927, 29–30, figs. 260–261, 264t, 514
Cremers 1928, 8–9
Behrens, "Zur Ästhetik des Fabrikbaus," 1929, 126,
    128
Grimme 1930, 7
Hamann and Hermand 1967, 529
Le Corbusier 1967, 213
Anderson 1968, chap. 7
Berlin, Architekten- und Ingenieur-Verein, 9 (1971),
    52–54, 97
Buddensieg 1975, 279–287
Posener 1979, 369, 371
Anderson 1981
Berlin, Technische Universität 1981, 2:153–157
Windsor 1981, 94–98
Hüter 1988, 246–248
Sembach et al. 1992, 84
See chapter 7 (and figures 7.3, 7.20–25) here

60. Berlin-Wedding, AEG factories on the
    Humboldthain, Gustav-Meyer-Allee
Designs for a monumental **AEG gate build-
    ing/Gate 4** (Tor 4) [Bu A72–76/
    A74–78]: three unbuilt designs; for a
    small executed gate, see no. 95 below
1909–1911

Mannheimer 1911
Hoeber 1913, 144, 147
Hoeber 1913b, 263
Anderson 1968, chap. 7
Buddensieg 1975, 295, 298
Anderson 1981, 67
See chapter 7 (and figure 7.20) here

61. **Potsdam**
**Secondary building (stables, garage, and
    tennis courts) for Frau Dr. Mertens**
    (Stall und Autogarage und Anlage eines
    Tennisplatzes); see also no. 93 below
Winter 1909–1910

Anon. 1911 (*Dekorative Kunst*)
Hoeber 1913, 115ff.

62. **Treptow bei Berlin, II. Ton-, Zement-
    und Kalkindustrieausstellung,** Summer
    1910
Three exhibition complexes listed below
1909–1910

General literature
Behrens, "Peter Behrens' Ausstellungsbauten," 1910
Schultze 1910, 348
Schur 1910, 747
Hoeber 1913, 123–128
Hegemann 1925, 2, 6, 15
Berlin, Architekten- und Ingenieur-Verein, 9 (1971),
    19, 30
Windsor 1981, 137–138

62a. **Courtyard of the Alliance of German
    Cement Products Manufacturers**

Meyer-Schönbrunn 1913
Le Corbusier 1967, fig. 7, 212f.
Buddensieg et al. 1979, 74; Engl. ed. 85

62b. **Courtyard of the Alliance of German
    Limestone Producers**

Pehnt 1989, 72–75

62c. **House of the Alliance of Calcareous
    Sandstone Producers**

63. **Brussels, Belgium, International
    Exposition,** opened April 1910
Behrens's several works listed below
1909–1910

General literature
*Weltausstellung Brüssel 1910. Deutsches Reich, Amtl.
    Katalog,* 1910
Mannheimer 1910b
Stoffers 1910, 80–83, 99, 105–109, 116, 119,
    130–131, 136–139, 219–220, 285–287,
    292, 312–319, 392–[414], pls. after pp. 418,
    428
Hoeber 1913, 118–123
Cremers 1928, 8

No. 62a. Perspective.

Windsor 1981, 135–137
Gebhardt in Pfeifer 1990, 126–132
See chapter 7 here

63a. Hall of the German Association of Engineers (Halle des Deutschen Ingenieurvereins)

Wertheimer in Stoffers 1910, 80
Breuer in Stoffers 1910, 105–106
Stoffers 1910, 285, 287, 292

63b. German Power Machinery Exhibition Hall (Deutsche Kraftmaschinenhalle)

Wertheimer in Stoffers 1910, 81–82
Breuer in Stoffers 1910, 105–106
Fritsche in Stoffers 1910, 312–319, 392–[414]
Hoeber 1913b, 264
Platz 1927, 121, fig. 181
Schmuckler 1927
Posener 1979, 498

63c. German Railway Exhibition Hall (Deutsche Eisenbahnhalle)

Wertheimer in Stoffers 1910, 82–83, 418, 428
Breuer in Stoffers 1910, 105–106
See figures 7.34–35 here

63d. Exhibition Space of the Delmenhorster Linoleumfabrik Anker-Marke

Breuer in Stoffers 1910, 99, 108–109, 139
Jefferies 1995, 244ff.

63e. Press Room (Presseraum)

Breuer in Stoffers 1910, 119, 130

63f. Library/Exhibition of the Association of German Publishers of Illustrated Magazines (Bibliotheksraum der Vereinigten deutschen Verleger illustrierter Zeitungen)

Breuer in Stoffers 1910, 131

64. Berlin, Keller & Reiner (Potsdamer Strasse 118b), Exhibition of Modern Interiors (Ausstellung moderner Wohnräume)
Reception room (Empfangszimmer)
Spring 1910

Mitteilungen der Berliner-Elektrizitätswerke, 6, no. 3 (March 1910), 38–43
Breuer 1910, 116, 121, 130–133
t. 1910, 448–451, 470–473 and plates
Le Corbusier 1912, 42
Hoeber 1913, 129–131
Platz 1933, 25, 115, fig. 207
Buddensieg et al. 1979, P36

65. Hennigsdorf bei Berlin
AEG Porcelain, Oilcloth and Lacquer factories (Porzellan-, Öltuch- und Lackfabrik) [Bu A138–140/A139–142]

General literature
Hoeber 1913, 147, 150–153
Anon. 1915 (*Der Industriebau*), 396–399
Hegemann 1925, 9–10, 15
Hirschberg 1929, 42–43
Posener 1979, 510
Negri 1993, [5]

65a. Porcelain Factory (Porzellanfabrik)
1910–Summer 1911; enlarged 1912

Mies van der Rohe 1924, 9

No. 65a. Interior view.

65b. Oilcloth Factory (Öltuchfabrik)
1911; completed September

65c. Lacquer Factory (Lackfabrik)
1911; completed September

66. Berlin-Wedding, AEG factories on the Humboldthain, Voltastrasse
AEG Small Motors Factory (Kleinmotoren-fabrik) [Bu A81–104/A83–105]
1910–1913

Mannheimer 1911
Mannheimer 1913
Hoeber 1913, 140–146
Hoeber 1913b, 263–264
Scheffler 1913, 160 and pl.
de Fries 1920–1921, 127
Behne [1922] 1961, 1164, 1167
Franz 1923, 6–11

Behne [1926] 1996, 108, 159
Platz 1927, 30
Cremers 1928, 9–10
Behrens, "Zur Ästhetik des Fabrikbaus," 1929, 128–129 (misidentification)
Posener 1934, 8–10
Weber 1961, 23
Hamann and Hermand 1967, 529
Anderson 1968, chap. 7
Berlin, Architekten- und Ingenieur-Verein, 9 (1971), 54–55, 97
Pehnt 1973, 65–67
Buddensieg 1975, 287–290
Drebusch 1976, 163–164
Posener 1979, 369–381
Anderson 1981
Berlin, Technische Universität 1981, 2:153–156
Windsor 1981, 94–99
Buddensieg 1987, 150–157
Neumeyer in Buddensieg 1987, 37–39
Posener in Kleihues 1987, cat. V42, 148–150, 307
Hüter 1988, 75, 246–249
Anderson 1991, 70–71
Buddensieg 1992, 73ff.
Jefferies 1995, 131–134
See chapter 7 (and figures 7.3, 7.26–28) here

67. Hagen, Westfälische Gewerbeausstellung (Westphalian Craft Exhibition)
Living room (Wohnzimmer)
1910

Rogge in Buddensieg et al. 1979, 117; Engl. ed. 501

68. Neuss am Rhein, Sternstrasse, Drususstrasse, and Stadtgraben
Idea sketch for **rental apartment house quarter** (Etagenhäuserviertel mittlerer Mietswohnungen)
1910

Hoeber 1913, 82–87
Hoeber 1917, 112
Siepe 1961, 12–18

69. Ahlsdorf bei Herzberg/Elster, Schlosspark
(former estate of Frau von Siemens)
Semicircular stone bench
1910

Hoeber 1913, 245
Kadatz 1977, 135

70. Cologne-Lindenthal
Interiors for Max Meirowsky: entrance
  vestibule, living hall (Wohndiele), bath,
  and dressing room
1910

Creutz 1911
Hoeber 1913, 130–134
F. Schumacher 1949, 222
Hamann and Hermand 1967, 409
Hagspiel in *Westdeutsche Impuls* (Cologne, 1984),
  47–48

No. 70. Living hall.

71. Berlin
AEG salesrooms (AEG-Verkaufsstelle) [Bu
  P2–9]

General literature
Mannheimer 1911
Hoeber 1913, 155–158, 162–166
Kadatz 1977, fig. 40
Schwartz 1996, 132–133

71a. **AEG Westend Salesroom,** Potsdamer
  Strasse 117 [Bu P2–3]
1910

71b. **AEG Salesroom,** Königgrätzer Strasse 4
  [Bu P4–9]
end 1910

Mitteilungen der Berliner-Elektrizitätswerke, 6, no. 12
  (December 1910), 178f.
Mitteilungen der Berliner-Elektrizitätswerke, 7, no. 3
  (March 1911), 34–40

72. Hennigsdorf bei Berlin, Rathenaustrasse
  14/15, opposite AEG factory land
AEG Workers' Housing (Zinshäuser für AEG
  Arbeiter) [Bu A183–189/A184–190]
1910–1911

Behrens, "Die Gartenstadtbewegung," *Berliner
  Tageblatt,* 1908
Hoeber 1913, 150–155, 225
Hoeber 1917, 114
Platz 1927, 158, fig. 273
Shand 1934, 85–86
Kadatz 1977, figs. 52, 55
Neumeyer 1978, 208–227, figs. 89–96
Neumeyer in Siepmann 1978, 238ff.
Posener 1979, 389, 397
Windsor 1981, 100–101
Posener in Kleihues 1987, 140–141
Hüter 1988, 251–253
Pommer and Otto 1991, 74, 89–90, 242 n. 46
Sembach et al. 1992, 153
See chapter 8 (and figure 8.11) here

73. Cologne-Deutz

Competition design in collaboration with
    Dortmunder Union: **Unanchored steel**
    suspension bridge "Kunst und
    Technik"

July 1910; jury of first stage, July 1911;
    though his was similar to the eventual
    winning design, Behrens was not invited
    to the 1912 second stage of the
    competition

Zentralblatt der Bauverwaltung, 30 (6 August 1910),
    420
Landsberg 1911
Zentralblatt der Bauverwaltung, 31 (26 July 1911),
    376
K. Bernhard 1912b
Hellwag 1913, 156
Hoeber 1913, 158–162, 166–168
K. Bernhard 1914, 1300
Kadatz 1977, figs. 59–60
Posener 1979, 498–499
Windsor 1981, 132
Hagspiel in *Westdeutsche Impuls* (Cologne, 1984), 45,
    48
Schäche 1991, 58

74. **Düsseldorf,** Mannesmannufer

Mannesmann Main Office Building
    (Mannesmann-Röhrenwerke
    Hauptverwaltung)

1910–1912; addition at rear by Hans Väth,
    1938, in consultation with Behrens (see
    no. 217 below)

Behrendt 1913
Hoeber 1913, 172–174, 177–182
Kalkschmidt 1913, 576
Franz 1917, 152–158
Hegemann 1925, 2, 6, 15
Behne [1926] 1996, 122
Platz 1927, 30–31, 142, figs. 270–272, 515
Cremers 1928, 12–13
Klapheck 1928, 15–24
Posener 1934, 12
Shand 1934, 85
Wolff 1939, 454

Hamann and Hermand 1967, 530
Anderson 1968, chap. 8
Kinser 1969, 28, 91
Anderson 1977, 67–68
Kadatz 1977, fig. 65
Posener 1979, 379–381
Windsor 1981, 127–129
Schäche in Bushart et al. 1985, 76–77
Hüter 1988, 241
Gebhardt in Pfeifer 1990, 101–102
Schäche 1991, 58
Schlüter 1991, 120–166
Busch 1993, 22, 47–51, 131, color pls. IV–VI
Jefferies 1995, 135–137, 216
See chapter 8 (and figures 8.34–40) here

75. **Hagen, Eppenhausen, Hohenhagen**

Goedecke house (see no. 36 above)

1910–1912

Hoeber 1913, 92, 95
Kaiserslautern 1966, cat. 145
Hesse-Frielinghaus 1966, 18
Anderson 1968, chap. 8
Stressig in Hesse-Frielinghaus et al. 1971, 419–421
Windsor 1981, 113–114
Windsor 1981b, 171–172
See chapter 8 (and figures 8.25–28) here

76. Berlin

Designs for the **AEG Rapid Transit Line**
    (Schnellbahn) **Gesundbrunnen-**
    Neukölln, elevated station at
    Gesundbrunnen? [Bu A174–176/
    A175–177]; neither the structural
    detailing nor the drawing of the rail
    viaduct of A176/A177 is in the manner
    of Behrens

1910–1912

Wittig 1922, 9
Bohle in Buddensieg et al. 1979, 199–204; Engl. ed.,
    198–203
Bohle-Heintzenberg 1980, 184f.
Bohle-Heintzenberg in Buddensieg and Rogge 1981,
    213
Windsor 1981, 131–132

77. Frankfurt-Osthafen

Frankfurter Gasgesellschaft (later Main-Gaswerke) **gasworks buildings:** director's house and gatehouse, office, bath and canteen building, storehouse and workshop, metering building, apparatus building, the towers, ammonia plant, machine house (Wohnhaus des Betriebsleiters und Fabrikportal, Bureaugebäude, Arbeiterwohlfahrtshaus, Werkstättenbau, Uhren- und Reglergebäude, Apparatenhaus, Wasserturm, Teer- und Ammoniahochbehälter, Ammoniakfabrik, Maschinenhaus)
1910–1912

Behne 1913
Hoeber 1913, 162–167, 169–175
Kalkschmidt 1913, 574–576
de Fries 1916
Müller-Wulckow 1917, 34
Behne [1926] 1996, 109
Platz 1927, 30, 115, 158, pl. VII
Cremers 1928, 11–12
Hamann and Hermand 1967, 529, 532
Anderson 1968, chap. 8
Pehnt 1973, 66–67
Drebusch 1976, 166–169
Kadatz 1977, fig. 61
Posener 1979, 389, 397, 439
Windsor 1981, 133–135
Buddensieg 1982, 38–40
Mohr and Müller 1984, 264–265
Buddensieg in Pfeifer 1990
Pfeifer 1990, 161, cat. 143
Jefferies 1995, 138
See chapter 8 (and figures 8.1–7) here

78. Berlin-Wedding, AEG factories on the Humboldthain, Voltastrasse, **Old Factory for Railway Equipment** (Alte Fabrik für Bahnmaterial); Johann Kraaz, architect, 1905ff. [Bu A49–51/A51–53]
Alterations to facade
Spring 1911

79. The Hague, Netherlands

Design for the **Kröller-Müller villa;** attribution to Behrens and Mies van der Rohe (Posener 1979, 161, 379)

February 1911: first contact; January 1912: decision to build a full-scale model of wood and canvas; resulted in Mme Kröller's decision against Behrens and the engagement of his assistant Ludwig Mies van der Rohe

Hoeber 1913, 200–205
Posener 1934, 11
F. Schumacher 1949, 222
Stressig in Hesse-Frielinghaus et al. 1971, 421–422
Posener 1979, 161, 170, 379
Windsor 1981, 117
Tegethoff in Ribbe and Schäche 1987, 473
Polano 1993
See chapter 8, note 45 here

No. 79. Perspective.

80. Berlin-Wedding, AEG factories on the Humboldthain, Brunnenstrasse 107a, Administration Building and Large Machine Hall

New roof garden (Neugestaltung des AEG Dachgartens)[Bu A105–110/A106–111]
1911

Rogge 1983, figs. 163–167

81. Berlin
Interiors for Dr. Ruge
1911

Hoeber 1913, 133–137

82. Bocholt in Westfalen
Design for a **water tower**
Summer 1911

Hoeber 1913, 167–169, 176

83. Berlin-Oberschöneweide, An der·
      Wuhlheide, on the banks of the Spree
Boathouse for the Elektra Rowing Club
      (for the employees of the AEG and
      BEW) [Bu A177–181/A178–182]
1911–1912

Hoeber 1913, 152–162
Müller-Wulckow 1928b, 7, 38
Kadatz 1977, figs. 56–58
Neumeyer 1978, 208–215, 227–236

No. 83. Exterior from street.

84. Berlin-Wedding, AEG factories on the
      Humboldthain, Voltastrasse 23–28
New Factory for Railway Equipment (Neue
      Fabrik für Bahnmaterial) [Bu A111–
      120/A112–121]
1911–1912

Hoeber 1913, 144–149
Hirschberg 1929, 41
Buddensieg 1975, 290–292
See figures 7.3, 7.29–30 here

85. Berlin-Wedding, AEG factories on the
      Humboldthain, Hussitenstrasse and
      Voltastrasse
AEG Assembly Hall for Large Machines
      (Montagehalle für Grossmaschinen) [Bu
      A121–136/A122–137]
1911–1912; four southeastern bays completed
      in summer 1928, under direction of
      Ernst Ziesel, architect

Hoeber 1913b, 264
Kalkschmidt 1913, 576
Scheffler 1913, 156ff. and plates
Anon. 1915 (*Der Industriebau*), 411–412
Franz 1917
Behne [1922] in *Bauwelt*, 52, nos. 41/42 (18
      October 1961), 1164f.
Müller-Wulckow 1925, 25
Behne [1926] 1996, 106, 158
Platz 1927, 30, 99–100, figs. 263, 264t
Schmuckler 1927
Behrens, "Zur Ästhetik des Fabrikbaus," 1929, 127,
      130
Hirschberg 1929, 41
Grimme 1930, 7
Heideck 1930, 518, 526
Heideck 1930b, 138–139
Posener 1934, 18
Banham 1960, 82f.
Weber 1961, 23
Anderson 1968, chap. 7
Berlin, Architekten- und Ingenieur-Verein, 9 (1971),
      55, 97–98
Buddensieg 1975, 290ff.
Drebusch 1976, 164

Posener 1979, 388–392, 397
Anderson 1981
Berlin, Technische Universität 1981, 2:153–156
Windsor 1981, 94–100
Posener in Kleihues 1987, cat. V39, 149, 307
Hüter 1988, 246–247
Buddensieg 1992, 73ff.
See chapter 7 (and figures 7.3, 7.29–32) here

86. Berlin-Zehlendorf (Dahlem), Peter-Lenné-
    Strasse 28–30
House of Dr. Theodor Wiegand, Director,
    Kgl. Altes Museum (now the seat of the
    Deutsches Archäologisches Institut)
1911–1912

Breuer 1913
Hoeber 1913, 191–199
Breuer 1914
Blätter für Architektur und Kunsthandwerk, 1 (1915),
    1–2, pls. 1–3
Stahl 1918–1919
de Fries 1924, viii, 62–70
Hegemann 1925, 2, 6, 15
Posener 1934, 11
Kaiserslautern 1966, cat. 146, fig. 74a
Hamann and Hermand 1967, 409
Anderson 1968, chap. 8
Jessen 1969, 518–524
Larsson in Speer 1978, 155
Neumeyer 1979, 242
Posener 1979, 161, 170, 379, 498
Peschken in Burckhardt 1980, 35–48
Anderson 1981, 54
Windsor 1981, 117–121
Posener in Kleihues 1987, cat. V32, 144–145
Buddensieg 1987, 19, 27
Hüter 1988, 74, 76
Borrmann 1989, 125, figs. 218–219
Anderson 1991, 71–72
Neumeyer 1991, 79–81, 90, 179
See chapter 8 (and figures 8.29–33) here

87. Berlin-Tempelhof, Colditz/Ecke
    Ordensmeisterstrasse
T-Z-Gitterwerks, office and factory
1911–1912

Hoeber 1913, 169f.
Kaiserslautern 1966, 29

88. Hagen, Delstern
Reconstruction of the **Crematorium** (see no.
    28 above; marble cladding had fallen off
    in the winter of 1910–1911)
Winter 1911–1912

Stressig in Hesse-Frielinghaus et al. 1971, 417

**89. Kelbra (near), Monument to Wilhelm I
    on an eminence called the Kyffhäuser**
    (Kyffhäuserdenkmal); Bruno Schmitz,
    architect, 1896
Design of the **burial place** (Grabstelle) **of the
    architect Bruno Schmitz** in the crypt of
    the monument
1911–1912

Buddensieg in Ribbe and Schäche 1987, 361

90. St. Petersburg, Russia, Isaacs Place
Imperial German Embassy (Kaiserliche
    Deutsche Botschaft)
1911–1913; with outbreak of war, interiors
    ravaged by the local populace, 4 August
    1914

Behrendt 1913
Hoeber 1913, 179–197
Kalkschmidt 1913, 576
Scheffler 1913b
K. Schaefer 1913
Paquet and Schäfer 1914
K. Schaefer 1914
Deutscher Werkbund 1914b, 75
de Fries 1916
Klopfer 1919, 36–37
Platz 1927, 28, 133, fig. 274
Cremers 1928, 11
Klapheck 1928, 17
Cortissoz 1930
Platz 1933, 25
Posener and Imbert 1934, 30
Wolff 1939, 453–454

Schüler 1940
H. G. E. in Sabais 1956, 331–332
Hamann and Hermand 1967, 408–409
Anderson 1968, chap. 8
Erben in Hesse-Frielinghaus et al. 1971, 79
Kadatz 1977, fig. 66
Koch in Speer 1978, 141–142
Neumeyer 1979, 247
Posener 1979, 369–381
Peschken in Burckhardt 1980, 35–48
Anderson 1981, 55
Windsor 1981, 121–124
Junghanns 1982, 30–31
Henn 1983, 73ff.
Buddensieg 1984
Buddensieg 1987, 16–17, 25
Tegethoff in Ribbe and Schäche 1987, 473
Hüter 1988, 75, 78, 246, 251
Speidel in Pfeifer 1990, 90–91
Anderson 1991, 70–71
Schäche 1991, 58
Sembach et al. 1992, 17, 74–75
Busch 1993, 52–53
Krawietz 1995, 75–81
See chapter 8 (and figures 8.44–46, 8.48–50) here

91. Berlin-Oberschöneweide, in the block
defined by Roedernstrasse 8–15,
Zeppelinstrasse 13–71, Fontanestrasse
8a–126, and An der Wuhlheide 4–12
and 14–22
Design for an **AEG housing estate** (Siedlung)
[Bu A190–195/A191–196]; **first,
urban-scale, unrealized project** (for
smaller realized project, see no. 113
below)
1911–1914

Kalkschmidt 1910, 29
Le Corbusier 1912, 44
Neumeyer 1978
Pommer and Otto 1991, 74, 114, fig. 200

No. 92. Street view.

No. 92. Interior of 1919–1920: view into main hall.

92. **Hannover,** Vahrenwalderstrasse
**Continental Kautschuk- und Guttapercha-
Kompanie (or Continental Gummi-
Werke), administration building**
1911–1914 (used as a warehouse for the
military during World War I; reconfigured
as an office building and completed,
1919–1920)

Hoeber 1913, 174–179, 183–187
Kalkschmidt 1913, 576
Cremers 1928, 13–14, pls. 42–45, 47, 79
Kadatz 1977, figs. 62–64
Windsor 1981, 129–131
Gebhardt in Pfeifer 1990, 102
Pfeifer 1990, 161, cat. 144
Schäche 1991, 58
Jefferies 1995, 135–139

93. Potsdam
Remodeling of the villa of Frau Dr. Mertens
Spring 1912

Hoeber 1913, 116ff.

94. Berlin, Berliner Gewerkschaftshaus, 2. Musterausstellung von Arbeitermöbeln (Second Model Exhibition of Workers' Furniture)
Furnishing of a two-room worker's dwelling with prototype furniture (Einrichtung einer Zweizimmer-Arbeiterwohnung)

94a. **Sitting/dining room with worker's kitchen** (Wohnzimmer mit Arbeiterküche)

94b. **Bedroom** (Arbeiterschlafzimmer)
Spring 1912; exhibited till November

Berlin, Kommission für vorbildliche Arbeiterwohnungen 1912
Bauwelt, 10, no. 19 (1912), Kunstbeilage, no. 9
Breuer 1912
Breuer 1912b
Fachblatt für Holzarbeiter 1912
Westheim 1914b, 465
Hoeber 1917, 118
Shand 1934, 85
Göldner 1955, 308
Stein 1956, 625–628
Günther in Siepmann 1978, 186–188
Henning in Thiekötter 1987, 304–314
Jefferies 1995, 224, 257

95. Berlin-Wedding, AEG factories on the Humboldthain, Gustav-Meyer-Allee
AEG goods entrance gate (Tor 4) [Bu A77–80/A79–82]
April-August 1912

Behrens, "Zur Ästhetik des Fabrikbaus," 1929, 128
Buddensieg 1975, 298
Anderson 1981, 67

96. Merseburg an der Saale
Design of **C. W. Julius Blancke-Werke AG, factories and housing quarter**
1912

Hoeber 1913, 203–206, 208–214
Windsor 1981, 141–142
Buddensieg in Ribbe and Schäche 1987, 361
See chapter 8 (and figure 8.12) here

97. Hennigsdorf bei Berlin (Rathenaupark; area of the AEG Hennigsdorf factories)
Boathouse for workers of AEG factories (Bootshaus für Arbeiter der AEG Fabriken Hennigsdorf) [Bu A182/A183]
1912

Negri 1993, [5]

98. Hellerau bei Dresden, Deutsche Werkstätten
Rooms of furniture for production by Deutsche Werkstätten
1912–1913

98a. **Dining room** (Speisezimmer) Nr. 15

98b. **Study** (Herrenzimmer) Nr. 27

98c. **Sitting room** (Salon) Nr. 47

Hellerau, Deutsche Werkstätten, [*Catalog*], 1913–1914, 46, 68, 90
Buddensieg in Ribbe and Schäche 1987, 361

99. Lübeck, a site between the Holstentor and the railroad station

Kaiser-Wilhelm-Volkshaus, preliminary design and competition designs for a cultural center

99a. **Preliminary design**
1912–1913

D. 1913, 94
Bong-Schmidt, *Lübeckische Blättern* (26 October 1913), 682f.
Scheffler 1914, 245
See figure 8.51 here

99b. **Four competition designs** ("Project 2" to "Project 5")
Spring/Summer 1913

Lübeckische Blättern (1913), 302f., 644–647, 665–667, 750f.; Mahn, 667–669, 683f.; Bong-Schmidt, 682f.; Piper, 699–702; Link, 729–731; Grube, 731–733; 728f.
Hellwag 1913
Lübeckische Blättern (1914), Moeller van den Bruck, 120–123; Behn, 135–137; Bong-Schmidt, 137f; Bendixen, 138f.; Mahn, 156–159
Scheffler 1914, 245f.
Anderson 1968, chap. 8
Kadatz 1977, fig. 67
Neumeyer 1979, 247
Windsor 1981, 141
See chapter 8 here

100. **Berlin, A. Wertheim Department Store, Exhibition of Modern Dwelling Interiors**

100a. **Dining room** (Speisezimmer)

100b. **Study** (Herrenzimmer)
1913

Breuer 1913c, 85, 90

101. **Berlin** N31, AEG-Apparatefabrik, Ackerstrasse 71–76 (pre-Behrens building)

AEG exhibition room (Ausstellungsraum) [Bu P13]
1913

Hoeber 1913, 104
Windsor 1985, 78

102. **Riga, Latvia**
AEG factory (Betriebsanlagen der AEG) [Bu A137/A138]
1913

Cremers 1928, 25
Siedler 1928, 766
Buddensieg 1975, 287

103. San Remo, Italy, Corso Mazzini
Design for a **spa hotel Majestic Palace** (Kurhotel)
1913–1914

Servaes 1916–1918
Cremers 1928, 164

104. **Berlin-Moabit, AEG Turbine Factory Complex,** Huttenstrasse 12–16
Additional stories on Annex A (Erhöhung von Anbau A) [Bu A33–37]
August 1913–April 1914

Negri 1993, [3]

105. **Hennigsdorf bei Berlin, Kreis Oranienburg, AEG Factories** (AEG Fabriken Hennigsdorf Werksgelände am Rathenaupark)
AEG Locomotive Factory (Lokomotivfabrik; several buildings) [Bu A141–148/ A143–150]
1913, construction of three halls; construction of the fourth hall, office buildings, boiler making shop, and forge by 1918

Behrens, "Zur Ästhetik des Fabrikbaus," 1929, 130
Hirschberg 1929, 42–43, 68
Posener 1934, 18
Negri 1993, [5]
Jefferies 1995, 134

106. **Cologne,** Unter-Sachsenhausen Strasse 37
Frank & Lehmann Building (Geschäftshaus
      der Firma Frank & Lehmann)
1913–1914

Cologne 1927, 47
Cremers 1928, 164
Anderson 1968, chap. 8
Hoepfner 1979, 14
Hagspiel in *Westdeutsche Impuls* (Cologne, 1984),
      45–46
Buddensieg in Ribbe and Schäche 1987, 353
See chapter 8 (and figure 8.43) here

107. **Cologne, Exhibition of the Deutscher**
      Werkbund 1914
Deutscher Werkbund Festhalle
1913–1914

Behrendt 1914c, 617–618
Bruckmann 1914, 625, 627
Deutscher Werkbund 1914b, 248
Hellwag 1914
Jatho 1914
Westheim 1914c, 984
Stahl 1914–1915, 174–176
Klapheck 1928, 103–105
Hamann and Hermand 1967, 409
Anderson 1968, chap. 8
Kadatz 1977, figs. 70–71
Posener 1979, 30, 231–233, 564
Windsor 1981, 138–141
Thiekötter in *Westdeutsche Impuls* (Cologne, 1984),
      60–113, 160–162
Buddensieg in Buderath 1990, 73
Gebhardt in Pfeifer 1990, 130–133
Anderson 1993b, 464–465
Schwartz 1996, 164
See chapter 8 (and figure 8.52) here

108. **Cologne, Exhibition of the Deutscher**
      Werkbund 1914
Exhibition rooms in Main Exhibition Hall
1914

108a. **Room "Peter Behrens"**

Kadatz 1977, fig. 68
Müller in *Westdeutsche Impuls* (Cologne, 1984), 267

108b. **Room "Gebr. Klingspor, Offenbach**
      a.M."

Deutscher Werkbund 1915, 36
Kadatz 1977, 84
Dal Co 1980, 85
Müller in *Westdeutsche Impuls* (Cologne, 1984), 267

108c. **Reception Room from the German**
      Embassy in St. Petersburg

Müller in *Westdeutsche Impuls* (Cologne, 1984), 267

109. Site unknown
Design for an **exhibition hall**
ca. 1913–1915

The Kaiserslautern publication dates this
to 1910 and specifies that it was for the
exhibition of automobiles. Schlüter dates
it to 1913. The contemporary reference
(R.) notes general exhibition use. Neither
reference gives a location or patron.

R. 1915, 381–382
Kaiserslautern 1966, fig. 63
Buddensieg in Ribbe and Schäche 1987, 361
Schlüter 1991, 270

No. 109. Perspective of interior.

110. Vienna, Austria
Design for a **Daimler-Werke Administration
      Building** (Verwaltungsgebäude)
1914

Cremers 1928, 164
Jefferies 1995, 138

111. Berlin
Design for the **AEG Rapid Transit Line**
      (Schnellbahn) **Gesundbrunnen-
      Neukölln, underground station at
      Neanderstrasse;** attribution to Behrens
      by Sabine Bohle
1914–1915?

Mitteilungen der Berliner-Elektrizitätswerke, 11,
      (1915), 165 (no attribution)
Bohle in Buddensieg et al. 1979, 199
Bohle-Heintzenberg 1980, 187f.

No. 112. Interior view.

112. **Hennigsdorf bei Berlin, Kreis
      Oranienburg** (south of AEG Fabriken
      Hennigsdorf Werksgelände am
      Rathenaupark)
Factory for the AEG Aeronautical Division
      (Hallen der AEG Flugtechnischen
      Abteilung) [Bu A149–151/A151–153]
1914–1915

Windsor 1981, 100
Negri 1993, [5]

113. **Berlin-Oberschöneweide,** block defined
      by Roedernstrasse, Zeppelinstrasse,
      Fontanestrasse, and An der Wuhlheide
AEG housing estate (Siedlung) [Bu A196–
      210/ A197–209]; smaller, realized
      project (see also no. 91 above)
1915

Behrens, "Waldsiedlung Berlin-Lichtenberg," 1920–
      1921, 329–330
Cremers 1928, 128 (misidentified)
Müller-Wulckow 1928, 63
Berlin, Architekten- und Ingenieur-Verein, 4, A
      (1970), 365
Kadatz 1977, figs. 47–49
Neumeyer 1978, 227–243, figs. 97–116
Hüter 1988, 252–253
Pommer and Otto 1991, 74

114. **Berlin-Lichtenberg,** Karlshorst,
      Hegemeisterweg, Drosselstieg, Fuchsbau
Forest Housing Estate (Waldsiedlung
      Lichtenberg)
1915–1916, project; 1919ff., construction

Hoeber 1917
Behrens, "Waldsiedlung Berlin-Lichtenberg,"
      1920–1921
Cremers 1928, 129–130 (pl. 128 is a misidentifica-
      tion of Behrens's Siedlung Oberschöneweide)
Berlin, Architekten- und Ingenieur-Verein, 4, A
      (1970), 370
Kadatz 1977, fig. 50

115. **Berlin-Moabit, AEG Turbine Factory
      Complex**
Munitions Factory (Munitionsfabrik), on
      Berlichingenstrasse [Bu A38–42]
1915– March 1916

116. **Berlin-Köpenick (Oberschöneweide),**
Ostendstrasse, Wilhelminenstrasse
Office and factory of the Nationale
Automobil-Gesellschaft (NAG; formerly
Neue Automobil AG [a subsidiary of
the AEG]; under the German Democratic Republic, Werk für Fernseh-
elektronik) [Bu A152–160/A154–162]
1915–1917

de Fries 1920–1921
Behne [1926] 1996, 108–109
Platz 1927, 30
Cremers 1928, 45–47
Kadatz 1977, figs. 42–46
Hüter 1988, 250, 252
Gebhardt in Pfeifer 1990, 103
Pfeifer 1990, cat. 145, p. 161
Haeder 1994
Jefferies 1995, 134–135
Kohlenbach, ca. 1998 (gives date of 1913–1917)

117. **Golpa, near Bitterfeld, Grosskraftwerk**
Zschornewitz, Georg Klingenberg, lead
architect; Behrens attributed as architectural consultant

117a. **Workers' housing estate**

117b. **House of the director of the works**
(Haus des Betriebsleiters)

117c. **Small transformer house**
(Transformatorenhäuschen)
1915–1919

Wilhelm in Buddensieg et al. 1979, 150–151; Engl.
ed. 151

118. **Brussels, Belgium, Social Welfare**
Exhibition (Soziale Fürsorge)
AEG Exhibition Pavilion [Bu A11–12]
1916

Buddensieg 1975, 296

119. Berlin-Moabit, AEG Turbine Factory
Complex

Project for the alteration and extension of the
Administration Building (Umbau und
Erweiterung des Verwaltungsgebäudes)
[Bu A163–169/A165–170]
May 1916

120. Istanbul, Turkey, Divan-Jolu-/Präfektur-
Strasse
Design (second prize) for the **House of**
German-Turkish Friendship (Haus der
Freundschaft)
1916–1917

Deutscher Werkbund und Deutsch-Türkische
Vereinigung 1918
Cremers 1928, 56–57
Hesse-Frielinghaus 1966, 21
Pehnt 1973, 71
Kadatz 1977, figs. 72–75
Posener 1979, 508, 512
Junghanns 1982, 47
Dal Co 1990, 212, 220–221, 225

121. **Berlin-Oberschöneweide,** Wilhelminenhofstrasse
AEG Kabelwerk Oberspree, Electric Cable
Factory Halls IV and VII (two groups
of three parallel halls each); not previously noted, attributed here to Behrens,
attribution confirmed by Landesdenkmalamt Berlin 1999; see also no. 139
below
1916–1917

The source of the photograph below is an article by Behrens, "Der Fabrikneubau," in *Das*
Echo (16 October 1919). It is captioned only
"Kabelwerk Oberspree." The article has ten
other photos of well-known Behrens factories,
none of which are discussed in the text or
specifically identifed as being by Behrens.

Although these Kabelwerk factory halls do
not appear in Cremers or Buddensieg or in any
list of Behrens's works, both the appearance of
the buildings and the context of the photograph

indicate that Behrens is the architect. The photograph has the appearance of dating from shortly after completion of the factories and Behrens's NAG factory (no. 116 above) in the background is complete, suggesting a date shortly after the NAG factory and obviously prior to the publication date.

In 1927–1929, Ernst Ziesel reworked this part of the Oberspree site for a new Fernmeldekabelfabrik. This involved a new four-story block parallel to existing low halls along the river Spree. Heideck 1930, p. 507, fig. 3, shows Ziesel's new bridge structure over the exisiting "Spreehalle," a low, single-story industrial building with brick detailing that also suggests Behrens's hand.

K. Bernhard 1912, 1146–1147
Behrens, "Der Fabrikneubau," 1919, 1295
Koeppen 1924, 191, 193
Hirschberg 1929 (pre-Behrens history, 10–11)
Heideck 1930, 505–511, 521–523
Haeder 1994
Kohlenbach, ca. 1998

No. 121. Three parallel factory halls with Behrens's NAG Factory and Administration Building (1914–1916) visible beyond.

122. **Hannover-Linden,** Schlorumpfsweg, **Hannover'sche Waggonfabrik**

122a. **Railway car assembly factory**
(Wagenmontagehalle)

No. 122b. Interior view.

122b. **Woodworking shop**
(Holzbearbeitungshalle)

1917

Behrens, "Der Fabrikneubau," 1919, 1294, 1296
Müller-Wulckow 1919
Hawa [Hannover'sche Waggonfabrik]-*Nachrichten,* 4 (January 1922)
Platz 1927, fig. 185
Cremers 1928, 164, pl. 48

123. **Basel and Winterthur, Switzerland Exhibitions of the Deutscher Werkbund;**
Behrens as lead architect

15 March 1917, opening, Gewerbemuseum, Basel; May/June 1917, Winterthur Museum

[Behrens] in Deutscher Werkbund 1917
F. 1917, 250–251
Hellwag 1918, 3
Wichmann 1978, 44

124. **Bern, Switzerland,** Kirchenfeldplatz **Exhibition building and exhibition of the Deutscher Werkbund**

1917

[Behrens] in Deutscher Werkbund 1917
Mitteilungen des Deutschen Werkbundes, no. 7 (1917)
Moeller van den Bruck 1917
Hellwag 1918

Cremers 1928, 139–141
Posener and Imbert 1934, 13, 30
Ammann 1940, 302–303
Hesse-Frielinghaus 1966, 22
Wichmann 1978, 44
Windsor 1981, 143–144
Junghanns 1982, 47, 50
Buddensieg in Ribbe and Schäche 1987, 348

125. Berlin-Spandau
Design for a **housing estate of row houses**
1917

Cremers 1928, 131
Kadatz 1977, fig. 76, p. 88 (misidentified as
    Grossenbaum)
Pommer and Otto 1991, 242 n. 47

126. Berlin-Wedding, AEG factories,
    Brunnenstrasse 107a
Design for an **AEG Administration Building
    on the Humboldthain** (Verwaltungs-
    gebäude am Humboldthain)
    [Bu A161–162/A163–164]
1917

Hüter 1988, 251
Buddensieg in Buderath 1990, 62
Schlüter 1991, 270

127. **Hannover, Hannover'sche Waggonfabrik,
    airplane factory buildings**

127a. **Hangar** (Flugzeugstarthalle)

127b. **Assembly building** (Montagehalle)
during World War I

Behrens, "Der Fabrikneubau," 1919, 1296
Müller-Wulckow 1919, 78, 102–106
Müller-Wulckow 1925, 55
Cremers 1928, 71, 164
Posener 1934, 10
Posener 1979, 389, 398
Windsor 1981, 144

128. Conceptual schemes for economical siting
    of low-income housing: "**Gruppenbau-
    weise**" from Behrens and Heinrich de
    Fries, *Vom sparsamen Bauen: Ein Beitrag
    zur Siedlungsfrage* (Berlin: Bauwelt,
    1918)
1917–1918

Weishaupt 1919
Behrens, "Das Wesen der neuen 'Gruppenbauweise',"
    1919, 622–624
See chapter 9 (and figure 9.15) here

129. **Neusalz an der Oder** (now Nowasól,
    Poland)
Plan for a sector of the city (Siedlungsplan)
1918

Cremers 1928, 132
Buddensieg in Ribbe and Schäche 1987, 362

130. **Hennigsdorf bei Berlin, Kreis
    Oranienburg**
AEG workers' housing (Zinshäuser für AEG
    Arbeiter) **in Paul-Jordan-Strasse** [Bu
    A211–213/A210–212]
1918–1919

Weishaupt 1919
Behrens, "Das Wesen der neuen 'Gruppenbauweise',"
    1919
Behrens, "Die Gruppenbauweise," 1919–1920
Platz 1927, fig. 507b
Taut 1927, 50, fig. 89
Cremers 1928, 130
Shand 1934, 85
Göldner 1955, 308
Kadatz 1977, figs. 53–54
Neumeyer 1978, 244–255, figs. 117–119
Windsor 1981, 143–144
Posener in Kleihues 1987, 140–141

131. **Forst (Brandenburg)**
Model workers' community (Muster-
    Gemeinschaftssiedlung für Arbeiter)
1919

Cremers 1928, 26–27, pl. 132
Shand 1934, 86
Windsor 1981, 145

132. **Altona-Othmarschen (Hamburg),**
Rosenhagenstrasse, Gutzkowstrasse,
Adickestrasse
Housing estate for the officers of Deutsche
Werft (Beamtensiedlung der Deutschen
Werft); Deutsche Werft AG was a sub-
sidiary of both the AEG and Gute-
hofnungshütte
ca. 1919–1921

Cremers 1928, 28f., pls. 136f.
Jessen 1968, 148
Körber 1978
Schlüter 1991, 247, 451–452

133. Design for **two-story buildings with flats**
opening to gardens on either side
(Doppelgärtenhäuser)
1920

Behrens, "Doppelgärtenhäuser," 1920
Cremers 1928, 27–28, 133–135
Shand 1934, 86
Göldner 1955
Kadatz 1977, figs. 77–78
See chapter 9 (and figure 9.16) here

134. Nowawes
Plan for a sector of the city (Bebauungsplan)
1920

Cremers 1928, 132

135. **Potsdam-Babelsberg**
Plan for a housing group (Siedlungsplan)
1920

Buddensieg in Ribbe and Schäche 1987, 362

136. Grossenbaum
Semidetached houses for a housing estate
(Siedlungshäuser)
1920

Cremers 1928, 131
Kadatz 1977, fig. 76 (misidentification of no. 125 above)

137. Erlangen
Design for the **Röntgeninstitut**
1920–1921

Buddensieg in Ribbe and Schäche 1987, 362

138. Oberhausen
Design for an **administration building for the**
Rombacher Hüttenwerke AG
(Concordia Bergbau AG)
1920–1921

Cremers 1928, 51
Günter 1975, 15, 47
Kadatz 1977, fig. 83
Busch 1993, 107–108, fig. 136

139. **Berlin-Oberschöneweide,**
Wilhelminenhofstrasse
AEG Kabelwerk Oberspree, addition to
Administration and Factory Building
(KWO Building A4 or No. 25)
ca. 1917? (attribute to Behrens?)
ca. 1920–24? (attribute to Behrens and/or Jean
Krämer?)

A building permit was issued for the northeast
part (to first stair tower and two bays beyond),
18 July 1905; architect Klemm. The 1905–
1906 building was of five stories with broad
segmental-arched windows, seemingly at all
floors (as still today on the northwest side,
though this is reworked after heavy damage in
World War II).

A building permit was issued for an addition to the southwest (to second stair tower
and three bays beyond), 13 May 1911; architect Klemm. The 1911–1912 building was of
five stories with broad rectangular windows (as
still today on the northwest side and the west-
ernmost part of the south side, which appear
to be only slightly reworked despite destruction at the upper floors in World War II).

No. 139. Exterior view from street.

The source of the photograph reproduced here is an article by W. Koeppen (1924). Koeppen notes, without specification, that Behrens built on this site (see no. 121 above), finding especially interesting Behrens's successful addition of stories to the Administration Building (p. 193). Koeppen gives no specific date, but his mention comes in the context of Behrens's work of ca. 1917.

The photograph would suggest that the fifth floor of the 1905 building was reworked with rectangular windows, a sixth floor was added to both the 1905 and 1911 parts, and a mansard roof with skylights was added. At least the top parts of the stair towers were necessarily transformed. The character and detail of the transformations and additions are consistent with Behrens's work.

However, Hirschberg (1929, p. 68) notes that a building at the Kabelwerk was reconstructed with additional stories in 1924 (though the completed work was published in 1924). Noting that the building was transformed from the ground up, he also refers to the installation of a monumental stair, a spacious hall, and exhibition and conference rooms also designed by the architect [Jean] Krämer. Osborn (1927), a monograph on

Krämer, neither mentions nor illustrates any work in Oberschöneweide by Krämer; nor does the small piece by P. Bucciarelli added to the 1996 reprint of that monograph. Kohlenbach (ca. 1998) credits the nearby Einbauhalle of the Akkumalatorenfabrik Oberspree (1925–1926) to Krämer. There is little literature on Krämer, but Buddensieg (in Buderath 1990, p. 68) places Krämer as a significant figure in Behrens's atelier from 1910 to at least late 1920, when he was involved in the design of the quite different Farbwerke Hoechst.

Thus Koeppen and Hirschberg provide a range of dates and alternative attributions to Behrens or Krämer; it is possible that the addition to the Kabelwerk was a joint work. If this building transformation is by Krämer, then it is in a manner most like Behrens's industrial work. In March 1999 Dr. Bernhard Kohlenbach of the Landesdenkmalamt Berlin agreed in the possibility of attribution to Behrens, but knows of no documentation. If it is by Behrens, I am more inclined to the ca. 1917 date, but locate it here in regard to the source materials of the 1920s.

Bernhard 1912b, 1146–1147
Koeppen 1924, 191, 193
Hirschberg 1929, 68
Haeder 1994
Kohlenbach, ca. 1998

140. **Oberhausen, Gutehofnungshütte,** Essener Strasse
Administration Building (Hauptverwaltung III), **Main Warehouse, Warehouse for Lubricants, and Gate**

140a. **Limited competition design** for a complex of buildings; neither the competition documents nor the designs survive
Summer-Fall 1920

Literature on the competition
Günter 1970, 365–372
Günter 1975, 15, 44
Buddensieg in Buderath 1990, 63 and n. 24
Schlüter 1991, 240–246

No. 140b. Complex from the rear: Main Warehouse, left, and Administration Building.

No. 140b. Administration Building, entry hall.

140b. Behrens's executed design
1921–1925

Müller-Wulckow 1925, 47
Platz 1927, 31–32, 133, fig. 465
Cremers 1928, 17–18, pls. III, 11–23
Häring 1928, 333
Klapheck 1928, 109–114, 182
Grimme 1930, 19
Posener and Imbert 1934, 14–16, 30
Günter 1970, 365–372
Günter 1975, 15, 44–48, figs. 21–24, 27, 31
Kadatz 1977, figs. 84–85
Günter in Siepmann 1978, 338–339
Windsor 1981, 157–158
Buddensieg in Ribbe and Schäche 1987, 354
Buddensieg in Buderath 1990, 63–64
Gebhardt in Pfeifer 1990, 104
Schlüter 1991, 238–278, figs. 161–185
Busch 1993, 108, 170–171, color pls. IX, XXIII,
    XXIV, figs. 48–50

141. Frankfurt-Hoechst
IG-Farben (later Farbwerke Hoechst),
    Hoechst Administration Building,
    and design for an **Autogarage**
1920–1924; Autogarage, 1922

Schürmeyer 1926
Platz 1927, 31, 118, 158, fig. 464
Cremers 1928, 15–17, pls. II, 2–10
Häring 1928, 331
Grimme 1930, 18
Vogelgesang 1930, 716–718
Posener and Imbert 1934, 14, 17, 30
Pehnt 1973, 52
Drebusch 1976, 165–168
Massobrio and Portoghesi 1976, 237, fig. 386
Kadatz 1977, 49, figs. 90–91, 133
Windsor 1981, 149–156
Simomura, *Space Design,* 255 (December 1985),
    49–52
Buddensieg in Ribbe and Schäche 1987, 353–354
Buderath 1990
Gebhardt in Pfeifer 1990, 104–105
Busch 1993, 134–135, fig. 175
See chapter 9 (and figures 9.4–7) here

No. 141. Axial view from stairwell to, and through, main hall.

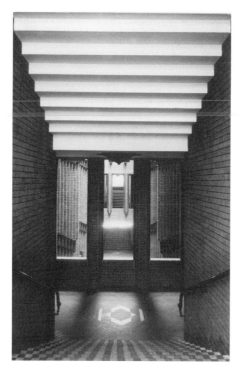

142. Düsseldorf, Breitestrasse
Design for the **Administration Building of the Stumm-Konzern** (Firma Gebr. Stumm GmbH)
1921

Anon. 1922 (*Deutsche Bauzeitung,* January 1922)
R. Meyer 1922
Cremers 1928, 49–50
Kadatz 1977, figs. 86–87
Schlüter 1991, 352–364, figs. 258–259
Busch 1993, 59, figs. 54–55
Neumann 1995, 171 (with additional bibliography)

143. **Leipzig, Messe,** fair of 28 August–3 September 1921
Exhibiton pavilion Reklameburg
1921

Cremers 1928, 164
Buddensieg in Ribbe and Schäche 1987, 354
Buddensieg in Buderath 1990, 71–72

144. Duisburg-Meiderich
Limited competition facade design for an **administration building for Rheinische Stahlwerke**
1921–1922

Anon. 1922 (*Deutsche Bauzeitung,* July 1922)
Schlüter 1991, 300–305
Busch 1993, 110

145. Berlin-Tiergarten
Competition design for a **high-rise office building** (Geschäftshochhaus) **on Kemperplatz**
end 1921–1922

[Taut (anon.)] 1922
Cremers 1928, 73
Kadatz 1977, fig. 82
Neumann 1995, 162

146. **Munich, Deutsche Gewerbeschau** exhibition, May-October 1922
Dombauhütte
1921–1922

Behrens, "Die Dombauhütte," 1923
Gut 1923, 9–10, 12
Platz 1927, 57
Cremers 1928, 20, pls. 83–88
Posener and Imbert 1934, 14, 30
Pehnt 1973, 52
Massobrio and Portoghesi 1976, 25, 353, figs. 218, 565
Windsor 1981, 156–158
Buddensieg in Ribbe and Schäche 1987, 354
Plischke 1989, 39
Buddensieg in Buderath 1990, 70–71
See chapter 9 (and figures 9.1–3) here

147. Cologne
Competition design for the **Stock Exchange and Kaufmannshaus AG, with a hotel** (Börsen- und Kaufmannshaus AG)
1923

Cremers 1928, 61–63
Kadatz 1977, figs. 88–89

148. **Vienna, Austria**
Behrens's dwelling (interiors)
n.d. (ca. 1923)

Cremers 1928, 119–120
Müller-Wulckow 1930, 66
Döllgast 1973, 1:36

149. **Berlin** (Magdeburger Strasse?)
Behrens's dwelling (interiors)
n.d. (ca. 1923?)

Cremers 1928, 121

150. **Vienna, Austria, Österreichisches**
    Museum, exhibition
Scholar's Study (Arbeitszimmer eines
    Gelehrten)
1923

Anon. 1924 (*Deutsche Kunst und Dekoration*)
Cremers 1928, 147–148
Anderson 1968, conclusion
Pehnt 1973, 33
Buddensieg in Ribbe and Schäche 1987, 354–355
See Conclusion (and figure 10.1) here

151. **Northampton, England,** 508
    Wellingborough Road
New Ways, house for W. J. Bassett-Lowke
1923–1926

Anon. 1926 (*Architectural Review*)
Cremers 1928, 108–112
Häring 1928, 332
Grimme 1930, 23
Cortissoz 1930
Ehmcke 1955, 13
Casabella 240, 29
Pevsner, *Buildings of England: Northamptonshire*
    (Harmondsworth: Penguin, 1961)
Hitchcock 1963, 346
Kadatz 1977, fig. 93
Windsor 1981, 161–162
Buddensieg in Buderath 1990, 72
Pfeifer 1990, 22, fig. 17
See chapter 9 (and figures 9.13–14) here

152. Design for **Terrace Housing**
    (Terrassenhäuser)
ca. 1924 (there are variants of this project;
    Cremers dated it 1920, but the earliest
    known publication is 1924)

Kunstblatt (1924), 104
Behrens, "Terrassen am Hause," 1927
Cremers 1928, 126–127
Döcker 1929, 125, fig. 198
Posener 1934, 21
Shand 1934, 86
Göldner 1955
Kadatz 1977, figs. 79–81
Tafuri 1980, 49
Windsor 1981, 145–146
Kirsch 1989, 178
Neumeyer 1991, 159
Pommer and Otto 1991, 112–115
See chapter 9 (and figure 9.17) here

153. **Essen-Rellinghausen**
Design for the **Parish Church, Communal**
    House, Vicarage and staff houses of St.
    Lambert (Kath. Pfarrkirche und
    Pfarrhäusern St. Lambert) (see also no.
    179 below); collaboration with Hans
    Döllgast
1924

Platz 1927, 57
Cremers 1928, 99–102
Kaiserslautern 1966, cat. 88
Kadatz 1977, figs. 95–96
Buddensieg in Buderath 1990, 72–73, 185 n. 50

154. **Mülheim-Ruhr**
Designs for the **mausoleum of Hugo Stinnes**
1924

Cremers 1928, 91
Kaiserslautern 1966, cat. 92, fig. 90
Jessen 1968, 149
Portoghesi 1970, 18
See chapter 9 (and figure 9.8) here

155. Berlin
Design for the **Radio Fair Hall** (Rundfunk-
    messehalle; Radio-Messehalle)
1924

Cremers 1928, 74–75
Kadatz 1977, fig. 104

156. Barcelona, Spain
Design of **wharf sheds** (Werftschuppen)
1924

Cremers 1928, 72
Kadatz 1977, fig. 107

157. Vienna, Austria
Design for the **Brigitte-Brücke**
1924

Cremers 1928, 77
Kadatz 1977, fig. 105

158. Neubabelsberg
Project for a **villa** ("Modell zu einer Villa in
    Neubabelsberg 1924" [in a list of works
    influenced by expressionism]; this may
    well be a mistake by Platz)
1924

Platz 1927, 57

159. **Vienna XIII, Austria,** Penzingerstrasse 20
Alexander Hoffmann house
1924

Cremers 1928, 115–116
Buddensieg in Buderath 1990, 185 n. 50

160. **Paris, France, Exposition Internationale
    des Arts Décoratifs et Industriels
    Modernes, 1925,** Quai de la
    Conférence, east of Pont Alexandre III
Austrian Pavilion, Wintergarden
    (Gewächshaus; Wintergartenhaus): the
    Austrian Pavilion was by Josef Hoffmann;
    Behrens designed the winter garden that
    was part of the popular Café Viennois

1924–1925

Paris 1925, 11–28, pl. following p. 60
Paris, *Exposition internationale des arts décoratifs . . . ,
    Rapport général* (Paris, 1928), 2:59
Cremers 1928, 144–146
Posener and Imbert 1934, 19, 30
Döllgast 1973, 1:34
Pehnt 1973, 38, 41
Massobrio and Portoghesi 1976, 17, 23, fig. 424
Posener 1979, 508
Windsor 1981, 162–163
Sekler 1985, 182–184, 403–404
Buddensieg in Ribbe and Schäche 1987, 354–355
Borrmann 1989, 162, fig. 259
See chapter 9 (and figures 9.9–10) here

161. **Salzburg, Austria**

161a. **College of St. Benedict, an extension of
    the Benedictine cloister of the Abbey
    of St. Peter** (Kolleg St. Benedikt in St.
    Peter); with Stadtbaumeister Franz
    Wagner and Hans Döllgast, who atypi-
    cally signed some of the drawings
1924–1926

Lux 1926
Scharff 1927
Hartig 1928
Cremers 1928, 22f., pls. 92–99
Anon. 1929 (*Pencil Points*)
Anon. 1930 (*Brooklyn Museum Quarterly*), 103
Grimme 1930, 22
Cortissoz 1930
Österreichische Kunst 1932, 19
Hanisch in Salzburg 1982, 216–220
Munich 1987, 19, 247
Buddensieg in Buderath 1990, 69, fig. 16
Mayr 1994
See chapter 9 (and figures 9.11–12) here

161b. **Milk house at the College** (Milch-
    häuschen am Collegiumsgebäude)

Cremers 1928, 97

162. **Vienna, Austria**
Three municipal social housing blocks
    (Volkswohnhäuser)
1924–1929

General literature
Behrens, "Die Gemeinde Wien als Bauherrin," 1928,
    976
Cremers 1928, 30–31
Hitchcock 1963, 346
Mang and Mang-Frimmel 1978
Tafuri 1980
Buddensieg in Ribbe and Schäche 1987, 355
Blau 1999
See chapter 9 here

162a. **Vienna XXII, Konstanziagasse 44**
1924–1925

Cremers 1928, 123
Mang and Mang-Frimmel 1978, cat. 372
Blau 1999, 311, 312, 372

162b. **Vienna XX, Winarsky-Hof,**
    Stromstrasse 36–38 (also known as
    Otto Haas-Hof), with Josef Frank, Josef
    Hoffmann, Oskar Strnad, and Oskar
    Wlach
1924–1925

Vienna 1926
Behrens, "Die Gemeinde Wien als Bauherrin," 1928
Cremers 1928, 122, 124–125
Grimme 1930, 22
Österreichische Kunst 1932, 23
Ungers 1969
Tafuri 1971, 301–303
Kadatz 1977, fig. 94
Mang and Mang-Frimmel 1978, cat. 320
Pommer and Otto 1991, 49, fig. 79
Blau 1999, 303–309, 372

162c. **Vienna V, Franz Domes-Hof,**
    Margaretengürtel 126–134
1928–1929

Grimme 1930, 22
Österreichische Kunst 1932, 22
Mang and Mang-Frimmel 1978, cat. 63
Blau 1999, 266, 311, 313, 373, 374
See figure 9.20 here

163. **Ida**
Monument to Hans Jäckh
n.d.

Cremers 1928, 98

164. **Salzburg, Austria**
Existing abbey church of St. Peter, enlarged
    choir
1925

Hartig 1928, 237–238
Mayr 1994

165. **Heidelberg, Waldfriedhof** [Bergfriedhof]
Monument of Reichspräsident Friedrich Ebert
1925; in 1967 completely remade, like the
    original, in Jurakalk

Cremers 1928, 81f.
Weiser 1929, 10
Grimme 1930, 23
Kaiserslautern 1966, cat. 157, fig. 91
Jessen 1968, 149
Windsor 1981, 160–161
Asche 1992, 298–299, 319

No. 165.

166. **Düsseldorf**
Design for **new buildings of the City Hall**
    (Rathaus-Neubauten)
1925

Cremers 1928, 58–60
Kordt 1963, 139
Kaiserslautern 1966, cat. 103, fig. 98
Kadatz 1977, figs. 109–111

167. Cologne
Design of **Exhibition Pavilion for the
    Association of German Mirror
    Manufacturers** (Verein Deutscher
    Spiegelglas-Fabriken)
1925

Cremers 1928, 142–143
Pehnt 1973, 39
Kadatz 1977, fig. 92
Windsor 1981, 163

168. Essen
Design for an **Industry Exhibition Hall**
    (Industrieausstellungshalle)
1925

Cremers 1928, 70
Vogelgesang 1930, 722
Posener 1934, 18
Kadatz 1977, figs. 97–98

169. Berlin
Design for the **administration building of a
    fire insurance corporation**
    (Verwaltungsbauten für eine
    Feuerversicherungsgesellschaft)
1925

Cremers 1928, 52

170. **Berlin-Mitte,** Jerusalemer Strasse 25
**Remodeled building facade and shop front for
    H. J. Wilm, Jewelers** (Ladenfront des
    Juweliers H. J. Wilm)
1925–1926 (conventional dating; or possibly
    1929–1930 [note group of earliest
    publications in 1930s])

Wilm 1930, 107
Anon. 1930 (*Zentralblatt der Bauverwaltung*)
Bt 1931, 221–223
Posener 1933, 43
A. Schumacher 1934, 126
Buddensieg in Ribbe and Schäche 1987, 363

171. Berlin
Design for a **study for Mr. Wilm**
    (Herrenzimmer Wilm); known from a
    perspective in the collection of the Pfalz-
    galerie, Kaiserslautern: C39/1/EZ IX/21
n.d.

172. Salzburg, Salzburger Festspielhaus
Design for the **renovation of the Stadtsaal**
    (realized by Clemens Holzmeister,
    1926); attributed to Behrens by Norbert
    Mayr, Salzburg, 1998 (personal commu-
    nication), with reference to a perspective
    in the collection of the Pfalzgalerie,
    Kaiserslautern: D1/1/EZ VII/135
1925–1926

Mayr in Tabor 1994

173. Brno (Brünn), Czechoslovakia (now
    Czech Republic)
Design for the **Hotel Ritz** (sometimes Hotel
    Stiassni)
1926

Cremers 1928, 63–64
Kaiserslautern 1966, cat. 105d
Kadatz 1977, figs. 100–101
Portoghesi 1970, 21

No. 173. Perspective.

174. Zagreb (Agram), Yugoslavia (now Croatia)

Design of an **administrative building** (Verwaltungsgebäude); attributed to Behrens in Kaiserslautern 1966, with reference to a drawing in the collection of the Pfalzgalerie, Kaiserslautern: C40/ 1/EZ VIII/21

1926

Kaiserslautern 1966, cat. 109

175. **Düsseldorf**, Kleverstrasse

"House of a Sculptor" in the Gesolei model estate (Haus eines Bildhauers in der Mustersiedlung Gesolei)

1926 (exhibition from May 1926)

Cremers 1928, 117–118
Buddensieg in Ribbe and Schäche 1987, 363
Gebhardt in Pfeifer 1990, 133–136

176. **Frankfurt, Exposition Grounds** (Messegelände, Frankfurter Internationale Messen)

House of Fashion (Haus der Moden): an exposition building as part of a competition design for the **new design of the fairgrounds** (Neugestaltung des Messegeländes); with Frankfurt architects Prof. von Loehr and Robert Wollmann

176a. **New design of the fairgrounds**
1926

M. [1927–1928?], 4

176b. **House of Fashion**
1926–1927

Anon. 1926 (*Die Baugilde*)
M. [1927–1928?], 1–2, 13–15
Kaiserslautern 1966, cat. 106, 160
Kadatz 1977, fig. 99

177. Cologne-Mülheim

Two (three?) competition designs with Fried. Krupp AG, Friedrich-Alfred-Hütte, Rheinhausen/Niederrhein, and Franz Schlüter AG for a **bridge over the Rhine**

177a. **"Aus einem Guss"** (first prize) and

177b. **"Ein Sprung"** (an open-web variant of "Aus einem Guss," among nine finalists)

A third design from Krupp, listed with collaborators as above, is **"Stufenweise"** (a truss bridge; not placed)

1926–1927

Kommerell 1927, 241–247, 263–271
Zimmermann 1927
Zimmermann 1927b
Schmuckler 1927, 97–98
Cremers 1928, 78
Grimme 1930, 17
Kaiserslautern 1966, cat. 111
Kadatz 1977, fig. 106

178. **Stuttgart, Deutscher Werkbund Exhibition "Die Wohnung," Weissenhof Siedlung**, 1927

General literature on the Weissenhof Siedlung
Deutscher Werkbund 1927b
Wedepohl 1927
Behrens, "Die Gemeinde Wien als Bauherrin," 1928, 976
Joedicke and Plath 1968
Daldrop 1978
Stuttgart, *info bau* 1987
Kirsch 1987; Eng. ed., 1989
Joedicke 1989
Pommer and Otto 1991

"Terrassenhaus" Behrens, Hölzelweg 3–5 (Am Weissenhof 30–32)
1926–1927

Behrens, "Etagenhaus und Kleinsiedlung," 1926
Behrens, "Terrassen am Hause," 1927
Lampmann 1927, 550–552
Nonn 1927, 407

Siedler 1928, 770
Ls 1928
Hajos and Zahn 1929, 112
Bohle-Heintzenberg 1980, 192f.
Bohle-Heintzenberg in Büddensieg and Rogge 1981, 213

186. **Zagreb** (Agram), **Yugoslavia** (now Croatia), Square of the Republic (the main square of the city, in 1994 known as Jelacic's Square)
Remodeling of the department store Haus Otto Stern
1927–1929; restoration 1986

Österreichische Kunst 1932, 36
Berckenhagen 1979, 248
Büddensieg in Buderath 1990, 185 n. 50

187. Salzburg, Austria, Westbahnhofstrasse
Invited competition design for a **spa** (Kurhaus)
1928

Salzburger Volksblatt, 166 (1928), 8
Salzburger Chronik (30 August 1928), 3
W. 1928–1929, 193–196
Salzburger Volksblatt, Jubiläumsausgabe (1930), 17, 21
Kaiserslautern 1966, cat. 118
Sekler 1985, 410
Mayr 1994, 11–12, cat. 132

188. Vienna-Dornbach, Austria
Design for a **church**
early 1928

Kaiserslautern 1966, cat. 120
Büddensieg in Ribbe and Schäche 1987, 363

189. Düsseldorf, Königsplatz
Limited competition design for an **office building of the Thyssen-Konzern**
1928

Cremers 1928, 52
Anon. 1928 (*Die Baugilde*), 976
Kaiserslautern 1966, cat. 116
Kadatz 1977, figs. 112–114

Schlüter 1991, 383–387, figs. 274–275
Busch 1993, 60, fig. 59

190. Düsseldorf
Design for the **office building of the Vereinigten Stahlwerke**
1928

Büddensieg in Ribbe and Schäche 1987, 363

191. Halle
Competition design for the **Stadthalle on the Lehmannsfelsen**
1928

Cremers 1928, 65–67
Weiser 1929, 10
Kaiserslautern 1966, cat. 117
Kadatz 1977, fig. 115

192. **Zilina** (Sillein), **Czechoslovakia** (now Slovakia)
Synagogue
1928–1929

Cremers 1928, 103–105
Weiser 1929, 6
Grimme 1930, 21
Österreichische Kunst 1932, 36
Kaiserslautern 1966, cat. 119
Kadatz 1977, fig. 103
Krawietz 1995, 300–301

193. Moscow, USSR (now Russia)
International competition design for the **Centrosoyus** (Zentrosojus): central office complex for the Union of the Cooperatives of the Soviet Union
1928–1929

Behrens, "Verwaltungsgebäude . . . ," 1929
Weiser 1929, 7–8
Grimme 1930, 20
Kaiserslautern 1966, cat. 124, figs. 95–96
Pfankuch in Waetzold 1977, Kat. 2/902–903; fig. 2/903
Büddensieg in Ribbe and Schäche 1987, 363
Busch 1993, 107–108, fig. 137

No. 193. Perspective.

194. **Berlin**

Competition design for a **new organization of Alexanderplatz** (for Behrens's buildings on the Alexanderplatz, see no. 202 below)

1928–1929

Wagner 1929, 37–39
Dietrich 1929, 62
Weiser 1929, 4–5
Grimme 1930, 20
Anon. 1930 (*Brooklyn Museum Quarterly*), 109

No. 194. Perspective, ink on vellum, traced over a base drawing; unsigned, here ascribed to Peter Behrens.

Posener 1934, 23
Büttner 1964
Kaiserslautern 1966, cat. 121, figs. 100, 102
Portoghesi 1970, 24–25
Berlin, Architekten- und Ingenieur-Verein, 9 (1971), 151–153
Volk 1972, 203ff., esp. 211–212
Kadatz 1977, figs. 124–125
Windsor 1981, 165
Scarpa 1986, ch. 4
Neumeyer in Buddensieg 1987, 72–76
Kleihues 1987, 309
Hüter 1988, 351–353
Bekiers in Kaiserslautern 1993, 56ff.
Krawietz 1995, 262, fig. 74
Neumann 1995, 166 (with additional bibliography)
See chapter 9 (and figure 9.25) here

195. Berlin-Mitte, Leipziger Strasse and Friedrichstrasse

Design for the **department store S. Adam**

1928–1930

Weiser 1929, 9
Grimme 1930, 21
Kaiserslautern 1966, cat. 125, figs. 97, 103
Portoghesi 1970, 23

196. **Kronberg im Taunus,** Falkensteinstrasse 19

Villa Clara Ganz

1928–1931 (dated drawings); some days after Kristallnacht (9 November 1938) Nazis set fire to the house; it was restored in the 1980s but much altered

Eisler 1932
Zimmermann 1932
P[aulsen] 1932
Riedrich 1932, 765–775, 778
Riedrich 1932b
Anon. 1932 (*American Architect*)
Shand 1932
Oud 1933, 253
Platz 1933, 25, pls. 225, 238, 332, 417, 422
Posener 1934, 24–29
Shand 1934, 86

Kaiserslautern 1966, cat. 128, fig. 104
Windsor 1981, 167–168
Buddensieg in Ribbe and Schäche 1987, 355
See chapter 9 (and figures 9.21–22) here

197. Berlin-Tiergarten, Platz der Republik
A design in the second competition for the
**extension of the Reichstag and design
of the Platz der Republik** (Erweiterungsbau des Reichstagsgebäudes und
Gestaltung des Platzes der Republik)
1929 (the first competition, in summer 1927,
was deemed to have produced no
satisfactory project; see Hüter 1988,
302–305)

Eiselen 1929
Anon. 1929 (*Die Baugilde*)
Gutkind 1929, 2002
Kiessling 1929
Anon. 1930 (*Deutsche Bauzeitung*)
Kaiserslautern 1966, cat. 110, fig. 101
Portoghesi 1970, 25
Kadatz 1977, fig. 116
Pfankuch in Waetzold 1977, Kat. 2/935–936
Lampugnani 1986, 154
Neumann 1995, 166 (with additional bibliography)

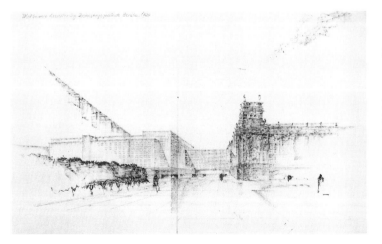

No. 197. Perspective.

198. Design for a **city sector composed of
high-rise, terraced apartments**
(Wohnhochhausstadt; Terrassenhoch-
häuser); Alexander Popp, coarchitect
1929

Anon. 1930 (*Bau- und Werkkunst*), 280–285
Österreichische Kunst 1932, 21
Kaiserslautern 1966, cat. 122
Portoghesi 1970, 26
Massobrio and Portoghesi 1976, 237, fig. 385
Buddensieg in Ribbe and Schäche 1987, 355

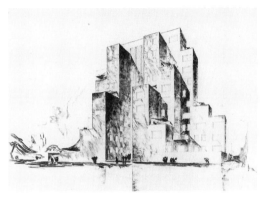

No. 198. Perspective.

199. Prague, Czechoslovakia (now Czech
Republic)
Design for **a bank building** (Bankhaus) **near
the Magazine** (Pulverturm)
1929

Kaiserslautern 1966, cat. 123, fig. 99
Portoghesi 1970, 26b
Buddensieg in Ribbe and Schäche 1987, 363

200. **Berlin-Zehlendorf (Schlachtensee)**,
Waldsängerpfad
Villa Kurt Lewin (Marcel Breuer completed
the interior design)
1929–1930

Riedrich 1932, 770, 772, 776–778
Behrens, "Ein Landhaus in Schlachtensee," 1932,
    16–17
Shand 1934, 40
Berlin, Architekten- und Ingenieur-Verein, 4, C
    (1975), 241
Berckenhagen 1979, 248
Windsor 1981, 166–170
Buddensieg in Ribbe and Schäche 1987, 354–355
Buddensieg 1987, 24, 30
Krawietz 1995, 266
See chapter 9 (and figures 9.23–24) here

201. **Projects for "Atlantropa,"** Herman
    Sörgel's project for lowering the water
    level of the Mediterranean Sea (projects
    by students of Behrens's master class at
    the Academy in Vienna, but Voigt also
    attributes some to Behrens)
1929–1932

Sörgel 1932
Voigt 1991

202. **Berlin-Mitte,** Alexanderplatz
Office buildings Berolina and Alexander (part
    of an urban transformation of
    Alexanderplatz; see no. 194 above)
1929–1932 (Anglo-American bombing raids in
    1945, followed by intense Nazi-Soviet
    fighting, left the buildings burned out
    but with structure intact; they were
    again occupied in 1950)

General literature
Behrens, "Die neuen Hochhäuser am
Alexanderplatz,"
1932
Salkind 1932
Riedrich 1932, 778
Riedrich 1932c
Werner 1932
Bösselmann 1933
Anon. 1933 (*Deutsche Bauzeitung*)
Dürbeck 1933
Posener and Imbert 1934, 20–24, 30

Kersten 1937, B272–273
Rave and Knöfel 1963, no. 117
Büttner 1964
Berlin, Architekten- und Ingenieur-Verein, 9 (1971),
    151–154, 193
Volk 1972, 211–216, with numerous images (220ff.)
Pfankuch in Waetzold 1977, Kat. 2/921–923
Kadatz 1977, figs. 126–132
Scarpa 1986, ch. 4
Buddensieg in Ribbe and Schäche 1987, 355–356
Hüter 1988, 351–353
Kaiserslautern 1993, figs. 102–103
See chapter 9 (and figures 9.25–27 and at no. 194)
    here

202a. **Berolina** ("Stahlhaus")
1929–1931

Anon. 1931 (*Wasmuths Monatshefte*)
Hegemann 1931

202b. **Cafe Braun** (first two floors of Berolina)

Riedrich 1932c, 906
Posener 1934, 20–24

202c. **Alexander** ("Aschingerblock")
1929–1932

Posener 1934, 21–23
P. Meyer 1940
Berlin, Architekten- und Ingenieur-Verein, 9 (1971),
    151–154, 193

203. **Linz, Austria**
State Tobacco Factory; Alexander Popp,
    coarchitect
1929–1938

General literature
Anon. 1930 (*Bau- und Werkkunst*), 273–281
Österreichische Kunst 1932, 11, 36
Ermers 1933
Shand 1933
Friedel 1936
H[offmann] 1936
Popp 1936
Anon. 1938 (*Architectural Forum*)
Buddensieg 1980, xxviii
Buddensieg in Ribbe and Schäche 1987, 355

Hüter 1988, 251
Gebhardt in Pfeifer 1990, 106–107

203a. Tobacco Warehouse
1929–1930

Anon. 1930 (*Bau- und Werkkunst*), 276–277
Ermers 1933, 8
Anon. 1938 (*Architectural Forum*), 198

203b. Cigarette Fabrication Building
1930–1932

Anon. 1930 (*Bau- und Werkkunst*), 275–278
Ermers 1933
Shand 1933
H[offmann] 1936
Anon. 1938 (*Architectural Forum*), 196–199
Pfeifer 1990, cover
See chapter 9 (and figure 9.28) here

203c. Small Fabrication Building, Administration Building, and Workers' Service (Wohlfahrts-) Building

Anon. 1930 (*Bau- und Werkkunst*), 278–279

203d. Pipe Tobacco Plant with north site entrance

H[offmann] 1936, 377
Anon. 1938 (*Architectural Forum*), 194

203e. Power Station

Anon. 1930 (*Bau- und Werkkunst*), 274
Anon. 1938 (*Architectural Forum*), 192, 195
Gebhardt in Pfeifer 1990, 106–107
Pfeifer 1990, 22

204. Linz-Urfahr, Austria
Design of **urban district** (Stadtverbauung) including the site of the Church of Peace (see no. 205 below); Alexander Popp, coarchitect
ca. 1929–1930

Österreichische Kunst 1932, 18

205. **Linz-Urfahr, Austria**
Design for the **Church of Peace** (Friedenskirche); Alexander Popp, coarchitect
ca. 1929–1932; realized in much altered form by others (1933–1949); only the lower part of the main facade and flanking chapels are as in the original design

Österreichische Kunst 1932, 16f.
J. Schmidt 1961, 14, 17, pl. 11

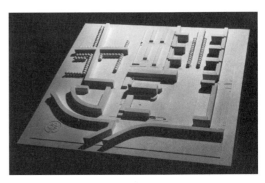

Nos. 204 and 205. Model showing northwest sector of urban design for Linz-Urfahr; the U-shaped complex at the center is the Church of Peace complex, with the entry to the church between the two apsidal chapels.

206. Linz, Austria
Urban plan for the crossing of Landstrasse, Mozartstrasse, and Rudigerstrasse; Alexander Popp, coarchitect
ca. 1930

Österreichische Kunst 1932, 18
J. Schmidt 1961, 22–23

207. Berlin-Mitte, Neue Wache (Karl Friedrich Schinkel, architect), Unter den Linden
Competition designs for a **Monument to the Fallen of the World War** (Kriegerdenkmal or Reichsehrenmal) in the Neue Wache
1930

P[aulsen] 1930
Behrendt 1930, 514f.
Blunck 1930, 82
Kaiserslautern 1966, cat. 113
Wangerin 1976, 50, 244
Berckenhagen 1978, 165
Berckenhagen 1979, 247–249, fig. 345
Buddensieg in Ribbe and Schäche 1987, 363
De Michelis 1991, 299–305 and bibliography

No. 209. Exterior view.

No. 207. Perspective (one of several designs).

208. Berlin, Deutsche Bauausstellung
Competition design for **development of the
    exhibition site** (Bebauung der
    Ausstellungsgelände)
1930

Kaiserslautern 1966, cat. 126, fig. 106

209. **Berlin-Westend,** Bolivarallee and
    Eichenallee
Apartment house
1930–1931

Rave and Knöfel 1963, no. 39
Hennig-Schefold 1966, 92
Berlin, Architekten- und Ingenieur-Verein, 4, A
    (1970), 277, 279
Berlin, Architekten- und Ingenieur-Verein, 4, B
    (1974), 71–73, 397, fig. 93
Buddensieg in Ribbe and Schäche 1987, 355, 363

210. **Berlin, Deutsche Bauausstellung,** 1931
"Haus Ring der Frauen" and Wilm pavilion
    (the exhibition pavilions were set in a
    formal garden of Behrens's design; see
    Riedrich 1931, 290)

210a. **"Haus Ring der Frauen";** Else Oppler-
    Legband, architectural collaborator
1931

Anon. 1931 (*Bau- und Werkkunst*), 225
Anon. 1931 (*Die Baugilde*)
Riedrich 1931
Schmuckler 1931, 138, 141
Taut [1931] in C[onrads] 1977, 1110
Riedrich 1932, 772, 778–780
Österreichische Kunst 1932, 36
Kaiserslautern 1966, cat. 127, fig. 105
Berlin, Architekten- und Ingenieur-Verein, 9 (1971),
    19–21, 31
Berckenhagen 1979, 248
Windsor 1981, 168–169
Buddensieg in Ribbe and Schäche 1987, 356–357
Borrmann 1989, 163, fig. 261
Motz in Pfeifer 1990, 49–50
Windsor 1994, 170
Krawietz 1995, 262, fig. 75

210b. **Exhibition pavilion for the firm H. J. Wilm, Goldsmith**
1931

Riedrich 1931, 290–292

211. Berlin, Deutsche Bauausstellung
Design for **Model Cemetery** (Musterfriedhof)
1931

Buddensieg in Ribbe and Schäche 1987, 363

212. Salzburg, Austria
Competition design for **development of the Arenberg district** (Verbauung der Arenberg-Gründe); Alexander Popp, coarchitect
1931 (competition, with continuing attempts at realization till 1934)

Wagner 1932, 81ff.
Kunz 1932, 5
Österreichische Kunst 1932, 20
Mayr 1994, 12–13, cat. 133–134

213. **Kreis Neustrelitz,** above the Zierksee
Behrens's villa (Landhaus) **Hohenlanke**
1931–1936

Behrens, "Ein Hof vor der Stadt," 1936
Buddensieg 1987, 355, 364
Krawietz 1995, 17–24, figs. 2–5, 7–18

214. Berlin
Design for **multistory pyramid-shaped blocks of flats** (Behrens's patent No. 578 164 Class 37f Group 701)
10 June 1933

Windsor 1994, 181

215. Hamburg, Heiligengeistfeld
Competition design for a **Congress, Sport, and Exhibition Hall** (Kongress-, Sport-, und Ausstellungshalle); Robert Schindler, engineering consultant; awarded one of four first prizes from 175 entrants
early 1934

Die Baugilde, 16, no. 11 (1934)
Langmaack 1934, 511–535
R. Schmidt 1934, 372–374
Kaiserslautern 1966, figs. 107a, b
Buddensieg in Ribbe and Schäche 1987, 357
Höhns 1991, 36–37
Krawietz 1995, 25–33
See chapter 9 (and figure 9.29) here

216. Washington, D.C.
Competition design for the **German Embassy** (Deutsche Botschaft) (limited competition, unbuilt as World War II intervened)
1937–1938

Schüler 1940, 66
Windsor 1994, 187
Krawietz 1995, 91–92

217. **Düsseldorf,** Mannesmannufer
Behrens as **artistic advisor for an addition to his Mannesmann Main Office Building** (see no. 74 above); architect: Regierungsbaumeister Dr. Hans Väth, leader of the Bauabteilung of the Mannesmann-Werke
26 January 1938: letter from Gundlach of the Secretariat of the Mannesmann-Werke to Behrens (typed copy of the letter in Pfalzgalerie, Kaiserslautern, uncataloged, in large brown case); above letter: "Der Bau muss am 1. März 1938 begonnen werden"

218. Berlin-Tiergarten, on the Nord-Süd-Achse envisioned by Albert Speer
Design for **AEG Main Administration Building** (Haupt-Verwaltungsgebäude) [Bu A170–173/A171–174]; in collaboration with Eugen Himmel and with design influence from Speer
1938–1939

Gut 1938, 1144, 1146
Wolff 1939
Koenig 1970
Speer 1970, 144–145
Windsor 1981, 171–173
Buddensieg in Ribbe and Schäche 1987, 353
Hüter 1988, 251
Borrmann 1989, 163, fig. 262
Schäche 1991, 77
Krawietz 1995, 99–133
See chapter 9 (and figure 9.30) here

Bibliography and Sources

1 Archival Materials

Throughout his career, Behrens was widely published; consequently we learn much from secondary sources documented in the bibliographies below.

There is no such thing as a proper Behrens Archive. Individual works are often documented in the archives of clients or municipal building authorities. No significant archive exists with relation to Behrens's work prior to his AEG career in Berlin, although his important association with Karl Ernst Osthaus is documented in extensive correspondence in the Karl Ernst Osthaus Museum, Hagen.

AEG archives were partially lost in the Second World War, yet important materials have been available through the AEG in Berlin, Braunschweig, and Frankfurt. In recent years this material has been redistributed: photographic materials to the Kunsthistorisches Institut of the Freie Universität, Berlin, and other materials including publications to the Deutsches Technikmuseum, Berlin.

In the interwar years, Behrens had offices in Berlin, Frankfurt, the Ruhr, and Vienna. In the late years, materials were dispersed among his younger associates, and no doubt much was lost. In the last twenty years some of these collections have reappeared and been placed in public collections. Behrens's daughter Petra Behrens gave her materials to the Kunstbibliothek, Berlin; his former assistant Karl Mittel gave his to the Pfalzgalerie, Kaiserslautern. The material I saw with Hans Döllgast in 1961 is apparently still in the family.

Professor Tilmann Buddensieg in the course of his studies of Behrens collected various materials, including glassware and china, industrial design objects, and the family photo albums (from Petra Behrens).

2 Writings by Behrens

Entries are normally listed chronologically by publication date. If an item is known to have been written significantly earlier than its publication, a note also appears at the date of authorship. Behrens himself often republished an essay unchanged or in slightly altered form; such repetitions are generally grouped under the reference to the first publication. Republications after Behrens's death are also listed with the original publication.

Numbers in brackets at the right side of an entry refer to Hoeber's bibliography (see Hoeber 1913), preceded by a "B" if the reference is to the bibliography of writings by Behrens.

1. "Die Darmstädter Künstler-Colonie." Sp. no., *Deutsche Kunst und Dekoration,* 3, no. 8 (May 1900). Containing "Die Grundstein-Legung des Künstler-Hauses," 353–355, with an excerpt of the address of Peter Behrens to the Grossherzog on the occasion, 354. See also next item.

2. "Die Dekoration der Bühne." *Deutsche Kunst und Dekoration,* 3, no. 8 (May 1900), 401–405.   [B 1]

    Excerpt from p. 401 published in Bahr 1900, 50.

3. *Feste des Lebens und der Kunst: Eine Betrachtung des Theaters als höchsten Kultursymbols.* Leipzig: Diederichs, 1900. (Written June 1900.)   [B 2]

    Dehmel 1922–1923, letter 302 to Gustav Kühl (2 February 1901), transmits two publications by Behrens (*Feste des Lebens* and, probably, "Lebensmesse") "in denen Sie wol [*sic*] stellenweise meine Hinterhand entdecken werden," and expresses enthusiasm for Darmstadt and against Vienna and the "Insel-gigerln."

    Diederichs 1967, 113–114, reproduces a Behrens letter of 25 July 1900 soliciting Diederichs's publication of Behrens's essay.

    Simon 1976 quotes Behrens's essay favorably (55) and notes its reliance on Fuchs (69).

    Excerpted by Posener in Siepmann 1978, 47ff.

    Extensive excerpt reprinted in Brauneck 1982, 46–50.

4. "Die dekorative Bühne: Gedanken und Vorschläge, die Dekoration der Bühne betreffend." *Darmstädter Bühne,* 2, no. 3 (23 September 1900), 1.

5. "Über Ausstellungen." *Rheinlande,* 1, no. 1 (October 1900), 33–34.

6. "Die 'Lebensmesse' von Richard Dehmel als festliches Spiel." *Rheinlande,* 1, no. 4 (January 1901), 28–40.   [B 3]

    Dehmel 1922–1923, letter 304 to Dr. R. de Campagnolle (27 February 1901), gives his account of "Lebensmesse," ending: "Denn die Bearbeitung von Behrens beruht auf meinen eigenen Angaben, ich hatte wirklich ein Drama einfachsten Stils vor Augen."

7. *Haus Peter Behrens; Provisorische Ausgabe vom 15 Mai 1901.* n.p. [Darmstadt], May 1901. Design of cover and book ornaments by Behrens.

    Illustrated in Buddensieg in Nürnberg 1980, 49, cat. 37.

8. *Haus Peter Behrens.* n.p., n.d. [Darmstadt, May 1901].   [B 4]

    Grautoff 1901 reprints a facsimile of two parts of the text, with the signet of the Rudhard'sche Giesserei, as an exemplar of Behrens-Schrift. Part one is the first half of "Einleitende Bemerkungen" as published in Buddensieg et al. 1979, D274; part two is from a descriptive text (the first half of the excerpt published in Fred 1901b).

An excerpt of the descriptive text, in English, published in Fred 1901b, 29–30.

"Einleitende Bemerkungen" reprinted in Buddensieg et al. 1979, D274, and as "The Peter Behrens House: Introductory Comments" in the English translation of Buddensieg, 207.

An abbreviated but better translation is in Neumeyer 1991, 146.

Illustrated in Buddensieg in Nürnberg 1980, 49, cat. 38.

9. "Vorrede." In *Das Zeichen: Festliche Handlung von Peter Behrens, Willem de Haan und Georg Fuchs.* n.p., n.d. [Darmstadt, 1901].

10. [Behrens's celebratory address (Festschrift) to Ernst Ludwig, Grand Duke of Hesse]. In [Darmstadt, Künstler-Kolonie], *Ein Dokument deutscher Kunst: Die Ausstellung der Künstler-Kolonie in Darmstadt. Zur Feier der Eröffnung 15. Mai 1901,* 7–13. Offenbach: Rudhard'sche Giesserei, [1901]. (Sixteen pages in Behrens-Schrift; sparing use of Behrens's ornament.) Reprint, Darmstadt: Roether, 1976.

    10a. Also published in [Darmstadt, Künstler-Kolonie], *Ein Dokument deutscher Kunst: Die Ausstellung der Künstler-Kolonie in Darmstadt—1901. Festschrift,* ed. [Peter Behrens?], 5–12. Munich: F. Bruckmann, [1901]. [B 5]

11. "Von der Entwicklung der Schrift!" In Rudhard'sche Giesserei, *Behrens: Schriften, Initialen und Schmuck nach Zeichnungen von Professor Behrens.* Offenbach: Rudhard'sche Giesserei, [n.d.; Behrens's text dated October 1902]. [B 6]

    11a. Behrens's essay republished in *Archiv für Buchgewerbe,* 40 (December 1903), 475–477. Translated in Burke 1992, appendix A, 34–36.

Title page of Behrens's essay and following page, 4–5, illustrated in Schauer 1963, 2: pl. 6.

12. Letter to Hermann Muthesius, from Darmstadt, 23 January 1903. In Siepmann 1978, 397, 402–405.

13. [Lecture, Grosse Saale des Kunstvereins, Bremen, 18 April 1903. See no. 15 below.]

14. [Behrens's introduction to his garden and nature theater]. In *Internationale Kunst- und grosse Gartenbauausstellung Düsseldorf 1904: Offizieller Führer.* Düsseldorf, 1904.

Fragments quoted in Max Osborn, "Die Düsseldorfer Ausstellung," *Kunst und Künstler,* 2, no. 12 (August-September 1904), 501–502. [46]

15. *Alkohol und Kunst.* Flensburg: Verlag von Deutschlands Grosslage II des I.O.G.T., 1905.

A lecture given at the IX. Internationalen Kongress gegen den Alkoholismus, Grosse Saale des Kunstvereins, Bremen, 18 April 1903 (see no. 13 above).

16. "Die Tapete in der modernen Zimmerausstattung." *Die Tapete,* 2 (2 April 1905), 3–5. [B 7]

17. "Architekt und Künstler." Lecture given in Oldenburg in 1905. Excerpt published in Otto Krebs, "Die architektonische Anlage der Nordwestdeutschen Kunstausstellung in Oldenburg," *Dekorative Kunst,* 9, no. 2 (November 1905), 88.

18. [Behrens's description of his design for a summer house, 1903–1904]. In Erich Haenel and Heinrich Tscharmann, *Das Einzelwohnhaus der Neuzeit,* 106–109. Leipzig: J. J. Weber, 1906. [54]

19. "Von der Weiterentwicklung der Kunstgewerbeschule zu Düsseldorf und der Angliederung von Baugewerbeklassen." Düsseldorf, 1906. Hauptstaatsarchiv Reg. Düsseldorf 11688.

Extensive quotations in Busch 1993, 19ff.

20. "Kunstschulen [a commentary on schools of applied arts]." In Karl Scheffler, *Kunst und Künstler,* 5, no. 5 (February 1907), 207. [B 8]

21. [A commentary on modern theater]. In Karl Scheffler, *Kunst und Künstler*, 5, no. 6 (March 1907), 236–237. [B 8a]

22. "Mein Sondergarten." *Offizielle Ausstellungszeitung der Internationalen Kunst- und Gartenbau-ausstellung: Mannheim 1907* (1 May 1907), 5–7. [B 9]

23. "Kunst in der Technik." *Berliner Tageblatt* (29 August 1907, Abendausgabe).

   Reprinted in Buddensieg et al. 1979, D274–275, and as "Art in Technology" in the English translation of Buddensieg, 207–208.

24. "Die Gartenstadtbewegung." *Berliner Tageblatt*, 37, no. 156 (5 March 1908, Abendausgabe). [B 10]

   Partial quotation in Müller 1974, 45.

25. "Die Gartenstadtbewegung." *Gartenstadt*, 2 (1908), 27.

   Reprinted in Posener 1979, 364–365.

26. "Was ist monumentale Kunst?" Lecture given in Hamburg on 8 April 1908. Partially published in Anton Lindner, "Peter Behrens in Hamburg," *Neue Hamburger Zeitung* (9 April 1908). [73]

27. "Was ist monumentale Kunst?" *Kunstgewerbeblatt*, n.s. 20, no. 3 (December 1908), 46, 48. [B 11]

   27a. Most fully published in *Weserzeitung* (15 December 1908).

   Commentary in Aschenbeck 1990.

28. "Kunst und Technik." *Berliner Tageblatt*, Beilage *Zeitgeist*, no. 4 (25 January 1909). "Important passages" of a speech in the AEG lecture room, 13 January 1909. For fuller development, see no. 34 below.

29. "Alfred Messel: Ein Nachruf." *Frankfurter Zeitung*, 53, no. 96 (6 April 1909, Morgenblatt), 1–2. [B 12]

30. "Die Zukunft unserer Kultur." *Frankfurter Zeitung*, 53, no. 103 (14 April 1909, Morgenblatt), 1–2. [B 13]

   Translated by Donald F. Friedman as "The Future of Our Culture," in Dal Co 1990, 303–305.

31. "Prof. Peter Behrens über Aesthetik in der Industrie." *AEG-Zeitung*, 11, no. 12 (June 1909), 5–7. [B 14]

   Reprinted in Buddensieg et al. 1979, D275–277, and as "Prof. Peter Behrens on Aesthetics in Industry" in the English translation of Buddensieg, 208–209.

   Commentary in Schwartz 1996, 69.

32. [Behrens's commentary on the Turbine Factory]. In "Die Turbinenhalle der A.E.G. zu Berlin." *Deutsche Techniker-Zeitung*, 27, no. 6 (12 February 1910), 87–90. [104]

   32a. With slight variations as "Neuzeitliche Industriebauten: 1. Die Turbinenhalle der Allgemeinen Elektrizitätsgesellschaft zu Berlin." In Düsseldorf, Rheinischer Verein für Denkmalpflege und Heimatschutz, *Mitteilungen*, 4, no. 1 (1 March 1910), 26–29. [B 15]

   This version reprinted in Buddensieg et al. 1979, D277–278, and as "The Turbine Hall of the Allgemeine Elektrizitätsgesellschaft zu Berlin, Designed and Described by Professor Peter Behrens, Neu-Babelsberg" in the English translation of Buddensieg, 210–211 (misdated to 1920).

   See also no. 58 below.

33. "Über die Kunst auf der Bühne." *Frankfurter Zeitung,* 54, no. 78 (20 March 1910, Morgenblatt), 1–3. [B 16]

Translated by Howard Fitzpatrick as "On the Art of the Stage," *Perspecta,* no. 26 (1990), 137–142, with an introduction by Stanford Anderson, 135–136.

34. "Kunst und Technik." *Elektrotechnische Zeitschrift,* 31, no. 22 (2 June 1910), 552–555. A lecture at the 18th annual convention of the Verband deutscher Elektrotechniker in Braunschweig, 26 May 1910; a fuller paper than no. 28 above.

34a. Also published as: "Bericht über die Jahresversammlung des Verbandes deutscher Elektrotechnischer am 26. und 27. Mai 1910 in Braunschweig." *Elektrotechnische Zeitschrift,* 31, nos. 27–32 (1910), Anlage A, 8 pp. [B 18']

34b. As "Kunst und Technik." *Der Industriebau,* 1, no. 8 (15 August 1910), 176–180, and 9 (15 September 1910), Beilage, lxxxi–lxxxv. [B 18]

Reprinted in Buddensieg et al. 1979, D278–285, and as "Art and Technology" in the English translation of Buddensieg, 212–219.

Italian translation as "Arte e tecnica," in Maldonado 1979, 115–130.

Commentary in Schwartz 1996, 18–24, 204.

35. "Peter Behrens' Ausstellungsbauten." *Zement und Beton,* 9, no. 31 (29 July 1910), 471–474. [B 17]

36. [A commentary on a new classical art; response to Ernst von Halle and Hermann Muthesius, "Die Stellung der Kunst in der Volkswirtschaft."] *Volkswirtschaftliche Blätter,* 9 (27 August 1910), 265–266. [B 19]

37. "Kunst und Technik." *Deutsche Wirtschafts-Zeitung,* 5, no. 20 (15 October 1910), cols. 919–932. [B 18']

Minor variations from no. 34 (and 34a–b) above.

38. [A commentary on the Gesellenhaus in Neuss]. In [Johannes Geller], *Festschrift zur Einweihung des katholischen Gesellenhaus zu Neuss.* Neuss, 1910. [137]

Extensive quotation in Siepe 1961, 9–10.

39. "Kunst und Technik." *Werkkunst,* 6 (1910–1911), no. 15, 124–125; no. 17, 131–133.

40. [Anonymous report on Behrens's lecture "Kunst und Technik" under the title] "Berichte über Versammlungen und Besichtigungen: Verein für deutsches Kunstgewerbe Berlin." *Deutsche Bauzeitung,* 45, no. 40 (20 May 1911), 346.

41. "Der moderne Garten." *Berliner Tageblatt,* 40, no. 291 (10 June 1911, Abendausgabe). [B 20]

Reprinted as *Peter Behrens. Der moderne Garten: 1911.* Berlin: Pückler Gesellschaft, Jahresgabe, 1981.

42. "Kunst und Technik." *Innendekoration,* 22 (July 1911), 294. [B 21]

Also a separate short quotation from Behrens: "Auf dem Weltmarkte können wir durch technische Leistungen allein keine führende Rolle auf die Dauer spielen, sondern nur durch ästhetische Leistungen."

43. "Kunst und Technik." *Deutsche Kunst und Dekoration,* 14 (1911), 264.

44. "Die Zukunft unserer Kultur" and "Kunst und Technik." *Mitteilungen des Verbandes technisch-wissenschaftlicher Vereine zu Magdeburg,* no. 7 (17 September 1911), 55–60. [B 18']

45. [A commentary on German script]. In "Den Gegnern der deutschen Schrift eine deutsche Antwort." Ed. Friedrich Seesselberg, *Werdandi,* 4, no. 1 (1911), 8.

46. "Ästhetik in Industriebau." *Neudeutsche Bauzeitung,* 8 (1912), 369.

47. [A commentary on the development of Berlin's urban form]. In *Berliner Morgenpost* (27
    November 1912). [B 22]

    See also no. 49 below.

48. [An address at the dedication of the main office building of Mannesmann]. In Düsseldorf,
    Mannesmannröhren-Werke, *Zur Erinnerung an die Einweihung des Verwaltungsgebäudes
    der Mannesmannröhren-Werke in Düsseldorf. 10. Dezember 1912,* 70–85. [Düsseldorf:
    Mannesmann, 1913].

    Partially reprinted in Buddensieg et al. 1979, D286, and as "Conclusion of Speech at
    Opening of New AEG [*sic*] Administration Building, Mannesmannröhren-Werke,
    Düsseldorf, 10 December 1912" in the English translation of Buddensieg, 220.

    See also no. 100 below.

    Critical comments noted by General Director Nikolaus Eich and referenced in Jefferies 1995,
    136.

49. "Berlins dritte Dimension: Zustimmung der Städtebauer." In *Berlins dritte Dimension: Offener
    Brief an Herrn Oberbürgermeister Wermuth,* 9–11. Berlin, 1913.

    Republication of no. 47 above.

50. "The Aesthetics of Industrial Buildings: Beauty in Perfect Adaptation to Useful Ends." *Scientific
    American Supplement,* 76 (23 August 1913), 120–121.

51. [Paul Zucker's report on Behrens's lecture "Prinzipien der architektonischen Schöpfung" under
    the title] "Vom I. Kongress für Ästhetik und Kunstwissenschaft zu Berlin vom 5.–7.
    Oktober 1913." *Deutsche Bauzeitung,* 47, no. 87 (29 October 1913), 796.

52. "Über den Zusammenhang des baukünstlerischen Schaffens mit der Technik." In Berlin,
    Kongress für Ästhetik und allgemeine Kunstwissenschaft, 7.–9. Okt. 1913, *Bericht,*
    251–265. Stuttgart: Enke, 1914.

    Repeats much of no. 34 above; includes critical responses.

    52a. Republished with slight variants as "Die Zusammenhänge zwischen Kunst und
    Technik." *Dokumente des Fortschritts,* 7 (March 1914), 134–141.

    52b. Republished with yet other slight variants in *Kunstwart und Kulturwart,* 27, no. 16
    (1914), 216–223.

    Discussed in M. Borissavliévitch, *Les théories de l'architecture: Essai critique sur les principales
    doctrines relatives a l'esthétique de l'architecture,* 20–21. [1926]; Paris: Payot, 1951.

    Commentary in Schwartz 1996, 205–208.

53. [A contribution, at the request of the young Le Corbusier, in defense of the Nouvelle Section de
    l'Ecole d'Art, La Chaux-de-Fonds]. In *Un mouvement d'art à La Chaux-de-Fonds—à propos
    de la Nouvelle Section de l'Ecole d'Art, La Chaux-de-Fonds.* Ed. Charles-Edouard Jeanneret.
    La Chaux-de-Fonds, n.d. [1914].

54. "Vom Rhythmus unserer Zeit." *Innendekoration,* 25 (1914), 472.

55. "Einfluss von Zeit- und Raumausnutzung auf moderne Formentwicklung." In Deutscher
    Werkbund, *Jahrbuch 1914,* 7–10. Jena: Diederichs, 1914.

    Reprinted in Fritz Schumacher, *Lesebuch für Baumeister,* 397–401. Berlin: Henssel, 1941.

    Also in Sabais 1956, 332–336; Posener 1979, 236–237.

    Excerpted in German, and in English as "Rhythm, Arrangement, and Town Planning," in

"Impetus and Departure: Façades of the Modern Movement." *Daidalos,* no. 6 (15 December 1982), 80–81.

Quoted in Kerp, *Westdeutsche Impuls* (Cologne, 1984), 57.

Referenced and quoted in Hüter 1988, 324, 326; Schwartz 1996, 208–209.

56. [A statement made after the confrontation between Hermann Muthesius and Henry van de Velde at the Deutscher Werkbund convention in Cologne, 1914]. In Hermann Muthesius, *Die Werkbund-Arbeit der Zukunft und Aussprache darüber. . . ,* 56–57. Jena: Diederichs, 1914.

56a. Also published in Platz 1927, 96–97; Posener 1964, 208.

Commentary in Platz 1933, 29–30; Shand 1934, 83, 85.

57. [Behrens as a signatory]. "An die Kulturwelt: Manifesto of the 93 German Intellectuals [1914]." In Ralph Haswell Lutz, ed., *Fall of the German Empire 1914–1918,* 1:74–75. Hoover War Library Publications, no. 1. Palo Alto: Stanford University Press, 1932.

58. *Über die Beziehungen der künstlerischen und technischen Probleme.* Technische Abende im Zentralinstitut für Erziehung und Unterricht, no. 5. Berlin: Mittler u. Sohn, 1917.

Reprints the text of no. 32a above, but with an altered description of the front of the Turbine Hall added as a footnote.

Republished in shorter version and with variants; see no. 77 below.

Partially reprinted in Kaiserslautern 1966, 9.

One of three Behrens writings cited in Behne 1926.

59. [Unattributed text, but by Behrens]. Deutscher Werkbund. *Deutscher Werkbund Ausstellung auf dem Kirchenfeldplatz: Bern 1917.* n.p., [1917].

Two fragments reprinted in Lotz 1932, 301.

59a. Same text, attributed to Behrens: "Einleitende Worte zur Ausstellung des Deutschen Werkbundes in Bern 1917." *Wieland,* 3, no. 7 (October 1917), cover and 2–7.

Buddensieg in Buderath 1990, 61, illustrates the *Wieland* cover (a crude drawing which Buddensieg shows was drawn over a photograph and convincingly attributes to Behrens).

60. [German art in Switzerland]. *Berliner Tageblatt* (8 July 1917).

61. "Neue Ziele der Baukunst." *Zentralblatt für das deutsche Baugewerbe,* 16, nos. 51–52 (21 December 1917), 497.

62. [Coauthor with] H[einrich] de Fries. *Vom sparsamen Bauen: Ein Beitrag zur Siedlungsfrage.* Berlin: Bauwelt, 1918.

Review or commentary: Weishaupt 1919 (detailed critique; for Behrens's response, see no. 72 below); Platz 1933, 101; Shand 1934, 86; Göldner 1955, 308; Buddensieg in Buderath 1990, 61; Neumeyer 1991, 141, 143.

63. [Berlin dwellings]. *Berliner Tageblatt* (2 August 1918).

64. "Neuzeitliche Forderungen bei der Errichtung von Bürohausbauten." [In unknown journal, not earlier than 1917; probably 1918–1920], 11–16. (The subject is Behrens's Mannesmann building. Known from a clipping in the Pfalzgalerie, Kaiserslautern, Mappe E1/1/EZ VI/1, but without source information. Suggested dates are from internal evidence in a footnote in a nonrelated article.)

65. *Die Kunststadt Potsdam: Ein Vorschlag.* n.p. [dated Neubabelsberg 10 May 1919].

66. [Behrens as a signatory (and author?)]. "Deutsche Architekten! [a proclamation calling for united front of architects in difficult times]." *Die Bauwelt,* 10, no. 23 (5 June 1919), 5–6.

In the following issue, from the same source: "Ziele und Aufgaben der deutschen Architekten."

Commentary in Pehnt 1973, 34.

67. [Development of Berlin]. *Berliner Tageblatt* (8 June 1919).

68. [On veterans' housing in the postwar period]. *Vorstand* (20 June 1919), 4, 6.

69. "Wiederaufbau der deutschen Baukunst." *Westdeutsche Wochenschrift für Politik,* 1, no. 13 (1919), 214–218.

70. "Reform der künstlerischen Erziehung." In Berlin, Zentrale für Heimatdienst, *Der Geist der neuen Volksgemeinschaft: Denkschrift für das deutschen Volk,* 93–106. Berlin: S. Fischer, 1919.

71. "Der Fabrikneubau." *Das Echo: Deutsche Export Revue,* no. 1936 (16 October 1919), 1294–1299. (Illustrated with Behrens's industrial buildings.)

   Largely repeated in a wider context in no. 109 below.

   Two paragraphs on workers' housing, not repeated in 1929, are reprinted in Buddensieg et al. 1979, D286, and as "The New Factory Architecture" in the English translation of Buddensieg, 221.

72. "Das Wesen der neuen 'Gruppenbauweise'." *Deutsche Bauzeitung,* 53, nos. 103–104 (24 December 1919), 620–624.

   See no. 62 above.

73. "Die Gruppenbauweise." *Wasmuth's Monatshefte für Baukunst,* 4 (1919–1920), 122–127.

74. "Etagenhaus und Kleinsiedlung." *Hamburger Kalendar,* 1 (1920), 132–138.

   Quoted in Pommer and Otto 1991, 240–241 n. 36.

75. "Das Ethos und die Umlagerung der künstlerischen Probleme." In *Der Leuchter: Weltanschauung und Lebensgestaltung. Jahrbuch der Schule der Weisheit,* ed. Graf Hermann Keyserling, 315–340. Darmstadt: O. Reichl, 1920 [on title page, but © 1921].

   No. 90 below is based on this article.

   A passage from pp. 324ff. is reprinted in Buddensieg et al. 1979, D287–288, and as "The Ethos and the Realignment of Artistic Problems" in the English translation of Buddensieg, 222–223.

   One of three Behrens writings cited in Behne 1926.

   Quoted in Buddensieg 1975, 290 n. 32.

   "Perhaps the most important literary work of Behrens" (Buddensieg in Buderath 1990, 64).

   Noted by Neumeyer in Buddensieg 1987b, 46.

76. "Doppelgärtenhäuser." *Die Volkswohnung: Zeitschrift für Wohnungsbau und Siedlungswesen,* 2, no. 2 (24 January 1920), 23–28.

77. "Über die Beziehungen der künstlerischen und technischen Probleme." In "Woningbouwnummer." *Wendingen,* 3 (March-April 1920), 4–21.

   See no. 58 above.

   Extensive quotation in Posener 1979, 567, 599–600.

78. [On *Wohnkultur*]. *Leipziger Mustermesse,* 4 (1920), 331.

79. "Werbende künstlerische Werte im Fabrikbau." *Das Plakat,* 11, no. 6 (June 1920), 269–273.

   Apart from the conclusion, similar to no. 71 above and no. 99 below.

   The conclusion is reprinted in Buddensieg et al. 1979, D287, and as "Artistic Values in

Factory Building and Their Effect as Publicity" in the English translation of Buddensieg, 221.

One of three Behrens writings cited in Behne 1926. (Passages are translated in the English translation of Behne, 107–108.)

80. "Bund der Erneuerung." *Die neue Rundschau,* 31, no. 9 (September 1920), 1051–1055. (Reports the founding, 16 June 1920, of an organization to realize the ideas of Karl Scheffler in his programmatic text "Sittliche Diktatur." Motto: "Vom Opfer zum Werk, vom Werk zur Gemeinschaft." Calls for refusal of all imported luxury goods; also living the simple life even in relation to local production.)

Excerpted in *Frankfurter Zeitung* (13 September 1920).

Reprinted as "Erneuerung," in [Ulrich Conrads, ed.], "Tendenzen der Zwanziger Jahre," *Bauwelt* (1977), 1080–1081.

81. [On *Siedlungen*]. *Berliner Tageblatt* (25 December 1920).

82. "Waldsiedlung Berlin-Lichtenberg." *Wasmuths Monatshefte für Baukunst,* 5 (1920–1921), 320–330.

83. "Karl Ernst Osthaus: Worte zu seinem Werk." *Frankfurter Zeitung,* no. 285 (19 April 1921, 1. Morgenblatt), 1–2.

Reprinted in Hesse-Frielinghaus 1966, 22–23.

84. "Ein norddeutscher Backsteinbau auf der Münchener Gewerbeschau." *Bau-Rundschau,* no. 20 (1921).

Quoted in Buddensieg in Buderath 1990, 185 n. 52.

85. "Arbeiten von Hugo Gorge—Wien." *Innendekoration,* 32 (September 1921), 260–265, illustrations to 286.

86. [On Behrens's Reklameburg]. *Leipziger Mustermesse,* 5 (1921), 291.

87. [On Behrens's Dombauhütte, Munich]. *Berliner Tageblatt* (11 January 1922).

88. "Zur Frage des Hochhauses." *Stadtbaukunst alter und neuer Zeit,* 2, no. 24 (15 March 1922), 369–371.

89. "Qualitätsarbeit." *Deutsche Zeitung für Spanien,* 7 (1922), no. 148, 2–3, and no. 149, 2–3.

90. "Stil?" *Die Form,* no. 1 (1922), 5ff.

Reprinted in Munich, Die Neue Sammlung, *Zwischen Kunst und Industrie* (1975), 181–184.

91. "Die neue Handwerks-Romantik." *Innendekoration,* 33, no. 10 (October 1922), 341.

92. [Two paragraphs from an address to the Versammlung Rheinischer Handwerkskammern, 1922]. In Lotz 1932, 302, 313.

93. "Von italienischen Gärten." *Gartenschönheit,* 3, no. 11 (November 1922), 250–252.

94. "Die Dombauhütte: Aus der Eröffnungsrede von Peter Behrens." *Deutsche Kunst und Dekoration,* 26 (January 1923), 220–230.

95. "A Letter from Austria." *Architecture* (London, July 1923), 454–459.

96. "Über neue Ziele." Reported by E. R. in *Hellweg,* 4 (1924), 872.

97. "The Work of Joseph Hoffmann." *Society of Architects Journal,* 5th ser., 2 (1924), 589–599.

98. "The Work of Joseph Hoffmann." *American Institute of Architects Journal,* 12 (October 1924), 421–426.

99. "Industriebau und Stadtgestaltung." *Der Neubau,* 7, no. 8 (24 April 1925), 97–102. (Projects from Behrens's Vienna *Meisterschule* are illustrated throughout and discussed on pp. 101–102, including designs by Alexander Popp, Hans Schreiner, and Georg Neidhardt.)

A passage (p. 100) on dramatic potentials of new techniques is reprinted in Buddensieg et al. 1979, D288–289, and as "Industrial Architecture and Urban Design" in the English translation of Buddensieg, 224.

100. "Administration Buildings for Industrial Plants." *American Architect,* 128 (26 August 1925), 167–174.

Translation of part of Behrens's address at the dedication of the Mannesmann building, 1912 (see no. 48 above).

101. "Seeking Aesthetic Worth in Industrial Buildings." *American Architect,* 128 (5 December 1925), 475–479.

102. [Coauthor with] Paul Bonatz, Karl Elkhart, Ludwig Hoffmann, Fritz Schumacher, and Hans Winterstein. "Zum Wettbewerb für einen Bebauungsplan des Messegeländes in Berlin." *Bauwelt,* 17, no. 4 (1926), 82–83.

102a. Text is identical to idem, "Zum Wettbewerb für den Bebauungsplan des Messe- und Ausstellungsgeländes in Berlin: Antwort der Technischen Preisrichter auf den 'Offenen Brief' Dr. Heiligenthals." *Der Städtebau,* 21 (1926), 21–23.

103. "Etagenhaus und Kleinsiedlung." *Blätter des Deutschen Roten Kreuzes,* nos. 8–9 (1926), 34–41. See also no. 74 above.

Kirsch 1987, 184, quotes Behrens's letter to Mies, 6 October 1926, Vienna, sending a copy of this article and soliciting an invitation to participate in the Weissenhof exhibition, Stuttgart (Mies van der Rohe Archiv).

104. "Terrassen am Hause." In Deutscher Werkbund, *Bau und Wohnung,* 16–25. Stuttgart: Fr. Wedekind, 1927.

Facsimile reprint, Stuttgart: K. Krämer, 1992.

Text excerpted in Stuttgart, *info bau 1987,* 17, and in both German and English in Joedicke 1989, 33.

105. "Zum Problem der technischen und tektonischen Beziehungen." *Das deutsche Bauwesen,* 3 (1927), 73ff.

Reprinted under same title (the 1927 Schinkel-Festrede of the Architekten-Verein zu Berlin) in Julius Posener, ed., *Festreden: Schinkel zu Ehren 1846–1980,* 281–290. Berlin: Architekten- und Ingenieur-Verein zu Berlin, 1981.

106. "Die Gemeinde Wien als Bauherrin." *Bauwelt,* 19, no. 41 (11 October 1928), 976–980.

107. "Joseph Hoffmann." In *Die Wiener Werkstätte 1903–1928.* Vienna, 1929.

Translated in Sekler 1985, 495–496.

108. "Verwaltungsgebäude des Konsumverein-Verbandes in Moskau [Zentrosojus]." *Die Baugilde,* 11, no. 9 (May 1929), 679–682.

109. "Zur Ästhetik des Fabrikbaus." *Gewerbefleiss,* 108, nos. 7–9 (July-September 1929), 125–130.

Partially reprinted in Buddensieg et al. 1979, D289–291, and as "On the Aesthetics of Factory Design" in the English translation of Buddensieg, 225–227.

110. "Zur Erziehung des baukünstlerischen Nachwuchses"/"The Education of the Rising Generation of Architects." In Karl Maria Grimme, ed., *Peter Behrens and His Academic Master-School, Vienna,* 9–16. Vienna: A. Luser, 1930. Text in German and English, translation by Louis H. Paulovsky.

111. "Neue Sachlichkeit in der Gartenformung." *Jahrbuch der Arbeitsgemeinschaft für deutsche Gartenkultur,* 1 (1930), [15]–19.

Partially reprinted in Ammann 1940, 302–303.

112. [An appreciation of Josef Hoffmann]. In "Josef Hoffmann zum sechzigsten Geburtstage." Sp. no., *Almanach der Dame* (Vienna, 15 December 1930), ed. Österreichischer Werkbund, 8–10.

113. "Die neuen Hochhäuser am Alexanderplatz in Berlin." *Der Bauingenieur,* 13, nos. 1–2 (1 January 1932), 10–12.

114. "Haus, in dem das Glück wohnt." *Berliner Lokal-Anzeiger* (1 January 1932), 4. Beiblatt.

115. [Excerpts from a lecture to the Versammlung Rheinischer Handwerkskammern 1922]. In Wilhelm Lotz, "Aus der Werkbund-Entwicklung: Arbeiten und Gedanken aus den ersten zwanzig Jahren." *Die Form,* 7, no. 10 (1932), 302, 313.

Excerpts reprinted in Hans Eckstein, ed., *50 Jahre Deutscher Werkbund,* 38, 43–44. Frankfurt: Metzner, 1958.

116. "Zeitloses und Zeitbewegtes." *Zentralblatt der Bauverwaltung,* 52, no. 31 (20 July 1932), 361–365. (Lecture at Prussian Akademie des Bauwesens, Berlin, 22 March 1932, centenary of the death of Goethe.)

A report on the lecture, with citations, in Riedrich 1932, 765–780.

A later lecture of the same title fully published; see no. 118 below.

117. "Ein Landhaus in Schlachtensee." *die neue linie* (November 1932), 16ff.

118. "Zeitloses und Zeitbewegtes." In "Zehn Jahre Architektur um Prof. Behrens." Sp. no., *Österreichische Kunst,* 3, no. 11 (November 1932), 5–10. (Lecture given in the Vienna Secession on the day prior to the opening of the exhibition "Zehn Jahre Architektur um Prof. Behrens.") Also, p. 35, Behrens's response to a question set by Else Hofmann on his experience of the atmosphere of Austrian art.

Commentary: W. D., "'Zeitloses und Zeitbewegtes': Vortrag von Peter Behrens in der Sezession." *Neue Freie Presse* (6 November 1932).

119. "Kunsterziehung der Deutschen." *Rheinisch-Westfälische Zeitung* (25 October 1933), 1ff.

120. "Die Baugesinnung des Faschismus." *die neue linie,* 5, no. 3 (November 1933), 11–13.

121. Vienna, Akademie der bildenden Künste. *Die Akademie der bildenden Künste. Neue Aufgaben und Ziele. Ansprache gehalten in der Aula der Akademie von Rektor Prof. Dr. Peter Behrens am 16. Dezember 1933.* Vienna: Schülerarbeit der Graphischen Lehr- und Versuchsanstalt, 1934.

122. "Das echte Handwerk." *Deutsche Zukunft* (22 July 1934), 15.

123. *Rede am Grabe Anton Hanaks.* Vienna, 1934. 6 pp.

124. "Ein Hof vor der Stadt." *Die Dame,* no. 10 (1936), 10–11, 50.

125. "Neue italienische Bauten." *die neue linie,* 9, no. 5 (January 1938), 36–38.

126. [A commentary on the relation of architecture and lettering]. In Georg Scheja and Eberhard Hölscher, *Die Schrift in der Baukunst,* 35. Berlin: Heintze und Blanckertz, [1938]. Translated in Burke 1992, appendix B, 36–37.

3 Selected Writings on Peter Behrens

Entries that begin in **boldface** are monographs, exhibition catalogs, and monographic issues of journals devoted to the work of Peter Behrens. The entries for each author are arranged in chronological order, as are the anonymous articles. Numbers in brackets at the right side of an entry refer to Hoeber's bibliography (see Hoeber 1913).

Ahlers-Hestermann, Friedrich. *Stilwende: Aufbruch der Jugend um 1900*. 1941; 2d ed. Berlin: Gebr. Mann, 1956.

Ammann, Gustav. "Nochmals Peter Behrens." *Werk,* 27 (1940), 302–303.

Anderson, Stanford. "Peter Behrens and the New Architecture of Germany, 1900–1917." Ph.D. diss., Columbia University, 1968.

> Five chapters and part of a sixth chapter of the dissertation appeared in the following journals:

> "Peter Behrens' Changing Concept of Life as Art." *Architectural Design,* 39 (February 1969), 72–78.

> "Modern Architecture and Industry: Peter Behrens and the Cultural Policy of Historical Determinism." *Oppositions,* no. 11 (Winter 1977), 52–71.

> "Modern Architecture and Industry: Peter Behrens, the AEG, and Industrial Design." *Oppositions,* no. 21 (Summer 1980), 78–97.

> "Modern Architecture and Industry: Peter Behrens and the AEG Factories." *Oppositions,* no. 23 (Winter 1981), 52–83.

> "Peter Behrens's Highest *Kultursymbol,* the Theater." *Perspecta,* no. 26 (1990), 103–134.

> "Peter Behrens' Engagement with Kunstwissenschaft: The Mannheim International Art Exhibition of 1907." Introductory essay to Kurt Asche, *Peter Behrens und die Oldenburger Ausstellung 1905: Entwürfe—Bauten—Gebrauchsgraphik* (Berlin: Gebr. Mann, 1992), 13–17, 323–324.

Anderson, Stanford. "The Legacy of German Neo-Classicism and Biedermeier: Behrens, Loos, Mies, and Tessenow." *Assemblage,* no. 15 (October 1991), 62–87.

Anderson, Stanford [1991b]. "Technology and Architecture: Three Historical Lessons." In Spiro Pollalis, ed., *Architecture: Design Implementation,* 28–32. Washington, DC: ACSA, 1991.

Anderson, Stanford [1991c]. "Architecture in a Cultural Field." In Taisto Mäkelä, ed., *Wars of Classification,* 8–35. Princeton: Princeton Architectural Press, 1991.

Anderson, Stanford. "*Sachlichkeit* and Modernity, or Realist Architecture." In Harry Mallgrave, ed., *Otto Wagner: Reflections on the Raiment of Modernity,* 322–360. Santa Monica: Getty Center, 1993.

Anderson, Stanford [1993b]. "Deutscher Werkbund—the 1914 Debate: Hermann Muthesius versus Henry van de Velde." In B. Farmer and H. Louw, eds., *Companion to Contemporary Architectural Thought,* 462–467. London: Routledge, 1993.

Anderson, Stanford. "Peter Behrens, Friedrich Naumann, and the Werkbund: Ideology in Industriekultur." In Roberto Behar, ed., *The Architecture of Politics: 1910–1940,* 8–21. Miami Beach: Wolfsonian Foundation, 1995.

Anonymous:

"Die Darmstädter Künstler-Kolonie." *Kunstgewerbeblatt*, n.s. 12, no. 2 (November 1900), 21–33.

"The International Exhibition of Modern Decorative Art at Turin: The German Section." *Studio*, 27, no. 117 (December 1902), 187–197.   [41]

[Tennis courts for Frau Dr. Mertens, Potsdam]. *Dekorative Kunst*, 14, no. 12 (September 1911), 540–541.   [150]

[Graphic coverage of Schroeder and Cuno houses, Hagen]. *Die Architektur des XX. Jahrhunderts*, 11, no. 4 (1911), 39–40, pls. 76–79.   [154]

[Graphic coverage of Mannesmann building, Düsseldorf]. *Die Architektur des XX. Jahrhunderts*, 14, no. 1 (1914), 2, pls. 3, 4.

"Einige Neubauten von Professor Peter Behrens, Berlin." *Der Industriebau*, 6, no. 8 (15 August 1915), 396–399; no. 9 (15 September 1915), 411–412.

"Beschränkter Wettbewerb zur Erlangung eines Entwurfes für ein Verwaltungsgebäude des Stumm-Konzernes in Düsseldorf." *Deutsche Bauzeitung*, 56, no. 3 (11 January 1922), 17–20; no. 6 (21 January 1922), 33–34.

"Das neue Verwaltungsgebäude der Rheinische Stahlwerke AG in Duisburg-Ruhrort." *Deutsche Bauzeitung*, 56, no. 60 (29 July 1922), 360.

["Arbeitszimmer eines Gelehrten" by Behrens]. *Deutsche Kunst und Dekoration*, 27 (April 1924), 43.

[Haus der Moden, Frankfurt]. *Die Baugilde*, 8 (1926), 30.

"'New Ways': The House of W. J. Bassett-Lowke, Esq., Northampton." *Architectural Review*, 60 (November 1926), 175–179 and pls.

"Wettbewerb August Thyssen-Haus, Düsseldorf." *Die Baugilde*, 10 (10 July 1928), 973–980, 1052f.

[Drawing for Benedictine cloister of Saint Peter, Salzburg]. *Pencil Points*, 10 (January 1929), 32.

"Wettbewerb Reichstag Erweiterung." *Die Baugilde*, 11, no. 24 (25 December 1929), 1989–2000.

"Erweiterungsbau des Reichstagsgebäudes: 2. Engerer Wettbewerb." *Deutsche Bauzeitung*, 64, no. 4 (11 January 1930), Beilage "Wettbewerbe" W1, 1–8.

"Peter Behrens–Alexander Popp." *Die Bau- und Werkkunst*, 6 (September 1930), 273–289.

"Bildnachrichten: Neue und alte Geschäftshäuser." *Zentralblatt der Bauverwaltung*, 50 (17 September 1930), 660.

"An Exhibition of Architectural Projects." *Brooklyn Museum Quarterly*, 17 (1930), 102–109.

"Ein neues Hochhaus in Berlin: Architekt Peter Behrens." *Wasmuths Monatshefte für Baukunst*, 15, no. 7 (1931), 289–293.

"Deutsche Bauausstellung—Berlin 1931." *Die Bau- und Werkkunst*, 7 (1931), 221–236.

"Haus 'Ring der Frauen' auf der Deutschen Bauausstellung, Berlin 1931." *Die Baugilde*, 13, no. 13 (1931), 1085.

"A House in the Taunus near Frankfort, Germany." *American Architect*, 142 (August 1932), 61–64.

[A. Dürbeck?] "Technisches vom Bau der Hochhäuser am Alexanderplatz in Berlin." *Deutsche Bauzeitung*, 67, no. 18 (3 May 1933), 355–362.

"Austrian State Tobacco Factory, Linz: P. Behrens and A. Popp." *Architectural Forum*, 68 (March 1938), 192–199.

Asche, Kurt. "Peter Behrens and the Planning Grid." *Daidalos,* no. 6 (15 December 1982), 85–88.

Asche, Kurt. "Die einspringende Ecke und die negative Fuge: Zwei konstruktive Details bei Peter Behrens und Mies van der Rohe." *Bauwelt,* 77, no. 11 (14 March 1986), 363–365.

Asche, Kurt. *Jugendstil in Oldenburg.* Vol. 2. Oldenburg: Nordwest-Zeitung, 1988.

Asche, Kurt. *Peter Behrens und die Oldenburger Ausstellung 1905: Entwürfe—Bauten— Gebrauchsgraphik.* Berlin: Gebr. Mann, 1992.

Aschenbeck, Nils. "Monument und Bedeutung: Eine Untersuchung anhand ausgesuchter Werke von Peter Behrens und Walter Gropius." *Archithese,* 20, no. 4 (July-August 1990), 14–21, 45.

Bahr, Hermann. *Bildung: Essays von Hermann Bahr.* Berlin and Leipzig: Insel Verlag, 1900.

Baird, George. *The Space of Appearance.* Cambridge: MIT Press, 1995.

Banham, Reyner. *Theory and Design in the First Machine Age.* London: Architectural Press, 1960.

Behne, Adolf. "Peter Behrens und die toskanische Architektur des 12. Jahrhunderts." *Kunstgewerbeblatt,* n.s. 23, no. 3 (December 1911), 45, 48–50.

Behne, Adolf. "Romantiker, Pathetiker und Logiker im modernen Industriebau." *Preussische Jahrbücher,* 154, no. 1 (October 1913), 171–174.

Behne, Adolf. "Fabrikbau als Reklame." *Das Plakat,* 11, no. 6 (June 1920), 274–276.

Behne, Adolf. "Vom Anhalter Bahnhof bis zum Bauhaus." *Soziale Bauwirtschaft,* no. 12. [Berlin?]: Verband Sozialer Baubetriebe, 1922. Rpt. [ed. Ulrich Conrads] as "Berlin. Dokumente europäischen Bauens," *Bauwelt,* 52, nos. 41–42 (16 October 1961), 1161–1173.

Behne, Adolf. *Der moderne Zweckbau.* Munich: Drei Masken, 1926. Written in 1923. Rpt., Berlin: Ullstein, 1964. Trans. Michael Robinson as *The Modern Functional Building.* Santa Monica: Getty Research Institute, 1996.

Behrendt. "Eine Gedächtnisstätte für die Gefallenen des Weltkrieges: Zum Umbau der Neuen Wache in Berlin." *Zentralblatt der Bauverwaltung,* 50, no. 29 (23 July 1930), 513–518, pl. 29.

Behrendt, Walter Curt. "Die deutsche Botschaft in Petersburg." *Die Zukunft,* 21 (24 May 1913), 259–265.

Behrendt, Walter Curt. "Über die deutsche Baukunst der Gegenwart." *Kunst und Künstler,* 12 (February-April 1914), 263–276, 328–336, 373–383.

Behrendt, Walter Curt [1914b]. "Das Pathos des Monumentalen." *Deutsche Kunst und Dekoration,* 34 (June 1914), 219–221.

Behrendt, Walter Curt [1914c]. "Die Deutsche Werkbundausstellung in Köln." *Kunst und Künstler,* 12 (September 1914), 615–626.

Berckenhagen, Ekhart. "Entwürfe von Peter Behrens und Heinrich Tessenow zum Ehrenmal Unter den Linden in Berlin." *Jahrbuch der Stiftung Preussischer Kulturbesitz,* 15 (1978), 155–165.

Berckenhagen, Ekhart. *Architektenzeichnungen 1470–1979.* Berlin: Volker Spiess, 1979.

Berg, [Max]. "Der neue Geist im Städtebau auf der Grossen Berliner Kunstausstellung." *Stadtbaukunst,* 8 (20 June 1927), 41–50.

Berlin, Architekten- und Ingenieur-Verein. *Berlin und seine Bauten.* Berlin, 1964ff.

Berlin, Kartell der vereinigten Verbände bildender Künstler Berlins. *Grosse Berliner Kunstausstellung 1927.* Berlin: Diehl, 1927.

Berlin, Kommission für vorbildliche Arbeiterwohnungen im Gewerkschaftshause. *Das Arbeitermöbel: Zwei Typen nach Entwürfen von Prof. Peter Behrens und Hermann Münchhausen.* Berlin: Die Kommission . . . , 1912.   [156a]

Berlin, Technische Universität. *Berlin: Von der Residenzstadt zur Industriemetropole.* 3 vols. Berlin: Technische Universität Berlin, 1981.

Bernhard, Karl. "Die neue Halle der Turbinenfabrik der AEG in Berlin." *Zentralblatt der Bauverwaltung,* 30, no. 5 (15 January 1910), 25–29.

Bernhard, Karl. "Die neue Halle für die Turbinenfabrik der Allgemeinen Elektricitäts-Gesellschaft in Berlin." *Zeitschrift des Vereines deutscher Ingenieure,* 55 (30 September 1911), 1625–1631; (7 October 1911), 1673–1682.

Bernhard, Karl. "Der moderne Industriebau in technischer und ästhetischer Beziehung." *Zeitschrift des Vereines deutscher Ingenieure,* 56 (20 July 1912), 1141–1147; (27 July 1912), 1185–1190; (3 August 1912), 1227–1233.

Bernhard, Karl [1912b]. "Der Wettbewerb um den Entwurf einer Strassenbrücke über den Rhein bei Köln." *Zeitschrift des Vereines deutscher Ingenieure,* 56, no. 38 (21 September 1912), 1531–1535.

Bernhard, Karl. "Rückblick auf den Kölner Brückenstreit." *Zeitschrift des Vereines deutscher Ingenieure,* 58, no. 32 (8 August 1914), 1300–1302.

Bernhard, Otto. "Gartenkunst." *Kunstgewerbeblatt,* n.s. 17, no. 2 (November 1905), 25–40.

Bilancioni, Guglielmo. *Il primo Behrens: Origini del moderno in architettura.* Florence: Sansoni, 1981.

Blau, Eve. *The Architecture of Red Vienna, 1919–1934.* Cambridge: MIT Press, 1999.

Bletter, Rosemarie Haag. "The Interpretation of the Glass Dream—Expressionist Architecture and the History of the Crystal Metaphor." *Journal of the Society of Architectural Historians,* 40 (March 1981), 20–43.

Blunck, Erich. "Umgestaltung der Neuen Wache in Berlin." *Deutsche Bauzeitung,* 64, nos. 65–66 (13 August 1930), Beilage "Wettbewerbe" W12, 81–85.

Board, H. "Die Kunstgewerbeschule zu Düsseldorf." *Dekorative Kunst,* 7, no. 11 (August 1904), 409–432 plus color plates.   [43]

Boche, Jutta. "Theater und Jugendstil—Feste des Lebens und der Kunst." In G. Bott, ed., *Von Morris zum Bauhaus,* 143–158. Hanau: Peters, 1977.

Bohle-Heintzenberg, Sabine. *Architektur der Berliner Hoch- und Untergrundbahn.* Berlin: Arenhövel, 1980.

Borrmann, Norbert. *Paul Schultze-Naumburg, 1869–1949.* Essen: Bacht, 1989.

Bösselmann, W. "Neugestaltung des Alexanderplatzes in Berlin." *Zentralblatt der Bauverwaltung,* 53 (8 February 1933), 68–71.

Bott, Gerhard. *Jugendstil: Vom Beitrag Darmstadts zur internationalen Kunstbewegung um 1900.* Darmstadt: Roether, 1965.

Bott, Gerhard. "Darmstadt und die Mathildenhöhe." In Gerhard Wietek, ed., *Deutsche Künstlerkolonien und Künstlerorte,* 154–162. Munich: Thiemig, 1976.

Bott, Gerhard, ed. *Von Morris zum Bauhaus: Eine Kunst gegründet auf Einfachheit.* Hanau: Hans Peters, 1977.

Branchesi, Lida. "Peter Behrens (1868–1940)." Ph.D. diss., University of Rome, 1965.

Brauneck, Manfred. *Theater im 20. Jahrhundert: Programmschriften, Stilperioden, Reformmodelle.* Reinbek: Rowohlt, 1982.

Breuer, Robert. "Peter Behrens." *Die Werkkunst,* 3, no. 10 (9 February 1908), [145–149].   [71]

Breuer, Robert. "Kunst und Technik." *Reclams Universum,* 25, no. 46 (2–8 August 1909), [1108].
                                                                                                      [96]

Breuer, Robert. "Peter Behrens und die Elektrizität." *Deutsche Kunst und Dekoration,* 13, no. 10 (July 1910), 264–266.   [120]

Breuer, Robert. "Arbeiter-Möbel von Peter Behrens." *Deutsche Kunst und Dekoration,* 15, no. 8 (May 1912), 131–133.   [157]

Breuer, Robert [1912b]. "Das Kunsthandwerk in Hessen." *Deutsche Industrie: Deutsche Kultur,* 8, no. 13 (1912).   [161]

Breuer, Robert. "Das Haus Wiegand in Dahlem bei Berlin." *Innendekoration,* 24 (November 1913), 430–447, with ill. to 450.

Breuer, Robert [1913b]. "Die Beziehungen des Arbeiters zur bildenden Kunst." *Dokumente des Fortschritts,* 6 (March 1913), 201–205.

Breuer, Robert [1913c]. "Gutbürgerlich." *Deutsche Kunst und Dekoration,* 17 (1913), 73–90.

Breuer, Robert. "Haus Dr. Wiegand in Dahlem." *Deutsche Kunst und Dekoration,* 17, no. 8 (1914), 121–130.

Breuer, Robert. "Das Bootshaus der Rudergesellschaft 'Elektra'." *Wasmuths Monatshefte für Baukunst,* 2 (1915–1916), 220–230.

Breysig, Kurt. "Das Haus Peter Behrens: Mit einem Versuch über Kunst und Leben." *Deutsche Kunst und Dekoration,* 5, no. 4 (January 1902), [133–194], incl. 74 ills.   [36']

Bruckmann, Peter. "Der Deutsche Werkbund und seine Ausstellung in Köln." *März,* 8 (2 May 1914), 620–629.

[Brussels. Exposition internationale 1910]. *Deutschland's Raumkunst und Kunstgewerbe auf der Weltausstellung zu Brüssel 1910. Vom Reichskommissar autorisierte Ausgabe.* Stuttgart: Hoffmann, 1910.   [130]

Brussels. Palais des Beaux-Arts. *Jugendstil.* Brussels, 1977.

Bt. "Neuere Bauten in Berlin." *Deutsche Bauzeitung,* 65, nos. 37–38 (6 May 1931), 218–225.

Buddensieg, Tilmann. "Neue Dokumente zur Baugeschichte der Fabriken am Humboldthain." In M. Sperlich and H. Borsch-Supan, eds., *Festschrift für Margarethe Kühn,* 271–299. Munich and Berlin: Deutscher Kunstverlag, 1975.

Buddensieg, Tilmann. "Documenti di architettura: Il Gaswerk di Peter Behrens." *Casabella,* 46, no. 479 (April 1982), 38–45, 63.

Buddensieg, Tilmann. "Die Kaiserlich Deutsche Botschaft in Petersburg von Peter Behrens." In Martin Warnke, ed., *Politische Architektur in Europa vom Mittelalter bis heute—Repräsentation und Gemeinschaft,* 374–398. Cologne: Dumont, 1984.

Buddensieg, Tilmann. "Peter Behrens." In Wolfgang Ribbe and Wolfgang Schäche, eds., *Baumeister. Architekten. Stadtplaner. Biographien zur baulichen Entwicklung Berlins,* 341–364. Berlin: Historische Kommission zu Berlin/Stapp Verlag, 1987.

Buddensieg, Tilmann, gen. ed. *Berlin 1900–1933: Architecture and Design. Architektur und Design.* New York: Cooper-Hewitt/Berlin: Gebr. Mann, 1987.

Buddensieg, Tilmann. "Der Vater, der Sohn und der künstlerische Beirat. Noch einmal zu Emil Rathenau, Walther Rathenau und Peter Behrens." In Tilmann Buddensieg et al., eds., *Ein Mann vieler Eigenschaften: Walther Rathenau und die Kultur der Moderne,* 123–139. Berlin: Wagenbach, 1990.

Buddensieg, Tilmann. "Von der Industriemythologie zur 'Kunst in der Produktion': Peter Behrens und die AEG." In Vittorio Magnago Lampugnani and Romana Schneider, eds., *Moderne Architektur in Deutschland 1900 bis 1950: Reform und Tradition*, 78–103. Stuttgart: Hatje, 1992.

Buddensieg, Tilmann, and Henning Rogge. "Formgestaltung für die Industrie: Peter Behrens und die Bogenlampen der AEG." In Gerhard Bott, ed., *Von Morris zum Bauhaus*, 117–142. Hanau: Hans Peters, 1977.

Buddensieg, Tilmann, with Henning Rogge, et al. Industriekultur: *Peter Behrens und die AEG 1907–1914*. Milan: Electa, 1978. (Catalog of a 1977 exhibition; not the same as the following entry.) Italian edition: *Cultura e industria*. Milan: Electa International, 1979.

Buddensieg, Tilmann, with Henning Rogge, et al. *Industriekultur: Peter Behrens und die AEG 1907–1914*. Berlin: Gebr. Mann, 1979; 2d printing, 1981 (with minor corrections); 3d printing, 1990 (unchanged). In English as *Industriekultur: Peter Behrens and the AEG 1907–1914*. Cambridge: MIT Press, 1984.

    N.B. Catalog numbers in the German and MIT Press editions sometimes differ; when so, both numbers are given, in that sequence.

Buddensieg, Tilmann, and Henning Rogge, eds. *Die nützlichen Künste: Gestaltende Technik und Bildende Kunst seit der Industriellen Revolution*. Berlin: Quadriga, 1981.

Buderath, Bernhard, ed. *Peter Behrens: Umbautes Licht*. Munich: Prestel, 1990.

Burckhardt, Lucius, ed. *The Werkbund: History and Ideology 1907–1933*. Woodbury, NY: Barron's, 1980.

Burke, Chris. "Peter Behrens and the German Letter: Type Design and Architectural Lettering." *Journal of Design History*, 5, no. 1 (1992), 19–37.

Busch, Wilhelm. *Bauten der 20er Jahre an Rhein und Ruhr*. Cologne: Bachem, 1993.

Bushart, Magdalena, et al., eds. *Entmachtung der Kunst: Architektur, Bildhauerei und ihre Institutionalisierung 1920 bis 1960*. Berlin: Frölich & Kaufmann, 1985.

Büttner, Horst. "Der Alexanderplatz in Berlin." *Deutsche Architektur*, 12 (1964), 736–739.

Carstanjen, Friedrich. "Peter Behrens: Mit einem sechs-farbigen Originalholzschnitt 'Der Kuss'." *Pan*, 4, no. 2 (September 1898), 117–120.   [13]

Carstanjen, Friedrich. "Nürnberger Handwerkskunst." *Dekorative Kunst*, 5, no. 9 (June 1902), 321–336.

Casabella **240**. Rogers, Ernesto, et al. "Peter Behrens." Sp. no., *Casabella continuità*, no. 240 (June 1960).

Chassé, Charles. "Didier Lenz and the Beuron School of Religious Art." *Oppositions*, no. 21 (Summer 1980), 98–103.

Claessens, François. "Quiet Objectivity." *Oase*, nos. 49–50 (1998), 86–107.

Cologne, Architekten- und Ingenieure-Verein. *Köln: Bauliche Entwicklung 1888–1927*. Cologne, 1927.

C[onrads], U[lrich], ed. "Tendenzen der zwanziger Jahre: Briefe, Glossen, Kritiken 1919–1931." *Die Bauwelt*, 68 (2 September 1977), 1079–1110.

Cortissoz, Royal. "Peter Behrens at the Brooklyn Museum." *New York Herald Tribune* (27 April 1930), § VIII, 9.

Cramer, Johannes, and Niels Gutschow. *Bauausstellungen*. Stuttgart: Kohlhammer, 1984.

Cremers, Paul Joseph. *Peter Behrens: Sein Werk von 1909 bis zur Gegenwart.* Essen: Baedeker, 1928.

Creutz, Max. "Amerika und die Weltausstellung in St. Louis 1904." *Dekorative Kunst,* 7, no. 12 (September 1904), 449–476.

Creutz, Max. "Das Krematorium von Peter Behrens in Hagen in Westfalen." *Kunstgewerbeblatt,* n.s. 20 (December 1908), 41–45.   [79]

Creutz, Max. "Das Haus Meirowsky in Cöln-Lindenthal." *Innendekoration,* 22, no. 7 (July 1911), 268–294, with ill. to 308.   [148]

D. "Stiftung eines Kaiser-Wilhelm-Volkshauses durch Herrn Senator Possehl." *Vaterstädtische Blätter* (Lübeck), no. 24 (16 March 1913), 93–94.

D., A. "Das neue katholische Gesellenhaus in Neuss." *Westdeutsche Bauzeitung,* 15, no. 2 (1911), 7, 9.

Dal Co, Francesco. "The Remoteness of *die Moderne.*" *Oppositions,* no. 22 (Fall 1980), 74–95.

Dal Co, Francesco. *Figures of Architecture and Thought: German Architecture Culture 1880–1920.* New York: Rizzoli, 1990.

Daldrop, Norbert W., et al. "Weissenhof—50 Years Later." *MD,* 24 (February 1978), 47–56.

Darmstadt, Hessisches Landesmuseum. *Kunsthandwerk um 1900: Jugendstil, art nouveau, modern style, nieuwe kunst.* Kataloge des Hessischen Landesmuseum, no. 1. Ed. Gerhard Bott and C. B. Heller. 2d rev. ed. Darmstadt: Roether, 1973.

Darmstadt, Hessisches Landesmuseum, et al. *Darmstadt: Ein Dokument deutscher Kunst.* 5 vols. Darmstadt: Roether, 1976.

Darmstadt, Hessisches Landesmuseum. *Jugendstil. Kunst um 1900.* Kataloge des Hessischen Landesmuseums, no. 12. Ed. Carl Benno Heller. Darmstadt: Roether, 1982.

[Darmstadt, Künstler-Kolonie]. *Die Ausstellung der Künstler-Kolonie: Darmstadt 1901. Hauptkatalog.* Darmstadt, [1901].

de Fries, Heinrich. "Die werdende Form: Zur Entwicklung der modernen Baukunst." *Die Rheinlande,* 26 (1916), 121–128.

de Fries, Heinrich. "Industriebaukunst." *Wasmuths Monatshefte für Baukunst,* 5 (1920–1921), 127–190.

de Fries, Heinrich. *Moderne Villen und Landhäuser.* Berlin: Wasmuth, 1924.

Dehmel, Richard. *Ausgewählte Briefe.* 2 vols. Berlin: Fischer, 1922–1923.

De Michelis, Marco. *Heinrich Tessenow: 1876–1950.* Milan: Electa, 1991.

Deutscher Werkbund. *Die Durchgeistigung der deutschen Arbeit.* Jena: Diederichs, 1911.   [145]

Deutscher Werkbund. *Der Verkehr. Deutscher Werkbund Jahrbuch 1914.* Jena: Diederichs, 1914.

Deutscher Werkbund [1914b]. *Deutscher Werkbund Ausstellung Cöln 1914: Offizieller Katalog.* Cologne and Berlin: Mosse, 1914.

Deutscher Werkbund. *Deutsche Form im Kriegsjahr. Deutscher Werkbund Jahrbuch 1915.* Munich: Bruckmann, 1915.

Deutscher Werkbund. *Die Wohnung.* Stuttgart: Ausstellungsleitung, 1927. (Catalog of the Weissenhof Siedlung.)

Deutscher Werkbund [1927b]. *Bau und Wohnung.* Stuttgart: Wedekind, 1927.

Deutscher Werkbund und Deutsch-Türkische Vereinigung. *Das Haus der Freundschaft in Konstantinopel: Ein Wettbewerb deutscher Architekten.* Munich: Bruckmann, 1918.

Diederichs, Eugen. *Selbstzeugnisse und Briefe von Zeitgenossen.* Düsseldorf: Diederichs, 1967.

Dietrich, Ulf. "Der Alexanderplatz in Berlin." *Der Städtebau,* 24 (1929), 57–63.

Döcker, Richard. *Terrassen Typ.* Stuttgart: Wedekind, 1929.

Dohrn, Wolf. "Das Vorbild der A.E.G.." *März,* 3, no. 17 (3 September 1909), 361–372.   [99]

Dohrn, Wolf. "Die Turbinenhalle der AEG in Berlin." *Der Industriebau,* 1, no. 6 (15 June 1910), 132–140.   [116]

Döllgast, Hans. *Journal retour.* 2 vols. Munich, 1973.

Drebusch, Günter. *Industriearchitektur.* Munich: Heyne, 1976.

Dresden. *III. Deutsche Kunstgewerbeausstellung Dresden 1906: Offizieller Katalog.* Dresden, 1906.

Dresden. III. Deutsche Kunstgewerbeausstellung Dresden 1906. *Die Raumkunst in Dresden 1906.* Berlin: Wasmuth, n.d. [1906?].

Dry, Graham. "Rheinauer Gartenmöbel: Die vergessenen Jugendstilmöbel von Beissbarth & Hoffmann." *Weltkunst,* no. 16 (15 August 1989), 2246–2250.

Dürbeck, A. "Die Stahlkonstruktion im Hochhaus 'Alexander' am Alexanderplatz zu Berlin." *Der Stahlbau,* 6 (9 June 1933), 102–104; (7 July 1933), 110–111.

[Dürbeck, A. See also Anon., *Deutsche Bauzeitung* (3 May 1933).]

Dürerbund-Werkbund Genossenschaft Hellerau bei Dresden. *Deutsches Warenbuch, Kriegsausgabe.* Ed. Joseph Popp. Munich, n.d. [ca. October 1915].

Düsseldorf. *Internationale Kunst- und grosse Gartenbauausstellung Düsseldorf 1904: Offizieller Führer.* Düsseldorf, 1904.

Dyroff, Hans-Dieter, ed. *Art Nouveau/Jugendstil Architecture in Europe.* New York: Saur, 1988.

Ehmcke, Fritz Helmuth. *Persönliches und Sachliches.* Berlin: H. Reckendorf, 1928.

Ehmcke, Fritz Helmuth. "Peter Behrens." *Neue deutsche Biographie.* Berlin, 1955, vol. 2.

Eiselen, F[ritz]. "Neuer Wettbewerb für die Erweiterung des Reichstagsbaus." *Deutsche Bauzeitung,* 63 (February 1929), Beilage "Wettbewerbe" W2, 35f.

Eisler, Max. "Peter Behrens: Landhaus einer Dame im Taunus." *Moderne Bauformen,* 31, no. 3 (March 1932), 117–132.

Engelhard, W. Freiherr von. "Von der Mannheimer Gartenbauausstellung 1907: III. Die Sondergärten des Prof. P. Schultze-Naumburg und des Prof. P. Behrens." *Die Gartenkunst,* 9, no. 11 (1 November 1907), 221–226.   [67]

Ermers, Max. "Staatliche Tabakfabrik in Linz: Architekten Peter Behrens und Alexander Popp." *Bauwelt,* 24 (5 October 1933), 7–8.

F., E. "Ausstellung des Deutschen Werkbundes in Basel." *Deutsche Kunst und Dekoration,* 20 (July 1917), 250–253.

Fahrner, Rudolf, ed. *Paul Thiersch: Leben und Werk.* Berlin: Gebr. Mann, 1970.

Fisher, Thomas. "Weissenhofsiedlung: Low Cost, High Design." *Progressive Architecture* (October 1988), 98–109.

Frankfurt-Hoechst, Farbwerke Hoechst. *Peter Behrens schuf "Turm und Brücke."* Dokumente aus Hoechster Archiven, no. 4. Frankfurt: Farbwerke Hoechst, 1964.

Franz, W. "Die Architektur im Industriebau." *Die Bauwelt,* 25 (1913), 113–118.

Franz, W. "Peter Behrens als Ingenieur-Architekt." *Die Kunst,* 36 (February 1917), 145–158.

Franz, W. *Fabrikbauten.* Leipzig: J. M. Gebhardt, 1923.

Fred, W. [pseudonym of Alfred Wechsler]. "Die Darmstädter Künstlerkolonie." *Kunst und Kunsthandwerk,* 4 (1901), 430–452.

Fred, W. [1901b]. "The Artists' Colony at Darmstadt." *The Studio,* 24 (November 1901), 21–30. Rpt. (with different figures), *Architectural Design,* nos. 1–2 (1980), 60–63.   [38]

Fred, W. "Die Turiner Ausstellung: Von der deutschen Abteilung." *Dekorative Kunst,* 5, no. 11 (September 1902), 433–445.

Friedel, Baron Salvator von, ed. *Die Neubauten und Betriebseinrichtungen der Tabakfabrik in Linz.* Salzburg: Kiesel, [1936].

Fuchs, Georg [Darmstadt, Künstler-Kolonie]. *Ein Dokument deutscher Kunst: Die Ausstellung der Künstler-Kolonie in Darmstadt. Zur Feier der Eröffnung 15. Mai 1901.* Rpt., Darmstadt: Roether, 1976.

Fuchs, Georg. "Die Vorhalle zum Hause der Macht und der Schönheit [Hamburger Vorhalle]." *Deutsche Kunst und Dekoration,* 6, no. 1 (October 1902), 1–44.   [40]

Fuchs, Georg. *Die Revolution des Theaters.* Munich and Leipzig: Georg Müller, 1909. Trans. ("condensed and adapted") C. C. Kuhn as *Revolution in the Theatre.* Ithaca: Cornell University Press, 1959.

Gmelin, L., ed. *Erste internationale Ausstellung für moderne dekorative Kunst in Turin 1902: Katalog der deutschen Abteilung.* Munich: Datterer & Cie, ca. 1902.

Göldner, Erich. "Gedanken zur Industrialisierung des Wohnungsbaues von Peter Behrens." *Baukunst und Werkform,* 8 (1955), 308–310.

Graul, Richard, ed. *Die Krisis im Kunstgewerbe: Studien über die Wege und Ziele der modernen Richtung.* Leipzig: Hirzel, 1901.

Grautoff, Otto. *Die Entwicklung der modernen Buchkunst in Deutschland.* Leipzig, n.d. [preface dated November 1901].

Gregotti, Vittorio. "L'architettura dell'espressionismo." *Casabella continuità,* no. 254 (August 1961), [24]–50.

Grimme, Karl Maria, ed. *Peter Behrens und seine Wiener akademische Meisterschule/Peter Behrens and His Academic Master-School, Vienna.* Captions by Alexander Popp. Vienna, Berlin, and Leipzig: Luser, 1930. (Text in German and English, trans. L. H. Paulovsky.)

Gropius, Walter. "Industriebauten." *Der Industriebau,* 3 (15 February 1912), 46–47.

Gropius, Walter. "Die Entwicklung moderner Industriebaukunst." In *Jahrbuch des Deutschen Werkbundes 1913,* 17–22. Jena: Diederichs, 1913.

Günter, Roland. "Zu einer Geschichte der technischen Architektur im Rheinland." In *Beiträge zur rheinischen Kunstgeschichte und Denkmalpflege,* Beiheft 16, 343–372. Düsseldorf: Rheinland, 1970.

Günter, Roland. *Oberhausen.* Düsseldorf: Schwann, 1975.

Gut, A[lbert]. "Die deutsche Gewerbeschau in München." *Zeitschrift für Bauwesen,* 73, nos. 1–3 (1923), 1–19.

Gut, A[lbert]. "Die deutsche Architekturausstellung in München." *Bauwelt,* 29 (15 December 1938), 1142–1146.

Gutkind, Erwin. "Der Wettbewerb um die Erweiterung des Reichstags." *Die Baugilde,* 11 (25 December 1929), 2001–2003.

Haeder, Alexander. "The Oberschöneweide Industrial Area." *Development Spreeknie,* pt. 5. Berlin: Berliner Landesentwicklung GmbH, 1994.

Haenel, Erich. "Ausstellung der Dresdener Werkstätten für Handwerkskunst." *Dekorative Kunst,* 7, no. 4 (January 1904), 146–167.

Haenel, Erich. *Die Wohnung der Neuzeit.* Leipzig: J. J. Weber, 1908.   [77]

Haenel, Erich, and Heinrich Tscharmann. *Das Einzelwohnhaus der Neuzeit.* 2 vols. Leipzig: Weber, 1906, 1910. [54, 131]

Hagen, Deutsches Museum für Kunst in Handel und Gewerbe. *Wanderausstellung des Deutschen Museums für Kunst in Handel und Gewerbe: Newark-Chicago-Indianapolis-Pittsburgh-Cincinnati-St. Louis.* Hagen: Deutsches Museum für Kunst in Handel und Gewerbe, 1912.

Hajos, Elisabeth, and Leopold Zahn. *Berliner Architektur 1919–1929: 10 Jahre Architektur der Moderne.* Berlin: Albertus, 1929. Rpt., Berlin: Gebr. Mann, 1996.

Hamann, Richard, and Jost Hermand. *Stilkunst um 1900.* Berlin (Ost): Akademie-Verlag, 1967.

Hamburg, Kunsthalle. *Kunst ins Leben: Alfred Lichtwarks Wirken für die Kunsthalle und Hamburg von 1886 bis 1914.* Ed. Helmut Leppien. Hamburg, 1987.

Häring, Hugo. "Die Sonderausstellung städtebaulicher Projekte Gross-Berlins in der grossen Berliner Kunstausstellung." *Stadtbaukunst,* 8 (20 June 1927), 50–55.

Häring, Hugo. "Neues Bauen." *Moderne Bauformen,* 27 (1928), 329–376. (Behrens, pp. 331–333: ills. of Hoechst, New Ways, and the Gutehofnungshütte buildings; short text with no specific reference to Behrens.)

Hartig, Michael. "Der Studienkollegbau zu St. Peter in Salzburg." *Die christliche Kunst,* 24 (May 1928), 234–240, pl. p. 225.

Hassler, Uta. "Max Läuger und die Gartenbauausstellung in Mannheim 1907." In Badische Kommunale Landesbank, *Jugendstil—Architektur um 1900 in Mannheim,* 257–293. Mannheim: Quadrat, 1986.

Haug, W. F., ed. *Warenästhetik: Beiträge zur Diskussion, Weiterentwicklung und Vermittlung ihrer Kritik.* Frankfurt: Suhrkamp, 1975.

Hegemann, Werner. "E. Fahrenkamp und der Sieg der Rheinländer im Schauseiten-Wettbewerb der 'D.A.Z.'." *Wasmuths Monatshefte für Baukunst,* 9, no. 1 (1925), 1–20.

Hegemann, Werner. "Berliner Plätze." *Der Städtebau,* 23, no. 10 (1928), 237–240.

Hegemann, Werner. "Berlin und die internationale Baukunst." *Der Querschnitt,* 10 (May 1931), 301–304.

Heinz, Dieter. "Haus Obenauer, Trillerweg 42." *Saarheimat,* 9, nos. 7–8 (1965), 233–238.

Heitmann, Karl Friedrich. "Das deutsche Kunstgewerbe auf der Weltausstellung in St. Louis." *Die Rheinlande,* 5, no. 1 (January 1905), 21–27.

Hellwag, Fritz. "Peter Behrens und die AEG." *Kunstgewerbeblatt,* n.s. 22, no. 8 (May 1911), 149–159. [146]

Hellwag, Fritz. "Lübeck: Das Kaiser-Wilhelm-Volkshaus." *Kunstgewerbeblatt,* n.s. 25, no. 3 (December 1913), 56–58.

Hellwag, Fritz. "Der Deutsche Werkbund und seine Ausstellung Köln 1914." *Kunstgewerbeblatt,* n.s. 26, no. 3 (December 1914), 41–59.

Hellwag, Fritz. "Die Ausstellung des Deutschen Werkbundes in Bern im Sommer 1917." *Moderne Bauformen,* 17, no. 1 (1918), 1–12.

Henn, Walter. "Die Bedeutung des Industriebaues für die Architektur des 20. Jahrhunderts." *Zentralblatt für Industriebau,* 29, no. 2 (1983), 73–80.

Hennig-Schefold, Monica. "Berliner Bauformen der zwanziger Jahre." *Werk,* 53 (March 1966), 82–107.

Hennig-Schefold, Monica, and Inge Schaefer. *Frühe Moderne in Berlin.* Winterthur: Werk, 1967.

Hermand, Jost. *Jugendstil: Ein Forschungsbericht 1918–1964.* Stuttgart: Metzler, 1965.

Hermand, Jost, ed. *Jugendstil.* Wege der Forschung, no. 110. Darmstadt: Wissenschaftliche Buchgesellschaft, 1971.

Herrmann, Wolfgang. *Deutsche Baukunst des 19. und 20. Jahrhunderts.* 2 vols. Basel: Birkhäuser, 1977. Vol. 2, *Von 1840 bis zur Gegenwart,* was printed in 1933 but suppressed; first published 1977.

Heskett, John. *Industrial Design.* New York: Oxford, 1980.

Heskett, John. *Design in Germany: 1870–1918.* London: Trefoil, 1986.

Hesse-Frielinghaus, Herta. *Peter Behrens und Karl Ernst Osthaus: Eine Dokumentation nach den Beständen des Osthaus-Archivs im Karl-Ernst-Osthaus-Museum, Hagen.* Hagen: Karl Ernst Osthaus Museum, 1966.

Hesse-Frielinghaus, Herta. *Hagener Architektur 1900–1914.* 2d ed. Münster: Westfälisches Amt für Denkmalpflege, 1987.

Hesse-Frielinghaus, Herta, et al. *Karl Ernst Osthaus—Leben und Werk.* Recklinghausen: Bongers, 1971.

Heuss, Theodor. "Das Werden der neuen Baukunst." *Die Hilfe,* 35 (15 August 1929), 397–398.

Heuss, Theodor. [Obituary of Peter Behrens]. *Die Hilfe,* 46, no. 5 (1940), 74–76.

Heyck, Ed., ed. *Moderne Kultur: Ein Handbuch der Lebensbildung und des guten Geschmacks.* 2 vols. Stuttgart and Leipzig: DVA, n.d.

Hirschberg, Heinrich. "Bau-Entwicklung der AEG-Fabriken." *Die Spannung,* 3, no. 1 (October 1929), 5–11; no. 2 (November 1929), 37–43; no. 3 (December 1929), 68–74.

Hitchcock, Henry-Russell. *Architecture: Nineteenth and Twentieth Centuries.* 2d ed. Baltimore: Penguin, 1963.

Hoeber, Fritz. *Peter Behrens.* Munich: Müller und Rentsch, 1913.

Hoeber, Fritz [1913b]. "Die Neubauten von Peter Behrens für die AEG." *Kunst und Künstler,* 11 (1913), 262–266.

Hoeber, Fritz. "Stadtbau und Verkehr." *Der Architekt,* 21 (1916–1918), 73–83.

Hoeber, Fritz. "Peter Behrens Gartenstadt Lichtenberg bei Berlin: Eine gute Lösung des Kleinwohnungsproblems." *Kunstgewerbeblatt,* n.s. 28, no. 6 (1917), 105–118.

Hoepfner, Wolfram, and Fritz Neumeyer. *Das Haus Wiegand von Peter Behrens in Berlin-Dahlem: Baugeschichte und Kunstgegenstände eines herrschaftlichen Wohnhauses.* Mainz: von Zabern, 1979.

H[offmann], H. "Peter Behrens und Alexander Popp, Wien: Staatliche Tabakfabrik Linz." *Moderne Bauformen,* 35 (July 1936), 365–388.

Hofmann, Albert. "Das künstlerische Ergebnis des Darmstadter 'Dokumentes'." *Deutsche Bauzeitung,* 36, no. 40 (17 May 1902), 253–259; no. 48 (14 June), 306–307, 310–312; no. 98 (6 December), 628, 630–631; no. 100 (13 December), 638, 640, 642–644.

Hofmann, Albert. "Die Baukunst auf der III. Deutschen Kunstgewerbeausstellung in Dresden." *Deutsche Bauzeitung* (1906), 483ff.

Högg, E. "Neue Wohnräume und neues Kunstgewerbe bei A. Wertheim." *Deutsche Kunst und Dekoration,* 8, no. 11 (August 1905), 646–698.

Höhns, Ulrich, ed. *Das ungebaute Hamburg: Visionen einer anderen Stadt in architektonischen Entwürfen der letzten hundertfünfzig Jahre.* Hamburg: Junius, 1991.

Hüter, Karl-Heinz. *Architektur in Berlin 1900–1933.* Dresden and Stuttgart: Kohlhammer, 1988.

Internationaler Kongress für Kunstgeschichte. *Akten des 25. Internationalen Kongresses für Kunstgeschichte.* Vol. 8, ed. Elisabeth Liskar: *Wien und die Architektur des 20. Jahrhunderts.* Vienna: Böhlau, 1986. Articles by G. Moeller, 77–81; H. Griepentrog, 83–86.

Jatho, Carl Oskar. "Werkbundgedanken." *Christliche Freiheit,* 30 (1914), col. 498.

Jaumann, Anton. "Neues von Peter Behrens." *Deutsche Kunst und Dekoration,* 12, no. 6 (March 1909), 343–361.   [85]

Jefferies, Matthew. *Politics and Culture in Wilhelmine Germany: The Case of Industrial Architecture.* Oxford and Washington: Berg, 1995.

Jessen, Hans B. "Der Baumeister Peter Behrens 1868–1940." *Nordelbingen,* 37 (1968), 146–149.

Jessen, Hans B. "Vorlage über Sitze des Deutschen Archäologischen Instituts zu Berlin." *Archäologischer Anzeiger,* 34 (1969), 511–524.

Joedicke, Jürgen. *Weissenhofsiedlung Stuttgart.* Stuttgart: Krämer, 1989. (In English and German.)

Joedicke, Jürgen, and Christian Plath. *Die Weissenhofsiedlung.* Stuttgart: Krämer, 1968.

Junghanns, Kurt. *Der Deutsche Werkbund: Sein erstes Jahrzehnt.* Berlin (Ost): Henschel, 1982.

Kabierske, Gerhard. "Hermann Billings Kunsthalle und die Jubiläumskunstausstellung von 1907." In Badische Kommunale Landesbank, *Jugendstil—Architektur um 1900 in Mannheim,* 225–256. Mannheim: Quadrat, 1986.

Kadatz, Hans-Joachim. *Peter Behrens: Architekt—Maler—Graphiker und Formgestalter 1868–1940.* Leipzig: Seemann, 1977.

Kaiserslautern, Pfalzgalerie. *Peter Behrens (1868–1940). Gedenkschrift mit Katalog aus Anlass der Ausstellung.* Ed. Wilhelm Weber. Kaiserslautern: Pfalzgalerie, 1966.

Kaiserslautern, Pfalzgalerie. *Peter Behrens: Berlin Alexanderplatz. Pläne, Zeichnungen und Photographien zum Wettbewerb und der Bebauung 1929–1932.* Kaiserslautern: Pfalzgalerie, 1993.

Kalkschmidt, Eugen. "Peter Behrens und die A.E.G. Ein Beitrag zur Kunst in der Industrie." *Die Grenzboten,* 69, no. 27 (6 July 1910), 24–30.   [121]

Kalkschmidt, Eugen. "Industriebauten von Peter Behrens." *Dekorative Kunst,* 16, no. 12 (September 1913), 573–576.

Karlsruhe, Badisches Landesmuseum. *Jugendstil: Eine Auswahl aus den Schausammlungen.* Ed. Irmela Franzke. Karlsruhe, 1978.

Kautzsch, Rudolf, ed. *Die neue Buchkunst: Studien im In- und Ausland.* Weimar: Gesellschaft der Bibliophilen, 1902.

Keller, M. A. "Richard Dehmel–Peter Behrens: Kunst und Theater um 1900." Thesis, University of Venice, 1980.

Kersten, C. "Skelettbauten in Eisenbeton." *Deutsche Bauzeitung,* 71, no. 17 (28 April 1937), B271–275.

Kiessling, Martin. "Der Reichstagswettbewerb [and response of Martin Wagner]." *Das neue Berlin,* 1, no. 12 (1929), 242–245.

Kinser, Bill, and Neil Kleinman. *The Dream That Was No More a Dream: A Search for Aesthetic Reality in Germany, 1890–1945.* New York: Harper, 1969.

Kirsch, Karin. *The Weissenhofsiedlung: Experimental Housing Built for the Deutscher Werkbund, Stuttgart, 1927.* 1987 (German ed.); New York: Rizzoli, 1989.

Klapheck, Richard. *Neue Baukunst in den Rheinlanden,* 15–24, 102–114. Düsseldorf: Schwann, [1928].

Kleihues, Josef Paul, ed. *750 Jahre Architektur und Städtebau in Berlin: Die Internationale Bauausstellung im Kontext der Baugeschichte Berlins.* Stuttgart: Hatje, 1987.

Klein, Rudolf. "Peter Behrens und der neue Garten." *Hochland,* 9 (July 1912), 466–471.   [162]

Klopfer, Paul. "Peter Behrens einst und jetzt." *Der Kunstwart,* 22, pt. 4 (August 1909), 218–220.
    [101]

Klopfer, Paul. *Das Wesen der Baukunst: Einführung in das Verstehen der Baukunst. Grundsätze und Anwendungen.* Leipzig: Leiner, 1919.

[Koch, Alexander, ed.] *Grossherzog Ernst Ludwig und die Darmst. Künstler-Kolonie.* Darmstadt: Alex. Koch, 1901. Rpt., Darmstadt: Verlag zur Megede, 1979.   [36]

Koch, Alexander, ed. *Internationale Ausstellung für Dekorative Kunst in Turin, MDCCCCII.* Darmstadt: A. Koch, 1902. Also as *L'exposition internationale des arts décoratifs modernes à Turin 1902.* Darmstadt: A. Koch, 1903.

Koch, Alexander, ed. *Nordwestdeutsche Kunst-Ausstellung Oldenburg 1905.* Darmstadt: A. Koch, 1905.

Koch, David. "Das Projekt von Peter Behrens zu einer evangelischen Kirche in Hagen i. W." *Die Rheinlande,* 7 (1907), 172–175.

Koenig, G. K. "Behrens and Thereabouts. Peter and Adolf: The Artist and the Housepainter." *Casabella,* no. 347 (April 1970), 2–5.

Kohlenbach, Bernhard. "Industriedenkmale in Oberschöneweide." Flier of Landesdenkmalamt, Berlin, ca. 1998. 4 pp.

Köln: Deutsche Kunstausstellung 1906. Katalog. Cologne, 1906.

Köln 1906: Das Tonhaus und das Krematorium in Hagen in Westfalen von Peter Behrens. Berlin: Wasmuth Verlag, 1906.   [53]

Kommerell, and W. Rein. "Engerer Wettbewerb um Entwürfe für eine feste Strassenbrücke über den Rhein in Köln-Mülheim." *Der Bauingenieur,* 8 (26 March 1927), 233–236; (2 April), 241–250; (9 April), 263–271; (16 April), 287–291.

Körber, Jürgen. "Ehemalige Beamtensiedlung der Deutschen Werft in Hamburg, Gross-Flottbeck." *Architekt* (October 1978), 452.

Kordt, Walter. "Die Kunstgewerbeschule von Peter Behrens in Düsseldorf (1903–1908)." *Die Heimat,* nos. 4–6 (April-June 1963), 81–85, 114–120, 137–139.

Kostka, Alexandre, and Irving Wohlfarth, eds. *Nietzsche and "An Architecture of Our Minds."* Los Angeles: Getty Research Institute, 1999.

Krause, Jürgen. *'Martyrer' und 'Prophet': Studien zum Nietzsche-Kult in der bildenden Kunst der Jahrhundertwende.* Berlin: Walter de Gruyter, 1984.

Krawietz, Georg. *Peter Behrens im Dritten Reich.* Weimar: Verlag und Datenbank für Geisteswissenschaften, 1995.

Krebs, Otto. "Die architektonische Anlage der Nordwestdeutschen Kunstausstellung in Oldenburg von Peter Behrens." *Dekorative Kunst,* 9, no. 2 (November 1905), 77–88.

Kunz, Otto. "Die Projekte der Erschliessung der Arenberg-Grunde." *Salzburger Volksblatt,* no. 41 (1932), 5.

Lampmann, Gustav. "Stuttgart 1927 'Die Wohnung'." *Zentralblatt der Bauverwaltung,* 47 (26 October 1927), 549–552, four pls.

Lampugnani, Vittorio Magnago. *Architektur als Kultur: Die Ideen und die Formen.* Cologne: DuMont, 1986.

Lancaster, Clay. "Oriental Contribution to Art Nouveau." *Art Bulletin,* 34 (1952), 297–310.

Landsberg, Th. "Der Wettbewerb für den Bau einer festen Strassenbrücke über den Rhein bei Köln." *Zentralblatt der Bauverwaltung,* 31, no. 77 (23 September 1911), 476–479.

Langmaack, Gerhard. "Unser Massenschicksal und der Weg der Baukunst: Eine kritische Untersuchung an dem Wettbewerb für eine Kongress-, Sport- und Ausstellungshalle in Hamburg." *Die Baugilde,* 16, no. 15 (1934), 511–535.

Lanzke, Hermann. *Peter Behrens: 50 Jahre Gestaltung in der Industrie.* Berlin: AEG, 1958.

Lasche, O. "Das Kraftwerk der AEG-Turbinenfabrik in Berlin." *Zeitschrift des Vereines deutscher Ingenieure,* 53 (24 April 1909), 648–655; (1 May 1909), 699–704.

Lasche, O. "Die neue Turbinenhalle der AEG." *AEG-Zeitung,* 12 (January 1910), cover, 1–4.

Lasche, O. "Die Turbinenfabrikation der AEG." *Zeitschrift des Vereines deutscher Ingenieure,* 55 (22 July 1911), 1198–1206; (29 July 1911), 1251–1260 and pls. 19–20.

Le Corbusier [Charles-Edouard Jeanneret]. *Etude sur le mouvement d'art décoratif en Allemagne.* La Chaux-de-Fonds: Haefeli & Co., 1912. Rpt., New York: Da Capo, 1968. Partially trans. into German by Stanislaus von Moos, *Werk,* 54 (April 1967), 211–215.   [163]

Lehmann, A. "Architektur auf der Jubiläumsausstellung Mannhiem 1907." *Moderne Bauformen,* 6 (1907), 217–264.   [61]

Lehnert, Georg, et al., eds. *Illustrierte Geschichte des Kunstgewerbes.* 2 vols. Berlin: Oldenbourg, 1907, 1909.

Lichtwark, Alfred. *Briefe an die Kommission für die Verwaltung der Kunsthalle.* 2 vols. Hamburg: Westermann, 1923.

Lotz, Wilhelm. "Aus der Werkbund-Entwicklung: Arbeiten und Gedanken aus den ersten zwanzig Jahren." *Die Form,* 7, no. 10 (1932), 300–324.

Loubier, Hans. *Die neue deutsche Buchkunst.* Stuttgart: Krais, 1921.

Ls. "Eröffnung der III. Teilstrecke der Schnellbahn Gesundbrunnen-Neukölln, Berlin." *Bautechnik,* 6 (4 May 1928), 261f.

Lux, Joseph August. "Peter Behrens." *Hohe Warte,* 4 (1908), 37–46.

Lux, Joseph August [1908b]. "Das künstlerische Problem der Industrie." *Innendekoration,* 19 (February-March 1908), 81–84, 107, 109.

Lux, Joseph August [1908c]. "Peter Behrens." In *Das neue Kunstgewerbe in Deutschland,* 171–177. Leipzig: Klinkhardt & Biermann, 1908.   [76]

Lux, Joseph August. "Salzburgs steinerne Sprache." *Deutsche Bauhütte,* 30 (8 September 1926), 256–257.

Lux, Joseph August, and Siedler. "Peter Behrens anlässlich seines 60. Geburtstages." *Die Baugilde,* 10, no. 11 (5 June 1928), 761–770.

M., F. "Die Messestadt Frankfurt a.M. und ihre Messebauten." Sonderdruck from *Neue Baukunst.* Berlin: M. Maul, n.d. [1927–1928?].

Madsen, S. Tschudi. *Sources of Art Nouveau.* New York: Wittenborn, 1955.

Maldonado, Tomas, ed. *Tecnica e cultura: Il dibattito tedesco fra Bismarck e Weimar.* Milan: Feltrinelli, 1979.

Mang, Karl, and Eva Mang-Frimmel. *Kommunaler Wohnbau in Wien: Aufbruch 1923–1934 Ausstrahlung.* 2d ed. Vienna: Stadt Wien, 1978.

Mannheim, Jubiläums-Ausstellung Mannheim 1907. *Internationale Kunst- und grosse Gartenbauausstellung: Offizieller Katalog der Kunst-Ausstellung.* Mannheim, 1907.

Mannheimer, Franz. "Fabrikenkunst." *Die Hilfe,* 16 (8 May 1910), 289–290.   [112]

Mannheimer, Franz [1910b]. "Die deutschen Hallen der Brüsseler Weltausstellung" *Der Industriebau,* 1 (15 September 1910), 193–207; (15 October 1910), 217–233.

Mannheimer, Franz. "Arbeiten von Professor Peter Behrens für die Allgemeine Elektrizitäts-gesellschaft." *Der Industriebau,* 2 (15 June 1911), 121–140 plus a color plate.   [147]

Mannheimer, Franz [1911b]. "Technische Schönheit." *Reclams Universum,* 27, vol. 2 (1911), 752–758.

Mannheimer, Franz. "A.E.G.-Bauten." In *Jahrbuch des Deutschen Werkbundes 1913,* 33–42. Jena: Diederichs, 1913.

Massobrio, Giovanna, and Paolo Portoghesi. *Album degli anni Venti.* Rome and Bari: Laterza, 1976.

Mayr, Norbert. *Peter Behrens 1868–1940: Entwürfe und Werke für Salzburg und Oldenburg. Teil II: Salzburg.* Salzburg: Salzburger Museum Carolino Augusteum, 1994.

[Meier-Graefe, Julius]. "Peter Behrens." *Dekorative Kunst,* 1, no. 8 (May 1898), 70–74.   [11.3]

Meier-Graefe, Julius. "Gemälde von Peter Behrens." *Dekorative Kunst,* 2, no. 2 (November 1898), 46, 67f.   [11.3]

Meier-Graefe, Julius. "Peter Behrens." *Dekorative Kunst,* 3, no. 1 (October 1899), 2–4, 16–25 (opp. p. 4, color plate of *The Kiss*).

Meier-Graefe, Julius. "Eine fürstliche Idee." *Dekorative Kunst,* 3, no. 7 (April 1900), 270–274.

Meier-Graefe, Julius. "Darmstadt." *Die Zukunft,* 9, no. 35 (1901), 478–486.

Meier-Graefe, Julius. "Darm-Athen." *Die Zukunft,* 10, no. 39 (1902), 195–201.

Meier-Graefe, Julius [1902b]. "Eine Renaissance?" *Die Zukunft,* 10, no. 39 (1902), 458–464.

Meier-Graefe, Julius. *Entwicklungsgeschichte der modernen Kunst: Vergleichende Betrachtung der bildenden Künste, als Beitrag zu einer neuen Ästhetik.* 3 vols. Stuttgart: Jul. Hoffmann, 1904. Trans. F. Simmonds and G. W. Chrystal as *Modern Art.* 2 vols. London and New York, 1908. Rpt., New York: Arno, 1968.   [47]

Meier-Graefe, Julius. "Peter Behrens, Düsseldorf." Sp. no., *Dekorative Kunst,* 8, no. 10 (July 1905).   [49]

Melani, Alfredo. "L'Art Nouveau at Turin: An Account of the Exposition." *Architectural Record,* 12 (November 1902), 584–599, and (December 1902), 734–750.

Mendelsohn, Erich. *Das Gesamtschaffen des Architekten: Skizzen, Entwürfe, Bauten.* Berlin: Mosse, 1930.

Meyer, Peter. "Architektur als Ausdruck der Gewalt." *Werk,* 27 (June 1940), 160–164.

Meyer, [Robert]. "Der Wettbewerb für Entwürfe zu einem Verwaltungsgebäude für den Stumm-Konzern in Düsseldorf." *Zentralblatt der Bauverwaltung,* 42 (14 January 1922), 21–23.

Meyer-Schönbrunn, F. *Peter Behrens.* Monographien Deutscher Reklamekünstler, 5. Hagen and Dortmund: Ruhfus, 1913.   [167]

Michel., Wilh[elm]. "Garten- und Veranda-Möbel." *Innendekoration,* 19 (March 1908), 115–122.

Mies van der Rohe, Ludwig. "Industrielles Bauen." *G,* no. 3 (1924), 8ff.

Moeller, Gisela. "Der frühe Behrens: Zu seinen kunstgewerblichen Anfängen in München und Darmstadt." *Wallraf-Richartz-Jahrbuch,* 44 (1983), 259–284.

Moeller, Gisela. "Peter Behrens in Düsseldorf: Die Jahre 1903 bis 1907." Ph.D. diss., Universität Bonn, 1988.

Moeller, Gisela. *Peter Behrens in Düsseldorf: Die Jahre 1903 bis 1907.* Weinheim: VCH, 1991.

Moeller van den Bruck, Arthur. "Die Ausstellung des Deutschen Werkbundes 1917 in Bern." *Dekorative Kunst,* 21, no. 3 (December 1917), 73–104.

Mohr, Christoph, and Michael Müller. *Funktionalität und Moderne.* Cologne: Muller, 1984.

Müller, Sebastian. *Kunst und Industrie: Ideologie und Organisation des Funktionalismus in der Architektur.* Munich: Hanser, 1974.

[Müller-Wulckow, Walter] Müller-Wulkow [*sic*], W. "Bauten im Frankfurter Osthafen: Die Gasfabrik im Industriegelände des Frankfurter Osthafens." *Der Industriebau,* 8, no. 3 (15 March 1917), [33]–44.

Müller-Wulckow, W[alter]. "Bauten von Prof. Peter Behrens für die Hannoversche Waggonfabrik Akt.-Ges. Hannover-Linden." *Der Industriebau,* 10, no. 6 (15 June 1919), 77–85; no. 7 (15 July 1919), 98–106.

Müller-Wulckow, Walter. *Bauten der Arbeit und des Verkehrs aus deutscher Gegenwart.* Königstein: Langewiesche, 1925.

Müller-Wulckow, Walter. *Wohnbauten und Siedlungen aus deutscher Gegenwart.* Königstein: Langewiesche, 1928.

Müller-Wulckow, Walter [1928b]. *Bauten der Gemeinschaft aus deutscher Gegenwart.* Königstein: Langewiesche, 1928.

Müller-Wulckow, Walter. *Deutsche Baukunst der Gegenwart.* Königstein: Langewiesche, n.d. [ca. 1930].

Munich, Technische Universität München. Winfried Nerdinger, ed. *Hans Döllgast.* Munich: Callwey, 1987.

Muthesius, Hermann. "Die Ausstellung der Darmstädter Künstler-Kolonie 1901." *Deutsche Monatsschrift für das gesamte Leben der Gegenwart,* 1, no. 11 (1902), 744–748.

Muthesius, Hermann. "Die Wohnungskunst auf der Weltausstellung in St. Louis 1904." *Deutsche Kunst und Dekoration,* 15 (1904–1905), 209–227.

Muthesius, Hermann. *Das moderne Landhaus und seine innere Ausstattung.* 2d ed. Munich, 1905.

Muthesius, Hermann. *Landhaus und Garten. Beispiele neuzeitlicher Landhäuser nebst Grundrissen, Innenräumen und Gärten.* Munich: Bruckmann, 1907.

Nacht. [Nachtlicht], Leo. *Turin 1902.* Berlin: Wasmuth, n.d. [1902].

[Nachtlicht, Leo, compiler]. St. Louis, Louisiana Purchase Exposition 1904, Imperial German Commission. *Descriptive Catalogue of the German Arts and Crafts at the Universal Exposition St. Louis 1904.* n.p.: Th. Lewald, 1904.

Nachtlicht, Leo, ed. [1904b] *Deutsches Kunstgewerbe St. Louis 1904.* Berlin: Wasmuth, n.d.

Negri, Chiara, and Raffaela Neri. "Behrens e Berlino: L'architettura per l'industria." Domus Itinerario no. 86. *Domus,* no. 745 (January 1993). 7 pp.

Nerdinger, Winfried. "Hans Döllgast: Cheerfully Puritanical Architecture." *Oase,* nos. 49–50 (1998), 108–114; see also photographs by Klaus Kinold, 115–119, 127–133.

Neumann, Dietrich. "Die Wolkenkratzer kommen!" In *Deutsche Hochhäuser der zwanziger Jahre: Debatten—Projekte—Bauten.* Braunschweig and Wiesbaden: Vieweg, 1995.

Neumeyer, Fritz. "Der Werkwohnungsbau der Industrie in Berlin und seine Entwicklung im 19. und frühen 20. Jahrhundert." Ph.D. diss., Technische Universität Berlin, 1978.

Neumeyer, Fritz. "Das Pathos des Monumentalen." In Burkhard Bergius et al., eds., *Architektur, Stadt, und Politik: Werkbund-Archiv Jahrbuch 4,* 241–252. Giessen: Anabas, 1979.

Neumeyer, Fritz. "Eine neue Welt entschleiert sich: Von Friedrich Gilly zu Mies van der Rohe." In Berlin Museum, *Friedrich Gilly 1772–1800 und die Privatgesellschaft junger Architekten,* 41–64. Berlin: Arenhövel, 1984.

Neumeyer, Fritz. *The Artless Word: Mies van der Rohe on the Building Art.* Cambridge: MIT Press, 1991.

Neumeyer, Fritz. "Nietzsche and Modern Architecture." In Alexandre Kostka and Irving Wohlfarth, eds., *Nietzsche and "An Architecture of Our Minds,"* 285–309. Los Angeles: Getty Research Institute, 1999.

Neuss, Katholisches Gesellenhaus. *Festschrift zur Einweihung des katholischen Gesellenhauses zu Neuss: 20. November 1910.* Neuss: Gesellschaft für Buchdruckerei, 1910.   [137]

Neuss, Katholisches Gesellenhaus. *Festschrift zur 100-Jahr-Feier der Kolpingsfamilie Neuss und Einweihung des wiedererrichteten Gesellenhauses.* Neuss: Gesellenhaus, 1952.

New York, Museum of Modern Art. *Art Nouveau: Art and Design at the Turn of the Century.* Ed. Peter Selz and Mildred Constantine. New York: Museum of Modern Art, 1959.

Niemeyer, W[ilhelm]. "Peter Behrens und die Raumästhetik seiner Kunst." *Dekorative Kunst,* 10, no. 4 (January 1907), 131–165; see also 166–176.   [55]

Nonn, Konrad. "Unabänderliches im Kleinwohnungsbau." *Wasmuths Monatshefte für Baukunst,* 11 (October 1927), 406–408.

Norberg-Schulz, Christian. *Casa Behrens: Darmstadt.* 2d ed. Rome: Officina, 1986.

Nürnberg, Germanisches Nationalmuseum. *Peter Behrens und Nürnberg, Geschmackswandel in Deutschland: Historismus, Jugendstil und die Anfänge der Industrieform.* Ed. Peter-Klaus Schuster. Munich: Prestel, 1980.

Offenbach, Gebr. Klingspor. *Behrens-Kursiv und Schmuck: Nach Zeichnungen von Professor P. Behrens.* Offenbach: [Gebr. Klingspor, n.d., ca. 1908].

Offenbach, Gebr. Klingspor. *Zum Geleit* [Behrens-Antiqua]. Offenbach: Gebr. Klingspor, [October 1908].

Offenbach, Gebr. Klingspor. *Behrens-Antiqua und Schmuck von Prof. Peter Behrens.* Offenbach: [Gebr. Klingspor, n.d., ca. 1908].

Offenbach, Gebr. Klingspor. *Die Mediaeval von Professor Peter Behrens.* Offenbach: Gebr. Klingspor, n.d.

Offenbach, Rudhard'sche Giesserei. *Behrens: Schriften, Initialen und Schmuck nach Zeichnungen von Professor Behrens.* Offenbach: Rudhard'sche Giesserei, n.d. [1902].

Osborn, Max. "Die modernen Wohnräume im Warenhaus von A. Wertheim zu Berlin." *Deutsche Kunst und Dekoration,* 6, no. 6 (March 1903), 263, 291–293.

Osborn, Max. "Die Düsseldorfer Ausstellung." *Kunst und Künstler,* 2, no. 12 (August-September 1904), 429–445, 496–504.

Osborn, Max. *Jean Krämer.* Berlin: Hübsch, 1927. Rpt., Berlin: Gebr. Mann, 1996.

Osborn, Max. *Berlin 1870–1929: Der Aufstieg zur Weltstadt.* Berlin: Hobbing, 1929. Rpt., Berlinische Bibliothek, I. Berlin: Gebr. Mann, 1994.

Österreichische Kunst. "Zehn Jahre Architektur um Prof. Behrens." Sp. no., *Österreichische Kunst,* 3 (November 1932).

Osthaus, Karl Ernst. "Peter Behrens." *Kunst und Künstler,* 6, no. 3 (December 1907), 116–124. [70]

Osthaus, Karl Ernst. "Eine Predigtkirche von Peter Behrens." *Westfälisches Kunstblatt,* 2, no. 1 (October 1908).

Osthaus, Karl Ernst. "Ein Fabrikbau von Peter Behrens." *Frankfurter Zeitung* (10 February 1910). [103]

Osthaus, Karl Ernst [1910b]. "Ein Fabrikbau von Peter Behrens." *Gartenstadt,* 4, no. 8 (August 1910), 88–92. [128]

Osthaus, Karl Ernst. "Die Gartenvorstadt an der Donnerkuhle." In *Jahrbuch des Deutschen Werkbundes 1912,* 93–96. Jena: Diederichs, 1912. [156]

Osthaus, Karl Ernst. "Das Schaufenster." In *Jahrbuch des Deutschen Werkbundes 1913,* 59–69. Jena: Diederichs, 1913.

Oud, J. J. P. "The European Movement: Towards a New Architecture." *The Studio,* 105 (1933), 249–256.

Paquet, Alfons, and Wilhelm Schäfer. "Die deutsche Botschaft in Petersburg." *Die Rheinlande,* 24 (1914), 347–370.

Paris, Exposition internationale des arts décoratifs et industriels modernes, 1925. *L'Autriche à l'Exposition internationale des arts décoratifs et industriels modernes: Paris 1925.* Vienna: Commission Exécutive, 1925.

P[aulsen, Friedrich]. "Wettbewerb für ein Ehrenmal in Berlin." *Bauwelt,* 21, no. 31 (1930), 986f.

Paulsen, Friedrich. "Haus am Taunus. Architekt: Professor Peter Behrens." *Bauwelt,* 23, no. 25 (23 June 1932), 617–620.

Pehnt, Wolfgang. *Expressionist Architecture.* New York: Praeger, 1973.

Pehnt, Wolfgang. *Die Erfindung der Geschichte: Aufsätze und Gespräche zur Architektur unseres Jahrhunderts.* Munich: Prestel, 1989.

Pfeifer, Hans-Georg, ed. *Peter Behrens: "Wer aber will sagen, was Schönheit sei?" Grafik, Produktgestaltung, Architektur.* Düsseldorf: Beton-Verlag, 1990. (Exhibition catalog, Düsseldorf, Fachhochschule Düsseldorf, Fachbereiche Architektur und Design.)

Platz, Gustav Adolf. *Die Baukunst der neuesten Zeit.* Berlin: Propyläen, 1927.

Platz, Gustav Adolf. *Wohnräume der Gegenwart.* Berlin: Propyläen, 1933.

Plischke, Ernst A. *Ein Leben mit Architektur.* Vienna: Löcker, 1989.

Polano, Sergio. "I Kroller e i loro architetti: Spiritus et Materia Unum." *Domus,* no. 745 (January 1993), 48–55. (Also in English.)

Pommer, Richard, and Christian F. Otto. *Weissenhof 1927 and the Modern Movement in Architecture.* Chicago: University of Chicago Press, 1991.

Popp, Alexander. "Die Meisterschule Behrens an der Wiener Akademie der bildenden Künste." *Bauwarte,* 5 (10 January 1929), 9–11.

Popp, Alexander. "Architekt und Industriebau." *Profil,* 4 (February 1936), 57–61.

Poppenberg, Felix. "Mannheimer Ausstellungsregie." *Die Werkkunst,* 2, no. 20 (30 June 1907), 309–314. [60]

Portoghesi, Paolo. "Disegni di Peter Behrens, 1922–1929." *Controspazio,* 2, nos. 1–2 (January–February 1970), 16–26.

Posener, Julius. "L'esthétique de la rue en Allemagne." *Architecture d'aujourd'hui,* 4, no. 3 (1933), 39–58.

Posener, Julius. *Anfänge des Funktionalismus. Von Arts and Crafts zum Deutschen Werkbund.* Berlin: Ullstein, 1964.

Posener, Julius. *Berlin auf dem Wege zu einer neuen Architektur: Das Zeitalter Wilhelms II 1890–1918.* Munich: Prestel, 1979.

Posener, Julius. "Vorlesungen zur Geschichte der neuen Architektur." Three sp. no. of *Arch+,* 48 (December 1979), 53 (September 1980), 59 (October 1981).

Posener, Julius, and José **Imbert.** "Peter Behrens." Sp. sect., *Architecture d'aujourd'hui,* 4th ser., 5, no. 2 (March 1934), 8–30.

Pudor, Heinrich. *Babel-Bibel in der modernen Kunst.* Berlin: Baumgärtel, 1905.

R. "Entwurf für eine Ausstellungshalle." *Der Industriebau,* 6 (1915), 381–382.

Rasch, Heinz and Bodo. *Wie bauen? Bau und Einrichtung der Werkbundsiedlung am Weissenhof in Stuttgart 1927.* Stuttgart: Wedekind, 1927.

Rasmussen, Steen Eiler. "Versuche zur Rettung des Gendarmenmarktes." *Der Städtebau,* 24, no. 3 (1929), 64–66.

Rave, Rolf, and H. J. Knöfel, eds. *Bauen seit 1900: Ein Führer durch Berlin.* Berlin: Ullstein, 1963.

[*Die Rheinlande*]. [Darmstadt Artists' Colony]. Sp. no., *Die Rheinlande,* 1, no. 4 (January 1901).

Ribbe, Wolfgang, and Wolfgang Schäche, eds. *Baumeister. Architekten. Stadtplaner. Biographien zur baulichen Entwicklung Berlins.* Berlin: Historische Kommission zu Berlin/Stapp Verlag, 1987.

Riedrich, Otto. "Haus Ring der Frauen auf der Deutschen Bauausstellung in Berlin." *Deutsche Bauzeitung,* 65, nos. 49–50 (17 June 1931), 289–293.

Riedrich, Otto. "Neue Arbeiten von Peter Behrens," incorporating "Die Baukunst und das Leben." *Baugilde,* 14, no. 16 (1932), 765–780.

Riedrich, Otto [1932b]. "Haus einer Dame im Taunus." *Die Kunst,* 33, no. 6 (March 1932), 124–132.

Riedrich, Otto [1932c]. "Die neuen Hochhäuser am Alexanderplatz in Berlin." *Deutsche Bauzeitung,* 66, no. 46 (9 November 1932), 901–906.

Roether, J., and Hans-Günther Sperlich. *Mathildenhöhe Darmstadt.* Darmstadt: E. Roether, 1958.

[Rogers, Ernesto. See *Casabella,* above.]

Rogge, Henning. *Fabrikwelt um die Jahrhundertwende am Beispiel der AEG Maschinenfabrik in Berlin-Wedding.* Cologne: DuMont, 1983.

Romein, Jan. *The Watershed of Two Eras: Europe in 1900.* Middletown, CT: Wesleyan University Press, 1978.

Ruettenauer, Benno. *Kunst und Handwerk.* Über Kunst der Neuzeit, 7. Strassburg: Heitz, 1902.

[39]

Sabais, Heinz Winfried. *Vom Geist einer Stadt: Ein Darmstadt Lesebuch.* Darmstadt: Roether, 1956.

Salkind. "Die Tragkonstruktionen der Hochhäuser am Alexanderplatz." *Der Bauingenieur,* 13 (1 January 1932), 12–15.

Salzburg, Amt der Salzburger Landesregierung. *St. Peter in Salzburg.* Ed. Heinz Dopsch and Roswitha Juffinger. Salzburg, 1982.

Scarpa, Ludovica. *Martin Wagner und Berlin: Architektur und Städtebau in der Weimarer Republik.* Braunschweig: Vieweg, 1986.

Schäche, Wolfgang. "Überlegungen zur Kontinuität der NS-Architektur." In Magdalena Bushart et al., eds., *Entmachtung der Kunst: Architektur, Bildhauerei und ihre Institutionalisierung 1920 bis 1960,* 74–85. Berlin: Frölich & Kaufmann, 1985.

Schäche, Wolfgang. *Architektur und Städtebau in Berlin zwischen 1933 und 1945: Planen und Bauen unter der Ägide der Stadtverwaltung.* Berlin: Gebr. Mann, 1991.

Schaefer, Herwin. *Nineteenth-Century Modern: The Functional Tradition in Victorian Design.* New York: Praeger, 1970.

Schaefer, K. "Nordwestdeutsche Kunstausstellung Oldenburg 1905." *Deutsche Kunst und Dekoration,* 9, no. 1 (October 1905), 1–68. [51]

Schaefen [*sic*], Dr. [Schaefer, 1905b]. "Die Nordwestdeutsche Kunstausstellung in Oldenburg." *Die Rheinlande,* 5, no. 11 (November 1905), 428–430.

Schaefer, Karl. "Ein Bismarckdenkmal von Peter Behrens auf dem Bookholzberge bei Gruppenbühren." *Bremer Nachrichten* (13 September 1908). [75]

Schaefer, Karl. "Kaiserl. Deutsche Botschaft in St. Petersburg." *Deutsche Kunst und Dekoration,* 16 (July 1913), 260–292.

Schaefer, Karl. "Das Gebäude der Kaiserlich Deutschen Botschaft in St. Petersburg." *Der Profanbau,* 10 (1914), part 1, 309–348. Also published as *Prof. Peter Behrens: Die deutsche Botschaft in St. Petersburg.* Leipzig: Arnd, 1914.

Schäfer, W[ilhelm]. "'Ein Dokument deutscher Kunst': Die Ausstellung der Künstlerkolonie Darmstadt 1901." *Die Rheinlande,* 1, no. 9 (June 1901), 38–40.

Schäfer, W[ilhelm] [1901b]. "Das Haus Peter Behrens." *Die Rheinlande,* 1, no. 11 (August 1901), 27–31, 48–49.

Schäfer, W[ilhelm]. "Die neue Kunstgewerbeschule in Düsseldorf." *Die Rheinlande,* 4, no. 1 (October 1903), 62–63; see also 57–59.

S[chäfer, Wilhelm]. "Gedanken zur Gartenbauausstellung in Düsseldorf: Jungbrunnen und Behrens-Garten." *Die Rheinlande,* 4, no. 10 (July 1904), 409–412.

S[chäfer, Wilhelm]. "Deutsche Kunstausstellung zu Köln 1906: Das Gebäude von Peter Behrens." *Die Rheinlande,* 5 (1905), 437–438.

Schäfer, Wilhelm. "In Hagen." *Die Rheinlande,* 9, no. 8 (August 1909), 265–272. [94]

Scharff, Richard. "Das Salzburger Benediktiner Kolleg." *Deutsche Bauzeitung,* 61, nos. 31–32 (16 April 1927), 265–267.

Schauer, Georg Kurt. *Deutsche Buchkunst 1890 bis 1960.* 2 vols. Hamburg: Maximilian-Gesellschaft, 1963.

Scheffler, Karl. "Das Haus Behrens." Sp. no., *Dekorative Kunst,* 5, no. 1 (October 1901). [37]

Scheffler, Karl. "Eine Bilanz." *Dekorative Kunst,* 6 (1903), 243ff.

Scheffler, Karl. "Die Jahrhundert-Ausstellung." *Die Zukunft,* 14, vol. 55 (1906), 88–95.

Scheffler, Karl. *Moderne Baukunst.* Berlin: Bard, 1907. [58]

Scheffler, Karl [1907b]. "Peter Behrens." *Die Zukunft,* 16, vol. 61 (23 November 1907), 270–276. [69]

Scheffler, Karl. "Kunst und Industrie." *Kunst und Künstler,* 6 (July 1908), 430–434. [74]

Scheffler, Karl. "Ein Garten von Peter Behrens." *Der gute Geschmack,* 1 (September 1911), title page, 11–14, 29–32. [149]

Scheffler, Karl. *Die Architektur der Grossstadt.* Berlin: Cassirer, 1913.

Scheffler, Karl [1913b]. "Das neue Haus der deutschen Botschaft in St. Petersburg." *Kunst und Künstler,* 11, no. 8 (May 1913), 414–431.

Scheffler, Karl. "Konkurrenzpolitik [Volkshaus, Lübeck]." *Kunst und Künstler,* 12, no. 5 (February 1914), 243–246.

Scheffler, Karl. *Die fetten und die mageren Jahre.* 2d rev. ed. Munich: List, [1948].

Scheibe, Werner. "Die Deutsche Werkbundausstellung in Köln." *Profanbau,* 10 (1914), part 1, 485–504.

Schlüter, Brigitte. "Verwaltungsbauten der rheinisch-westfälischen Stahlindustrie 1900–1930." Ph.D. diss., Universität Bonn, 1991.

Schmalenbach, Fritz. *Jugendstil: Ein Beitrag zu Theorie und Geschichte der Flächenkunst.* Würzburg: Triltsch, 1935.

Schmid, Max. "Baukunst und Innendekoration auf der Ausstellung für christliche Kunst in Düsseldorf 1909." *Moderne Bauformen,* 8, no. 9 (1909), 385–456.   [100]

Schmidt, Justus. *Neues Linz.* Munich and Berlin: Deutscher Kunstverlag, 1961.

Schmidt, Rudolf. "Der Wettbewerb zur Gewinnung von Ideen für eine Kongress-, Sport- und Ausstellungshalle auf den Heiligengeistfeld in Hamburg." *Wasmuths Monatshefte für Baukunst,* 18, no. 8 (August 1934), 369–379.

Schmuckler, Hans. "Fortschritte des Eisenbaues im 20. Jahrhundert." *Deutsche Bauzeitung,* 61 (9 July 1927), Beilage "Konstruktion und Ausführung" K14, 93–100.

Schmuckler, Hans. "Stahlbau und Schweisstechnik auf der deutschen Bauausstellung." *Deutsche Bauzeitung,* 65 (21 October 1931), Beilage "Konstruktion und Ausführung" K18, 137–144.

Schmutzler, Robert. *Art Nouveau.* New York: Abrams, 1978.

Schneider, Camillo Karl. "Gartengestaltung." *Dekorative Kunst,* 8, no. 4 (January 1905), 166–175; no. 6 (March 1905), 240–250; no. 11 (August 1905), 458–463.

Schüler, Edmund. *Die Kunst im Deutschen Reich* (Ausgabe B: *Die Baukunst*), 4 (April 1940), 65–66.

Schultze, F[riedrich]. "Die zweite Ton-, Zement- und Kalkindustrieausstellung in Berlin." *Zentralblatt der Bauverwaltung,* 30, no. 52 (29 June 1910), 345–348.

Schumacher, Adolf. *Ladenbau.* Stuttgart and Basel: J. Hoffmann, 1934.

Schumacher, Fritz. "Die Ausstellung der Darmstädter Künstlerkolonie." *Dekorative Kunst,* 4, no. 11 (August 1901), 417–431.

Schumacher, Fritz [1901b]. *Das Bauschaffen der Jetztzeit und historische Ueberlieferung.* Leipzig: Diederichs, 1901. Rpt., Nendeln and Liechtenstein: Kraus, 1976.

Schumacher, Fritz. "Hans Poelzig und Peter Behrens." In *Selbstgespräche: Erinnerungen und Betrachtungen,* 216–222. Hamburg: Springer, 1949.

Schur, Ernst. "Die Raumkunst in Dresden 1906." *Die Rheinlande,* 6 (1906), 56–[72].

Schur, Ernst [1906b]. "Baukunst auf der Kölner Ausstellung." *Die Rheinlande,* 6 (1906), 122–132.

Schur, Ernst. "Die II. Ton-, Zement-, und Kalkindustrie-Ausstellung." *Zement und Beton,* 9, no. 48 (25 November 1910), 743–747.

Schürmeyer, Walter. "Das technische Betriebsgebäude der Farbenindustrie-A.-G., Höchst a.M." *Deutsche Bauzeitung,* 60, no. 33 (24 April 1926), 273–277 and pl. 33; no. 34 (28 April 1926), 281–284.

Schwartz, Frederick J. *The Werkbund: Design Theory and Mass Culture before the First World War.* New Haven: Yale University Press, 1996.

Sedlmayr, Hans. *Art in Crisis: The Lost Center.* 1948; Chicago: Regnery, 1958.

Sekler, Eduard. *Josef Hoffmann: The Architectural Work.* Princeton: Princeton University Press, 1985.

Seling, Helmut, ed. *Jugendstil: Der Weg ins 20. Jahrhundert.* Heidelberg and Munich: Keyser, 1959.

Selle, Gert. *Jugendstil und Kunst-Industrie: Zur Ökonomie und Ästhetik des Kunstgewerbes um 1900.* Ravensburg: Otto Maier, 1974.

Selle, Gert. *Die Geschichte des Design in Deutschland von 1870 bis heute: Entwicklung der industriellen Produktkultur.* Cologne: DuMont, 1978.

Sembach, Klaus-Jürgen, et al. *1910. Halbzeit der Moderne: van de Velde, Behrens, Hoffmann und die Andere.* Stuttgart: Hatje, 1992. (Exhibition catalog, Westfälisches Landesmuseum für Kunst und Kulturgeschichte, Münster.)

Senger, Alexander von. "Der Baubolschewismus und seine Verkoppelungen mit Wirtschaft und Politik." *Nationalsozialistische Monatshefte,* 5, no. 51 (June 1934), 497–507.

Servaes, Franz. "Das Kurhotel der Zukunft: Ein Bauplan von Peter Behrens." *Der Architekt,* 21 (1916–1918), 41–58.

Shand, P. Morton. "A Villa in the Taunus Mountains by Professor Peter Behrens." *Architectural Review,* 72 (October 1932), 121–123.

Shand, P. Morton. "The Largest Cigarette Factory in the World." *Architectural Review,* 73 (February 1933), 56.

Shand, P. Morton. "Scenario for a Human Drama [seven part series, pts. 2 and 3 concern Behrens]." *Architectural Review,* 76 (August, September 1934), 39–42, 83–86. Rpt., without original figs., as "The Machine: Peter Behrens," *Architectural Association Journal,* no. 827 (January 1959), 173–178.

Siedler. "Peter Behrens." *Die Baugilde,* 10, no. 11 (5 June 1928), 763–770.

Siepe, Elmar. "Das Gesellenhaus und eine städtebauliche Studie von Peter Behrens in Neuss." *Neusser Jahrbuch* (1961), cover and 9–18.

Siepmann, Eckhard, ed. *Kunst und Alltag um 1900.* Jahrbuch des Werkbund-Archivs 3. Lahn-Giessen: Anabas, 1978.

Simon, Hans-Ulrich. *Sezessionismus: Kunstgewerbe in literarischer und bildender Kunst.* Stuttgart: Metzler, 1976.

Simons, Anna. "Der staatliche Schriftkursus in Neubabelsberg." *Kunstgewerbeblatt,* n.s. 21, no. 6 (March 1910), 101–113.   [108]

Singer, Hans W. "Arts and Crafts at Dresden." *International Studio,* 22 (1904), 53–58.

Sörgel, Herman. *Atlantropa.* Zurich: Fretz & Wasmuth/Munich: Piloty & Loehle, [1932].

Speer, Albert. *Inside the Third Reich.* New York: Macmillan, 1970.

Speer, Albert. *Architektur: Arbeiten 1933–1942.* 1978; rpt., Frankfurt and Berlin: Propyläen, 1995.

Spickernagel, Ellen. "Unerwünschte Tätigkeit: Die Hausfrau und Wohnungsform der Neuzeit." *Kritische Berichte,* 20, no. 4 (1992), 80–96.

Stahl, Fritz. "Die Architektur der Werkbund-Ausstellung." *Wasmuths Monatshefte für Baukunst,* 1 (1914–1915), 153–[204].

Stahl, Fritz. "Landhaus Wiegand in Dahlem." *Wasmuths Monatshefte für Baukunst,* 3 (1918–1919), 265–285.

Stein, Egon. "Der Übergang zu Normung, Typung und Industrialisierung im Bauwesen." *Wissenschaftliche Zeitschrift der Technischen Hochschule Dresden,* 6, no. 3 (1956–1957), 619–629.

Stoeving, Curt. "A. Wertheim: Neue Wohn-Räume, neues Kunstgewerbe, dem Hause eigen, nach Entwürfen von Künstlern unter Leitung von Prof. Curt Stoeving." *Deutsche Kunst und Dekoration,* 8, no. 11 (August 1905), 643–646.

Stoffers, Gottfried, ed. *Deutschland in Brüssel 1910: Die deutsche Abteilung der Weltausstellung.* Cologne: DuMont Schauberg, 1910.

Stuttgart, Staatlicher Hochbau Baden-Württemberg. "Weissenhof 1927–87." Sp. no. *info bau 87,* 14, no. 2 (1987), including a reprint of *info bau 83,* 10, no. 2 (1983).

Sutter, Conrad. "Die Architektur auf der Deutschen Kunstausstellung in Köln 1906." *Architektonische Rundschau,* 23, no. 4 (1907), 29–36.

t. "Die moderne Ausstellung bei Keller und Reiner." *Berliner Architekturwelt,* 12, no. 12 (March 1910), 447–451, 470–473.   [107]

Tabor, Jan, ed. *Kunst und Diktatur: Architektur, Bildhauerei und Malerei in Österreich, Deutschland, Italien und der Sowjetunion 1922–1956.* Baden: Grasl, 1994.

Tafuri, Manfredo. "Austromarxismo e città: 'Das rote Wien'." *Contropiano,* 2 (1971), 259–311.

Tafuri, Manfredo, ed. *Vienna rossa: La politica residenziale nella Vienna socialista, 1919–1933.* Milan: Electa, 1980.

[Taut, Bruno (anon.)]. "Architektonische Lösung: Ecke Bellevue- und Viktoriastrasse am Kemperplatz in Berlin." *Frühlicht,* 1, no. 3 (Spring 1922). Rpt. in *Frühlicht 1920–1922: Eine Folge für die Verwirklichung neuen Baugedankens,* 159–163. Berlin: Ullstein, 1963.

Taut, Bruno. *Bauen: Der neue Wohnbau.* Leipzig and Berlin: Klinkhardt & Biermann, 1927.

Thiekötter, Angelika, and Eckhard Siepmann, eds. *Packeis und Pressglas: Von der Kunstgewerbebewegung zum Deutschen Werkbund.* Werkbund Archiv, vol. 16. Giessen: Anabas, 1987.

Tummers, Nic. *Der Hagener Impuls: M. Lauweriks Werk und Einfluss auf Architektur und Formgebung um 1910.* Hagen: Linnepe, 1972.

Ungers, O. M., and Joachim Schlandt. *Die Wiener Superblocks.* Berlin: Technische Universität Berlin, 1969.

Very, F. "Peter Behrens." Thesis, Istituto Universitario di Architettura, Venice, 1973.

Vienna, City of. *Die Wohnhausanlage der Gemeinde Wien: Winarskyhof im XX. Bezirk.* Vienna, 1926.

Vogelgesang, Shepard. "Peter Behrens, Architect and Teacher." *Architectural Forum,* 52 (May 1930), 715–725.

Voigt, Wolfgang, et al. "Atlantropa." *Bauwelt,* 82 (17 May 1991), 938–965.

Volk, Waltraud. *Berlin, Hauptstadt der DDR: Historische Strassen und Plätze heute.* 2d rev. ed. Berlin: Verlag für Bauwesen, 1972.

Völter, Ernst. "Linden, Platz der Republik, Reichstagserweiterung und Durchbruch." *Die Baugilde,* 9 (1927), 1098–1101.

W., A. "Kurhausanlage in Salzburg." *Die Bau- und Werkkunst,* 5 (1928–1929), 193–196.

Wach, Hugo. "Der Entwurf zu einer protestantischen Kirche für Hagen von Professor Peter Behrens in Neubabelsberg." *Die Kirche,* 7, no. 1 (1909), 10–15.   [82]

Waentig, Heinrich. *Wirtschaft und Kunst: Eine Untersuchung über Geschichte und Theorie der modernen Kunstgewerbebewegung.* Jena: Fischer, 1909.

Waetzold, Stephan, et al., eds. *Tendenzen der Zwanziger Jahre. 15. europäische Kunstausstellung Berlin 1977.* Berlin: Dietrich Reimer, 1977.

Wagner, Martin. "Das Formproblem eines Weltstadtplatzes: Wettbewerb der Verkehrs-A.G. für die Umbauung des Alexanderplatzes." *Das Neue Berlin,* 1, no. 2 (1929), 33–39.

Wagner, [Martin?]. "Wettbewerb: Verbauung der Arenberggründe in Salzburg." *Die Bau- und Werkkunst,* 8, no. 4 (April 1932), 81ff.

Weber, Helmut. *Walter Gropius und das Faguswerk.* Munich: Callwey, 1961.

[Wechsler, Alfred. See Fred, W.]

Wedepohl, Edgar. "Die Weissenhof-Siedlung der Werkbund-Ausstellung 'Die Wohnung', Stuttgart 1927." *Wasmuths Monatshefte für Baukunst,* 11, no. 10 (October 1927), 391–402.

Weigle, Hermann. "Die Mannheimer Jubiläumsausstellung: Gartenbau- und Kunstausstellung." *Architektonische Rundschau,* 23, no. 11 (1907), 85–96 and pls. 81–88.

Weiser, Armand. "Ein neuer Stil?" *Die Bau- und Werkkunst,* 6, no. 1 (October 1929), 1–16.

Weishaupt. "Das Wesen der neuen 'Gruppenbauweise'." *Deutsche Bauzeitung,* 53, no. 72 (6 September 1919), 430–432; no. 73 (10 September), 433–434; no. 74 (13 September), 439–440; no. 76 (20 September), 450–455; and no. 84 (18 October), 498–502.

Werner, Hermann, ed. *Moderner Berliner Zweckbau: Verwaltungsgebäude.* Berlin and Leipzig: Deutsche Architektur-Bücherei, 1932.

Der Westdeutsche Impuls 1900–1914: Kunst und Umweltgestaltung im Industriegebiet. A series of exhibitions under the above title, beginning in March 1984; listed below by individual catalogs:

Cologne, Kölnischer Kunstverein. *Die Deutsche Werkbund-Ausstellung, Cöln 1914.* Cologne: Kölnischer Kunstverein, 1984.

Düsseldorf, Kunstmuseum. *Düsseldorf: Eine Grossstadt auf dem Weg in die Moderne.* Düsseldorf: Kunstmuseum, 1984.

Hagen, Karl Ernst Osthaus Museum. *Die Folkwang-Idee des Karl Ernst Osthaus.* Hagen: Karl Ernst Osthaus Museum, 1984.

Hagen, Karl Ernst Osthaus Museum. *Beiheft mit Liste der Ausgestellten Werke und Kurzbiographien.* Hagen: Karl Ernst Osthaus Museum, 1984.

Krefeld, Kaiser Wilhelm Museum. *Von der Künstlerseide zur Industriefotografie: Das Museum zwischen Jugendstil und Werkbund.* Krefeld: Kaiser Wilhelm Museum, 1984.

Westheim, Paul. "Kleinwohnungseinrichtungen." *Sozialistische Monatshefte,* 20 (1914), 464f.

Westheim, Paul [1914b]. "Anpassung oder Typenschöpfung? Entwickelungsperspektiven des Kunstgewerbes." *Sozialistische Monatshefte,* 20 (1914), 979–989.

Wichmann, Hans. *Aufbruch zum neuen Wohnen. Deutsche Werkstätten und WK-Verband (1898–1970).* Basel and Stuttgart: Birkhäuser, 1978.

Wilhelm, Sibylle. *"Kunstgewerbebewegung": Ästhetische Welt oder Macht durch Kunst?* Frankfurt: P. Lang, 1991.

Wilm, Hubert. "Vom Sammeln neuer Goldschmiedearbeiten." *Werk und Kunst,* 1, no. 4 (1930), 105–108.

Windsor, Alan. *Peter Behrens: Architect and Designer.* New York: Whitney Library of Design, 1981. In German as *Peter Behrens, Architekt und Designer.* Stuttgart: DVA, 1985.

Windsor, Alan [1981b]. "Hohenhagen." *Architectural Review,* 152 (September 1981), 169–175.

Windsor, Alan. "Peter Behrens and the Aesthetics of Engineering." *Royal Institute of British Architects Transactions,* no. 7 (1985), 70–81.

Windsor, Alan. "Letters from Peter Behrens to P. Morton Shand, 1932–1938." *Architectural History*, 37 (1994), 165–187.

Wittig, Paul. *Die Architektur der Hoch- und Untergrundbahn in Berlin.* Berlin, 1922.

Wolff, H. "Der Neubau des Hauptverwaltungsgebäudes der AEG in Berlin." *Die Kunst im Dritten Reich* (Ausgabe B: *Die Baukunst*), 3 (October 1939), 447–454.

Worringer, Wilhelm. "Zum Problem der modernen Architektur." *Neudeutsche Bauzeitung*, 7 (1911), 496–500.

Wrede, Kraft-Eike. *Karl Ernst Osthaus und das Theater: Peter Behrens' Inszenierung des 'Diogenes' von Otto Erich Hartleben für die Hagener Sommerschauspiele (1909).* Hagen: Karl Ernst Osthaus Museum, 1984.

Zimmermann, H. "Der Wettbewerb um die Strassenbrücke über den Rhein in Köln-Mülheim." *Zentralblatt der Bauverwaltung*, 47 (2 February 1927), 37–38. Also excerpt of jury report (9 March 1927), 112–113.

Zimmermann, H. [1927b]. "Die Entscheidung über die Köln-Mülheimer Strassenbrücke." *Zentralblatt der Bauverwaltung*, 47 (6 July 1927), 338–339.

Zimmermann, H. K. "Ein Landsitz am Taunus erbaut von Prof. Peter Behrens, Berlin." *Deutsche Kunst und Dekoration*, 35 (April 1932), 32–40.

Zobel, Victor. "Mannheimer Ausstellungsgärten II." *Dekorative Kunst*, 10, no. 11 (August 1907), 465–472.

Zurich, Kunstgewerbemuseum. *Objekte des Jugendstils aus der Sammlung des Kunstgewerbemuseums Zürich.* Ed. Erika Gysling-Billeter. Bern: Benteli, 1975.

Illustration Credits

Aachen, Suermondt-Ludwig-Museum; photographer, Anne Gold (**figure 5.5**)

AEG-Archiv (**figures 5.1–2, 5.8–9, 6.8, 7.2–5, 7.14, 7.25, 7.28, 7.30–32, list of works nos. 49, 112**)

    AEG Zeitung, 2 (1900–1901), suppl. (**figure 5.7**)

    AEG Zeitung (May 1905 and May 1907) (**figure 6.1**)

    Mitteilungen der Berliner Elektricitätswerke, 3 (1907), 130 (**figure 6.2**)

    Mitteilungen der Berliner Elektricitätswerke, 4 (August 1908), 119 (**figure 5.6**)

Ahlers-Hestermann, F., *Stilwende,* opp. p. 56 (**figure 1.12**)

Amherst, University of Massachusetts

    Innendekoration, 19 (March 1908), 121, 115 (**figure 4.10, list of works no. 38**)

    Innendekoration, 24 (November 1913), 439 (**figure 8.33**)

Amsterdam, Stedelijk Museum (**figure 4.11**)

Author (**figures 2.10 [drawing based on one in the Bauordnungsamt, Hagen, dated May 1912], 7.12, 8.4, 8.6–7, 8.10, 8.40, 8.43, 9.4, 9.13, 9.24, list of works no. 165**)

    Berlage, H. P., *Grundlagen und Entwicklung der Architektur* (Rotterdam: W. L. & J. Brusse, [1908]), 64, 56 (**figures 4.4–5**)

    Krefeld, Kaiser-Wilhelm-Museum, *Linie und Form* (1904), frontispiece, tailpiece (**figures 1.21–22**)

    Ring, no. 4 (April 1909), 13 (**figure 4.14**)

Beenken, H., *Schöpferische Bauideen der deutschen Romantik* (Mainz: Matthias-Grünewald-Verlag, 1952), fig. 37; original lost, formerly Technische Hochschule, Berlin (**figure 7.16**)

Behrens, P., and H. de Fries, *Vom sparsamen Bauen* (Berlin: Bauwelt, 1918), fig. 9 (**figure 9.15**)

Berlin, Architekten- und Ingenieur-Verein

    Berlin und seine Bauten, part 4, vol. C (1975), 241 (**figure 9.23**)

    100 Jahre Schinkel-Wettbewerb (Berlin, 1955), 42 (**figure 1.3**)

Berlin, Bauhaus-Archiv (**figure 9.25**)

Berlin, Bildarchiv Preussischer Kulturbesitz
    Das Echo, 38 (16 October 1919), 1295 (**list of works no. 121**)

Berlin, Brandenburgisches Landesamt für Denkmalpflege Messbildarchiv
    Photo Messbildanstalt 1910 (**figure 8.8**)
    Photo Staatl. Bildstelle 1928 (**figures 7.6–7**)

Berlin, Deutsches Technikmuseum
    AEG-Zeitung (1910), fig. 4 (**figure 7.10**)
    Die Spannung (1929), 40, fig. 4 (**figure 7.27**)

Berlin, Kunstbibliothek (**figures 1.7** [photo K.-H. Poulmann], **2.5, 2.9, 3.3, 8.22, list of works no. 70**)

Beuron, Beuroner Kunstverlag (**figures 1.25, 2.14**)

Bonn, Foreign Office (**figure 8.45**)

Brussels, Bibliothèque Royale Albert 1er, Van de Velde Archive (**figures 1.8, 1.10**)

Brussels, Musée Horta (**figure 1.9**)

Buchwald, H., *Form from Process* (Cambridge: Harvard University, Carpenter Center, 1967), fig. 15 (**figure 6.10**)

Cambridge, Harvard University, Fine Arts Library
    American Architect (August 1932), 62 (**figure 9.21**)
    Dekorative Kunst, 5, no. 1 (October 1901), 26 (**figure 3.12**)
    Dekorative Kunst, 10, no. 4 (January 1907), 144 (**figure 5.10**)
    Die Kunst im Dritten Reich, Ausgabe B: *Die Baukunst,* 3 (October 1939), 447 (**figure 9.30**)
    Kunstgewerbeblatt, n.s. 20 (December 1908), 47 (**figure 2.15**)
    Kunstgewerbeblatt, n.s. 21 (June 1910), 180 (**list of works no. 62a**)

Cambridge, Fogg Art Museum, Harvard University Art Museums, Gift of William Gray from the collection of Francis Calley Gray; photographer, Rick Stafford. © President and Fellows of Harvard College, Harvard University (**figure 10.2**)

Cambridge, Massachusetts Institute of Technology
    Dekorative Kunst, 7 (August 1904), 412, 430 (**figures 4.1–2**)
    Deutsche Bauzeitung (1902), 257 (**figure 3.4**)
    Deutsche Bauzeitung (3 October 1934), 797 (**figure 9.26**)
    Deutsche Bauzeitung (September 1938), 259 (**figure 9.29**)
    Der Industriebau, 1, no. 6 (15 June 1910), 135, 136 (**figures 7.8, 7.13**)
    Der Industriebau, 2, no. 6 (15 June 1911), 132, 128 (**figures 7.21, 7.26**)
    Der Industriebau, 8 (15 March 1917), 42, 34 (**figures 8.1, 8.5**)
    Photographer Paul Birnbaum (**figures 8.30, 8.32, list of works no. 209**)
    Zeitschrift des Vereines deutscher Ingenieure, 55, no. 39 (30 September 1911), 1627 (**figure 7.9**)

Cremers, P. J., *Peter Behrens* (Essen: Baedeker, 1928), pls. 7, 133, 127 (**figures 9.7, 9.16–17**)

Krefeld, Deutsches Textilmuseum, inv. no. 06490; digitally reproduced and multiplied by Professor Julie Dorsey, MIT (**endpapers**)

Kreitmaier, J., *Beuroner Kunst: Eine Ausdrucksform der christlichen Mystik,* 5th ed. (Freiburg im Br.: Herder, 1923), pl. 3 (**figure 1.6**)

Kunstgewerbeblatt, n.s. 22 (1910), 43 (**figure 3.15**)

Lauweriks, J. L. M., *Handarbeit für Knaben und Mädchen - 4: Holzarbeit* (Leipzig: Teubner, [n.d.]), 11–12, pl. VIII (**figures 4.8–9**)

Lessing, Erich (**figure 8.9**)

Liège, Ville de Liège, Musées d'archéologie et d'arts décoratifs, Musée Curtius (**figure 8.42**)

Linz, Stadtmuseum (**list of works nos. 204–205**)

London, Architectural Review (**figure 9.28**)
 Architectural Review (1932), 121 (**figure 9.22**)

London, British Architectural Library, RIBA (**figure 9.14**)

Los Angeles, Getty Institute (**figures 1.30, 6.5**)

Lübeck, Archiv der Hansestadt (**figure 8.51**)

Marburg, Bildarchiv Foto Marburg (**frontispiece, figures 1.2, 2.7–8, 2.11–12, 4.3, 4.7, 4.13, 5.4, 6.7, 7.20, 7.33–35, 8.21, 8.24, 8.27, 8.34, 9.19, list of works nos. 39, 79, 83, 92 [first]**)

Moderne Bauformen, 13, no. 1 (1914), pl. 4 (**figure 1.28**)

I. K. H. Moritz Landgraf von Hessen, Kronberg im Taunus (collection of the Hessische Haus-stiftung, Kronberg); photo: Kulturinstitut der Stadt Darmstadt (**figure 2.4**)

Munich, Architekturmuseum, Technische Universität (**figures 1.14, 9.2–3**)

Munich, Collection Hans Döllgast (1961) (**figure 9.8**)

New York, Columbia University, Avery Architectural and Fine Arts Library
 Blätter für Architektur und Kunsthandwerk, 28 (January 1915), 1 (**figure 8.31**)
 G, no. 3 (1924), 9 (**list of works no. 65a**)
 Der Neubau, 6 (1924), 191, fig. 4 (**list of works no. 139**)
 Wasmuths Monatshefte für Baukunst, 1 (1914–1915), fig. 170 (**figure 8.52**)

New York, The Museum of Modern Art
 Ludwig Mies van der Rohe, project for a house with a court (ca. 1934), interior perspective. Pencil, cut-out reproduction (of unidentified sculpture) on illustration board, 30 x 40 in. (76.2 x 101.6 cm). The Mies van der Rohe Archive, The Museum of Modern Art, New York. Gift of the architect. ©1999 The Museum of Modern Art, New York (**figure 4.16**)
 Mies van der Rohe, project for a concert hall (1942). Collage over photograph, 29 1/2 x 62 in. (75 x 157.5 cm). The Mies van der Rohe Archive, The Museum of Modern Art, New York. Gift of the architect. ©1999 The Museum of Modern Art, New York (**figure 4.17**)

New York, The New York Public Library, Astor, Lenox and Tilden Foundations: Art and Architecture Collection, Miriam and Ira D. Wallach Division of Art, Prints and Photographs
 Werkkunst (February 1908), [147] (**figure 8.15**)

Oberhausen, Gutehofnungshütte (**list of works no. 140b [both]**)

Offenbach, Klingspor Museum (**figure 3.11**)

Otterlo, Rijksmuseum Kröller-Müller (**figure 1.4**)

Petersen, Knud Peter, Berlin (**figure 7.11**)

Philadelphia Museum of Art. Purchased: Fiske Kimball Fund; photographer, Graydon Wood (**figure 1.16**)

Die Rheinlande, 1 (January 1901), 30, 38 (**figures 3.13–14**)

Saarbrücken, Collection Obenauer (**figures 8.13–14, 8.17–20**)

Schauer, G. K., *Deutsche Buchkunst 1890 bis 1960* (Hamburg, 1963), 1:44 (**figure 4.18**)

Schmutzler, R., *Art Nouveau,* 244 (**figure 1.1**)

Schürer, Arnold, Bielefeld
  Georg Malkowsky, ed., *Die Pariser Weltausstellung in Wort und Bild* (Berlin: Kirchoff & Co., 1900), 361 (**figure 5.3**)

Schweizerische Bauzeitung (1913), pl. 71 (**figure 8.38**)

Sekler, Professor Eduard, Cambridge, Massachusetts (**figures 1.20, 1.27, 9.9**)

Semper, Gottfried, *Über die bleiernen Schleudergeschosse der Alten* (Frankfurt, 1859), pls. 2, 3 (**figures 6.3–4**)

Spiluttini, Margherita, Vienna (**figures 1.24, 1.26, 1.29**)

Thonet, *Michael Thonet* (Vienna, 1896), pl. I (**figure 6.9**)

Touring Club Italiano, *Attraverso l'Italia: Firenze* (Milan, 1962), pl. XV; photographer, Ezio Quiresi (**figure 2.16**)

Trier, Rheinisches Landesmuseum (**figure 8.47**)

Über Land und Meer, 83, no. 4 (October 1899), 59, 61 (**figures 2.1, 3.1**)

Vienna, Österreichisches Nationalbibliothek (**figures 9.10–12, 10.1**)

Werner, H., ed., *Moderner Berliner Zweckbau, Band I: Verwaltungsgebäude* (Berlin and Leipzig: Deutsche Architektur-Bücherei, 1932), unnumbered plate (**figure 9.27**)

Zurich, Museum Bellerive (Marlen Perez) (**figure 1.11**)

Index

Works discussed in the text are indexed under both maker and location. Works mentioned only in the "List of Architectural Works by Peter Behrens" (pp. 323–371) are indexed under location (works in the List executed for the AEG also appear under the AEG entry). Unless otherwise noted, cities referred to are in Germany.

Behrens, Peter (*cont.*)

Berlin (*cont.*)